Lecture Notes in Computer Science 14952

Founding Editors

Gerhard Goos
Juris Hartmanis

Editorial Board Members

Elisa Bertino, *Purdue University, West Lafayette, IN, USA*
Wen Gao, *Peking University, Beijing, China*
Bernhard Steffen, *TU Dortmund University, Dortmund, Germany*
Moti Yung, *Columbia University, New York, NY, USA*

The series Lecture Notes in Computer Science (LNCS), including its subseries Lecture Notes in Artificial Intelligence (LNAI) and Lecture Notes in Bioinformatics (LNBI), has established itself as a medium for the publication of new developments in computer science and information technology research, teaching, and education.

LNCS enjoys close cooperation with the computer science R & D community, the series counts many renowned academics among its volume editors and paper authors, and collaborates with prestigious societies. Its mission is to serve this international community by providing an invaluable service, mainly focused on the publication of conference and workshop proceedings and postproceedings. LNCS commenced publication in 1973.

Anne E. Haxthausen · Wendelin Serwe
Editors

Formal Methods for Industrial Critical Systems

29th International Conference, FMICS 2024
Milan, Italy, September 9–11, 2024
Proceedings

Editors
Anne E. Haxthausen
Technical University of Denmark
Lyngby, Denmark

Wendelin Serwe
Inria Grenoble
Montbonnot Cedex, France

ISSN 0302-9743 ISSN 1611-3349 (electronic)
Lecture Notes in Computer Science
ISBN 978-3-031-68149-3 ISBN 978-3-031-68150-9 (eBook)
https://doi.org/10.1007/978-3-031-68150-9

© The Editor(s) (if applicable) and The Author(s), under exclusive license
to Springer Nature Switzerland AG 2024

This work is subject to copyright. All rights are solely and exclusively licensed by the Publisher, whether the whole or part of the material is concerned, specifically the rights of translation, reprinting, reuse of illustrations, recitation, broadcasting, reproduction on microfilms or in any other physical way, and transmission or information storage and retrieval, electronic adaptation, computer software, or by similar or dissimilar methodology now known or hereafter developed.
The use of general descriptive names, registered names, trademarks, service marks, etc. in this publication does not imply, even in the absence of a specific statement, that such names are exempt from the relevant protective laws and regulations and therefore free for general use.
The publisher, the authors and the editors are safe to assume that the advice and information in this book are believed to be true and accurate at the date of publication. Neither the publisher nor the authors or the editors give a warranty, expressed or implied, with respect to the material contained herein or for any errors or omissions that may have been made. The publisher remains neutral with regard to jurisdictional claims in published maps and institutional affiliations.

This Springer imprint is published by the registered company Springer Nature Switzerland AG
The registered company address is: Gewerbestrasse 11, 6330 Cham, Switzerland

If disposing of this product, please recycle the paper.

Preface

The International Conference on Formal Methods in Industrial Critical Systems (FMICS), organized by ERCIM, is the key conference at the intersection of industrial applications and formal methods. The aim of the FMICS series is to provide a forum for researchers and practitioners who are interested in the development and application of formal methods in industry. FMICS brings together scientists and engineers who are active in the area of formal methods and interested in exchanging their experiences in the industrial usage of these methods. FMICS also strives to promote research and development for the improvement of formal methods and tools for industrial applications.

This volume contains the papers presented at the 29th International Conference on Formal Methods in Industrial Critical Systems (FMICS 2024), which was held during September 9–11, 2024. The symposium took place in Milan, Italy, and was organized alongside the 26th International Symposium on Formal Methods (FM 2024), the 18th International Conference on Tests and Proofs (TAP 2024), the 34th International Symposium on Logic-Based Program Synthesis and Transformation (LOPSTR), the 25th International Symposium on Principles and Practice of Declarative Programming (PPDP), and the 20th International Conference on Formal Aspects of Component Software (FACS).

This year we received 25 abstracts that ended up in 22 paper submissions. We selected a total of 14 papers for presentation during the conference and inclusion in these proceedings with an acceptance rate of 63%. The submissions were reviewed by an international Program Committee (PC) of 35 members from a mix of universities, industry, and research institutes. All submissions went through a rigorous single-blind review process overseen by the Program Committee Chairs. Each submission received at least three review reports and was actively and thoroughly discussed by the PC. Program Committee members coauthoring a submission were excluded from the reviewing and discussions about this submission.

The program included two invited keynotes: one by Thierry Lecomte, from CLEARSY, on the modeling and verification of system properties for mission-critical software applications, and one, shared with the Industry Day of FM, by Byron Cook, from Amazon, about industrial usage and challenges of automated reasoning tools.

We are grateful to all involved in FMICS 2024. We thank the authors for submitting and presenting their work at FMICS 2024 and the PC members and sub-reviewers for their accurate and timely reviewing. We also thank the invited speakers, session chairs, and attendees, all of whom contributed to making the conference a success. We are also grateful to the providers of the EasyChair system, which was used to manage the submissions, to Springer for sponsoring the Best Paper Award and for publishing the proceedings, to Inria for sponsoring the invited talk by Thierry Lecomte, to ERCIM for sponsoring the invited talk by Byron Cook, and to the Steering Committee of FMICS for their trust and support. We thank the General Chairs of FM 2024, Matteo Pradella and

Matteo Rossi, for providing the logistics that enabled and facilitated the organization of FMICS 2024.

June 2024

Anne E. Haxthausen
Wendelin Serwe

Organization

Program Committee Chairs

Anne Haxthausen — Technical University of Denmark, Denmark
Wendelin Serwe — Inria Grenoble, France

Steering Committee

Maurice ter Beek — ISTI-CNR, Italy
Alessandro Fantechi — Università di Firenze, Italy
Hubert Garavel — Inria, France
Tiziana Margaria — University of Limerick and LERO, Ireland
Radu Mateescu — Inria, France
Jaco van de Pol — Aarhus University, Denmark

Program Committee

Bernhard Aichernig — TU Graz, Austria
Davide Basile — ISTI CNR, Pisa, Italy
Alessandro Cimatti — Fondazione Bruno Kessler, Italy
Pedro R. D'Argenio — Universidad Nacional de Córdoba, Argentina
Jennifer Davis — Collins Aerospace, USA
Luca di Stefano — TU Wien, Austria
Hugues Evrard — Google, France
Alessandro Fantechi — Universitá di Firenze, Italy
Wan Fokkink — Vrije Universiteit Amsterdam, The Netherlands
Martin Fränzle — Carl von Ossietzky Universität Oldenburg, Germany
Pierre-Loïc Garoche — ENAC, France
Matthias Güdemann — UAS Munich, Germany
Klaus Havelund — California Institute of Technology, USA
Anne Haxthausen — Technical University of Denmark, Denmark
Holger Hermanns — Universität des Saarlandes, Germany
Peter Höfner — Australian National University, Australia
Bertrand Jeannet — Dassault Systèmes, France
Joseph Kiniry — Galois, Inc., USA

Jan Křetínský	Masaryk University, Czech Republic
Kim Larsen	Aalborg University, Denmark
Thierry Lecomte	CLEARSY, France
Tiziana Margaria	University of Limerick and LERO, Ireland
Lina Marsso	University of Toronto, Canada
Stephan Merz	Inria Nancy, France
Stefan Mitsch	DePaul University, USA
David Monniaux	CNRS, Verimag, France
Charles Pecheur	Université Catholique de Louvain, Belgium
Cristina Seceleanu	Mälardalen University, Sweden
Wendelin Serwe	Inria Grenoble, France
Laura Titolo	AMA Inc/NASA LaRC, USA
Jaco van de Pol	Aarhus University, Denmark
Virginie Wiels	ONERA, France
Anton Wijs	Eindhoven University of Technology, The Netherlands
Jim Woodcock	University of York, UK
Zhen Zhang	Utah State University, USA

Additional Reviewers

Peter Backeman
Jonas Hansen
Paul Kröger
Stefanie Mohr
Sabine Rieder
Steffan Sølvsten
Lars B. van den Haak

Sponsors

ERCIM

INRIA

Springer

Contents

Real-Time Systems/Robotics

Safe Linear Encoding of Vehicle Dynamics for the Instantiation of Abstract Scenarios 3
   Jan Steffen Becker

Evaluating the Effectiveness of Digital Twins Through Statistical Model Checking with Feedback and Perturbations 21
   Valentina Castiglioni, Ruggero Lanotte, Michele Loreti, and Simone Tini

UPPAAL-Based Modeling and Verification of ROS 2 Multi-threaded Execution and Operating System Reservations 40
   Lukas Dust, Rong Gu, Cristina Seceleanu, Mikael Ekström, and Saad Mubeen

Semantics and Verification

Formalising the Industrial Language SMMT in mCRL2 63
   Jordi E. P. M. van Laarhoven, Olav Bunte, Louis C. M. van Gool, and Tim A. C. Willemse

Fault Tree Inference Using Multi-objective Evolutionary Algorithms and Confusion Matrix-Based Metrics 80
   Lisandro A. Jimenez-Roa, Nicolae Rusnac, Matthias Volk, and Mariëlle Stoelinga

Logika: The Sireum Verification Framework 97
   Robby, John Hatcliff, and Jason Belt

Case Studies

Fuzzing an Industrial Proprietary Protocol 119
   Eduard Baranov, Axel Legay, and Martin Vivian

Modelling and Analysis of DTLS: Power Consumption and Attacks 136
   Lise Bech Gehlert, Malthe Peter Højen Jørgensen, Christoffer Brejnholm Koch, Tobias Møller, Signe Kirstine Rusbjerg, Tobias Worm Bøgedal, Danny Bøgsted Poulsen, René Rydhof Hansen, and Daniel Lux

Verifying a Radio Telescope Pipeline Using HaliVer: Solving Nonlinear
and Quantifier Challenges 152
  Lars B. van den Haak, Anton Wijs, Marieke Huisman,
  and Mark van den Brand

Reconstructing the High-Level Structure of Legacy Code via Software
Model Checking: An Experience Report 170
  Roberto Cavada, Alessandro Cimatti, Alberto Griggio, Stefano Tonetta,
  Federico Bonafini, Matteo Campidelli, and Andrea Zasa

Formal Analysis and Monitoring of Legacy Safety-Critical Interlocking
Systems with the Use of Certified Industrial Tools 182
  Dalay Almeida, Florian Jamain, and Thierry Lecomte

Neural Networks

Unifying Syntactic and Semantic Abstractions for Deep Neural Networks 201
  Sanaa Siddiqui, Diganta Mukhopadhyay, Mohammad Afzal,
  Hrishikesh Karmarkar, and Kumar Madhukar

Multimodal Model Predictive Runtime Verification for Safety
of Autonomous Cyber-Physical Systems 220
  Alexis Aurandt, Phillip H. Jones, Kristin Yvonne Rozier,
  and Tichakorn Wongpiromsarn

Surrogate Neural Networks Local Stability for Aircraft Predictive
Maintenance 245
  Mélanie Ducoffe, Guillaume Povéda, Audrey Galametz,
  Ryma Boumazouza, Marion-Cécile Martin, Julien Baris,
  Derk Daverschot, and Eugene O'Higgins

Author Index 259

Real-Time Systems/Robotics

Safe Linear Encoding of Vehicle Dynamics for the Instantiation of Abstract Scenarios

Jan Steffen Becker[✉]

German Aerospace Center (DLR) e.V., Institute of Systems Engineering
for Future Mobility, Oldenburg, Germany
jan.becker@dlr.de

Abstract. In the automotive domain, scenario-based development is the answer to the increasing complexity of highly automated driving functions. Scenario-based methods cluster the large scenario space by so-called abstract scenarios which can be used to sample an infinite number of concrete scenarios. Because abstract scenarios constrain driving maneuvers by excessive use of additional constraints, constraint solving techniques may be required to find concrete scenario instances. In order to guarantee correctness of simulation runs with respect to the abstract scenario, realistic vehicle dynamics need to be considered during the instantiation process. This paper proposes a new encoding scheme for simple, but realistic vehicle dynamics into linear constraint systems for the generation of correct-by-construction concrete scenarios. The correctness of the construction is formally proven, and applicability shown by demonstrating the method on a set of basic driving maneuvers.

Keywords: scenario-based testing · simulation · vehicle dynamics · constraint solving · abstract scenario

1 Introduction

In the scenario-driven development of highly automated vehicles, scenarios are used at different levels of abstraction [24,26]. This paper looks at two abstraction levels: *abstract* and *concrete* scenarios. While a concrete scenario [24] describes one specific event sequence in a fixed scenery, abstract scenarios [26] focus on the relations between traffic participants and the environment. Thereby, an abstract scenario may cover a variety of scenes and event sequences – it subsumes an infinite number of concrete scenarios. In a scenario-based testing process [27], for example, abstract scenarios are used to cluster the test space into adequate scenario classes. Scenario class mining may be data-driven or based on expert knowledge, and supported by criticality analysis [26]. Test execution, and experimental evaluation (e.g., in the context of criticality analysis), however, requires sampling of concrete scenarios from the scenario classes.

Formal languages for abstract scenarios, such as OpenSCENARIO DSL [33], SCENIC [14], or Traffic Sequence Charts [7], allow the user to specify complex spatial and temporal relations between traffic participants. These various constraints may interact in a way that turns instantiation of abstract scenarios into a tough challenge. As a simple example, speed and distance constraints later on in a scenario can restrict valid placements of traffic participants at the beginning of the scenario.

As a quite generic solution, this work proposes to use constraint solving to generate concrete scenarios that satisfy all the constraints. Given an abstract scenario, the constraint system must guarantee that

– the concrete scenario is executable on a simulator with realistic vehicle dynamics, and
– the simulation conforms to the abstract scenario, i.e., all the constraints in the abstract scenario are fulfilled.

This requires that knowledge about vehicle dynamics is incorporated into the constraint solving problem. In this work an approach is presented, how both abstract scenarios and vehicle dynamics can be encoded into a linear constraint solving problem. The focus is on the encoding of vehicle dynamics.

The reminder of the paper is structured as follows: Sect. 2 summarizes related work, and Sect. 3 gives an overview on the SMT-based scenario instantiation approach. In Sect. 4, the complete construction for encoding vehicle dynamics is presented, followed by a correctness proof in Sect. 5. An experimental evaluation is described in Sect. 6. The paper concludes with a short discussion in Sect. 7.

2 Related Work

A range of description languages for traffic scenarios has been proposed so far [22]. Most of them follow the concepts defined by Ulbrich et al. [37], who define a scenario as a sequence of scenes, where the temporal evolution between the scenes is described by events and actions. Bach et al. [1] present a model-based scenario description language in a graphical modeling environment. Zhang et al. [38] decide for a textual language for scripting driving scenarios on two different abstraction levels. Menzel et al. [23] propose to derive so-called logical scenarios from natural language scenario descriptions in an engineering process. Logical scenarios are equipped with parameter ranges and probability distributions that allow to sample test cases that follow well-known characteristics. Schuldt et al. [35] propose testing strategies based on logical scenarios. ASAM OpenSCE-NARIO XML has evolved to a widely accepted industry standard for logical and concrete driving scenarios and has been adopted by academic and industrial driving simulators such as ESMINI, Vires VTD, and CARLA. These description languages all use a similar set of driving maneuvers as scenario building blocks. This allows an efficient execution by simulation software, but only a limited level of abstraction.

Neurohr et al. [26,27] therefore propose the use of formalized abstract scenario descriptions. The authors present concepts for exploiting abstract scenarios for testing [27] and criticality analysis [21,26] of automated driving functions.

Textual domain-specific languages for abstract scenarios are M-DSL [11], OpenSCENARIO DSL [33], and Scenic [14]. These languages combine maneuvers and textual constraints. Because they still rely on maneuver actions, their interpretation is simulator-dependent. While Scenic comes with an execution engine that implements a guided simulation approach, the support of OpenSCENARIO DSL is still limited. Since version 0.9.15, the CARLA ScenarioRunner[1] implements a subset of OpenSCENARIO DSL.

Zone graphs [5] and traffic sequence charts (TSCs) [7,8] are graphical specification languages for abstract scenarios. TSCs have a mathematically defined semantics [9], and have been proposed for a wide range of applications, including simulation [2] and monitoring [16]. In contrast to the aforementioned languages, TSCs rely exclusively on seamless declarative scene descriptions. Therefore, simulation requires constraint solving [2,3]. Similar approaches are followed by, e.g., Eggers et al. [10], Klischat and Althoff [19], and Goyal et al. [15].

There are different approaches for solving constraint systems arising from traffic scenarios. A pure discrete approach is presented by Schwammberger [36]. Above cited work [2,3,10,19] sketches some solutions that consider vehicle dynamics to some extend. General-purpose numeric solvers for hybrid systems such as PHAVer [12] and SpaceEx [13] generate precise solutions, but scale bad for the large state space induced by traffic scenarios. Plaku et al. [29,30] overcome this limitation by combining simulation techniques with temporal model checking.

Bézier curves are widely used for path planning (e.g., in [6,17,32]). The cited works use them in combination with a single track vehicle dynamics model (sometimes also called bicycle model). Kong et al. [20] show experimentally that a more complex dynamic model (that considers tire forces) has no advantages over the simple model with respect to control design.

3 Encoding of Abstract Scenarios

According to Ulbrich et al., "a scenario describes the temporal development between several scenes in a sequence of scenes" [37]. This is realized differently in the different scenario description languages. In this paper, a simplified form of traffic sequence charts (TSCs) [7] is used as an example specification language. A TSC describes an abstract scenario as a sequence of so-called *spatial views*. A spatial view is a graphical representation of a scene with a well-defined mathematical semantics. Figure 1 shows a TSC describing an overtake maneuver. The placement of symbols (roads, crossings, vehicles) in a spatial view describes spatial relations between the depicted objects in both an x and y direction. For simplicity, we assume straight roads and orthogonal crossings, and describe spatial relations with respect to vehicle bounding boxes (in a Cartesian coordinate system) and lane boundaries. The dashed boxes are so-called somewhere boxes and are used to finer control the spatial relation—the objects outside the box are put in relation to the box borders, instead of the object inside the box.

---

[1] https://github.com/carla-simulator/scenario_runner/tree/v0.9.15 accessed on 2024-04-19.

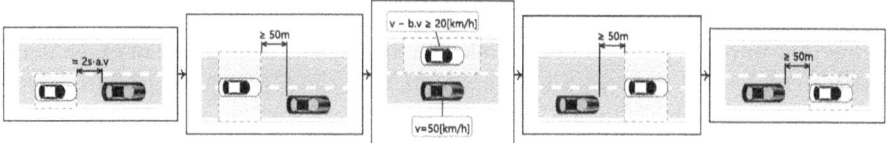

Fig. 1. An overtaking maneuver as TSC

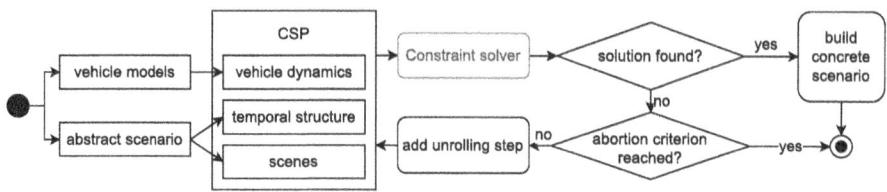

Fig. 2. Strategy for scenario instantiation

Example 1. Using the dashed lane marking as the x-axis of the global coordinate system, the first spatial view in Fig. 1 can be expressed as

$$-w < b.\underline{y} < b.\bar{y} < 0 \land -w < a.\underline{y} < a.\bar{y} < 0 \land b.\underline{x} - a.\bar{x} = 2\,\text{s} \cdot a.v,$$

where $\underline{x}$, $\bar{x}$, $\underline{y}$, and $\bar{y}$ denote bounding boxes (see Fig. 3) of the white (a) and the black (b) vehicles. The variable w denotes lane width, so the interval $[-w, 0]$ is the y-range covered by the lane that contains the vehicles.

The encoding process for an abstract scenario into a constraint solving problem (CSP) follows the idea of bounded model checking and is displayed in Fig. 2. First, we split the time domain of the scenario into N intervals $T_i = [t_{i-1}, t_i)$ (for $i = 1, 2, \ldots, N$) of fixed length $t_i - t_{i-1} = \Delta$, called slices. Note, that a scene may hold during more then one slice, so the number of slices can be larger than the number of scenes. Usually, one starts with the minimal number of slices, and adds further slices until a solution is found or an abortion criterion (e.g., maximum number of slices or timeout) reached. On each time slice $i = 1, 2, \ldots, N$, we describe each scene (indexed by j) in the scenario with a constraint ϕ_j^i. This constraint is further described later on in Sect. 4. The temporal structure of the abstract scenario is encoded with boolean state variables. A seamless sequence of five scenes – as in our running example – can be encoded by introducing a Boolean variable s_j^i for each scene $j = 1, 2, \ldots, 5$ and slice index $i = 1, 2, \ldots, N$ together with a constraint

$$\overbrace{\bigwedge_{i=1}^{N-1} \left((s_1^{i+1} \to s_1^i) \land \bigwedge_{j=1}^{4} (s_{j+1}^{i+1} \to (s_{j+1}^i \lor s_j^i)) \right)}^{(a)} \land \overbrace{\left(s_1^1 \land \bigwedge_{j=2}^{5} \neg s_j^1 \right)}^{(b)} \land \overbrace{s_5^N}^{(c)}.$$

Part (a) of the formula says that scene $j+1$ may be 'active' on slice $i+1$ only if itself or its predecessor was active on slice i. The sub-term $(s_1^{i+1} \to s_1^i)$ handles

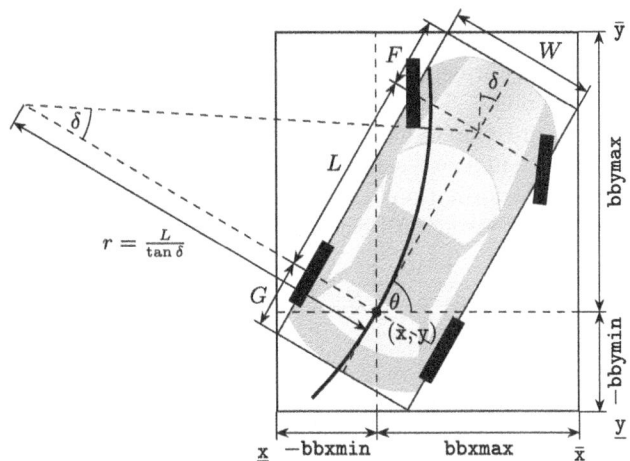

Fig. 3. The simple single track model

this rule for the first scene which has no predecessor. Furthermore, only the first scene is active on the first slice (part (b)), and the last scene in the end (part (c)). The link between the spatial and temporal aspects of the scenario is done by adding a series of implications $\bigwedge_{j,i} \left(sc_j^i \to \phi_j^i \right)$ ranging over all slices and scenes.

4 Encoding Vehicle Dynamics and Scenes

In this work, a simple single track vehicle dynamics model [34] is used. The single track model (Fig. 3) assumes that the longitudinal axis of the vehicle is tangential to the vehicles trajectory, and touches the trajectory at the center of the (stable) rear axis, which is used as a reference point for the vehicle position. The direction of the longitudinal axis is called the *heading angle* θ and is at the same time the direction of movement. In steady state cornering, the vehicle follows a circle with radius $r = \frac{L}{\tan \delta}$ depending on wheel base L and steering angle δ.

4.1 Encoding Trajectories as Splines

We model vehicle trajectories as Bézier splines of fixed degree $n \geq 2$. Bézier curves [31] of degree n are defined by interpolation between $n+1$ points $\mathbf{p}_0, \ldots \mathbf{p}_n$, where $\mathbf{p}_0$ and $\mathbf{p}_n$ are endpoints of the curve, and $\mathbf{p}_1, \ldots, \mathbf{p}_{n-1}$ are bend-points.

Definition 1 (Bézier curve). *A Bézier curve of degree n with control points $\mathbf{p}_0, \ldots, \mathbf{p}_n \in \mathbb{R}^2$ is a parametric curve $\mathbf{p} : [0,1] \to \mathbb{R}^2$ given by*

$$\mathbf{p}(s) := \sum_{k=0}^{n} \mathcal{B}_k^n(s) \mathbf{p}_k \quad \text{with} \quad \mathcal{B}_k^n(s) := \binom{n}{k} (1-s)^k s^{n-k}$$

called the Bernstein basis polynomial. A Bézier spline is a connected curve that is piecewise defined by Bézier curves.

Bézier curves have the following properties [31] that are of interest for this work:

(P1) A Bézier curve is always located within the polygon (convex hull) spanned by its control points.

(P2) Bézier curves are closed under linear combinations and affine transformations; Bézier curves of same degree can be combined/transformed by applying the transformation/combination (pairwise) to the control points.

(P3) The first derivative is again Bézier curve of degree $n-1$:

$$\dot{\mathbf{p}}(s) = \sum_{k=0}^{n-1} \mathcal{B}_k^{n-1}(s) n (\mathbf{p}_{k+1} - \mathbf{p}_k)$$

By applying *degree elevation*, we can express it as a Bézier curve of degree n with control points $\dot{\mathbf{p}}_0 = n(\mathbf{p}_1 - \mathbf{p}_0)$, $\dot{\mathbf{p}}_n = n(\mathbf{p}_n - \mathbf{p}_{n-1})$, and $\dot{\mathbf{p}}_k = k(\mathbf{p}_k - \mathbf{p}_{k-1}) + (n-k)(\mathbf{p}_{k+1} - \mathbf{p}_k)$ for $k = 1, \ldots, n-1$.

We describe the trajectories of vehicles by Bézier splines, using one spline segment per time slice. The spline uniquely defines both the path and the speed profile of a vehicle. A trajectory $\mathbf{p} : [t_0, t_N] \to \mathbb{R}^2$ of N slices is described by a sequence of $N \in \mathbb{N}$ Bézier curves $\mathbf{p}^1, \ldots, \mathbf{p}^N$ such that

$$\mathbf{p}(t) = \mathbf{p}^i(s) \quad \text{for } t \in [t_{i-1}, t_i) \text{ and } s = \frac{t - t_{i-1}}{\Delta}. \tag{1}$$

Note that velocity and acceleration at time point $t \in [t_{i-1}, t_i)$ scale by Δ^{-1} (resp. Δ^{-2}) and are given by

$$\mathbf{v}(t) = \frac{\mathrm{d}}{\mathrm{d}t}\mathbf{p}^i((t - t_{i-1})\Delta^{-1}) = \Delta^{-1}\dot{\mathbf{p}}^i(s) \text{ and } \mathbf{a}(t) = \frac{\mathrm{d}}{\mathrm{d}t}\mathbf{v}(t) = \Delta_i^{-2}\ddot{\mathbf{p}}^i(s). \tag{2}$$

4.2 Encoding of Scenes

In the following, we consider only a single time slice and vehicle. So, we can drop the superscripts and refer to the Bézier curve for the current slice as $\mathbf{p}$. It is described by $n+1$ control points $\mathbf{p}_0, \ldots, \mathbf{p}_n$. We encode the kth control point $\mathbf{p}_k$ by a pair of variables x_k and y_k. Furthermore, we approximate speed v, longitudinal acceleration acc, heading angle θ, and the bounding box dimensions $bound \in BB := \{\texttt{bbxmin}, \texttt{bbxmax}, \texttt{bbymin}, \texttt{bbymax}\}$ by save lower and upper bounds $bound^l$, $bound^u$ (for $bound \in BB$), $v^l(s)$, $v^u(s)$, $acc^l(s)$, $acc^u(s)$, θ^l, and θ^u (lower bounds are denoted by superscript l and upper bounds by superscript u). In case of bounding box dimensions and heading angle, these are variables; in case of v and acc these are Bernstein polynomials. For simplicity, w.l.o.g. we assume all used Bézier splines and Bernstein polynomials (including derivatives such as velocity and acceleration) having same the degree n. A practical implementation, however, will reduce the number of free variables by encoding velocity and acceleration bounds with at most n (resp. $n-1$) control points.

Given some scene as a monotone Boolean combination of linear constraints, we can utilize properties (P1) and (P2) of Bézier splines and conservatively approximate each linear constraint using the Bézier control points and lower/upper bounds introduced above.

Example 2. A sufficient condition for a 2-seconds distance between two vehicles a and b can be expressed as

$$\bigwedge_{k=0}^{n} \left((b.x_k + b.\texttt{bbxmin}^l) - (a.x_k + a.\texttt{bbxmax}^u) \geq 2\,\text{s} \cdot (a.v_k^u - b.v_k^l) \right).$$

4.3 Encoding of Vehicle Dynamics

The CSP constructed from the abstract scenario must ensure that

- the trajectory is possible within the single track model, and
- the variables, resp. values, $bound^l$, $bound^u$ (for $bound \in BB$), $v^l(s)$, $v^u(s)$, $acc^l(s)$, $acc^u(s)$, θ^l, and θ^u are valid lower/upper bounds for $bound(\theta(t))$, $v(t)$, $\dot{v}(t)$, and $\theta(t)$.

This is done by constructing some constraint system denoted Φ in the following, that is instantiated for each vehicle and time slice. It includes a special linear approximation of the single track model equations of motion.

Definition 2. *The single track model's equations of movement are*

$$\dot{x}(t) = v(t)\cos\theta(t), \qquad \dot{y}(t) = v(t)\sin\theta(t), \qquad \dot{\theta}(t) = v(t)\frac{\tan\delta(t)}{L}$$

and are subject to the constraints

$$|\delta(t)| \leq \delta_{\max} \quad \text{and} \quad a_{lat}(t) := |\dot{\theta}(t)v(t)| \leq a_{lat,\max} := 0.4\text{g}.$$

The construction for Φ uses a discretization of the heading angle θ. We choose a finite set $\mathcal{I}$ of heading intervals. Each interval $I = [\bar{\theta} - \eta, \bar{\theta} + \eta] \in \mathcal{I}$ is characterized by a *primary heading angle* $\bar{\theta} \in [-\pi, \pi]$ and a *heading angle deviation* $\eta \in [0, \pi/2)$. The selection of heading intervals depends on the abstract scenario. For example, a U-turn scenario requires that the union of heading intervals contains at least a half circle, while in an overtaking scenario a small heading range may be sufficient. The to-be-constructed constraint Φ ensures that on each slice the vehicle heading is within one of the intervals. From this interval, linear constraints for the vehicle movement within the slice are derived. In order to simplify the construction, we project the vehicle trajectory into a rotated coordinate system where the x-axis points into the primary heading direction.

Construction 1. *Given some interval $I = [\bar{\theta} - \eta, \bar{\theta} + \eta]$ and variables x_k, y_k (for $k = 0, \ldots, n$) describing Bézier curve control points, define*

$$X(I)_k := x_k \cos\bar{\theta} + y_k \sin\bar{\theta} \quad \text{and} \quad Y(I)_k := -x_k \sin\bar{\theta} + y_k \cos\bar{\theta}.$$

Analogously, denote the control points of the projected first and second derivatives (see property (P3)) by $(\dot{X}(I)_k, \dot{Y}(I)_k)^T$ resp. $(\ddot{X}(I)_k, \ddot{Y}(I)_k)^T$.

In the rotated coordinate system, the vehicle moves roughly in X-direction, with a deviation of $\pm\eta$. Because the speed on a curve segment is determined by the distance between control points, the curvature increases when the vehicle accelerates (or brakes) on a curved segment (visually, the segment is skewed which leads to a sharper bend). In order to make handling of the curvature easier, the following construction distinguishes between straight and curved segments. Acceleration and deceleration along the rotated $X(I)$ axes are allowed on straight ($\eta = 0$) segments only, otherwise $\ddot{X}(I)$ is kept constant. Furthermore, a Boolean variable rws differentiates forward (rws = 0) from reverse (rws = 1) driving.

Construction 2. *Given a set $\mathcal{I}$ of heading intervals, the simple single track model is approximated by a constraint*

$$\Phi := \Phi_{cont} \wedge \bigvee_{I \in \mathcal{I}} ((\neg \text{rws} \rightarrow \Phi_{fwd}(I)) \wedge (\text{rws} \rightarrow \Phi_{rws}(I)))$$

with $\Phi_{fwd}(I) :\equiv \Phi_H(I) \wedge \Phi_{BB}(I) \wedge \Phi_{valid}(I) \wedge \Phi_v(I) \wedge \Phi_{acc}(I)$ *where*

$$\Phi_{cont} :\equiv \mathbf{p}_n = \mathbf{p}'_0 \wedge \dot{\mathbf{p}}_n = \dot{\mathbf{p}}'_0 \wedge (\dot{\mathbf{p}}_n = \mathbf{0} \rightarrow \theta^l = \theta^u = \theta^{l'} = \theta^{u'}) \wedge (\dot{\mathbf{p}}_n \neq \mathbf{0} \rightarrow (\text{rws} \leftrightarrow \text{rws}'))$$

$$\Phi_{BB}(I) :\equiv \bigwedge_{bound \in BB} \left(bound^l \leq \min_{\theta \in I} bound(\theta) \wedge bound^u \geq \max_{\theta \in I} bound(\theta) \right)$$

$$\Phi_H(I) :\equiv [\theta^l, \theta^u] \supseteq I \wedge \bigwedge_{k=0}^{n} \left(\dot{X}(I)_k \geq 0 \wedge |\dot{Y}(I)_k| \leq \dot{X}(I)_k \tan \eta \right)$$

$$\Phi_{valid}(I) :\equiv \bigwedge_{k=0}^{n} \left(\underbrace{\ddot{X}(I)_k = 0}_{\eta > 0 \text{ only}} \wedge \left| \frac{\ddot{Y}(I)_k}{\Delta^2} \right| \leq a_{lat,max} \wedge \dot{X}(I)_k \geq \frac{2(n-1)L\tan(\eta)}{\tan(\delta_{max})} \right)$$

$$\Phi_v(I) :\equiv \bigwedge_{k=0}^{n} \begin{cases} v_k^l = v_k^u = \Delta^{-1} \dot{X}(I)_k & \text{for } \eta = 0 \\ v_k^l \leq \Delta^{-1} \dot{X}(I)_k \wedge v_k^u \geq \frac{\dot{X}(I)_k + \tan(\frac{\eta}{2})|\dot{Y}(I)_k|}{\Delta} & \text{for } \eta > 0 \end{cases}$$

$$\Phi_{acc}(I) :\equiv \bigwedge_{k=0}^{n} \begin{cases} acc_k^l = acc_k^u = \Delta^{-2} \ddot{X}(I)_k & \text{for } \eta = 0 \\ acc_k^l \leq -|\Delta^{-2} \ddot{Y}(I)_k| \wedge acc_k^u \geq |\Delta^{-2} \ddot{Y}(I)_k| & \text{for } \eta > 0 \end{cases}$$

The constraint $\Phi_{rws}(I)$ is the same as $\Phi_{fwd}(I)$ except for the following replacements: $\dot{X}(I)_k$ by $-\dot{X}(I)_k$, v_k^l by $-v_k^u$, and v_k^u by $-v_k^l$.

In the construction, Φ_{cont} ensures that the next segment starts with the heading and speed at the end of the current segment. On each segment, $\Phi_{fwd}(I)$ and $\Phi_{rws}(I)$ encode forward resp. backwards movement within a heading interval I. Here, $\phi_H(I)$ ensures that the movement direction on the current slice is within the given interval. The remaining constraints ensure that curvature and lateral acceleration are within validity range of the single track model ($\phi_{valid}(I)$), and that bounding box ($\phi_{BB}(I)$), velocity ($\phi_v(I)$), and acceleration ($\phi_{acc}(I)$) bounds are valid.

5 Correctness

This section sketches the correctness proofs for the construction. Recall that the constraint Φ from Construction 2 is instantiated for every slice and vehicle. Each solution of the resulting constraint system contains control point values that can be used to construct a vehicle trajectory according to Eq. (1). In the following, it is shown that the generated trajectory is a solution for the simple single track model equations. Then, it is shown that the values for $v^l, v^u, acc^l, acc^u, \ldots$ are correct lower and upper bounds for velocity, acceleration, heading, and bounding box dimensions. For reasons of space, the proofs show the case for forward driving only. Proofs for reversing are analogous.

Lemma 1. *A trajectory $\mathbf{p}$ as defined in Eq. (1) satisfies the simple single track model differential equations with*

$$v(t) = |\dot{\mathbf{p}}(t)|, \ \delta(t) = \arctan(\kappa'(t)L), \ and \ \kappa'(t) = \frac{\dot{x}(t)\ddot{y}(t) - \ddot{x}(t)\dot{y}(t)}{(\dot{x}(t)^2 + \dot{y}(t)^2)^{3/2}} \ if \ v(t) \neq 0$$

(else $\kappa'(t) = 0$), provided the control points $\mathbf{p}_k = \mathbf{p}_k^i$, $\mathbf{p}_k' = \mathbf{p}_k^{i+1}$ ($i = 0, \ldots, n$) satisfy Φ as defined in Construction 2.

Proof. Given some time point t, call the ith slice, with $t_{i-1} \leq t \leq t_i$, the *current slice*. Assuming that the constraint Φ holds, there is some heading range $I_i = [\bar{\theta}_i - \eta_i, \bar{\theta}_i + \eta_i] \in \mathcal{I}$ such that $\Phi_H(I_i)$ and $\Phi_{valid}(I_i)$ hold. Furthermore, Φ_{cont} holds. The ODE system for the single track model can also be formulated as a linear ODE

$$\dot{\mathbf{h}}(t) = \begin{bmatrix} 0 & -v(t)\kappa(t) \\ v(t)\kappa(t) & 0 \end{bmatrix} \mathbf{h}(t) \qquad \dot{\mathbf{p}}(t) = v(t)\mathbf{h}(t) \tag{3}$$

with the constraint $|\mathbf{h}(t)| = 1$. It can be easily verified that the single track model ODEs solve the above linear ODE if $\mathbf{h}(t) = (\cos\theta(t), \sin\theta(t))^T$ and $\kappa(t) = \frac{\tan\delta(t)}{L}$. We show that the ODEs in Eq. 3 hold on the current slice when setting

$$\mathbf{h}(t) = \begin{cases} (\cos\bar{\theta}_i, \sin\bar{\theta}_i)^T & \text{if } v(t) = 0 \\ \dot{\mathbf{p}}(t)/v(t) & \text{else.} \end{cases} \tag{4}$$

and $\delta(t)$ as in the Lemma. In case $v(t) \neq 0$, this is true by some basic analysis:

$$\dot{\mathbf{h}}(t) = \frac{d}{dt}\frac{\dot{\mathbf{p}}(t)}{v(t)} = \frac{d}{dt}\begin{bmatrix} \frac{\dot{x}(t)}{\sqrt{\dot{x}(t)^2+\dot{y}(t)^2}} \\ \frac{\dot{y}(t)}{\sqrt{\dot{x}(t)^2+\dot{y}(t)^2}} \end{bmatrix} = \begin{bmatrix} \frac{\ddot{x}(t)\dot{y}(t)^2 - \ddot{y}(t)\dot{x}(t)\dot{y}(t)}{(\dot{x}(t)^2+\dot{y}(t)^2)^{3/2}} \\ \frac{\ddot{y}(t)\dot{x}(t)^2 - \ddot{x}(t)\dot{x}(t)\dot{y}(t)}{(\dot{x}(t)^2+\dot{y}(t)^2)^{3/2}} \end{bmatrix}$$

$$= \begin{bmatrix} -\kappa'(t)\dot{y}(t) \\ \kappa'(t)\dot{x}(t) \end{bmatrix} = \begin{bmatrix} 0 & -v(t)\kappa(t) \\ v(t)\kappa(t) & 0 \end{bmatrix} \mathbf{h}(t)$$

(note that $\kappa'(t) = \kappa(t)$). In case $v(t) = 0$, we have to show that $\dot{\mathbf{h}}(t) = 0$. Constraint $\Phi_{valid}(I)$ allows $v(t) = 0$ only if $\eta_i = 0$. By $\Phi_H(I)$ and Construction 1, this implies that we are on a straight segment with $\dot{\mathbf{p}}(t') = (\cos \bar{\theta}_i, \sin \bar{\theta}_i)^T v(t')$, and therefore $\mathbf{h}(t') = (\cos \bar{\theta}_i, \sin \bar{\theta}_i)^T$ constant for all $t' \in [t_{i-1}, t_i]$. So, $\dot{\mathbf{h}}(t) = 0$.

The remaining part, showing that no discontinuities at time slice boundaries occur, is a direct consequence of the constraint Φ_{cont}. □

For the following lemmas and proofs, we fix some Bézier spline trajectory and construct $v(t)$ and $\delta(t)$ as in Lemma 1. Furthermore, we fix some time slice $[t_{i-1}, t_i]$ and some heading interval $I = [\bar{\theta} - \eta, \bar{\theta} + \eta]$ with $\bar{\theta} \in \mathbb{R}, \eta \in [0, \pi/2)$. Again, we drop the superscripts. Recall that Construction 1 uses a rotated version of the trajectory segment given by control points $(X_k, Y_k)^T$, depending on $\bar{\theta}$. We use it in form of Bernstein polynomials $X(s) := \sum_{k=0}^{n} \mathcal{B}_k^n(s) X_k$ and $Y(s) := \sum_{k=0}^{n} \mathcal{B}_k^n(s) Y_k$.

Lemma 2. *If both the heading constraint $\Phi_H(I)$ and the constraint $\Phi_{valid}(I)$ hold, then $|\kappa(t)| \leq \frac{\tan(\delta_{\max})}{L}$ and $|a_{lat}(t)| \leq a_{lat,\max}$ for all $t \in [t_{i-1}, t_i]$.*

Proof. Fix some $t \in [t_{i-1}, t_i]$ and let $s = (t - t_{i-1})\Delta^{-1}$. By property (P1) of Bézier curves, the constraints $\Phi_{valid}(I)$ and $\Phi_H(I)$ imply

$$\Delta v(t) = \sqrt{\dot{X}^2(s) + \dot{Y}^2(s)} \geq \dot{X}(s) \geq 0 \text{ and } |\dot{Y}(s)| \leq \dot{X}(s) \tan \eta$$

for all $s \in [0, 1]$ (recall that speed is invariant to rotation and, by Eq. (2), scaled by Δ^{-1}). The curvature of the trajectory is invariant to rotation and, with the above inequalities, bounded by

$$|\kappa(t)| = \frac{|\dot{X}(s)\ddot{Y}(s) - \ddot{X}(s)\dot{Y}(s)|}{(\dot{X}^2(s) + \dot{Y}^2(s))^{3/2}} \leq \frac{|\ddot{Y}(s)| + |\ddot{X}(s)|\tan\eta}{\dot{X}^2(s) + \dot{Y}^2(s)} \leq \frac{|\ddot{Y}(s)| + |\ddot{X}(s)|\tan\eta}{\Delta^2 v^2(s)}$$

Similar, lateral acceleration $a_{lat}(t) = \kappa(t) v^2(t)$ is bounded by

$$a_{lat}(t) \leq \frac{|\ddot{Y}(s)| + |\ddot{X}(s)|\tan\eta}{\Delta^2}.$$

In the case $\eta = 0$, the bound $|\dot{Y}(s)| \leq \dot{X}(s) \tan \eta$ implies $\dot{Y}(s) = 0$ for all $s \in [0, 1]$, so $\ddot{Y}(s) = 0$. As a consequence of the above equations, both $a_{lat}(t) = 0$ and $\kappa(t) = 0$.

For $\eta > 0$, the constraint $\Phi_{valid}(I)$ forces $\dot{X}(s) > 0$ and $\ddot{X}(s) = 0$. This simplifies the above approximation for a_{lat} to $a_{lat}(t) \leq |\ddot{Y}(s)|\Delta^{-2}$. Furthermore, it means that $\dot{X}(s)$ is constant. Recall that $\dot{X}$ and $\dot{Y}$ are Bernstein polynomials of degree n with $\dot{X}_0 = \dot{X}_1 = \cdots = \dot{X}_{n-1} = \dot{X}(s) > 0$, and control points of $\dot{Y}$ can be bounded by $|\dot{Y}_i| \leq \dot{X}(s)\tan(\eta)$ for $i = 0, 1, \ldots, n-1$. By Bézier curve properties, $\ddot{Y}(s)$ is bounded by

$$|\ddot{Y}_i(s)| \leq (n-1)|\dot{Y}_{i+1} - \dot{Y}_i| \leq 2(n-1)\dot{X}(s)\tan(\eta).$$

Using $\dot{X}(s)$ as a lower bound for $\Delta \cdot v(t)$, it is

$$|\kappa(s)| \leq \frac{2(n-1)\dot{X}(s)\tan(\eta)}{\dot{X}^2(s)} = \frac{2(n-1)\tan(\eta)}{\dot{X}(s)}.$$

With the bounds $\left|\frac{\ddot{Y}(s)}{\Delta^2}\right| \leq a_{lat,\max}$ and $\dot{X}(s) \geq \frac{2(n-1)L\tan(\eta)}{\tan(\delta_{\max})}$ implied by $\Phi_{valid}(I)$ follows $|a_{lat}(s)| \leq a_{lat,\max}$ and $|\kappa(t)| \leq \frac{\tan(\delta_{\max})}{L}$. □

Lemma 3. *If both the heading constraint $\Phi_H(I)$ and $\Phi_v(I)$ hold, then $v^l(t) \leq v(t) \leq v^u(t)$ for all $t \in [t_{i-1}, t_i]$.*

Proof. Fix some time point $t \in [t_{i-1}, t_i]$ and let $s := (t - t_{i-1})\Delta^{-1}$. Define $v_X := \Delta^{-1}\dot{X}(s)$ and $v_Y = \Delta^{-1}\dot{Y}(s)$ and recall that $v(t) = \sqrt{v_X^2 + v_Y^2}$ and $v_X \geq 0$. So, $v^l(t) \leq v_X \leq v(t)$.

In case $\eta = 0$, the constraint $|\dot{Y}(s)| \leq \dot{X}(s)\tan\eta$ implied by $\Phi_H(I)$ enforces $v_Y = 0$. Hence, $v(t) = v_X$ and by definition $v^u(t) = v_X = v(t)$.

The remaining case is $\eta > 0$. Recall (from the above proofs) that then $v_X > 0$. Because $v(t) = \sqrt{v_X^2 + v_Y^2} > 0$ and $0 < |v_Y| \leq v_X \tan\eta$ we can find some (unique) $\eta' \in [-\eta, +\eta]$ such that $v_X = v(t)\cos\eta'$ and $v_Y = v(t)\sin\eta'$. It is

$$v(t) = v(t)\cos(\eta') + v(t)(1 - \cos(\eta')) = v(t)\cos(\eta') + \frac{1 - \cos(\eta')}{\sin(\eta')}v(t)\sin(\eta')$$

$$= v_X + \frac{1 - \cos(\eta')}{\sin(\eta')}v_Y = v_X + \tan\left(\frac{\eta'}{2}\right)v_Y$$

and by monotony of tan on the interval $(-\pi, +\pi)$

$$\leq v_X + \tan\left(\frac{\eta}{2}\right)|v_Y| = \Delta^{-1}\dot{X}(s) + \Delta^{-1}\tan\left(\frac{\eta}{2}\right)|\dot{Y}(s)| \leq v^u(s)$$

by definition of $\Phi_v(I)$. So, the lemma holds. □

Lemma 4. *If both $\Phi_H(I)$, $\Phi_{valid}(I)$, and $\Phi_{acc}(I)$ hold, then $acc^l(t) \leq acc(t) \leq acc^u(t)$ for all $t \in [t_{i-1}, t_i]$.*

Proof. Fix some time point $t \in [t_{i-1}, t_i]$ and let $s := (t - t_{i-1})\Delta^{-1}$. The acceleration $acc(t) = \dot{v}(t)$ is invariant to rotation of the spline segment. Therefore

$$acc(t) = \frac{\ddot{X}(s)\dot{X}(s) + \ddot{Y}(s)\dot{Y}(s)}{\Delta^2\sqrt{\dot{X}(s)^2 + \dot{Y}(s)^2}}.$$

If $\eta = 0$, then by constraint $\Phi_H(I)$, it is $\dot{Y}(s) = \ddot{Y}(s) = 0$ and therefore $acc(t) = \Delta^2\ddot{X}(s) = acc^l(t) = acc^u(t)$. If $\eta > 0$, then $\Phi_{valid}(I)$ enforces $\ddot{X}(s) = 0$. Together with $\sqrt{\dot{X}(s)^2 + \dot{Y}(s)^2} \geq |\dot{Y}(s)|$ follows $|acc(t)| \leq \Delta^{-2}|\ddot{Y}(s)|$. The lemma follows with the definition of $\Phi_{acc}(I)$. □

Corollary 1 (Correctness of Construction 2). *Bézier splines satisfying Construction 2 are valid trajectories for the simple single track model, with valid bounds for velocity and acceleration.*

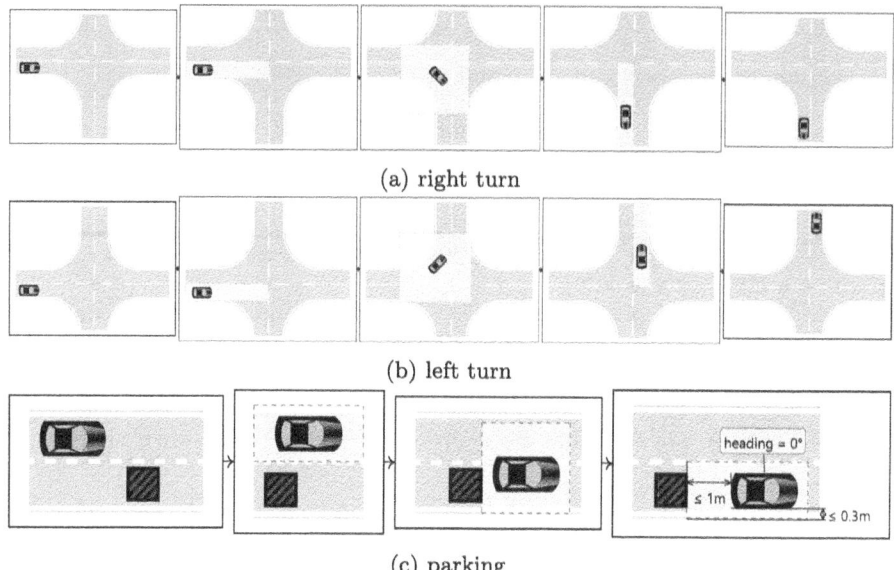

Fig. 4. Additional demonstration scenarios

6 Demonstration

In order to demonstrate the applicability of the approach, this section presents trajectories generated from four different abstract scenarios: an overtaking (Fig. 1), a right turn (Fig. 4a), a left turn (Fig. 4b), and a parking scenario (Fig. 4c). The four scenarios have been selected in order to contain a majority of the basic driving maneuvers that commonly occur in urban traffic scenarios. In particular, they map to the basic maneuvers identified by Hartjen et al. [18] as follows:

- Overtaking: keep velocity, follow lane, change lane, follow object[2], passing
- Left/right turn: follow lane, approach/cross junction, left/right turn[3]
- Parking: driveaway[4], halt, approach object, reversing, park

The vehicle dynamics encoding given in this paper has been integrated into the scenario instantiation framework for TSCs that has been presented in previous work [2,3]. As a CSP solver, Z3 [25] is used. The TSCs (temporal structure and spatial views) given in Figs. 1 and 4 are translated to BMC problems using the encoding scheme sketched in Sect. 3 and the related work [2,3]. Vehicle dynamics are encoded with quadratic Bézier splines ($n = 2$) using Construction 2 given in this paper. Table 2 lists the heading intervals $\mathcal{I}$, unrolling depth N, and

---

[2] keep distance to other vehicle.
[3] 90° turn on junction.
[4] acceleration from standstill.

Table 1. Vehicle parameters for the demonstration scenarios

parameter	variable	value
max. Ackermann steering angle	δ_{max}	45.0°
front	F	0.8 m
wheel base	L	2.8 m
rear	G	0.7 m
width	W	1.8 m

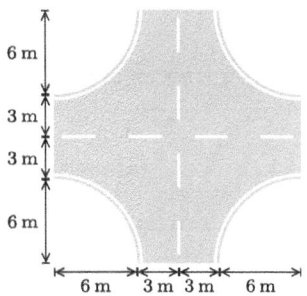

Fig. 5. Dimensions of the crossing in the demonstration scenarios

Table 2. Heading intervals, number of slices (N), and slice length (Δ) for the demonstration scenarios

scenario	intervals $\mathcal{I}$	#slices N	slice length Δ
overtaking	$[0,0]°$, $[-10,10]°$	20	2 s
parking	$[0,0]°$, $[-15,15]°$, $[15,15]°$, $[0,30]°$	8	3 s
left turn	$[0,0]°$, $[0,45]°$, $[45,90]°$, $[90,90]°$	8	3 s
right turn	$[0,0]°$, $[0,-45]°$, $[-45,-90]°$, $[-90,-90]°$	8	3 s

step size Δ used in each scenario. All scenarios use a fictive vehicle model with a maximum speed of 120 km/h, (20 km/h when reversing), maximum acceleration of 1 ms^{-2} (both forward and reverse), and braking deceleration of -5 ms^{-2}. The single track model vehicle parameters (except heading ranges which are scenario-dependent) are listed in Table 1. All scenarios use a lane width of 3 m. The crossing in the turning scenario has a corner radius of 6 m as shown in Fig. 5.

For each of the SMT problems, the solver can find a satisfying model within less than 10 s[5]. The resulting trajectories are plotted in Fig. 6. The blue shaded areas show the outer bounding box approximation calculated by the solver. Note that the inequalities $\Phi_{BB}(I)$ in Construction 2 allow the solver to assume any bounding approximation box that fits the vehicle, so the bounding boxes are not necessarily tight. It can be observed that the solver tends to choose the maximum bounding box that satisfies the current spatial view.

The presented concrete scenarios show that trajectories can be found for all basic maneuvers. The trajectories are correct by construction with respect to the chosen vehicle model and abstract scenario. However, the single track vehicle model simplifies actual vehicle dynamics. For example, side slip of the tires is neglected. As a consequence, when a simulator executes the scenario with a more accurate vehicle physics model, the simulated trajectory may differ from the

---

[5] The results have been produced using Z3 v4.8.14 running on a Windows 10 notebook with Intel Core i7-1185G7 CPU @ 3.00 GHz and 16 GB RAM.

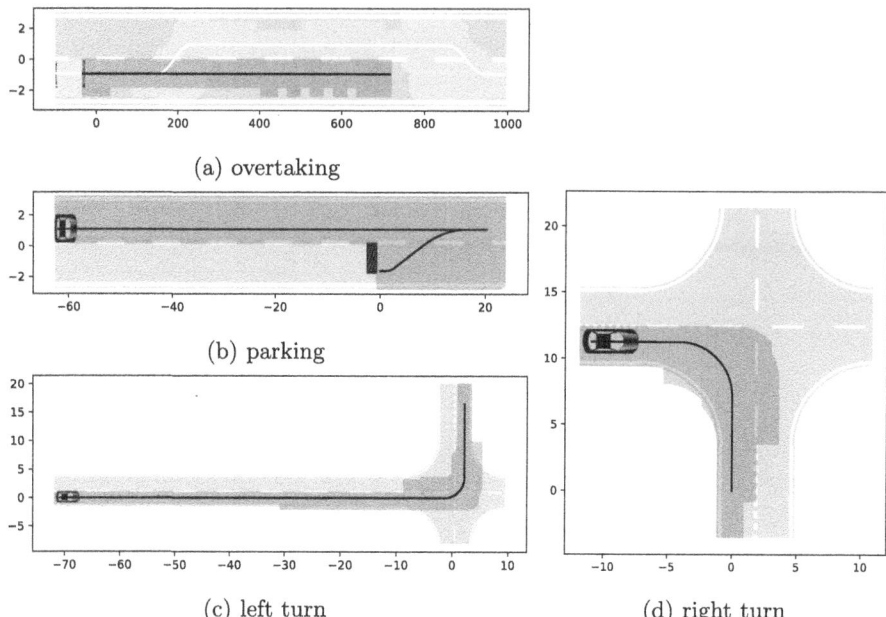

Fig. 6. Generated trajectories; the solid lines show vehicle trajectories, and the shaded areas the bounding box approximation; axes are in Meters

ideal one calculated by the CSP solver. In order to give an upper bound for the simulation error for the demonstration scenarios, the generated trajectories have been executed with the CARLA 14.0 driving simulator. As a vehicle, the CARLA built-in model of an Audi A2 has been chosen, which has nearly the same wheel base as our fictive vehicle. In the experiment, a custom controller implementation has been used that operates in the simulation loop. In each simulation step, the controller calculates throttle/brake and steering values by comparing the current actual and calculated vehicle states. Table 3 shows the maximum error in each experiment, in terms of lateral (lat) and longitudinal (lon) distance of the actual reference point to the calculated trajectory, heading angle (heading), and absolute distance error in the corners of the vehicle bounding box (bounds).

The results show that the lateral error is with a maximum of 4.0 cm in the right turn maneuver quite moderate. They are comparable to what has been achieved by Kong et al. [20] using a model predictive controller. This indicates that the single track model is adequate for trajectory planning. The comparatively larger longitudinal error is due to the sensitivity of the implemented controller with respect to acceleration changes, which are quite prominent in the overtaking maneuver for other. This can probably be reduced, e.g., by replacing the used discrete PID controller by a model predictive control algorithm [20]. The controller aims at minimizing the error in the vehicle reference point located at the rear axes. As a consequence, the bounding box error is dominated by the heading and longitudinal errors. Choosing another reference point in the simulation may reduce this effect.

Table 3. Error between ideal and simulated trajectories

scenario (vehicle)	lat	lon	heading	bounds
overtaking (ego)	4.0 cm	14.9 cm	0.6°	14.9 cm
overtaking (other)	<0.1 cm	11.8 cm	<0.1°	11.9 cm
right turn (ego)	2.0 cm	3.6 cm	1.5°	9.0 cm
left turn (ego)	2.8 cm	10.0 cm	1.7°	10.0 cm
parking (ego)	0.5 cm	13.4 cm	0.4°	13.4 cm

7 Conclusion

This paper describes a method for encoding abstract scenarios to linear constraint solving/BMC problems. The encoding of vehicle dynamics, given in detail in Sect. 4, uses a simple single track model. The main ideas are to describe the vehicle trajectories as Bézier splines that are parameterized by time. So, the solution of the constraint problem determines the position of every vehicle to every point in time. Linear constraints give safe bounds for velocity and acceleration, by a discretization of the heading angle.

Due to the linearizations and over-approximations, heading intervals, number, and length of time slices must be appropriately chosen for the abstract scenario. While finer discretizations increase the covered scenario space, they also increase the complexity of the CSP problem. The practical demonstration in Sect. 6 shows that the approach can generate trajectories for a majority of basic driving maneuvers, and that the simple vehicle dynamics yields trajectories that can be executed under realistic driving physics. In this paper only one solution has been generated for each abstract scenario. The approach may be combined with model enumeration techniques (e.g. all-SMT [28] or recursive blocking [4]) in order to systematically generate different scenarios. Because of the enormous search space, strategies for finding an optimal coverage need to be developed. This subject to ongoing research.

So far, the approach has been applied to simulation [2] (where also first scalability results have been published) and consistency analysis [3] of TSCs. Future applications include the application to maritime and railway scenarios. This future research will address the above shortcomings of the approach.

References

1. Bach, J., Otten, S., Sax, E.: Model based scenario specification for development and test of automated driving functions. In: 2016 IEEE Intelligent Vehicles Symposium (IV), pp. 1149–1155 (2016). https://doi.org/10.1109/IVS.2016.7535534
2. Becker, J., et al.: Simulation of abstract scenarios: towards automated tooling in criticality analysis, pp. 42–51 (2022). https://doi.org/10.5281/zenodo.5907154
3. Becker, J.S.: Partial consistency for requirement engineering with traffic sequence charts. In: Automotive Software Engineering (ASE2020) (2020)

4. Bjørner, N., de Moura, L., Nachmanson, L., Wintersteiger, C.M.: Programming Z3. In: Bowen, J., Liu, Z., Zhang, Z. (eds.) SETSS 2018. LNCS, vol. 11430, pp. 148–201. Springer, Cham (2019). https://doi.org/10.1007/978-3-030-17601-3_4
5. Butz, M., et al.: SOCA: domain analysis for highly automated driving systems. In: 2020 IEEE 23rd International Conference on Intelligent Transportation Systems (ITSC), pp. 1–6 (2020). https://doi.org/10.1109/ITSC45102.2020.9294438
6. Choi, J.W., Curry, R., Elkaim, G.: Path planning based on Bézier curve for autonomous ground vehicles. In: Advances in Electrical and Electronics Engineering-IAENG Special Edition of the World Congress on Engineering and Computer Science 2008, pp. 158–166. IEEE (2008)
7. Damm, W., Kemper, S., Möhlmann, E., Peikenkamp, T., Rakow, A.: Using traffic sequence charts for the development of HAVs. In: ERTS 2018. 9th European Congress on Embedded Real Time Software and Systems (ERTS 2018), Toulouse, France (2018). https://hal.science/hal-01714060
8. Damm, W., Kemper, S., Möhlmann, E., Peikenkamp, T., Rakow, A.: Traffic sequence charts: a visual language for capturing traffic scenarios. In: Embedded Real Time Software and Systems - ERTS2018 (2018)
9. Damm, W., Möhlmann, E., Peikenkamp, T., Rakow, A.: A formal semantics for traffic sequence charts. In: Lohstroh, M., Derler, P., Sirjani, M. (eds.) Principles of Modeling. LNCS, vol. 10760, pp. 182–205. Springer, Cham (2018). https://doi.org/10.1007/978-3-319-95246-8_11
10. Eggers, A., Stasch, M., Teige, T., Bienmüller, T., Brockmeyer, U.: Constraint systems from traffic scenarios for the validation of autonomous driving. In: Third International Workshop on Satisfiability Checking and Symbolic Computation, Part of FLOC 2018 (2018)
11. Foretellix Ltd.: Measurable scenario description language reference. Technical report, Foretellix Ltd. (2020). https://www.foretellix.com/wp-content/uploads/2020/07/M-SDL_LRM_OS.pdf. Accessed 19 Apr 2024
12. Frehse, G.: PHAVer: algorithmic verification of hybrid systems past HyTech. In: Morari, M., Thiele, L. (eds.) HSCC 2005. LNCS, vol. 3414, pp. 258–273. Springer, Heidelberg (2005). https://doi.org/10.1007/978-3-540-31954-2_17
13. Frehse, G., et al.: SpaceEx: scalable verification of hybrid systems. In: Gopalakrishnan, G., Qadeer, S. (eds.) CAV 2011. LNCS, vol. 6806, pp. 379–395. Springer, Heidelberg (2011). https://doi.org/10.1007/978-3-642-22110-1_30
14. Fremont, D.J., et al.: Scenic: a language for scenario specification and data generation. Mach. Learn. **112**(10), 3805–3849 (2023). https://doi.org/10.1007/s10994-021-06120-5
15. Goyal, S., Griggio, A., Kimblad, J., Tonetta, S.: Automatic generation of scenarios for system-level simulation-based verification of autonomous driving systems. arXiv preprint arXiv:2311.09784 (2023)
16. Grundt, D., Köhne, A., Saxena, I., Stemmer, R., Westphal, B., Möhlmann, E.: Towards runtime monitoring of complex system requirements for autonomous driving functions (2022). https://doi.org/10.48550/arXiv.2209.14032
17. Han, L., Yashiro, H., Nejad, H.T.N., Do, Q.H., Mita, S.: Bezier curve based path planning for autonomous vehicle in urban environment. In: 2010 IEEE Intelligent Vehicles Symposium, pp. 1036–1042. IEEE (2010)
18. Hartjen, L., Philipp, R., Schuldt, F., Friedrich, B., Howar, F.: Classification of driving maneuvers in urban traffic for parametrization of test scenarios. In: 9. Tagung Automatisiertes Fahren (2019)

19. Klischat, M., Althoff, M.: Synthesizing traffic scenarios from formal specifications for testing automated vehicles. In: 2020 IEEE Intelligent Vehicles Symposium (IV), pp. 2065–2072. IEEE (2020)
20. Kong, J., Pfeiffer, M., Schildbach, G., Borrelli, F.: Kinematic and dynamic vehicle models for autonomous driving control design, pp. 1094–1099 (2015). https://doi.org/10.1109/IVS.2015.7225830
21. Kramer, B., Neurohr, C., Büker, M., Böde, E., Fränzle, M., Damm, W.: Identification and quantification of hazardous scenarios for automated driving. In: Zeller, M., Höfig, K. (eds.) IMBSA 2020. LNCS, vol. 12297, pp. 163–178. Springer International Publishing, Cham (2020). https://doi.org/10.1007/978-3-030-58920-2_11
22. Ma, J., Che, X., Li, Y., Lai, E.M.K.: Traffic scenarios for automated vehicle testing: a review of description languages and systems. Machines **9**(12), 342 (2021)
23. Menzel, T., Bagschik, G., Isensee, L., Schomburg, A., Maurer, M.: From functional to logical scenarios: detailing a keyword-based scenario description for execution in a simulation environment. In: 2019 IEEE Intelligent Vehicles Symposium (IV), pp. 2383–2390 (2019). https://doi.org/10.1109/IVS.2019.8814099
24. Menzel, T., Bagschik, G., Maurer, M.: Scenarios for development, test and validation of automated vehicles. In: 2018 IEEE Intelligent Vehicles Symposium (IV), pp. 1821–1827. IEEE (2018). https://doi.org/10.1109/IVS.2018.8500406
25. de Moura, L., Bjørner, N.: Z3: an efficient SMT solver. In: Ramakrishnan, C.R., Rehof, J. (eds.) TACAS 2008. LNCS, vol. 4963, pp. 337–340. Springer, Heidelberg (2008). https://doi.org/10.1007/978-3-540-78800-3_24
26. Neurohr, C., Westhofen, L., Butz, M., Bollmann, M.H., Eberle, U., Galbas, R.: Criticality analysis for the verification and validation of automated vehicles. IEEE Access **9**, 18016–18041 (2021). https://doi.org/10.1109/ACCESS.2021.3053159
27. Neurohr, C., Westhofen, L., Henning, T., de Graaff, T., Mohlmann, E., Bode, E.: Fundamental considerations around scenario-based testing for automated driving. In: 2020 IEEE Intelligent Vehicles Symposium (IV), pp. 121–127. IEEE (2020). https://doi.org/10.1109/IV47402.2020.9304823
28. Phan, Q.S., Malacaria, P.: All-solution satisfiability modulo theories: applications, algorithms and benchmarks. In: 2015 10th International Conference on Availability, Reliability and Security, pp. 100–109 (2015). https://doi.org/10.1109/ARES.2015.14
29. Plaku, E., Kavraki, L.E., Vardi, M.Y.: Hybrid systems: from verification to falsification. In: Damm, W., Hermanns, H. (eds.) CAV 2007. LNCS, vol. 4590, pp. 463–476. Springer, Heidelberg (2007). https://doi.org/10.1007/978-3-540-73368-3_48
30. Plaku, E., Kavraki, L.E., Vardi, M.Y.: Falsification of LTL safety properties in hybrid systems. Int. J. Softw. Tools Technol. Transfer **15**(4), 305–320 (2013)
31. Prautzsch, H., Boehm, W., Paluszny, M.: Bézier and B-Spline Techniques. Springer, Heidelberg (2013)
32. Qian, X., Navarro, I., de La Fortelle, A., Moutarde, F.: Motion planning for urban autonomous driving using Bézier curves and MPC. In: 2016 IEEE 19th International Conference on Intelligent Transportation Systems (ITSC), pp. 826–833. IEEE (2016)
33. Rauschert, A., Amid, G.: ASAM OpenSCENARIO DSL 2.1.0: release presentation. Presentation (2024). https://www.asam.net/standards/detail/openscenario-dsl/. Accessed 08 May 2024
34. Schramm, D., Hiller, M., Bardini, R.: Single track models. In: Schramm, D., Hiller, M., Bardini, R. (eds.) Vehicle Dynamics, pp. 223–253. Springer, Heidelberg (2014). https://doi.org/10.1007/978-3-540-36045-2_10

35. Schuldt, F., Reschka, A., Maurer, M.: A method for an efficient, systematic test case generation for advanced driver assistance systems in virtual environments. In: Winner, H., Prokop, G., Maurer, M. (eds.) Automotive Systems Engineering II, pp. 147–175. Springer, Cham (2018). https://doi.org/10.1007/978-3-319-61607-0_7
36. Schwammberger, M.: An abstract model for proving safety of autonomous urban traffic. Theor. Comput. Sci. **744**, 143–169 (2018)
37. Ulbrich, S., Menzel, T., Reschka, A., Schuldt, F., Maurer, M.: Defining and substantiating the terms scene, situation, and scenario for automated driving. In: 2015 IEEE 18th International Conference on Intelligent Transportation Systems, pp. 982–988. IEEE (2015)
38. Zhang, X., Khastgir, S., Jennings, P.: Scenario description language for automated driving systems: a two level abstraction approach. In: 2020 IEEE International Conference on Systems, Man, and Cybernetics (SMC), pp. 973–980. IEEE (2020)

Evaluating the Effectiveness of Digital Twins Through Statistical Model Checking with Feedback and Perturbations

Valentina Castiglioni[1](✉), Ruggero Lanotte[2], Michele Loreti[3], and Simone Tini[2]

[1] Eindhoven University of Technology, Eindhoven, The Netherlands
v.castiglioni@tue.nl
[2] University of Insubria, Como, Italy
[3] University of Camerino, Camerino, Italy

Abstract. We present DT-STARK, an extension of the STARK tool aimed at the verification and evaluation of the *effectiveness* of digital twins, i.e., their ability to direct the physical counterparts. To this end, we introduce *feedback* in STARK, a special mechanism that allow us to model the communications, and their effects, between the digital and the physical (perturbed) twin in a concise, clean fashion. We can then exploit the features of STARK to compare the behaviour of the twins, to verify properties over them, and to measure effectiveness. We provide some examples of the use of our tool by applying it to the evaluation of the effectiveness of digital twins in two robotic scenarios.

1 Introduction

Digital Twins (DT) [23,26,48], introduced over two decades ago, promised a revolutionary approach to system development, offering real-time monitoring, simulation, optimisation, and accurate prediction. This innovative approach has received considerable attention across various sectors, including smart cities, manufacturing, healthcare, and automotive industries (see, e.g., [9,25,31,41,50,51]).

The essence of DT lies in creating a virtual replica of physical systems, facilitating real-time interaction between virtual and physical counterparts to enhance decision-making processes and ensure coherent system execution. This approach aims to reduce failures, costs, and time, enhancing user safety and system efficiency [23,24]. Hence, the main objective is to closely represent the physical counterparts, aiming to anticipate system behaviours and outcomes, incorporating simulation models for predictive analysis [20,21]. We formalise this intuition in the notion of *effectiveness* of the DT, a measure of how well the DT can direct the physical counterpart. However, challenges arise due to inherent disparities between the Physical Twin (PT) and the DT, particularly in decision-making and feedback processes (see e.g., [49]). Factors such as environmental variations, sensor and actuator imprecision, challenges in building faithful and predictive models, are all limiting the predictive precision of DT, thus affecting its effectiveness. Hence, connecting modelling to the real world highlights the imperative for thorough validation, ensuring fidelity. For DT, this becomes fundamental. Therefore, validation and verification [6,44] represent the foundations in the development of digital models such as DT. Underlining this process is the recognition that the validity of the model depends on specific experimental conditions and defined objectives. This calls for a quantitative approach to validation and verification, rather than a qualitative one. Statistical model checking techniques [2,35] allow us to establish whether the probability that a given system satisfies a given property is above or below a given threshold, or to evaluate the probability of satisfaction. Hence, we can apply them to DT to express a credibility percentage that reflects the nature of model evaluation. However, to the best of our knowledge, statistical model checking is usually employed to verify correctness properties, such as safety [47], of digital models without their physical counterparts. Indeed, those properties are examined under a degree of uncertainty and noise, but the focus is solely on evaluating the robustness of the digital model, rather than the *effectiveness* of the DT. This paper provides a first step towards filling this gap.

Our Contribution: DT-STARK. We introduce DT-STARK (https://github.com/quasylab/jspear/tree/digital_twins), an extension of the *Software Tool for the Analysis of Robustness in the unKnown environment* (STARK) [14,17], as a tool for the formal verification and evaluation of the effectiveness of a DT when the PT is operating in an unpredictable environment and with uncertain data.

STARK, developed for Cyber-Physical Systems, is based on the *evolution sequence model* [11,13], for the representation of systems behaviour, and on the *Robustness Temporal Logic* (*RobTL*) [12,16], for the specification of properties. Briefly, evolution sequences are sequences of probability measures over sets of application-relevant data, called *data states*, each representing the result of the interaction of the agents (the cyber component) with the environment (the physical component) at a given time step. RobTL is a temporal logic for the evaluation of system robustness, which is specified as a temporal property of *distances* between nominal and perturbed behaviours of a system. RobTL formulae are defined by means of two simple languages: one to specify the effect of *perturbations* over an evolution sequence, and one to specify *distance expressions* between evolution sequences, in particular nominal and perturbed ones. The intuition is that we can use evolution sequences to simulate the behaviour of DT and PT: since the PT is deployed in the environment, its behaviour will be subject to perturbations. Hence, given the evolution sequence representing the behaviour of the DT, its perturbed version will model the behaviour of the PT. The objective of the DT is then to monitor the behaviour of the PT: it uses the data collected from it to run some predictive analysis, and, when necessary, it sends commands to the PT in order to ensure a coherent behaviour and possibly counter the effects of perturbations. However, the current version of STARK does not provide a mechanism allowing us to model this kind of communication.

We remedy this problem by introducing the *feedback* mechanism. Briefly, the feedback will be attached to the agent (the controller) of the PT, so that it will have direct access to the data related to its behaviour. The feedback will also have access to the evolution sequence of the DT so that it can simulate the decision-making procedure based on the current data. The communication between the twins is then simulated by letting the feedback apply the effects of those decisions directly to the data states. Indeed, the feedback mechanism allows us to abstract from the implementation details of the communication between the two twins, in favour of a clear representation of its effects on the behaviour of the PT. We leave as future work the development of an accurate, detailed communication mechanism in DT-STARK.

We showcase the features of our approach by providing two case studies on a robotic scenario inspired by industrial and healthcare applications.

Originality and Relevance. To the best of our knowledge, DT-STARK is the only existing tool for the analysis of effectiveness, and formal verification, of DT. Indeed, while the novel feedback mechanism is key to encode the communication between twins, the smoothness and efficiency of the analysis are due to the attributes of STARK. The unique features of RobTL and evolution sequences, that make (DT-)STARK so versatile and widely applicable, play a significant role also in the application context of DT.

RobTL. RobTL allows us to express properties of distances between nominal and perturbed evolution sequences over a finite time horizon, by also providing the means to specify the perturbations and the distances. To the best of our knowledge, RobTL is the only existing temporal logic that compares the behaviour of *two systems* to evaluate the validity of formulae. Usually, in the quantitative setting, we have that properties are specified over *a single trajectory* of a system, or across trajectories *of the same* system. The former case corresponds to the classic approach of PCTL, probabilistic LTL, and their variants [5,33,46], and to those in [19,22], where a single trajectory of a single system is compared to the set of the behaviours that satisfy a given property (specified in a suitable temporal logic, like, e.g., STL). The latter case is the *hyperproperty* [18] approach of, e.g., HyperPCTL [1] or HPSTL [4], where one can express quantitative dependencies, in the form of bounds on probabilistic weights, between *different independent trajectories* of the system. With RobTL we can specify properties based on the comparison of *all possible trajectories* of *two different systems*. This is a key feature in the evaluation of the effectiveness of a DT. By means of RobTL, and thus of DT-STARK, we can easily measure the distance between the intended behaviour of the system (i.e., that of the DT) and that of the PT when it is subject to perturbations while under control of the DT. If the distance is below a desired threshold, then we can establish that the feedback mechanism, i.e., the interaction with the DT, is effective.

The Evolution Sequence Model. The evolution sequence model follows a discrete-time, data-driven approach: the behaviour of the system is modelled in terms of the modifications that the interaction of the agents with the environment induces on a set of application-relevant data, called *data state*. Due to the unpredictability of the environment and potential approximations in the specification of agents, those modifications are modelled as continuous *distributions* on the attainable data states. The *evolution sequence* of a system is then defined as the sequence of the distributions over data states that are obtained at each time step.

The reason why we chose this model over classical and more established ones, like Labelled Markov Chains and Stochastic Hybrid Systems [10,30], is purely technical. The most prominent consequence of the design choices in this model is that the behaviour of the system is not given by a set of traces/trajectories, but by the combination of their effects. This means a property of an evolution sequence takes into account all potential behaviours of the system. This is fundamental in the validation and verification of DT [37], since even the slightest modification induced by uncertainty on behaviour is taken into account.

2 Case Studies

To explain how to apply our approach, and showcase its functionalities, we consider two instances of a simple robotic scenario, in which a single TURTLE-like robot [38] has to follow a determined path inside a working area, by going from one waypoint to another. The working area can be an industrial plant, or a warehouse, or even a hospital. We use waypoints to model both, the fact that the robot has to follow a determined path (e.g., to reduce the risk of collisions in a fully automated plant), and that it has to reach specific locations (e.g., to receive/deliver materials, goods, medicines, etc.).

The scripts with the experiments conducted on the case studies (Sect. 5 below) are available at https://github.com/quasylab/jspear/blob/digital_twins/examples/turtle/.

The Robot. Our focus in this paper is not to determine how a DT takes its decisions, but rather to show how to use formal verification methods to measure the effectiveness of the interaction between the two twins. For this reason, we abstract from several implementation details of the robot, and opt for a simple model of its behaviour. In particular, we chose to use the TURTLE robot, developed by Tech United Eindhoven at the Eindhoven University of Technology, as a reference, due to its dimensions (making it suitable for both, moving around without disrupting other operations, and transporting some material), and its swerve drive platform [32] that allows it to rotate around its vertical axis, and to move on uneven surfaces with a lower risk of getting stuck or slipping away with respect to other platforms. These features will allow us to further simplify the mathematical modelling in the various scenarios, thus favouring a clearer analysis of behaviour. For instance, we do not implement the selection procedure of waypoints, and we assume that obstacle avoidance has already been taken into account in that: the path between two waypoints is always clear. Hence, the controller of the robot will be responsible for managing the acceleration actuator, to set the moving speed, and the wheels actuator, to set the direction. Specifically, when in a waypoint location, the robot first sets its direction towards the next waypoint, and rotates accordingly. At the next time step, the robot starts moving: the controller decides, with a certain frequency, whether to accelerate or to brake based on its current (evaluated) position and the required braking distance, given the current position and (sensed) speed.

Industrial Plant. The first case study concerns the use of the robot to transport some material inside an industrial plant. We will make use of this case study as a running example to highlight all the features of DT-STARK. Hence, we will give a detailed description of it in the examples throughout the paper, and we limit ourselves to remark here that the main challenges for the DT will consist in:

1. Ensuring that the robot actually stops in proximity of each waypoint. In this way, it can correctly receive or deliver the material.
2. Counter the effects of perturbations on the speed sensor of the robot.

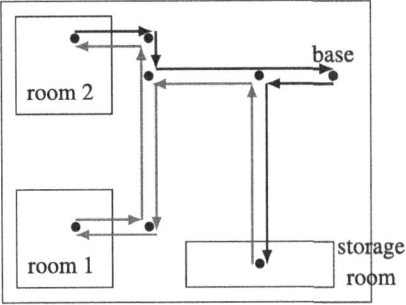

Fig. 1. Sketch of the hospital. In blue the path to be followed when loaded. (Color figure online)

Smart Hospital. The recent pandemic led to the development of intelligent systems, like autonomous robots, that can safely traverse physical spaces hosting patients to sanitise a room, or to deliver medicines, instruments, etc. [40].

Our second case study is inspired by this setting, and it is sketched in Fig. 1. The robot starts from its base, and has to reach the storage room to receive some medicines and instruments that have to be delivered in two rooms. To do so, the robot has to follow a given path along the corridors of the hospital. We will use perturbations to mimic the fact that the robot will have to modify its current direction in order to avoid obstacles, like people walking in the same corridor. Hence, the DT will have the following tasks:

1. Ensure that the robot reaches the desired waypoints.
2. Ensure that the medicines and instruments that are transported are not damaged by changes in the direction made at "high" speed.
3. Ensure that the delivery is completed.

3 The STARK Tool

In this section we describe the evolution sequence model and RobTL.

3.1 The Evolution Sequence Model

We recall the main elements of the evolution sequence model [13]. Systems consist of a set of *agents*, modelling the cyber component, and an *environment*, modelling the physical component, whose interaction produces changes on a *data space* $\mathcal{D}$, containing the values assumed by *variables* from a *finite* set $\mathcal{V}$, representing: (i) physical quantities, (ii) sensors, (iii) actuators, and (iv) internal variables of agents.

For each $x \in \mathcal{V}$, the domain $\mathcal{D}_x \subseteq \mathbb{R}$ is either *finite*, or a *compact* subset of $\mathbb{R}$ (and thus Polish), and equipped with the Borel σ-algebra $\mathcal{B}_x$. Then, $\mathcal{D} = \bigtimes_{x \in \mathcal{V}} \mathcal{D}_x$ and we equip it with the product σ-algebra $\mathcal{B}_\mathcal{D} = \bigotimes_{x \in \mathcal{V}} \mathcal{B}_x$ [8]. Let $\Pi(\mathcal{D}, \mathcal{B}_\mathcal{D})$ be the set of distributions over $(\mathcal{D}, \mathcal{B}_\mathcal{D})$. We call *data state* the current state of the data space, and represent it by a mapping $\mathbf{d} \colon \mathcal{V} \to \mathbb{R}$, with $\mathbf{d}(x) \in \mathcal{D}_x$ for all $x \in \mathcal{V}$.

At each step, the agents and the environment induce some changes on the data state, providing a new data state at the next step. Those modifications are subject to the presence of uncertainties, meaning that it is not always possible to determine exactly the values assumed by data at the next step. Hence, we model the changes induced at each step as a distribution on the attainable data states. We can assume two measurable functions ag, env: $\mathcal{D} \to \Pi(\mathcal{D}, \mathcal{B}_\mathcal{D})$ defining, respectively, the effects on data states of the agents and of the environment (see [13] for the details). In particular, ag maps each data state onto a discrete distribution, whereas env maps them onto continuous distributions. The behaviour of the system is then expressed by its *evolution sequence*, i.e., the sequence of the distributions obtained at each step by combining the effects of ag with those of env. In [13, Prop. 3.15] we proved that the function $\text{env}(\text{ag}(\mathbf{d}))(\mathbb{D}) = \sum_{\mathbf{d}' \in \text{supp}(\text{ag}(\mathbf{d}))} \text{ag}(\mathbf{d})(\mathbf{d}') \cdot \text{env}(\mathbf{d}')(\mathbb{D})$ is a well defined *Markov kernel*, and the evolution sequence is the *Markov process* generated by it: $\text{env}(\text{ag}(\mathbf{d}))(\mathbb{D})$ expresses the probability to reach a data state in $\mathbb{D}$ from $\mathbf{d}$ in one computation step. Indeed, each system is characterised by a kernel env(ag) starting from an *initial distribution* over $\mathcal{D}$.

Definition 1. *The evolution sequence of a system* s *having* μ *as initial distribution is a countable sequence* $\mathcal{S}_\mu = \mathcal{S}_\mu^0, \mathcal{S}_\mu^1, \ldots$ *of distributions in* $\Pi(\mathcal{D}, \mathcal{B}_\mathcal{D})$ *s.t., for all* $\mathbb{D} \in \mathcal{B}_\mathcal{D}$:

$$\mathcal{S}_\mu^0(\mathbb{D}) = \mu(\mathbb{D}) \quad \text{and} \quad \mathcal{S}_\mu^{i+1}(\mathbb{D}) = \int_\mathcal{D} \text{env}(\text{ag}(\mathbf{d}))(\mathbb{D}) \, d\mathcal{S}_\mu^i(\mathbf{d}).$$

Example 1. We briefly describe the behaviour of the controller of the robot, and of the environment in the industrial case study. We assume that the robot is initially still, i.e., its physical and sensed speed (respectively, p_speed and s_speed) are set to 0.0 m/s, and has to set its direction θ, i.e., the value of the wheels actuators, towards the first waypoint. The robot turns during the first time step, and will start moving afterwards. To do so, the controller has to set the value of the acceleration actuator acc. For simplicity, we assume that the robot can either accelerate, with a constant positive acceleration A m/s^2, or brake, with a constant negative acceleration $-$B m/s^2. The decision of whether to accelerate or brake, is taken by the controller every TIMER steps, on the basis of both the speed of the robot and its gap from the next waypoint. The gap is given by the difference between the physical distance p_distance from the waypoint, and the braking distance of the robot, i.e., the space required to stop if the robot starts breaking immediately. Since the objective of the robot is to stop as close as possible to the established waypoint, it starts braking as soon as the gap is negative. Once the waypoint is reached, the procedure described above is repeated to reach the next waypoint. The position (x, y) of the robot, its speed, and the gap from the next waypoint are updated by the environment, at each time step, according to the motion laws and the values of the actuators.

3.2 RobTL

Robustness Temporal Logic (RobTL) [12, 16] is the only temporal logic allowing one to express temporal properties of distances over systems behaviours. It uses atomic propositions of the form $\Delta(\exp, \mathbf{p}) \bowtie \eta$ to evaluate, at a given time step, the *distance*, specified by an *expression* exp, between a given evolution sequence and its perturbed version, obtained by some *perturbation* p, and to compare it with the threshold η. Atomic propositions are then combined with classic Boolean and temporal operators, in order to extend and compare these evaluations over the chosen time horizon. Hence, there are three main components constituting RobTL formulae: 1. A language Exp to specify *distance expressions*; 2. A language P to specify *perturbations*; 3. Classic Boolean and temporal operators to specify requirements on the *evolution of distances in time*.

Distance Expressions. We use expressions in Exp to define distances over evolution sequences. The idea is to introduce a *distance over distributions on data states* measuring their differences with respect to a *given target*, and then use the operators of the logic to extend it to the evolution sequences, while possibly taking into account *different targets and perturbations over time*. Following [11], to capture a particular task, we use a *rank function* $\rho \colon \mathcal{D} \to [0, 1]$ assigning to each data state $\mathbf{d}$ a rank in $[0, 1]$. These ranks are used to define a ground distance on data states, expressing how much they differ with respect to the point of view identified by the rank. Then we use ρ to obtain a *distance on data states*, i.e., the 1-bounded *metric* m_ρ defined for all $\mathbf{d}_1, \mathbf{d}_2 \in \mathcal{D}$ by:

$$m_\rho(\mathbf{d}_1, \mathbf{d}_2) = |\, \rho(\mathbf{d}_2) - \rho(\mathbf{d}_1) \,|$$

Note that $m_\rho(\mathbf{d}_1, \mathbf{d}_2)$ expresses the distance between $\mathbf{d}_2$ and $\mathbf{d}_1$ according to ρ. Then, we need to lift the metric m_ρ to a metric over $\Pi(\mathcal{D}, \mathcal{B}_\mathcal{D})$. To this end, we make use of the *Wasserstein lifting* [52]: for any two distributions μ, ν on $(\mathcal{D}, \mathcal{B}_\mathcal{D})$, the Wasserstein lifting of m_ρ to a distance between μ and ν is defined by

$$\mathbf{W}(m_\rho)(\mu, \nu) = \inf_{\mathfrak{w} \in \mathfrak{W}(\mu,\nu)} \int_{\mathcal{D} \times \mathcal{D}} m_\rho(\mathbf{d}, \mathbf{d}') \, \partial \mathfrak{w}(\mathbf{d}, \mathbf{d}')$$

where $\mathfrak{W}(\mu, \nu)$ is the set of the couplings of μ and ν, namely the set of joint distributions $\mathfrak{w}$ over the product space $(\mathcal{D} \times \mathcal{D}, \mathcal{B}(\mathcal{D} \times \mathcal{D}))$ having μ and ν as left and right marginal, respectively, i.e., $\mathfrak{w}(\mathbb{D} \times \mathcal{D}) = \mu(\mathbb{D})$ and $\mathfrak{w}(\mathcal{D} \times \mathbb{D}) = \nu(\mathbb{D})$, for all $\mathbb{D} \in \mathcal{B}(\mathcal{D})$.

Definition 2 (Distance expressions). *Expressions in* Exp *are defined as follows:*

$$\exp ::= <^\rho \mid \mathbf{F}^I \exp \mid \mathbf{G}^I \exp \mid \exp \mathbf{U}^I \exp \mid$$
$$\min(\exp, \exp) \mid \max(\exp, \exp) \mid \sum_{k \in K} w_k \cdot \exp_k \mid \sigma(\exp, \bowtie \zeta)$$

where ρ ranges over rank functions, I is an interval, K is a finite set of indexes, $w_k \in (0, 1]$ for each $k \in K$, $\sum_{k \in K} w_k = 1$, and $\zeta \in [0, 1]$.

Distance expressions are evaluated over a pair of evolution sequences and a time step: given two evolution sequences $\mathcal{S}_1, \mathcal{S}_2$ and a time step τ, the evaluation of expressions in the triple $\mathcal{S}_1, \mathcal{S}_2, \tau$ is given by function $[\![\cdot]\!]^\tau_{\mathcal{S}_1, \mathcal{S}_2} \colon \mathrm{Exp} \to [0, 1]$ which is defined inductively over expressions as follows:

- $[\![<^\rho]\!]^\tau_{\mathcal{S}_1, \mathcal{S}_2} = \mathbf{W}(m^\rho_\tau)(\mathcal{S}_1^\tau, \mathcal{S}_2^\tau)$;
- $[\![\mathbf{F}^I \exp]\!]^\tau_{\mathcal{S}_1, \mathcal{S}_2} = \min_{t \in I + \tau} [\![\exp]\!]^t_{\mathcal{S}_1, \mathcal{S}_2}$;

- $[\![\mathtt{G}^I\,\mathtt{exp}]\!]^{\tau}_{\mathcal{S}_1,\mathcal{S}_2} = \max_{t \in I+\tau}[\![\mathtt{exp}]\!]^{t}_{\mathcal{S}_1,\mathcal{S}_2}$;
- $[\![\mathtt{exp}_1\,\mathtt{U}^I\,\mathtt{exp}_2]\!]^{\tau}_{\mathcal{S}_1,\mathcal{S}_2} = \min_{t \in I+\tau} \max\left\{[\![\mathtt{exp}_2]\!]^{t}_{\mathcal{S}_1,\mathcal{S}_2}, \max_{t' \in I+\tau, t'<t}[\![\mathtt{exp}_1]\!]^{t'}_{\mathcal{S}_1,\mathcal{S}_2}\right\}$;
- $[\![\mathtt{min}\,(\mathtt{exp}_1,\mathtt{exp}_2)]\!]^{\tau}_{\mathcal{S}_1,\mathcal{S}_2} = \min\{[\![\mathtt{exp}_1]\!]^{\tau}_{\mathcal{S}_1,\mathcal{S}_2}, [\![\mathtt{exp}_2]\!]^{\tau}_{\mathcal{S}_1,\mathcal{S}_2}\}$;
- $[\![\mathtt{max}\,(\mathtt{exp}_1,\mathtt{exp}_2)]\!]^{\tau}_{\mathcal{S}_1,\mathcal{S}_2} = \max\{[\![\mathtt{exp}_1]\!]^{\tau}_{\mathcal{S}_1,\mathcal{S}_2}, [\![\mathtt{exp}_2]\!]^{\tau}_{\mathcal{S}_1,\mathcal{S}_2}\}$;
- $[\![\sum_{k \in K} w_k \mathtt{exp}_k]\!]^{\tau}_{\mathcal{S}_1,\mathcal{S}_2} = \sum_{k \in K} w_k \cdot [\![\mathtt{exp}_k]\!]^{\tau}_{\mathcal{S}_1,\mathcal{S}_2}$;
- $[\![\sigma(\mathtt{exp}, \bowtie \zeta)]\!]^{\tau}_{\mathcal{S}_1,\mathcal{S}_2} = \begin{cases} 0 & \text{if } [\![\mathtt{exp}]\!]^{\tau}_{\mathcal{S}_1,\mathcal{S}_2} \bowtie \zeta, \\ 1 & \text{otherwise.} \end{cases}$

Example 2. The rank function $\rho_E(\mathbf{d}) = \sqrt{(\mathtt{x} - \mathtt{wp}_\mathtt{x})^2 + (\mathtt{y} - \mathtt{wp}_\mathtt{y})^2}/\mathtt{max_E}$ assigns to a data state $\mathbf{d}$ of the robot a rank in $[0, 1]$ corresponding to the normalised value of its distance from the current waypoint $(\mathtt{wp}_\mathtt{x}, \mathtt{wp}_\mathtt{y})$. Here, $\mathtt{max_E}$ is the maximal distance from the current waypoint that can be observed in the executions of the system. This value is estimated by employing the simulation module of DT-STARK. Intuitively, given two data states $\mathbf{d}_1$ and $\mathbf{d}_2$ reached at the same step in two different evolutions, $|\rho_E(\mathbf{d}_1) - \rho_E(\mathbf{d}_2)|$ measures how much one of the two evolution is closer to the next target with respect to the other. Based on ρ_E we define the atomic distance $<^{\rho_E}$ mapping two distributions to the Wasserstein distance [52] between their ranks, and the distance expression $\mathtt{dMax}(u, v) = \mathtt{G}^{[u,v]} <^{\rho_E}$ returning the maximum of $<^{\rho_E}$ over the interval $[u, v]$. Notice that, as the ranks, both $<^{\rho_E}$ and $\mathtt{dMax}(u, v)$ are reals in $[0, 1]$.

Perturbations. A perturbation is the effect of unpredictable events, that can be repeated or different in time, on the current state of the system. In [12,16], a perturbation is therefore modelled as a time-dependent function that maps a data state into a distribution over data states. Specifically, a perturbation p is a list of mappings in which the i-th element describes the effects of p at time i, and that is specified in the following language:

Definition 3 (Perturbations). *Perturbations in* P *are defined as follows:*

$$\mathtt{p} ::= \quad \mathtt{nil} \quad | \quad \mathfrak{p}@\tau \quad | \quad \mathtt{p}_1; \mathtt{p}_2 \quad | \quad \mathtt{p}^n \quad | \quad \mathtt{p}^\infty$$

where p *ranges over* P, n *and* τ *are finite natural numbers, and:*

- nil *is the perturbation with* no effects;
- $\mathfrak{p}@\tau$ *is an* atomic perturbation, *i.e., a function* $\mathfrak{p}\colon \mathcal{D} \to \Pi(\mathcal{D}, \mathcal{B}_\mathcal{D})$ *such that the mapping* $\mathbf{d} \mapsto \mathfrak{p}(\mathbf{d})(\mathbb{D})$ *is* $\mathcal{B}_\mathcal{D}$-*measurable for all* $\mathbb{D} \in \mathcal{B}_\mathcal{D}$, *and that is applied after* τ *time steps from the current instant;*
- $\mathtt{p}_1; \mathtt{p}_2$ *is a* sequential perturbation, *i.e., perturbation* $\mathtt{p}_2$ *is applied at the time step subsequent to the (final) application of* $\mathtt{p}_1$;
- $\mathtt{p}^n$ *is an* iterated perturbation, *i.e., perturbation* p *is applied for a total of n times;*
- $\mathtt{p}^\infty$ *is a* persistent perturbation, *i.e.,* p *is applied along the whole evolution.*

The semantics of perturbations is defined by means of two auxiliary functions: $\mathtt{effect}(\mathtt{p})$, that describes the effect of p at the current step, and $\mathtt{next}(\mathtt{p})$, that identifies the perturbation that will be applied at the next step. These two functions are defined inductively over the structure of p. Due to space limitations, we omit their formal definition (which is similar to that of functions changes and succ in Sect. 4.1 below), and refer the interested reader to [12]. We make use of effect and next to define the mapping $\langle\!\langle \cdot \rangle\!\rangle \colon \mathrm{P} \to (\mathcal{D} \times \mathbb{N} \to \Pi(\mathcal{D}, \mathcal{B}_\mathcal{D}))$ such that, for all $\mathbf{d} \in \mathcal{D}$ and $i \in \mathbb{N}$:

$$\langle\!\langle \mathrm{p} \rangle\!\rangle(\mathbf{d}, i) = \mathsf{effect}(\mathsf{next}^i(\mathrm{p}))(\mathbf{d}),$$

where $\mathsf{next}^0(\mathrm{p}) = \mathrm{p}$ and $\mathsf{next}^i(\mathrm{p}) = \mathsf{next}(\mathsf{next}^{i-1}(\mathrm{p}))$, for all $i > 0$.

Now we can define the perturbation of an evolution sequence.

Definition 4 (Perturbation of an evolution sequence). *Given an evolution sequence $\mathcal{S}_\mu$, with μ as initial distribution, and a perturbation p, we define the perturbation of $\mathcal{S}_\mu$ via p as the evolution sequence $\mathcal{S}_\mu^\mathrm{p}$ obtained as follows:*

$$\mathcal{S}_\mu^{\mathrm{p},0}(\mathbb{D}) = \int_\mathcal{D} \langle\!\langle \mathrm{p} \rangle\!\rangle(\mathbf{d}, 0)(\mathbb{D}) \, \eth \, \mu(\mathbf{d})$$

$$\mathcal{S}_\mu^{\mathrm{p},i+1}(\mathbb{D}) = \int_\mathcal{D} \left(\int_\mathcal{D} \langle\!\langle \mathrm{p} \rangle\!\rangle(\mathbf{d}', i+1)(\mathbb{D}) \, \eth \, \mathsf{env}(\mathsf{ag}(\mathbf{d}))(\mathbf{d}') \right) \eth \, \mathcal{S}_\mu^{\mathrm{p},i}(\mathbf{d}),$$

where function $\mathsf{env}(\mathsf{ag})$ *is the Markov kernel that generates* $\mathcal{S}_\mu$.

Example 3. We consider the perturbation $\mathfrak{p}_{speed,o} = (\mathfrak{p}_{speed,o}@0)^\infty$, where $\mathfrak{p}_{speed,o}(\mathbf{d})$ is the distribution of the random variable $O(o, \mathbf{d})$, for o uniformly distributed in $[0, 1]$, defined for all $\mathbf{d} \in \mathcal{D}$ by $O(o, \mathbf{d}) = \mathbf{d}'$, where $\mathbf{d}'(\mathtt{s\_speed}) = \mathbf{d}(\mathtt{p\_speed}) - o * \mathtt{MAXOFFSET}$, for a constant $\mathtt{MAXOFFSET}$, and $\mathbf{d}'(x) = \mathbf{d}(x)$ for all other variables. Note that $\mathfrak{p}_{speed,o}$ is a persistent perturbation. At each step $\mathfrak{p}_{speed,o}$ is applied immediately (this is given by _@0) and tricks the controller of the robot by letting it sense a speed which is lower than the real one. This may lead the robot to skip the next waypoint.

RobTL Formulae. We use formulae in RobTL for the specification and analysis of distances between nominal and perturbed evolution sequences over a finite time horizon.

Definition 5 (RobTL). *RobTL consists in the set of formulae* L *defined by:*

$$\varphi ::= \top \mid \Delta(\mathsf{exp}, \mathrm{p}) \bowtie \eta \mid \neg \varphi \mid \varphi \wedge \varphi \mid \varphi \, \mathcal{U}^I \, \varphi$$

where φ ranges over L, exp *ranges over expressions in* Exp, p *ranges over perturbations in* P, $\bowtie \in \{<, \leq, \geq, >\}$, $\eta \in [0, 1]$, *and* $I \subseteq [0, \mathfrak{h}]$ *is a bounded time interval.*

Formulae are evaluated in an evolution sequence and a time instant. The semantics of classic Boolean and temporal operators is standard, and it is based on the evaluation of the atomic formulae, which is defined as follows:

$$\mathcal{S}, \tau \models \Delta(\mathsf{exp}, \mathrm{p}) \bowtie \eta \text{ iff } [\![\mathsf{exp}]\!]^\tau_{\mathcal{S}, \mathcal{S}_{|\langle\!\langle \mathrm{p} \rangle\!\rangle, \tau}} \bowtie \eta,$$

where the evolution sequence $\mathcal{S}_{|\langle\!\langle \mathrm{p} \rangle\!\rangle, \tau}$ is defined as:

$$(\mathcal{S}_{|\langle\!\langle \mathrm{p} \rangle\!\rangle, \tau})^t = \begin{cases} \mathcal{S}^t & \text{if } t < \tau, \\ \mathcal{S}_{\mathcal{S}^\tau}^{\mathrm{p}, t-\tau} & \text{if } t \geq \tau. \end{cases}$$

Example 4. Consider the distance $\texttt{dMax}(u,v)$ in Example 2 and the perturbation $\texttt{p}_{speed,o}$ in Example 3. A RobTL atomic formula $\varphi_{(u,v,o,\eta)}$ expressing that the distance $\texttt{dMax}(u,v)$ between the nominal behaviour and its perturbation via $\texttt{p}_{speed,o}$ is below a threshold η can be defined as follows:

$$\varphi_{(u,v,o,\eta)} = \Delta(\texttt{dMax}(u,v), \texttt{p}_{speed,o}) \leq \eta \tag{1}$$

4 DT-STARK

Our objective is to provide the means to measure the effectiveness of a DT when the PT is operating in an unpredictable environment and with uncertain data.

One, naive, approach would consist in a direct encoding of the two twins in STARK: we model the controller of the DT as an agent, and then we simulate its behaviour in a given environment. The behaviour of the DT corresponds, thus, to the nominal evolution sequence. Conversely, to obtain the behaviour of the PT we let the same agent interact with a perturbed environment. We can then use distance expressions, and RobTL formulae, to check how close the behaviour of the two twins is. While this approach gives us a measure of the robustness of the DT against perturbations, it does not allow us to encode the monitoring function of the DT over the physical one: the DT receives data from the PT and, based on simulations and predictions, sends commands to it in order to ensure that its behaviour is as intended.

At the moment, STARK does not offer a similar communication mechanism between systems. Hence, we propose an extension of it, DT-STARK available at https://github.com/quasylab/jspear/tree/digital_twins, that enriches STARK with a special mechanism, henceforth called *feedback*, allowing us to simulate the communication between the two twins, and, thus, to implement the monitoring activity of the DT. We can exploit the features of RobTL to measure the effectiveness of the DT.

4.1 The Feedback Mechanism

We use the feedback mechanism to abstract from the implementation details of the communication between the two twins: the feedback has access to the data of the PT and to the behaviour of the DT so that it can modify, up to a certain extent, the behaviour of the former to comply with the one of the latter.

For instance, consider a self-driven vehicle that has to turn. The idea is that the feedback checks for the status of the steering wheel and of the accelerator, and it compares them to their values in the corresponding state of the DT. If the speed of the vehicle is too high given the steering angle, or the angle is not correct, the mechanism will adjust the behaviour of the vehicle by either imposing to decelerate, or to change the steering angle. In DT-STARK, this is obtained by applying the feedback to the perturbed system (modelling the PT), so that it can have access to its data state $\mathbf{d}$. The mechanism takes as input the evolution sequence of the nominal system (modelling the DT), and determines whether to take action or not by comparing the values of the variables to be monitored (corresponding to actuators) in the two systems, at the current time step. Indeed, the magnitude of the modifications imposed by the feedback is limited by physical and safety constraints: the speed of the vehicle can only be reduced by a certain amount per second, depending on the braking force of the vehicle and the conditions of the road; the steering angle cannot be changed abruptly, to limit the risk of a collision or of spinning out. Hence, each variable will only be modified up to a certain percentage.

Following the purely data-driven approach of the evolution sequence model, the communication between the two twins is abstracted by implementing the procedure sketched above as a mapping f_S over data states: the data state $f_S(\mathbf{d})$ is obtained by applying to $\mathbf{d}$ the modifications imposed by the feedback as formalised in f_S. Specifically, to better encode the communication, the feedback is applied to the data states obtained from an application of the controller ag of the PT: the DT checks for the current data and the decisions taken by the physical counterpart (given by $\text{ag}(\mathbf{d})$) and it reacts to them by sending modification commands. These are abstracted in the application of the feedback to the data states, given by $f_S(\text{ag}(\mathbf{d}))$. We remark that f_S can be defined arbitrarily by the user, that can therefore autonomously decide how to use the behaviour S to establish the modifications. Moreover, we allow for choosing the time step at which the feedback will be applied: we use $f_S@\tau$ to denote that f_S will be applied (to the data states reached) after τ steps from the current one. This feature allows us to establish the frequency of the feedback.

Function $f_S@\tau$ defines an *atomic feedback*. Since we may wish to apply the same feedback iteratively, or different modifications in time, we also offer the possibility to define *iterated* and *sequential feedback*.

The informal discussion above is formalised in the following definition.

Definition 6 (Feedback). *Feedback in F are defined as follows:*

$$f ::= \text{id} \mid f_S@\tau \mid f_1;f_2 \mid f^n \mid f^\infty$$

where f ranges over F, n, τ are finite natural numbers, S is an evolution sequence, and:

- id *is the feedback with no effects, i.e., at each time step it behaves like the identity function* $\text{id}: \mathcal{D} \to \mathcal{D}$ *such that* $\text{id}(\mathbf{d}) = \mathbf{d}$ *for all* $\mathbf{d} \in \mathcal{D}$;
- $f_S@\tau$ *is an atomic feedback, i.e., a function* $f_S: \mathcal{D} \to \mathcal{D}$ *that is applied after τ time steps from the current instant;*
- $f_1;f_2$ *is a sequential feedback, i.e., feedback f_2 is applied at the time step subsequent to the (final) application of f_1;*
- f^n *is an iterated feedback, i.e., feedback f is applied for a total of n times;*
- f^∞ *is a persistent feedback, i.e., feedback f is applied along the whole evolution.*

The semantics of feedback is then defined by means of two auxiliary functions: changes(f), that describes the effect of f at the current step, and succ(f), that identifies the feedback that will be applied at the next step. Both functions are defined inductively over the structure of f as follows:

$$\text{changes}(\text{id}) = \text{id}$$

$$\text{changes}(\mathfrak{f}_S@\tau) = \begin{cases} \text{id} & \text{if } \tau > 0 \\ \mathfrak{f}_S & \text{if } \tau = 0 \end{cases}$$

$$\text{changes}(\mathfrak{f}^n) = \text{changes}(\mathfrak{f})$$

$$\text{changes}(\mathfrak{f}_1;\mathfrak{f}_2) = \text{changes}(\mathfrak{f}_1)$$

$$\text{changes}(\mathfrak{f}^\infty) = \text{changes}(\mathfrak{f})$$

$$\text{succ}(\text{id}) = \text{id}$$

$$\text{succ}(\mathfrak{f}_S@\tau) = \begin{cases} \mathfrak{f}_S@(\tau-1) & \text{if } \tau > 0 \\ \text{id} & \text{otherwise} \end{cases}$$

$$\text{succ}(\mathfrak{f}^n) = \begin{cases} \text{succ}(\mathfrak{f}); \mathfrak{f}^{n-1} & \text{if } n > 0 \\ \text{id} & \text{otherwise} \end{cases}$$

$$\text{succ}(\mathfrak{f}_1;\mathfrak{f}_2) = \begin{cases} \text{succ}(\mathfrak{f}_1); \mathfrak{f}_2 & \text{if } \text{succ}(\mathfrak{f}_1) \neq \text{id} \\ \mathfrak{f}_2 & \text{otherwise} \end{cases}$$

$$\text{succ}(\mathfrak{f}^\infty) = \text{succ}(\mathfrak{f}); \mathfrak{f}^\infty.$$

As for perturbations, we can identify the semantics of a feedback $\mathfrak{f}$ with the list of its effects in time. Hence, we make use of changes and succ to define the mapping $\ulcorner \cdot \urcorner \colon F \to (\mathcal{D} \times \mathbb{N} \to \mathcal{D})$ such that, for all $\mathbf{d} \in \mathcal{D}$ and $i \in \mathbb{N}$:

$$\ulcorner \mathfrak{f} \urcorner(\mathbf{d}, i) = \text{changes}(\text{succ}^i(\mathfrak{f}))(\mathbf{d}),$$

where $\text{succ}^0(\mathfrak{f}) = \mathfrak{f}$ and $\text{succ}^i(\mathfrak{f}) = \text{succ}(\text{succ}^{i-1}(\mathfrak{f}))$, for all $i > 0$.

As briefly discussed above, to model the communication between the two twins, the effects of the feedback are applied to the data states *after* the effects of the agents, and *before* those of the environment. This allows us to simulate the reaction of the DT to the decisions taken by the PT. We abstract this procedure by letting the agent (the PT) set its actuators according to the data at its disposal; the feedback (the DT) compares those values to those assumed in the nominal system, and, if necessary, it modifies them to make the behaviour compliant to the expected one. This double modification is done within the same time step, before the environment reacts to the activity of the agent. Moreover, as a consequence, the feedback has no effect on the initial distribution of an evolution sequence.

Definition 7 (Feedback of an evolution sequence). *Given an evolution sequence $\mathcal{S}_\mu$, with μ as initial distribution, and a feedback $\mathfrak{f}$, we define the* feedback of $\mathcal{S}_\mu$ via $\mathfrak{f}$ *as the evolution sequence $\mathcal{S}_\mu^{\mathfrak{f}}$ obtained as follows:*

$$\mathcal{S}_\mu^{\mathfrak{f},0}(\mathbb{D}) = \mu(\mathbb{D})$$

$$\mathcal{S}_\mu^{\mathfrak{f},i+1}(\mathbb{D}) = \int_\mathcal{D} \text{env}(\ulcorner \mathfrak{f} \urcorner(\text{ag}(\mathbf{d}), i+1))(\mathbb{D}) \, \eth \, \mathcal{S}_\mu^{\mathfrak{f},i}(\mathbf{d}),$$

where $\text{env}(\ulcorner \mathfrak{f} \urcorner(\text{ag}(\mathbf{d}), i))(\mathbb{D})$ *stands for* $\sum_{\mathbf{d}' \in \text{supp}(\text{ag}(\mathbf{d}))} \text{ag}(\mathbf{d})(\mathbf{d}') \cdot \text{env}(\ulcorner \mathfrak{f} \urcorner(\mathbf{d}', i))(\mathbb{D})$.

Thanks to the modular design of the back-end of STARK, the feedback mechanism can be smoothly integrated in it. The main difference between DT-STARK and the original tool is in the module for the simulation of evolution sequences, which is modified to allow for the application of the effects of the feedback. All other modules, i.e., the ones for the application of perturbations, the evaluation of distances, and the statistical model checker for RobTL formulae, then automatically interact with the new simulation method, without the need for further modifications.

Example 5. We define the persistent feedback $f_{speed\&dir} = (f_{s\&d}@0)^\infty$, where function $f_{s\&d}$ is applied immediately at each step (this is given by @0) and is defined as $f_{s\&d}(\mathbf{d}) = \mathbf{d}'$, with:

- $\mathbf{d}'(\texttt{acc}) = \begin{cases} -\texttt{B} & \text{if } \mathbf{d}(\texttt{s\_speed}) > \texttt{m\_s\_speed} + \texttt{SpeedD} \\ \mathbf{d}(\texttt{acc}) & \text{otherwise} \end{cases}$

- $\mathbf{d}'(\texttt{wp}_\texttt{x}) = \begin{cases} \texttt{m\_wp}_\texttt{x} & \text{if } \mathbf{d}(\texttt{cur}_\texttt{wp}) < \texttt{m\_cur}_\texttt{wp} \\ \mathbf{d}(\texttt{wp}_\texttt{x}) & \text{otherwise} \end{cases}$

- $\mathbf{d}'(\texttt{wp}_\texttt{y}) = \begin{cases} \texttt{m\_wp}_\texttt{y} & \text{if } \mathbf{d}(\texttt{cur}_\texttt{wp}) < \texttt{m\_cur}_\texttt{wp} \\ \mathbf{d}(\texttt{wp}_\texttt{y}) & \text{otherwise} \end{cases}$

- $\mathbf{d}'(\theta) = \begin{cases} \texttt{m\_}\theta & \text{if } \texttt{cur}_\texttt{wp} < \texttt{m\_cur}_\texttt{wp} \\ \mathbf{d}(\theta) & \text{otherwise} \end{cases}$

and $\mathbf{d}'(x) = \mathbf{d}(x)$ for all other variables. Here, acc is the actuator of the accelerator, $(\texttt{wp}_\texttt{x}, \texttt{wp}_\texttt{y})$ are the coordinates of the current waypoint, $\texttt{cur}_\texttt{wp}$ identifies the position of the current waypoint in the list of the waypoints, and θ is the steering angle. For each variable x, the average value assumed by x in the nominal evolution of DT at the same step is denoted with m_x. Intuitively, this feedback forces the robot to slow down if it is too fast, and to focus on the next waypoint if the previous one has been already passed.

5 Experiments

Industrial Plant. Consider the distances $<^{\rho_E}$ and $\texttt{dMax}(u,v)$ in Example 2, the perturbation $\mathtt{p}_{speed,o}$ in Example 3, the formula $\varphi_{(u,v,o,\eta)}$ in Example 4 and the feedback $f_{speed\&dir}$ in Example 5. In Fig. 2a we showcase the paths followed by the robot in three scenarios: nominal evolution, perturbed evolution without feedback and perturbed evolution with feedback. The waypoints list is $(1,3), (13,3), (7,7), (23,14), (20,31), (32,40), (35,30)$. The plot shows that the perturbation affects the behaviour of the robot, but the feedback is able to neutralise it. Pointwise evaluations of distance $<^{\rho_E}$ between the nominal and the perturbed behaviour in the scenarios without and with feedback are showed in Fig. 2b and Fig. 2c, respectively. These plots confirms the effectiveness of the DT. Finally, Fig. 2d shows the evaluation of $\varphi_{(100,200,1.0,\eta)}$ for several values of η.

Smart Hospital. Due to space restrictions, we give only a bird's-eye view on the results that we obtained. We refer the interested reader directly to the script at https://github.com/quasylab/jspear/blob/digital_twins/examples/turtle/ for more details, including the (initial) values of variables and parameters.

In Fig. 3a we report the path followed by the robot in the nominal system, i.e., the one established by the DT in the absence of perturbations, and the one followed by the physical robot. The latter is subject to the persistent perturbation $\mathtt{p}_{obs} = (\mathtt{p}_{obs,\delta}@0)^\infty$ that simulates continuous changes in the direction due to obstacle avoidance. In fact, function $\mathtt{p}_{obs,\delta}$ applies an offset δ uniformly distributed in $[-\theta_{\text{OFF}}/2, \theta_{\text{OFF}}/2]$, for a

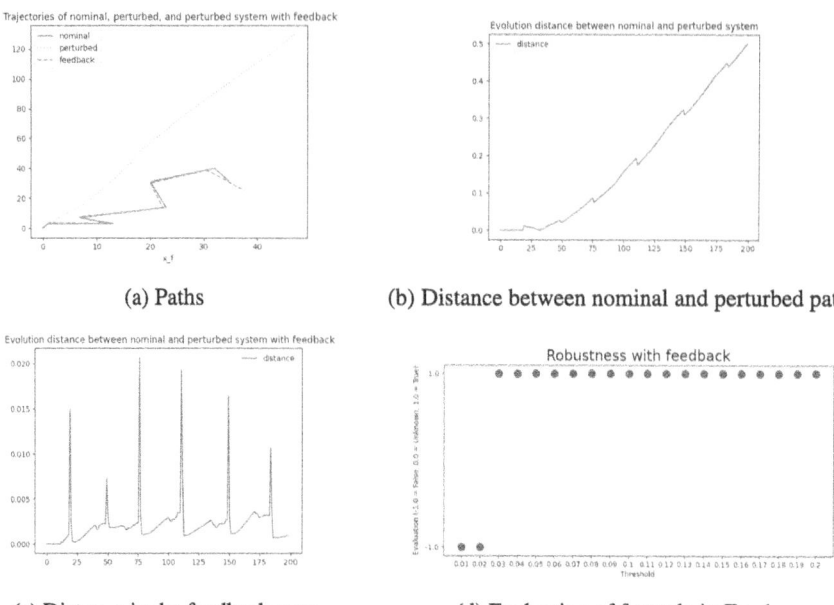

Fig. 2. Analysis of the industrial plant case study.

chosen parameter θ_{OFF}, to the current direction. Indeed, while it is unlikely for the robot to incur in continuous disruptions, we can use this heavy perturbation to show the effectiveness of the feedback mechanism. We recall that, besides guaranteeing that the robot reaches the designed waypoints, the feedback has also to guarantee that the medicines and instruments that it carries are not damaged on the way. Hence, we define the feedback as $f = (f_S@0)^\infty$ where function f_S is such that:

1. Whenever the robot is carrying something, encoded by get_medicine $= 1$, then the robot cannot travel at a speed higher than MAX_SPEED_WITH_MED. Hence, function f_S forces the robot to stop accelerating, and thus to gently decelerate, whenever its speed is close to the threshold.
2. Whenever the current direction of the robot deviates too much from the one in the nominal system, the feedback acts on the wheels actuator to point it towards the correct waypoint. Also in this case, the feedback determines the magnitude of the change according to whether the robot is carrying something and its current speed.
3. f_S behaves like $f_{s\&d}$ with respect to waypoint selection.

In Fig. 3b we report the evaluation of the atomic distance between the speed, and the direction assumed in the two systems. We remark that the peaks in the difference between the directions are due to temporal delays in reaching the same waypoint.

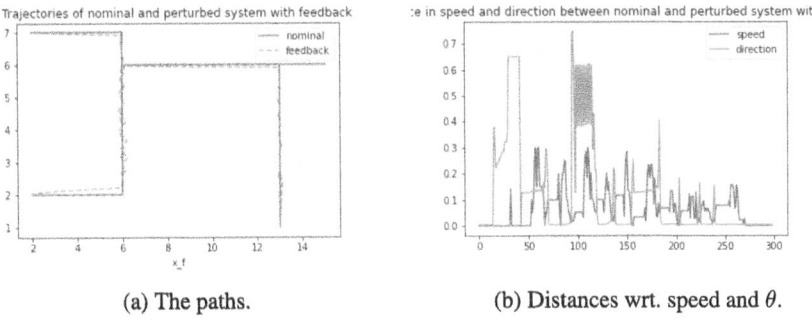

(a) The paths. (b) Distances wrt. speed and θ.

Fig. 3. Analysis of the smart hospital case study.

6 Related Work

To the best of our knowledge, statistical model checking, and more broadly, model checking, are utilised for verifying correctness properties, such as safety and security (see e.g. [34]), of digital models without their physical counterparts. Consequently, interactions and feedback are not considered. While some of these works share similarities with our study by examining safety under a degree of uncertainty and noise, they focus solely on evaluating the robustness of the digital model, rather than the effectiveness of the digital twin. For instance, in [3], the authors verify the planned manoeuvres of an automated car on the road using reachable sets. This approach enables the verification of potential collisions with other traffic participants taking in account sensor noise, uncertain friction coefficient, and uncertain initial states.

In the literature, instead of model checking, other techniques for evaluating the discrepancy in valuation of digital twins, such as Bayesian inference, have been studied. These techniques often rely on validation techniques [44,45], model calibration [43], and conformance checking approaches [39]. For a comprehensive overview, an exhaustive survey can be found in [42]. It's worth noting that recently, [37] introduced the new concept of online validation of digital twins. The techniques proposed in this research enable the continuous updating of a digital model in terms of both inputs and logic, facilitating short-term decision-making. The proposed methodology is subject to several limitations, as, for instance, it is designed for validating digital models with limited data and it is focused on manufacturing system data.

In the literature, we can find several tools for (statistical) model checking and formal verification, like HyTECH [28], PRISM [29], Storm [27], UPPAAL [7], etc. While these tools have been successfully applied to the verification of Cyber-Physical Systems, we could find fewer applications in the context of DT. For instance, in [47], PRISM is used for the analysis of security properties of DT, modelled as Markov Decision Processes. In [36], DT are modelled as time automata networks whose properties are verified in UPPAAL. However, in the former case, only the behaviour of the DT is taken into account. In the latter case, as the paper concerns building DT, the interaction with the PT is considered, but there is no analysis of behaviour in the presence of uncertainty and perturbations.

7 Concluding Remarks

We presented DT-STARK, that extends the STARK tool with a feedback mechanism that allows us to encode the communication between the digital and the physical twin. Thanks to it, we can use RobTL formulae to evaluate the effectiveness of the DT, namely how much it is able to direct the PT that is operating under the effect of uncertainty and perturbations. To the best of our knowledge, DT-STARK is the only formal tool that allows for this kind of analysis.

Given the high level of abstraction in the current implementation, the next step in the development of DT-STARK will consist in switching from discrete step modelling to a time-point modelling, by refining the techniques we introduced in *Bio*-STARK [15] for the robustness analysis of biological systems. This will allow us not only to check for discrepancies in time in the behaviour of the two twins, but also to account for potential delays in the communication between them, and thus in the application of feedback, and their consequences. Moreover, for a more accurate simulation of behaviour, we plan to extend (DT-)STARK with ODE modelling.

Acknowledgements. This study received funding from the European Union - NextGenerationEU - National Recovery and Resilience Plan (NRRP) - MISSION 4 COMPONENT 2, INVESTMENT N. 1.1, CALL PRIN 2022 D.D. 104 02-02-2022 - MEDICA Project, CUP N.J53D23007180006.

This publication is part of the project *NODES* which has received funding from the MUR - M4C2 1.5 of PNRR with grant agreement no. ECS00000036.

References

1. Ábrahám, E., Bonakdarpour, B.: HyperPCTL: a temporal logic for probabilistic hyperproperties. In: McIver, A., Horvath, A. (eds.) QEST 2018. LNCS, vol. 11024, pp. 20–35. Springer, Cham (2018). https://doi.org/10.1007/978-3-319-99154-2_2
2. Agha, G., Palmskog, K.: A survey of statistical model checking. ACM Trans. Model. Comput. Simul. **28**(1), 6:1–6:39 (2018). https://doi.org/10.1145/3158668
3. Althoff, M., Dolan, J.M.: Reachability computation of low-order models for the safety verification of high-order road vehicle models. In: American Control Conference (ACC) 2012, pp. 3559–3566. IEEE (2012). https://doi.org/10.1109/ACC.2012.6314777
4. Arora, S., Hansen, R.R., Larsen, K.G., Legay, A., Poulsen, D.B.: Statistical model checking for probabilistic hyperproperties of real-valued signals. In: Legunsen, O., Rosu, G. (eds.) SPIN 2022. LNCS, vol. 13255, pp. 61–78. Springer, Cham (2022). https://doi.org/10.1007/978-3-031-15077-7_4
5. Baier, C.: Probabilistic model checking. In: Dependable Software Systems Engineering, NATO Science for Peace and Security Series - D: Information and Communication Security, vol. 45, pp. 1–23. IOS Press (2016). https://doi.org/10.3233/978-1-61499-627-9-1
6. Banks, J.: Handbook of Simulation - Principles, Methodology, Advances, Applications, and Practice. Wiley, Hoboken (1998)
7. Behrmann, G., David, A., Larsen, K.G.: A tutorial on UPPAAL. In: Bernardo, M., Corradini, F. (eds.) SFM-RT 2004. LNCS, vol. 3185, pp. 200–236. Springer, Cham (2004). https://doi.org/10.1007/978-3-540-30080-9_7
8. Bogachev, V.I.: Measure Theory, vol. 2. Springer, Heidelberg (2007). https://doi.org/10.1007/978-3-540-34514-5

9. Brosinsky, C., Westermann, D., Krebs, R.: Recent and prospective developments in power system control centers: adapting the digital twin technology for application in power system control centers. In: 2018 IEEE International Energy Conference (ENERGYCON), pp. 1–6 (2018). https://doi.org/10.1109/ENERGYCON.2018.8398846
10. Cassandras, C.G., Lygeros, J. (eds.): Stochastic Hybrid Systems. No. 24 in Control Engineering, 1st edn. CRC Press, Boca Raton (2007). https://doi.org/10.1201/9781315221625
11. Castiglioni, V., Loreti, M., Tini, S.: How adaptive and reliable is your program? In: Peters, K., Willemse, T.A.C. (eds.) FORTE 2021. LNCS, vol. 12719, pp. 60–79. Springer, Cham (2021). https://doi.org/10.1007/978-3-030-78089-0_4
12. Castiglioni, V., Loreti, M., Tini, S.: RobTL: a temporal logic for the robustness of cyber-physical systems. CoRR abs/2212.11158 (2022). https://doi.org/10.48550/arXiv.2212.11158
13. Castiglioni, V., Loreti, M., Tini, S.: A framework to measure the robustness of programs in the unpredictable environment. Log. Methods Comput. Sci. **19**(3) (2023). https://doi.org/10.46298/LMCS-19(3:2)2023
14. Castiglioni, V., Loreti, M., Tini, S.: STARK: a software tool for the analysis of robustness in the unknown environment. In: Jongmans, S.S., Lopes, A. (eds.) COORDINATION 2023. LNCS, vol. 13908, pp. 115–132. Springer, Cham (2023). https://doi.org/10.1007/978-3-031-35361-1_6
15. Castiglioni, V., Loreti, M., Tini, S.: Bio-STARK: a tool for the time-point robustness analysis of biological systems. In: Proceedings of CMSB 2024. LNCS. Springer (2024, to appear)
16. Castiglioni, V., Loreti, M., Tini, S.: RobTL: robustness temporal logic for CPS. In: Proceedings of CONCUR 2024. LIPIcs. Schloss Dagstuhl - Leibniz-Zentrum für Informatik (2024, to appear)
17. Castiglioni, V., Loreti, M., Tini, S.: STARK: a tool for the analysis of CPSs robustness. Sci. Comput. Program. **236**, 103134 (2024). https://doi.org/10.1016/j.scico.2024.103134
18. Clarkson, M.R., Schneider, F.B.: Hyperproperties. J. Comput. Secur. **18**(6), 1157–1210 (2010). https://doi.org/10.3233/JCS-2009-0393
19. Donzé, A., Maler, O.: Robust satisfaction of temporal logic over real-valued signals. In: Chatterjee, K., Henzinger, T.A. (eds.) FORMATS 2010. LNCS, vol. 6246, pp. 92–106. Springer, Heidelberg (2010). https://doi.org/10.1007/978_3_642-15297-9_9
20. Esterle, L., Gomes, C., Frasheri, M., Ejersbo, H., Tomforde, S., Larsen, P.G.: Digital twins for collaboration and self-integration. In: 2021 IEEE International Conference on Autonomic Computing and Self-Organizing Systems Companion (ACSOS-C), pp. 172–177 (2021). https://doi.org/10.1109/ACSOS-C52956.2021.00040
21. Esterle, L., Porter, B., Woodcock, J.: Verification and uncertainties in self-integrating system. In: 2nd IEEE International Conference on Autonomic Computing and Self-Organizing Systems Companion, ACSOS-C 2021, pp. 220–225. IEEE (2021). https://doi.org/10.1109/ACSOS-C52956.2021.00040
22. Fainekos, G.E., Pappas, G.J.: Robustness of temporal logic specifications for continuous-time signals. Theor. Comput. Sci. **410**(42), 4262–4291 (2009). https://doi.org/10.1016/j.tcs.2009.06.021
23. Frasheri, M., et al.: Addressing time discrepancy between digital and physical twins. Robot. Auton. Syst. **161**, 104347 (2023). https://doi.org/10.1016/j.robot.2022.104347
24. Fuller, A., Fan, Z., Day, C., Barlow, C.: Digital twin: enabling technologies, challenges and open research. IEEE Access **8**, 108952–108971 (2020). https://doi.org/10.1109/ACCESS.2020.2998358
25. Gahlot, S., Reddy, S.R.N., Kumar, D.: Review of smart health monitoring approaches with survey analysis and proposed framework. IEEE Internet Things J. **6**, 2116–2127 (2019). https://doi.org/10.1109/JIOT.2018.2872389

26. Grieves, M., Vickers, J.: Digital twin: mitigating unpredictable, undesirable emergent behavior in complex systems. In: Kahlen, J., Flumerfelt, S., Alves, A. (eds.) Transdisciplinary Perspectives on Complex Systems, pp. 85–113. Springer, Cham (2017). https://doi.org/10.1007/978-3-319-38756-7_4
27. Hensel, C., Junges, S., Katoen, J.P., Quatmann, T., Volk, M.: The probabilistic model checker STORM. Int. J. Softw. Tools Technol. Transfer **24**(4), 589–610 (2022). https://doi.org/10.1007/s10009-021-00633-z
28. Henzinger, T.A., Ho, P.H., Wong-Toi, H.: HYTECH: a model checker for hybrid systems. In: Grumberg, O. (ed.) CAV 1997. LNCS, vol. 1254, pp. 460–463. Springer, Cham (1997). https://doi.org/10.1007/3-540-63166-6_48
29. Hinton, A., Kwiatkowska, M., Norman, G., Parker, D.: PRISM: a tool for automatic verification of probabilistic systems. In: Hermanns, H., Palsberg, J. (eds.) TACAS 2006. LNCS, vol. 3920, pp. 441–444. Springer, Heidelberg (2006). https://doi.org/10.1007/11691372_29
30. Hu, J., Lygeros, J., Sastry, S.: Towards a theory of stochastic hybrid systems. In: Lynch, N., Krogh, B.H. (eds.) HSCC 2000. LNCS, vol. 1790, pp. 160–173. Springer, Heidelberg (2000). https://doi.org/10.1007/3-540-46430-1_16
31. Ibrahim, M., Rassõlkin, A., Vaimann, T., Kallaste, A.: Overview on digital twin for autonomous electrical vehicles propulsion drive system. Sustainability **14**(2) (2022). https://doi.org/10.3390/su14020601
32. Kempers, S.T., et al.: Tech united Eindhoven middle size league winner 2022. In: Eguchi, A., Lau, N., Paetzel-Prüsmann, M., Wanichanon, T. (eds.) RoboCup 2022. LNCS, vol. 13561, pp. 337–348. Springer, Cham (2023). https://doi.org/10.1007/978-3-031-28469-4_28
33. Kwiatkowska, M.Z., Norman, G., Parker, D.: Stochastic model checking. In: Bernardo, M., Hillston, J. (eds.) SFM 2007. LNCS, vol. 4486, pp. 220–270. Springer, Heidelberg (2007). https://doi.org/10.1007/978-3-540-72522-0_6
34. Lanotte, R., Merro, M., Zannone, N.: Impact analysis of coordinated cyber-physical attacks via statistical model checking: a case study. In: Huisman, M., Ravara, A. (eds.) FORTE 2023. LNCS, vol. 13910, pp. 75–94. Springer, Cham (2023). https://doi.org/10.1007/978-3-031-35355-0_6
35. Legay, A., Lukina, A., Traonouez, L., Yang, J., Smolka, S.A., Grosu, R.: Statistical model checking. In: Steffen, B., Woeginger, G. (eds.) Computing and Software Science - State of the Art and Perspectives. LNCS, vol. 10000, pp. 478–504. Springer, Cham (2019). https://doi.org/10.1007/978-3-319-91908-9_23
36. Li, S., Yang, Q., Xing, J., Chen, W., Zou, R.: A foundation model for building digital twins: a case study of a chiller. Buildings **12**(8) (2022). https://doi.org/10.3390/buildings12081079
37. Lugaresi, G., Gangemi, S., Gazzoni, G., Matta, A.: Online validation of digital twins for manufacturing systems. Comput. Ind. **150**, 103942 (2023). https://doi.org/10.1016/j.compind.2023.103942
38. Martinez, C.L., et al.: Tech united Eindhoven team description. Technical report, Eindhoven University of Technology (2014). https://www.techunited.nl/media/files/TDP2014.pdf
39. Naderifar, V., Sahran, S., Shukur, Z.: A review on conformance checking technique for the evaluation of process mining algorithms. TEM J. **8**(4), 1232 (2019). https://doi.org/10.18421/TEM84-18
40. Pinciroli, R., Trubiani, C.: Model-based performance analysis for architecting cyber-physical dynamic spaces. In: Proceedings of ICSA 2021, pp. 104–114. IEEE (2021). https://doi.org/10.1109/ICSA51549.2021.00018
41. Qi, Q., Tao, F.: Digital twin and big data towards smart manufacturing and industry 4.0: 360 degree comparison. IEEE Access **6**, 3585–3593 (2018). https://doi.org/10.1109/access.2018.2793265

42. Riedmaier, S., Danquah, B., Schick, B., Diermeyer, F.: Unified framework and survey for model verification, validation and uncertainty quantification. Arch. Comput. Methods Eng. **28**, 2655–2688 (2021). https://doi.org/10.1007/s11831-020-09473-7
43. Sankararaman, S., Mahadevan, S.: Integration of model verification, validation, and calibration for uncertainty quantification in engineering systems. Reliab. Eng. Syst. Saf. **138**, 194–209 (2015). https://doi.org/10.1016/j.ress.2015.01.023
44. Sargent, R.G.: Verification and validation of simulation models. In: Proceedings of the 2010 Winter Simulation Conference, pp. 166–183 (2010). https://doi.org/10.1109/WSC.2010.5679166
45. Sargent, R.G.: Verification and validation of simulation models. J. Simul. **7**, 12–24 (2013). https://doi.org/10.1057/JOS.2012.20
46. Sen, K., Viswanathan, M., Agha, G.: On statistical model checking of stochastic systems. In: Etessami, K., Rajamani, S.K. (eds.) CAV 2005. LNCS, vol. 3576, pp. 266–280. Springer, Heidelberg (2005). https://doi.org/10.1007/11513988_26
47. Shaikh, E., Al-Ali, A., Muhammad, S., Mohammad, N., Aloul, F.A.: Security analysis of a digital twin framework using probabilistic model checking. IEEE Access **11**, 26358–26374 (2023). https://doi.org/10.1109/ACCESS.2023.3257171
48. Sharma, A., Kosasih, E., Zhang, J., Brintrup, A., Calinescu, A.: Digital twins: state of the art theory and practice, challenges, and open research questions. J. Ind. Inf. Integr. **30**, 100383 (2022). https://doi.org/10.1016/j.jii.2022.100383
49. Sifakis, J., Harel, D.: Trustworthy autonomous system development. ACM Trans. Embed. Comput. Syst. **22**(3) (2023). https://doi.org/10.1145/3545178
50. Soe, R.M.: FINEST twins: platform for cross-border smart city solutions. In: Proceedings of the 18th Annual International Conference on Digital Government Research, pp. 352–357. Association for Computing Machinery (2017). https://doi.org/10.1145/3085228.3085287
51. Umeda, Y., et al.: Development of an education program for digital manufacturing system engineers based on 'digital triplet' concept. Procedia Manuf. **31**, 363–369 (2019). https://doi.org/10.1016/j.promfg.2019.03.057
52. Vaserstein, L.N.: Markovian processes on countable space product describing large systems of automata. Probl. Peredachi Inf. **5**(3), 64–72 (1969)

UPPAAL-Based Modeling and Verification of ROS 2 Multi-threaded Execution and Operating System Reservations

Lukas Dust[✉], Rong Gu, Cristina Seceleanu, Mikael Ekström, and Saad Mubeen

Mälardalen University, Västerås, Sweden
{lukas.dust,rong.gu,cristina.seceleanu,mikael.ekstrom,
saad.mubeen}@mdu.se

Abstract. In this paper, we propose a formal modeling approach in UPPAAL to simulate and verify multi-threaded robotics middleware execution based on ROS 2. In the modeling process, we consider middleware-specific scheduling by creating formal models that simulate the execution behavior of a ROS 2-based system. Furthermore, we show how to model potential underlying operating system's influences on execution, by modeling reservation servers. We propose timed automata templates to model the multi-threaded execution of ROS 2 systems and the reservations of the underlying operating system in UPPAAL. We show how to use the created templates to simulate a ROS 2 application. We demonstrate the application of the formal models and model checking in various ROS 2 experiments. Furthermore, we validate the created models by comparing the observed execution traces in experiments on ROS 2 systems and the simulated traces of our models. Overall, this paper showcases the application and usefulness of model-based verification of distributed middleware applications, including internal scheduling and influences of underlying operating system actions.

Keywords: Robot Operating System 2 · Pattern-Based Modeling · Model Checking

1 Introduction

Middleware implementations such as the open-source project Robot Operating System 2 (ROS 2) [16] aim to standardize processes while facilitating the rapid development and prototyping of applications across various domains. In the robotics domain, ROS 2 and its predecessor ROS [18] have seen increased interest in academia and industry [3]. ROS 2-based robotic systems often operate in populated environments, leading to safety-critical applications. To guarantee safety, strict timing requirements are given to the utilized hardware and software, hence the system must follow real-time demands. To meet the required real-time support, ROS 2 utilizes Data Distribution Service (DDS) for real-time communication and execution. Since supporting ROS will end in 2025 [17], robotic systems using ROS have to be updated to ROS 2. Nevertheless, the missing analysis and documentation of ROS 2 might lead to unexpected behavioral consequences for robotic systems.

Initial investigation on ROS 2 real-time capabilities in the form of theoretical response-time analysis and end-to-end timing analysis has been conducted in the literature [7,9,23]. Proposed methods allow analytical verification of ROS 2 systems but require extensive system knowledge and manual analysis, and are hard to automate. As a middleware, ROS 2 execution relies on an underlying operating system (OS) that schedules an inbuilt module called *executor*. The executor acts as a ROS 2 specific scheduler, which conducts the scheduling of the ROS 2 executable functions, called *callbacks*. Callbacks in ROS 2 are triggered by the arrival of data in the DDS communication channels or through timer events. Furthermore, the callbacks are specific to the communication channel and timer. Each main system component of ROS 2 systems, called *node*, consists of at least one executor. The internal scheduling and execution of ROS 2 nodes in the mainline single-threaded executor have been analyzed in the literature [7,9,11]. An initial analysis of the multi-threaded executor that utilizes multiple threads of the underlying OS has been performed by Xu et al. [15] and Sobhani et al. [21]. Xu et al. [15] have observed that in the multi-threaded executor, response time might be worse when utilizing multiple threads compared to a single-thread execution, due to blocking. Such a phenomenon can threaten the timing requirements of safety-critical systems and deserves further analysis.

Nevertheless, in robotic systems, verification and testing are mostly based on trial-and-error approaches [19]. These approaches are not systematic and may miss errors that happen rarely. Furthermore, due to missing standardization, they are hard to automate. In contrast, formal methods, such as *model checking* [6], with tools such as UPPAAL [1,13] and SPIN [2,14], can comprehensively analyze such systems. Specifically, model checking gives a mathematical and rigorous analysis of complex systems with an automatic exploration of the model's entire state space. Exhaustive verification can be conducted to verify given requirements. Nevertheless, the drawback to model checking is the process of formal modeling, which is complicated and has a steep learning curve. Previously, we have proposed an approach to simplifying the process of formal modeling of ROS 2 Nodes utilizing single-threaded executors [10]. The approach uses *timed automata* (TA) [4] as model templates in the model checker UPPAAL [1,13].

In this paper, we adapt and refine our earlier approach [10] to verify the stated blocking issue in multi-threaded executors. The previously created analysis assumes that the thread in the underlying OS is continuously available. Hence, the calculated response time can be optimistic (underestimated) in systems with limited resources. Nevertheless, this is different from reality. Therefore, in this paper, we introduce *reservation-based scheduling* in our formal models to initially model influences of underlying OS scheduling. These lead us to the following research questions: **RQ1**: Given the behavioral semantics of multi-threaded executors in ROS 2, how to verify the design of ROS 2-based systems concerning callback blocking? **RQ2**: How to incorporate underlying operating system influences in the verification? **RQ3**: What are the reusable patterns for modeling multi-threaded execution and underlying OS reservations in ROS 2 systems?

The contributions in this paper are as follows:

- We propose UPPAAL Timed Automata templates for modeling multi-threaded execution of ROS 2 systems, simplifying the complex construction of formal models that require configuration of parameters (in Sect. 3).
- We show how to incorporate the underlying OS' influence on the scheduling of middleware applications into formal modeling and model-checking of ROS 2, which has not been addressed in the literature so far (in Sect. 3.5).
- We validate our formal models of the ROS 2 multi-threaded executor by experiments, where we compare real ROS 2 execution traces to simulated traces in UPPAAL (in Sect. 4).
- We show the vulnerabilities caused by the blocking in multi-threaded executors of ROS 2 by using our formal models.

2 Background

For a better understanding of the reader, in this section, we start with an introduction to the concepts of ROS2 and reservation-based scheduling. Next, we briefly overview Timed Automata and UPPAAL and introduce an existing example of pattern-based verification of single-threaded execution of ROS 2.

2.1 ROS 2

As an open-source middleware, the goal of ROS 2 is to enable fast prototyping and implementation of distributed robotic systems. The development and improvement of ROS 2 is continuous, with stable versions being released.

ROS 2 System Model. The main components of ROS 2 systems are the so-called *nodes*, which are capable of communication through designated channels in the DDS. With the *publisher-subscriber* and *service-client* communication methods, there are two approaches to communication.

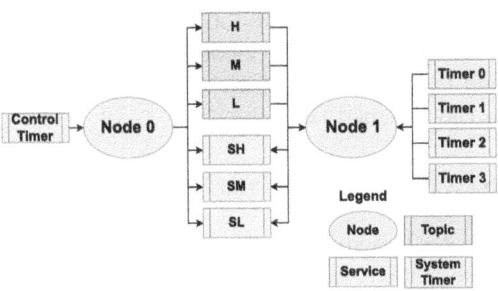

Fig. 1. Schematic example of ROS 2 systems containing two nodes and communication channels. (Color figure online)

We give an example of a ROS 2 system with two nodes in Fig. 1. Green ellipses represent nodes. The communication channels for *publisher-subscriber* communication, called *topics*, are shown in red, and the channels for *service-client* communication, called *services*, are shown in blue. Each node using the *publisher-subscriber* communication can send data through a specific topic as a *publisher*. The messages are then received by all nodes that are subscribed to that topic. The *service-client* communication is directional. A node can request the execution of a server function in another node, where a response from the server function triggers a client callback in the requesting node. Generally, the arrival of data in the connected DDS channels triggers the execution of a callback in the receiving node, defined explicitly by the channel. Furthermore, system timers (yellow) can be assigned to a node and trigger the execution of specific callbacks in that node.

ROS 2 Scheduling and Execution. The execution of ROS 2 nodes relies on an underlying OS. Furthermore, each node contains a ROS 2 specific scheduler module to schedule the callbacks, called *the executor*. The executor can be set to single-threaded [9] and multi-threaded [15], utilizing a single thread or multiple threads of the host OS. In this paper, we focus only on the multi-threaded executors. Generally, the execution of callbacks is non-preemptive, meaning that a callback execution can not be interrupted by another callback execution. Furthermore, the scheduling is set-based, where so-called *ready-sets* are created to store one instance of each released callback. The creation of the ready-set is done at distinct points in the scheduling procedure (*polling point*). Execution order is determined after the callback type (subscriber, service, client, timer) and the callback initialization time. For the scheduling algorithm, there are two options: *mutually exclusive* and *reentrant* execution. In mutually exclusive execution, callbacks are not allowed to be executed in parallel despite the existence of multiple threads. In reentrant execution, callbacks can be executed in parallel on multiple threads.

2.2 Reservation Based Scheduling

The utilization of reservation servers is known as a method to make an operating system's influences deterministic. Hence, it is a good starting point for analysis of middleware applications and the influence of underlying OS [9]. In this paper, we assume it is table-driven reservation-based scheduling. In table-driven reservation-based scheduling, threads are assigned to run inside reservation servers. A reservation server, denoted by R_t, consists of a set of statically configured time slots (reservation table) and a period, denoted by p_t. A time slot consists of a start time and an end time, repeating with every p_t. A thread is assigned to R_t and can only run in the assigned time slots.

2.3 Timed Automata and UPPAAL

In this section, we give an introduction to Timed Automata (TA) alongside an introduction to the TA-based model checker UPPAAL. As the formal definitions of TA are not required to understand the paper, and due to space constraints, we direct readers to the literature [4,13] for a comprehensive and precise exposition of these concepts.

A Timed Automaton (TA) [4] is a tuple including a finite set of locations, with an initial location, a finite set of non-negative real-valued variables called *clocks*, a finite set of actions, a finite set of edges, a set of *guards*, that is, conjunctive formulas of constraints, a set of clocks in the locations that are reset on the edge, and a partial function assigning invariants to locations. Furthermore, the semantics of a TA are defined as a labeled transition system, with delay and action transitions. UPPAAL [13] is a tool for modeling, simulating, and performing model checking on an extension of Timed Automata (TA) called UPPAAL *Timed Automata* (UTA). Within UPPAAL, UTA are structured as *templates* (see Fig. 2) that can be instantiated. UTA expands the capabilities of TA by introducing features like data variables, synchronization channels, urgent and committed locations, and more. Additionally, UPPAAL enables the composition of UTA in parallel as a network of UTA (NUTA), synchronized via *channels*. Figure 2 illustrates a NUTA implemented in UPPAAL. In this depiction, blue circles represent *locations* interconnected by directional *edges*. Double-circled locations are the *initial* locations (e.g. L0). Encircled "u" denotes *urgent* locations (e.g. L3), and encircled "c" denotes *committed* locations (e.g. L4). UTA imposes constraints such that time does not progress in urgent and committed locations. Committed locations have even stricter rules: the subsequent edge traversal must initiate from one of them. Edges allow assignments for resetting clocks (e.g., c1:=0), updating data variables (e.g., v1:=para1), guards (e.g., c1>=10), and synchronization channels (e.g., a! and a?). At location L1, an invariant c1<=15 dictates that clock c1 can never surpass 15 time units. In UPPAAL, templates of UTA can incorporate parameters (e.g., para1 in TA1) that receive values upon instantiation.

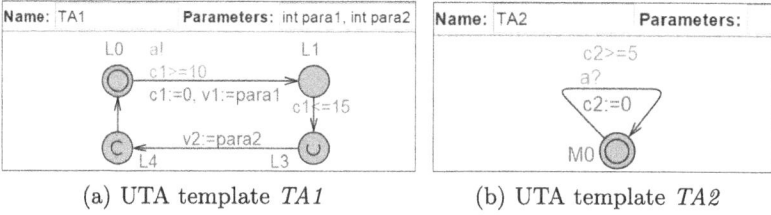

(a) UTA template *TA1*   (b) UTA template *TA2*

Fig. 2. An example of UTA templates in UPPAAL (Color figure online)

The UPPAAL queries that we verify in this paper are **supremum evaluations**: sup{con}:list computes the supremum of the expressions in the list only when the condition (i.e., con) is *true*.

2.4 Pattern-Based Verification of ROS 2 Systems

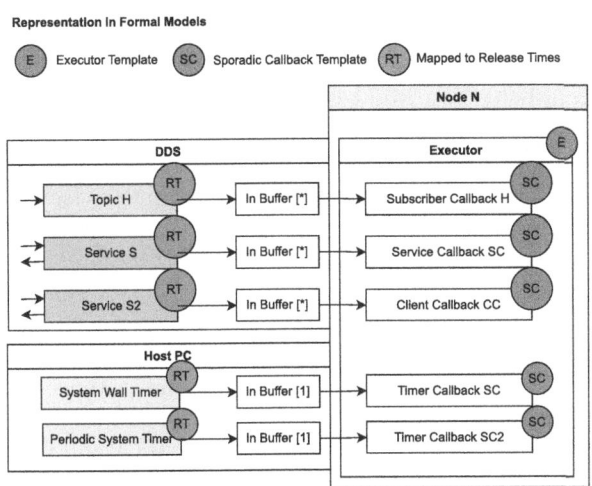

Fig. 3. System abstractions in [10]

Our previous work [10] presents pattern-based verification of ROS 2 systems using single-threaded executors in UPPAAL. UTA templates are created to allow simple system composition for verification of buffer sizes and callback latencies. An overview of the main abstractions of ROS 2 system components can be found in Fig. 3. To model the scheduling of ROS 2 callbacks in a single-threaded executor, two types of UTA templates are needed, the executor templates and the callback templates. The executor UTA template allows the modeling of an individual ROS 2 executor by one initialized executor UTA. Each callback in a ROS 2 application can be modeled by one initialized callback UTA. A vital abstraction is the representation of releases of callbacks through release times. While in real ROS 2 applications, the callbacks are released on the arrival of data or on a timer event, in the formal models, it is assumed that with system analysis, the release times (representing the arrival or data or timing events) and the execution times of the callbacks are sufficient to model the scheduling of a ROS 2 application formally. We refer to [10] for more details on the implementation.

3 Modeling and Verification in UPPAAL

In this section, we present our approach to modeling ROS 2 nodes and applications with instances of formal model templates. Therefore, we describe the abstractions and representation of features in the formal model templates. Next, we present the formal model templates for the callbacks and the multi-threaded executor[1]. That is followed by a demonstration of how to compose UTA to a model of the ROS 2 system and verify the latency of callbacks.

---
[1] The complete model is available: https://sites.google.com/view/ubvros2nodes.

3.1 Feature Selection and Abstraction

We build the formal models to simulate the execution of a ROS 2 system and perform verification on callback latency in multi-threaded executors. We define *callback latency* as the time from the release of a callback (e.g., the arrival of data) until the execution of the instance has finished. To model the *multi-threaded execution* of ROS 2 nodes, we use similar abstractions as presented in our previous work [10]. We create two types of UTA templates to represent the callbacks and the executor, respectively. The templates require specific input parameters to allow the modeling of execution behavior. We abstract the arrival of data and timer events to callback release times, meaning that instead of modeling the communication explicitly, we pass the arrival times of messages as release times to the models. Furthermore, we pass the execution time as a parameter to the callback UTA. Nevertheless, while in [10] each initialized executor UTA modeled a complete executor, in this paper, each instantiated executor UTA represents a specific thread of one executor only. Furthermore, to model callback execution, we configure the UTA template to model the execution of the callback on a defined thread of the executor. Hence, to model a callback execution on a multi-threaded executor, the callback must be composed of one instance of the UTA callback template for each assigned thread. When two threads and one callback exist in an executor, we need to instantiate two callback UTA and two executor UTA. We allow interaction through synchronized channels between the executor UTA and the callback UTA by passing an executor ID, unique for the general executor, and a thread ID, unique for the individual thread, to the executor and callback UTA templates. Executor UTA sharing the same executor ID, hence representing the same multi-threaded executor, interact with each other through shared global variables. Callback UTA, sharing the same callback ID, modeling the same callback in different threads interact through synchronized channels and shared variables.

3.2 Modeling of Callbacks

In this section, we present our created callback UTA. Each instance of a callback UTA represents a specific callback on a specific thread. That means, that a callback executing on two threads needs to be modeled by two callback UTA. To indicate multiple callback UTA modeling the same callback, a parameter, called *callbackID* is passed to the UTA, that is unique to each callback in the system, but equal the UTA modeling the same callback on the different threads. To assign a callback UTA to an executor and its thread, the parameters *executorID* and *threadID* are used as inputs to the UTA. Both parameters are needed to enable interaction between a callback UTA and all UTA modeling the executor the callback is assigned to, as well as to identify the individual executor UTA, the specific callback UTA is executing on. Additional input parameters to the callback UTA are the input buffer size, a finite set of release times, the worst case execution time and the type of callback. The type of callback is either *timer*, *subscription*, *service* or *client*. A simplified overview of the created callback UTA template is given in Fig. 4. Due to the multiple threads, the callback UTA can be released, polled, and reset at multiple locations. Hence, we group edges and mark them with the same label. The first kind of edges, marked with the *RELEASE* statement, are taken when a release time of the callback has been reached. The edge updates the variable *nextReleaseTime* and initializes a designated timer that keeps track of the latency of each individual release instance. Furthermore, the callback UTA synchronizes via a broadcast channel with all executor UTAs that model the executor to whom the callback is assigned.

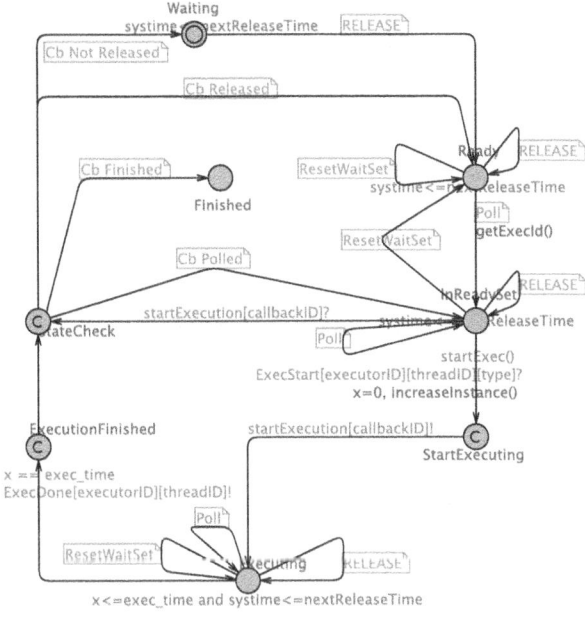

Fig. 4. Simplified UTA of a Callback

The edges labeled with *Poll* are initialized by a synchronized channel with the executor UTA, modeling the polling by the corresponding executor. Internally, the callback UTA counts polling instances. All edges labeled with *ResetWaitSet* are initialized by a synchronized channel with the executor UTA signaling when the callback has been removed from the ready set without being executed.

In the Waiting location, the callback waits to be released to then move to the Ready location. Following, the callback waits for the executor to include the callback in the ready set. That can be done via a synchronized channel poll by each executor UTA that models the executor that the callback is assigned to. The function *getExecId* on the edge calculates the priority of the callback. In the InReadySet location, the callback waits to be executed. When the UTA of the assigned thread and executor starts the execution of the callback, via the synchronized channel *ExecStart*, guarded by *startExec()* to ensure the callback priority is high enough to be executed, the callback moves to the StartExecuting location. Furthermore, the function *increaseInstance* updates internal counters that track execution instances. Next, the callback UTA synchronizes to all callback UTA that model the same callback on different threads to move them to the StateCheck location. In the Executing location, the callback waits until the execution time has passed before it moves to the ExecutionFinished location. A synchronized channel *ExecDone* synchronizes with the executor UTA to signal the end of the execution. `ExecutionFinished` leads to the `StateCheck` location and allows the checking of the variables representing the latency when the execution has finished. From the `StateCheck` location, the callback can move to the `Waiting`, `Ready`, `InReadySet`, and `Finished` location, dependent on the number of releases and polls.

3.3 Modeling of the Multi-threaded Executor

Next, we present our model of the multi-threaded executor. The model follows the ROS 2 execution semantics presented in the literature [15]. While in the ROS 2 executors, it is possible to configure different callback groups with different settings in one executor, for simplicity, we assume all callbacks in an executor are assigned to one callback group with the same settings. As explained, we create the UTA templates so that each instance of the UTA models an individual thread of a multi-threaded executor. When utilizing the UTA templates to model a multi-threaded executor, there are as many initialized instances of the executor UTA sharing the same executor ID as there are threads existing in the executor. The UTA instances differ by the thread ID only. An overview of our UTA template is presented in Fig. 5. Executor UTA instances sharing the same executor ID interact with each other through shared global variables. Hence, the shared variables called *locks* are used to interact between the instances of the same executor on different threads. Generally, there are two types of locks. The first one, denoted by `lock`, serves to lock the executor, whereas a thread instance of the executor performs scheduling actions. The second lock called `canBeTakenFrom`, models the availability of the callback group to represent the mutually exclusive behavior by blocking other callbacks from being executed while a callback from the same group is currently under execution. When the execution is set to being `Reentrant`, the second lock is not activated. As the state of the locks must be readable and writable from each executor UTA sharing the same executor ID at any given state, they are implemented as shared variables and not synchronized channels. The executor UTA starts in `WaitForLock`, where it is modeled to wait for the lock to be returned or a new callback to be released, leading to the `Idle` location. In the `Idle` location, it is checked if the thread can obtain the lock. When possible, the thread executes by moving to the `FetchCb` location while locking other executor threads by setting the *lock* variable to true. To limit the model's state space, we separate between two edges to allow the modeling of a maximal simulation time, where one edge would lead to a deadlock after a defined time. On the edge leading to the `FetchCb` location, a function *nextCb* is executed. In this function, a variable called *cbType* is determined as the type of callback contained in the ready set that is next to be scheduled. The order of callback types is *timers*, *subscriptions*, *services*, and then *clients*, where timers in the ready set will always be scheduled first. When the ready set is empty, or the execution of callbacks is blocked (in the mutually exclusive setting), indicated by the lock `canBeTakenFrom`, the variable *cbType* is set to *empty*.

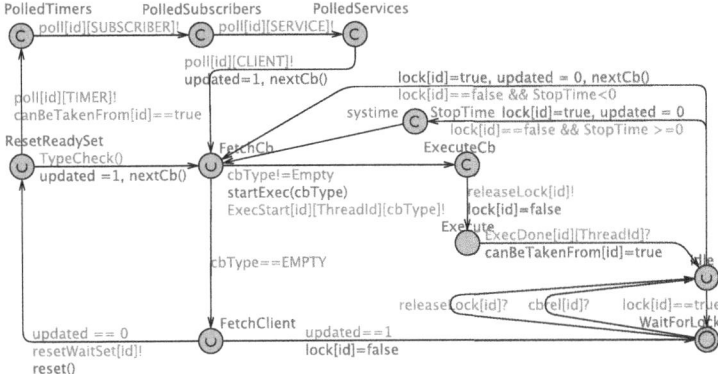

Fig. 5. Simplified UTA of a Multi-Threaded Executor Thread

When callbacks are ready for execution, the executor starts scheduling the callback by utilizing a synchronized channel. Next, the lock is released to allow other executor threads to perform scheduling actions. Following, the executor waits in the Execute location until the callback execution is finished, modeled by a synchronized channel initialized from the callback template. Upon the end of execution, the executor moves to the Idle location, where it checks if it can obtain the lock to perform further scheduling actions. When the executor is in the FetchCb location and the *cbType* is *empty*, hence there are no callbacks in the ready set available, or the type of the executor is mutually exclusive, and a callback is executing in another thread, the executor moves to the ResetReadySet location. On the incoming edge, the ready set is reset by a synchronized transition to the callback UTA and the UTA internal *reset* function. Following, available callbacks are polled via the synchronized channels. Alternatively, the TypeCheck checks if the execution is mutually exclusive and another callback is executed in a different thread. In that case, the ready set remains empty. Next, with the function *nextCb*, the executor goes through the ready set to check for the type of the next available callback to execute. Following, the executor moves to the WaitForLock location if no callback is available or the execution is blocked.

3.4 System Declaration and Verification in UPPAAL

To compose a system of the UTA templates, the user needs to define the system declaration. The system declaration is C-like code, where templates are initialized with parameters to system components. With the chosen approach, it is possible to verify individual nodes. Each executor thread needs to be modeled using an individual UTA instance. Furthermore, each callback needs to be modeled with an individual UTA instance for each thread it might execute. Next, the simulator can be used to generate random system traces based on the formal model. Furthermore, the verifier can be used to define properties that can be checked for. In our model, we incorporate timers that keep track of the elapsed time from the release of a callback. Hence, it is possible to use the *supremum* evaluation, including all UTA of a callback thread, to determine the maximum latency for each callback, serving as a measure that incorporates the blocking time of a callback. With the shown example in Eq. 1, the maximum value for the timer of the actual instance of execution is checked at location ExecutionFinished for the individual instance in all UTA instances (in the given case, 2 instances for two threads) of the callback.

$$\sup\{\text{cb\_t0.ExecutionFinished or cb\_t1.ExecutionFinished}\}: \\ \text{cb.releaseTimers[cb.instance]} \qquad (1)$$

3.5 Modeling of Operating System Reservations

This section presents our approach to including operating system reservations in the model-based verification proposed before. We introduce a new UTA template that acts as a new layer in the models to model OS reservations. With the chosen approach, we create model templates representing the reservation servers and adapt the callback and executor templates to incorporate the blocking behavior.

Modeling Reservation Servers. First, we define a formal model that represents the behavior of reservation servers. The model will interact with the callback and executor UTA via a global variable representing a lock to show whether the thread is available or not. Again, as the state of the lock must be readable from each executor and callback UTA sharing the same executor ID at any given state, they are implemented as shared variables and not as synchronized channels.

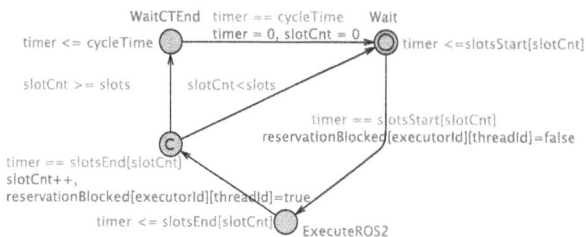

Fig. 6. UTA Template of a Reservation Server

In our implementation, each thread receives its own reservation server, modeled by the lock being an array of the size of the executor ID and thread ID. As shown in Fig. 6, the reservation server consists of two modes, *blocking* and *allowing* the execution. Initially, execution is blocked, and the server waits to reach the first time slot where execution is allowed. When the start time is reached, the reservation server moves to the execution location and sets the lock to false. It stays in the location until the upper bound of the time slot is reached, before transitioning back to the waiting state and setting the lock to true. When the last time slot has been executed, the server goes to location WaitCTEnd, waits until the period has elapsed, and then resets the timer and the slot counter to restart the reservations.

Adaptation of the ROS 2 Component Templates. To model the influence of reservations on the execution, we incorporate the blocking behavior into the callback and executor UTA. The interaction between the callback and executor UTA and the reservation server UTA is modeled by the shared variable *reservationBlocked*. Hence, we need to change the outgoing edges of locations where the underlying OS can block the execution. Note, the changes are additions to the UTA shown in Fig. 4 and Fig. 5, and while they are implemented in our created models, for simplicity, they are not shown in the figures. In the executor UTA, the critical locations are the *WaitForLock* and *Idle*. In the other locations where the underlying OS can block the execution, that is, the locations of execution of callbacks, the executors are blocked by the callback UTA. Hence, we add blocking in the *WaitForLock* and *Idle* only by adding guards to outgoing edges to check for the availability of reservations. In the callback model, there are multiple locations where the underlying OS can block the execution. Nevertheless, some of these locations model behavior that is independent of the reservations. Releases of callbacks are handled independently of the thread. Hence, no blocking by reservations occurs. In the callback model, the crucial location is the `Executing` location. To allow blocking of the execution, we increase the execution time by the blocking time. We implement this behavior by a self-loop edge that increases the target time by one if the thread is blocked in the current execution step. In the callback UTA, all other locations are urgent or committed locations, so they occur at the same time as the modified locations start or end.

System Declaration. To declare a ROS 2 Node, we must utilize the callbacks, the executor, and the reservation server template. We assign each executor thread its reservation server, using the same executor ID and thread ID, respectively.

4 Evaluation

In this section, we evaluate and validate the created model templates. In the first subsection, we present the used experiment systems and their setup. Next, we use the models of the multi-threaded executor without reservation-based scheduling and compare the generated system traces from UPPAAL 4.0 with observed execution in two real ROS 2 systems. In the scenarios, we show the criticality of blocking and the rising latency of callbacks while utilizing multiple threads. Next, we evaluate the reservation-based scheduling templates on two scenarios using the two experiment systems. For reservation-based scheduling, we evaluate the models against synthetic execution traces carefully designed by hand based on the execution semantics.

4.1 Experimental Setup

We create two experiment systems that are composed of ROS 2 nodes to validate our created models. Both systems are built and executed on a single computer assuming 100% availability of underlying OS resources.

System 1: ROS 2 Experiment System. The first system is based on the experimentation system in [9] and [10]. We use the system with a similar scenario to allow comparability to the execution of the single-threaded executor. The experiment system, shown in Fig. 1, consists of two nodes, of which Node 1 is the node to be verified. Node 0 is for the sake of controlling the experiments.

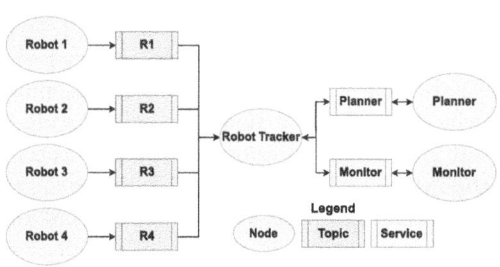

Fig. 7. Schematic of the Robotic System.

The nodes communicate over three publisher-subscriber channels, named after their priority in Node 1 (H, M, L). Furthermore, the control Node can call three servers in Node 1 (SH, SM, SL). Despite the communication, there are four timers in Node 1 and a control timer in Node 0. The system is used to create execution scenarios and validate the observed behavior with the generated UPPAAL model traces.

System 2: Centralized Robotic System. The second system is an abstraction of a centralized multi-agent robotic system. In the centralized system depicted in Fig. 7, four robots periodically publish their status information to a central server called the Robot Tracker. The Robot Tracker's task is to collect the robots' status information and send it to other central nodes, such as the Planner and the Monitor, via a server request for further processing. As the node collects the data in a data structure, simultaneous access to the data storage must be avoided. Hence, we assume the execution will be mutually exclusive. In a realistic system, there would be further processing after the planner and monitor and a feedback loop back to the robots. For simplicity, in our evaluation, we focus on the execution of the Robot Tracker.

4.2 Multi-threaded Execution

In this subsection, we evaluate the created models of the multi-threaded executor (without reservation-based scheduling) to compare observed traces with real system traces. Given the presented experiment systems, we create two scenarios.

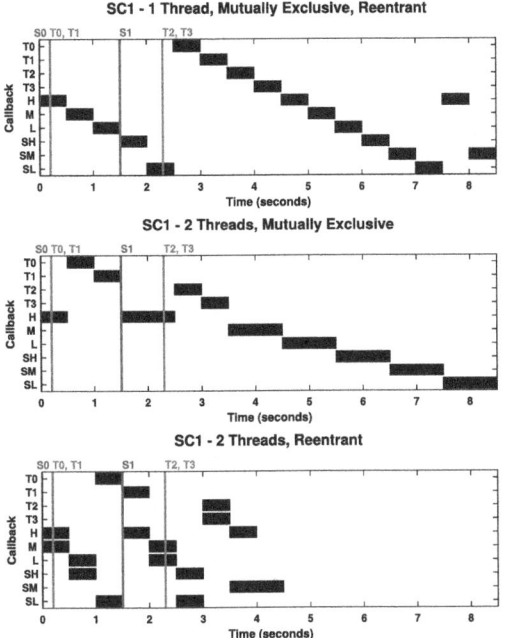

Fig. 8. Observed Execution Traces SC1 (Color figure online)

Scenario 1. In the first scenario, we use the experiment system from Fig. 1 to execute the scenario presented in the literature [9]. The following message sequence S0 is released during initialization (0 s), releasing callbacks $<L$; M; H; SH; SL; L; M; H; SH; $SL>$ simultaneously. A message sequence S1 is sent at 1.5 s and triggers releases of callbacks $<SM$; SM; $H>$. Timers 0 and 1 are configured to release after 0.3 s, while Timers 2 and 3 release after 2.3 s. Each callback is configured to execute for 500 ms. Next, we execute the system with the multi-threaded executor, first utilizing one thread, the two mutually exclusive threads, and finally two reentrant ones. During execution, we observe the trace, shown in Fig. 8. In the figure, the sequence releases are marked in blue, while the timer releases are marked in red. After this, we initialize the system using the model templates in the UPPAAL models. We use the simulator in UPPAAL to generate system traces. We validate that the observed trace is contained in the randomly generated traces. Next, we utilize the UPPAAL verifier to determine the worst-case latency for each callback using the model.

Table 1. Observed Latency in System Execution and UPPAAL Simulation SC1

	1 Thread		2 Threads Mutually Exclusive		2 Threads Reentrant	
CB	Observed	UPPAAL	Observed	UPPAAL	Observed	UPPAAL
T0	2,8	2,8	0,8	0,8	1,3	1,3
T1	3,3	3,3	1,3	1,3	1,8	1,8
T2	1,7	1,7	0,7	0,7	1,2	1,2
T3	2,2	2,2	1,2	1,2	1,2	1,2
H	6,5	6,5	2,0	2,0	2,5	2,5
M	5,5	5,5	4,5	4,5	2,5	2,5
L	6,0	6,0	5,5	5,5	2,5	2,5
SH	6,5	6,5	6,5	6,5	3,0	3,0
SM	7,0	7,0	6,0	6,0	3,0	3,0
SL	7,5	7,5	8,5	8,5	3,0	3,0

In Table 1, we compare the observed results with the results from the real system execution. We observe the latencies to be precisely as the observed latencies in the real system. In the scenario, it is important to note that the latency for individual callbacks such as SL is higher when utilizing two threads in the mutually exclusive setting than when utilizing a single thread. This is due to the second thread resetting the ready set and the callback getting blocked by other arriving callbacks. Furthermore, we see multiple callback instances executed consecutively despite the staggered release, which might be undesired.

Robotic System. Next, we utilize the robotic system and model and verify the Robot Tracker Node using the multi-threaded executor with one and two threads, respectively, executing mutually exclusive. In this scenario, we show the criticality of blocking when using multiple threads. Utilizing the robotic system, we create the following scenario. We assume all callbacks will be executed for 200 ms, respectively. The robots send their status information periodically each second. The Planner sends a service request at 0.7 and 1.7 s, while the Monitor sends requests at 0.3 and 1.3 s. In Fig. 9, we show the observed execution traces from the execution. In blue, we mark the release of status data from the robots. We mark the service requests from the Planner and the Monitor in red. Next, we model the scenario with our UPPAAL templates and use the UPPAAL simulator to generate system traces. The execution traces match with the observed traces in the simulator.

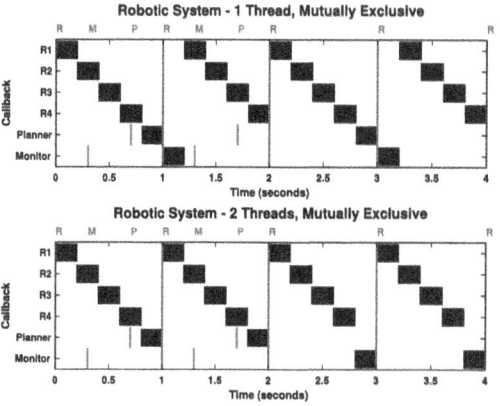

Fig. 9. Observed Execution Traces (Color figure online)

Next, we use the verifier to evaluate the maximum latencies using Eq. 1. The results are presented in Table 2. We can see that the latencies match in all cases. In the scenario, it can be seen that in the case of two utilized threads, the latency of the Monitor is significantly higher (2.7 s to 1.9 s) than a single thread. That is because the Planner internally has a higher priority than the Monitor. In ROS 2's set-based scheduling, one instance of each released callback is included in the ready set at the polling point. In the execution on a single thread, the following polling instance will not happen until all callbacks in the ready set have been executed. When using two threads mutually exclusive, the second thread is idle and resets the ready set. Hence, a new ready set is built before scheduling a callback with one instance of each released callback. This is critical, as the lower priority callbacks can get

Table 2. Results Robotic System

	1 Thread		2 Threads Mutually Exclusive	
CB	Observed	UPPAAL	Observed	UPPAAL
R1	0,4	0,4	0,2	0,2
R2	0,6	0,6	0,4	0,4
R3	0,8	0,8	0,6	0,6
R4	1,0	1,0	0,8	0,8
Planner	1,3	1,3	0,3	0,3
Monitor	1,9	1,9	2,7	2,7

blocked by multiple instances of the same higher priority callbacks. Hence, in extreme cases, starvation can occur. The blocking is limited to a single instance of higher-priority callbacks in a single thread. Such behavior can be observed in the formal models, and the blocking is verified through simulation traces and the calculation of worst-case callback latency.

4.3 Reservation-Based Scheduling

In the following, two simple examples show the application of reservation-based scheduling in the formal models. The first example is a synthetic example showing the correctness of the approach, while the second example is a small-scale robotic system. For simplicity, the evaluation is performed on the formal models and traces generated by theoretical analysis, given the behavioral semantics of the executor.

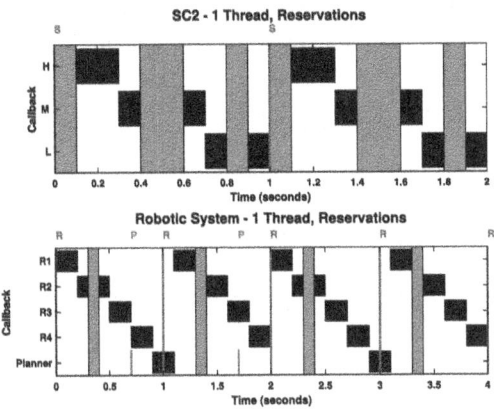

Fig. 10. Observed Execution Traces

Scenario 2 (SC2). In this scenario, we utilize the experiment system in Fig. 1 to validate the models of the reservation servers. We create a simple scenario in which the topics H, M, and L are released each second and executed for 0.2 s. The reservation server is configured to execute the ROS 2 thread between 0.1 to 0.4 s, 0.6 to 0.8 s, and 0.9 to 1 s, repeating each second.

Robotic System. In this scenario, we utilize the robotic system to execute 90 Percent of reservations, blocking the reservation server from 0.3 to 0.4 s each second. The planner requests the service at 0.7 and 1.7 s. The execution time of the callbacks is set to 0.2 s.

Results. In Fig. 10, we show the system traces observed in UPPAAL. The black boxes show the execution of the callbacks. In grey, we mark the time slots blocked by the underlying OS reservations. The traces align with the calculated traces, resulting from careful manual analysis given the ROS 2 execution semantics. Furthermore, we validate the observed worst-case latencies by calculating them by hand following the ROS 2 semantics. Our initial observation is that the blocking effect of the underlying OS reservations rightfully extends the execution time of callbacks. Despite the execution delay due to the blocking, in the Robotic System, the order of callback execution changes compared to a scenario with full thread availability. The second instance of the Planner is executed after the third instance of R4, while with full availability of the OS thread, it would be executed after the second instance of R4. The observed behavior matches the manually calculated behavior. Hence, it verifies a correct implementation of the reservations blocking and halting the scheduling and execution of the callbacks. The models show, once again, that despite the ROS 2 internal scheduling of callbacks being non-preemptive, the underlying OS thread that executes the ROS 2 executor can be preempted, causing additional latencies.

4.4 Answer to the Research Questions

Based on the conducted modeling actions and the experimental evaluation, we answer the research questions in this section. **RQ1**: Given the behavioral semantics of multi-threaded executors in ROS 2, how to verify the design of ROS 2-based systems concerning callback blocking?

The blocking of callbacks in a ROS 2-based system can be verified by formally determining the worst-case callback latency. The callback latency measures the time from the release of the callback until the end of its execution. Hence, knowing the execution time, and the latency of the callback can serve as a measure for the blocking. To calculate the callback latency in given scenarios, we apply formal modeling and model-checking with automated exploration of the full state space. During the modeling process, we utilize pattern-based modeling and simplify the process of modeling for future model users by creating formal model templates that can be applied by filling them with parameters.

RQ2: How to incorporate underlying operating system influences in the formal verification?

In the formal modeling process in this paper, we create reusable formal model templates to model the behavior of table-driven reservation servers. The servers take time slots as inputs, allowing a synchronized thread of the multi-threaded executor template to execute. The formal model templates of the executor and the callbacks are modified to pause the execution during the blocking stages. The assumption of reservation servers is the best practice in theoretical analysis. Hence, incorporating reservation servers into the models is the first step in incorporating the underlying execution of a host operating system.

RQ3: What are the patterns for modeling multi-threaded execution and underlying OS reservations in ROS 2 systems, which can be reused in verification?

In the first step, we utilize similar abstractions as defined in [10]. Communication can be abstracted to release callback times, reducing models' complexity. This paper assumes callbacks to be sporadic, with defined release times that can be obtained from system analysis and passed to the models as system parameters. Furthermore, we utilize further patterns presented in [10], such as dividing the model into callback and executor templates. Nevertheless, to model the multi-threaded execution, each callback and executor need to be represented individually with a formal model instance for each thread. Therefore, we identify each executor with an ID and each executor thread with an individual thread ID passed to the formal model templates. We create formal model templates that are specific and synchronized with the executors' threads to model the reservation servers. Moreover, we adapt the callback and executor templates to lock the execution in the blocked time slots. The validity of the selected patterns is shown through experiments.

5 Related Work

While the response time analysis for ROS 2 callbacks in a node using the single-threaded executor and reservation-based scheduling has been receiving increased attention in the literature [7,22], the same problem assuming a multi-threaded executor setting is less investigated.

Xu et al. [15] and Shobani et al. [21] propose a comprehensive response-time analysis framework for chains running on ROS 2 multi-threaded executors, for which the latter work analyzes chains with both arbitrary and constrained deadlines, taking into account the effect of mutually-exclusive callback groups. However, these works do not employ formal verification to confirm the analytical results and get new insights into the blocking issue of ROS 2 multi-threaded executors. In their work, Halder et al. [12] present an approach aimed to model and verify ROS 2 communication between nodes, utilizing UPPAAL. While their approach shares similarities with ours, in the sense that the authors incorporate low-level parameters into their TA models to verify queue overflow, they do not address callback latency verification for multi-threaded executors. Moreover, their work lacks the validation of formal models, a step that we undertake in our research by simulation experiments.

Webster et al. [24] present a formal verification method for industrial robotic programs utilizing the SPIN model checker. Their emphasis is on refining behavior and verifying specific robot requirements. While their approach is demonstrated on an operational personal robotic system, it is not tailored to ROS. Furthermore, it centers solely on verifying high-level decision-making rules. Carvalho et al. [8] introduce a model-checking technique designed to verify system-wide, architectural-level safety properties in message-passing systems. Their method is based on formalizing ROS launch configurations and the loosely defined behaviors of individual nodes. They employ an Alloy extension called Electrum along with its Analyzer for this purpose. In contrast, our work concentrates on lower-level model checking of multi-threaded executors' scheduling and shows the vulnerabilities caused by potential blocking in multi-threaded executors of ROS 2, via pattern-based modeling and verification in UPPAAL.

Anand and Knepper [5] introduce ROSCoq, a Coq framework tailored for building certified systems within ROS. This framework leverages CoRN's theory of constructive real analysis to handle computations involving real numbers. Their methodology follows a "correct-by-construction" approach, which differs from ours but complements it, yet the authors do not focus on multi-threaded executors. An interesting approach, yet never applied in the ROS 2 context, is the schedulability analysis based on *schedule-abstraction graphs* [20] that relies only on reachability-based task schedulability verification, without the possibility of verifying possibly interesting richer properties such as (bounded) liveness.

6 Conclusion and Future Work

In this paper, we adapt the concept of using pattern-based verification for ROS 2-based systems, to show and allow verification of the vulnerabilities to block multi-threaded executors in ROS 2, by employing formal models and UPPAAL. To simplify the application of formal modeling, we create formal model templates that allow simple modeling of multi-threaded execution of ROS 2. The models are configured to allow simple verification of callback latencies and generation of execution examples where high latency is detected. Furthermore, we validate the created formal models by experiments. During the experiments, we compare observed system traces of real ROS 2 executions with the generated traces from the models. Additionally, in this paper, we make a first attempt to incorporate the effects of the underlying operating system into the scheduling of middleware applications. Therefore, we create formal model templates that can model underlying reservation servers with defined periods of execution and blocking times. In two experiments, we show how to utilize the reservation servers in verification.

With the current state of the models, some efforts to reduce the state space are beneficial, in order to reduce complexity and enable verification of complex systems. Evaluation and improvements in complexity are especially beneficial in models containing the reservation servers. Nevertheless, our approach in this paper presents a first evaluation of formal modeling of multi-threaded execution and incorporation of underlying OS reservations and shows the feasibility of formal modeling. Further implementation of correctness properties, such as the absence of buffer overflow, would strengthen the applicability of the designed formal models and model-checking. Nevertheless, to simplify the demonstration of model-checking in the context of callback blocking, we leave the design of further verification properties to future work. Furthermore, future adaptations can be done on the extension towards a holistic modeling of communication and further automation of the verification process.

References

1. UPPAAL (2024). https://uppaal.org/
2. Verifying Multi-threaded Software with SPIN (2024). https://spinroot.com/spin/whatispin.html
3. Albonico, M., Dordevic, M., Hamer, E., Malavolta, I.: Software engineering research on the robot operating system: a systematic mapping study. J. Syst. Softw. **197**(C) (2023). https://doi.org/10.1016/j.jss.2022.111574
4. Alur, R., Dill, D.L.: A theory of timed automata. Theor. Comput. Sci. **126**, 183–235 (1994)
5. Anand, A., Knepper, R.: ROSCoq: robots powered by constructive reals. In: Urban, C., Zhang, X. (eds.) ITP 2015. LNCS, pp. 34–50. Springer, Cham (2015). https://doi.org/10.1007/978-3-319-22102-1_3
6. Baier, C., Katoen, J.P.: Principles of Model Checking. MIT Press, Cambridge (2008)

7. Blaß, T., Casini, D., Bozhko, S., Brandenburg, B.B.: A ROS 2 response-time analysis exploiting starvation freedom and execution-time variance. In: IEEE Real-Time Systems Symposium, pp. 41–53. IEEE (2021)
8. Carvalho, R., Cunha, A., Macedo, N., Santos, A.: Verification of system-wide safety properties of ROS applications. In: 2020 IEEE/RSJ International Conference on Intelligent Robots and Systems (IROS) (2020)
9. Casini, D., Blaß, T., Lütkebohle, I., Brandenburg, B.: Response-time analysis of ROS 2 processing chains under reservation-based scheduling. In: 31st Euromicro Conference on Real-Time Systems, pp. 1–23 (2019)
10. Dust, L., Gu, R., Seceleanu, C., Ekström, M., Mubeen, S.: Pattern-based verification of ROS 2 nodes using UPPAAL. In: Cimatti, A., Titolo, L. (eds.) FMICS 2023. LNCS, vol. 14290, pp. 57–75. Springer, Cham (2023). https://doi.org/10.1007/978-3-031-43681-9_4
11. Dust, L., Persson, E., Mikael, E., Saad, M., Emmanuel, D.: Quantitative analysis of communication handling for centralized multi-agent robot systems using ROS2. In: IEEE International Conference on Industrial Informatics (2022)
12. Halder, R., Proença, J., Macedo, N., Santos, A.: Formal verification of ROS-based robotic applications using timed-automata. In: 2017 IEEE/ACM 5th International FME Workshop on Formal Methods in Software Engineering (FormaliSE), pp. 44–50 (2017)
13. Hendriks, M., et al.: UPPAAL 4.0. In: Third International Conference on the Quantitative Evaluation of Systems - (QEST 2006) (2006)
14. Holzmann, G.J.: The model checker SPIN. IEEE Trans. Softw. Eng. **23**(5), 279–295 (1997)
15. Jiang, X., Ji, D., Guan, N., Li, R., Tang, Y., Wang, Y.: Real-time scheduling and analysis of processing chains on multi-threaded executor in ROS 2. In: 2022 IEEE Real-Time Systems Symposium (RTSS), pp. 27–39 (2022). https://doi.org/10.1109/RTSS55097.2022.00013
16. OpenRobotics: Ros 2: Documentation (2023). https://docs.ros.org/en/humble
17. OpenRobotics: ROS: Distributions (2024). http://wiki.ros.org/Distributions
18. Quigley, M., et al.: ROS: an open-source robot operating system. In: ICRA Workshop on Open Source Software, Kobe, Japan, vol. 3, p. 5 (2009)
19. Rajkumar, R., Lee, I., Sha, L., Stankovic, J.: Cyber-physical systems: the next computing revolution. In: Proceedings of the 47th Design Automation Conference, pp. 731–736 (2010)
20. Ranjha, S., Gohari, P., Nelissen, G., Nasri, M.: Partial-order reduction in reachability-based response-time analyses of limited-preemptive DAG tasks. Real-Time Syst. **59**, 201–255 (2023)
21. Sobhani, H., Choi, H., Kim, H.: Timing analysis and priority-driven enhancements of ROS 2 multi-threaded executors. In: 2023 IEEE 29th Real-Time and Embedded Technology and Applications Symposium (RTAS), pp. 106–118. IEEE (2023)
22. Tang, Y., et al.: Response time analysis and priority assignment of processing chains on ROS2 executors. In: IEEE Real-Time Systems Symposium, pp. 231–243 (2020)
23. Teper, H., Günzel, M., Ueter, N., von der Brüggen, G., Chen, J.J.: End-to-end timing analysis in ROS2. In: 2022 IEEE Real-Time Systems Symposium (RTSS), pp. 53–65 (2022)
24. Webster, M., et al.: Toward reliable autonomous robotic assistants through formal verification: a case study. IEEE Trans. Hum.-Mach. Syst. **46**(2), 186–196 (2016)

Semantics and Verification

Formalising the Industrial Language SMMT in mCRL2

Jordi E. P. M. van Laarhoven[1]([✉])[iD], Olav Bunte[2], Louis C. M. van Gool[1], and Tim A. C. Willemse[2][iD]

[1] Canon Production Printing, Venlo, The Netherlands
{jordi.vanlaarhoven,louis.vangool}@cpp.canon
[2] Eindhoven University of Technology, Eindhoven, The Netherlands
{o.bunte,t.a.c.willemse}@tue.nl

Abstract. The proprietary State Machine Modelling Tool (SMMT), developed and maintained at Canon Production Printing, can be used to model software components using state machines and generate executable production code. We have reverse-engineered the semantics that is associated to models specified in SMMT and subsequently formalised their semantics in the mCRL2 language. Using this formalisation, we have been able to detect subtle bugs in the implementation of the SMMT tool. Moreover, our formalisation allows for verifying the models specified in SMMT before the code is generated, offering users the option to thoroughly verify their designs.

1 Introduction

In the past decades we have witnessed an increased use of *Domain-Specific Languages* (DSLs) and the associated *Model-Driven Engineering* (MDE) paradigm for developing software solutions. Central to this trend is the idea that DSLs democratise the development of systems because they rely on concepts that are in close alignment with the problem domain, allowing domain specialists to describe solutions in concepts native to them. Indeed, there is some truth to the promise of higher productivity and improved maintainability of code offered by MDE: models typically hide a great deal of the intricate complexities of implementation details and permit practitioners to focus on what matters.

At Canon Production Printing, there have been a number of initiatives to introduce DSLs in daily work. For instance, a DSL called CSX [10] for specifying finishers was introduced a few years ago; it supports fully automated exploration of the configuration space of finishers. A more generic DSL called OIL [5,6] was introduced close to a decade ago. It was first introduced to model the interaction between components, but had gradually grown into a language that helped to alleviate the burden of manually programming components with complex control logic by supporting code generation for the components themselves. However, despite the expressive power and the support for separation of concerns, which both help to keep the models concise, OIL has not gained large scale adoption.

More recently, an alternative to OIL emerged at Canon Production Printing. This alternative was developed to closely resemble the state machines of the Boost Statechart Modelling (SCM) C++ library, with which developers at Canon Production Printing are very familiar. In contrast to OIL, the SCM library was designed to offer the building blocks that closely resemble those used in the existing state machines at Canon Production Printing. Moreover, inspired by OIL, it added some constructs that give it additional expressive power and flexibility.

To simplify modelling software components using the SCM library, the State Machine Modelling Tool (SMMT) was created. SMMT has been developed in the language workbench JetBrains MPS [22]. It allows the engineers to model the behaviour of software components both textually and graphically and allowing the engineers to automatically generate executable C# and C++ code from the state machines. Currently, SMMT is reasonably well adopted, with at least 26 models of software components being written in the tool and code, generated from these models, being included in production software.

While OIL has been endowed with a formal semantics, model checkers and dedicated consistency requirements checkers, SMMT, which has not been designed with verification in mind, seems a step backwards from a Formal Methods' point of view since it has none of these facilities. To mend this situation, we have provided an operational semantics for SMMT and formalised the semantics in the mCRL2 language [11,12] and toolset [7,9]. In this paper, we report on our efforts doing so. For the sake of brevity, we focus on a small but representative subset of the language; for the semantics of the full set of language constructs in use we refer to [18].

We furthermore illustrate the added benefits of having a tool-supported formal semantics of a DSL by analysing the 26 SMMT models available to us. Our formalisation reveals a subtle bug in the code generator of SMMT; this bug causes models to behave in unintended ways. Moreover, we have identified various models that violate the (implicitly assumed, but not enforced) static semantics. Such violations may manifest themselves when seemingly innocuous changes to the code generator are made. Finally, we have analysed several generic properties of the SMMT models, revealing several further issues with a few models. Our work thus adds to a growing body of evidence that formalising a DSL is both feasible and leads to improvements in the quality of the models.

The language constructs of SMMT are such that there does not seem to be a simple mapping of the language to the process algebra of a language such as mCRL2. In particular, concepts such as hierarchy and priority are difficult to map onto operators typically offered by process algebras. For this reason, we formalise the SMMT language largely in the data language of mCRL2 and use only a very restricted set of process algebraic operators. We compare and contrast the approach we take in this paper to encodings of other languages we have formalised in mCRL2 and briefly discuss the implications of our approach.

Related Work. Apart from the DSLs already mentioned, there are various other DSLs that have been formalised. For instance, formalisations of widely-used state machine modelling languages such as UML, SysML, Activity Diagrams, *etc.* can be found in the literature, see *e.g.* [1,4,13,17,19,20,24].

Beyond the domain of state machine-like languages, DSLs also appear in other domains. In [23], the authors introduce a DSL, called IDL, for specifying behavioural models and properties of interlocking systems. IDL has been used for real-world stations and lines in Denmark. Another tool used for the Railway domain is OnTrack [16], which is based on a DSL and which can support workflows for railway verification. In [3], the authors describe their B formalisation of Bossa, a DSL that is tailored to the development of process schedulers with applications in the context of Linux. And in [21], the authors describe a DSL called Rebel (a formal specification language for software for financial enterprise systems) offering simulation and checking of specifications using SMT solvers.

The mCRL2 language has been used previously for formalising DSLs. For example, in [14,15] the authors describe an mCRL2 formalisation of CERN's FSM language, and introduce dedicated algorithms, based on SMT solving, for verifying FSM models. An mCRL2 formalisation of the DEZYNE language is discussed in [2]; this language is commercialised by the Dutch company Verum B.V. A more in-depth discussion of the differences between the mCRL2-formalisations of these languages and the SMMT language can be found in Sect. 6.

Organisation. In Sect. 2, we give a very brief, informal overview of the SMMT language. We present a formal semantics of the language in Sect. 3, and in Sect. 4, we describe our formalisation of this semantics in the mCRL2 language. In Sect. 5, we discuss the validity of our formalisation and the issues we found in an existing set of models. We discuss lessons learnt in Sect. 6 and wrap up in Sect. 7.

2 The SMMT Language

At Canon Production Printing the Model-Driven Software development methodology was adopted a couple of decades ago. Modelling software was used to design models consisting of state machines that modelled the expected behaviour of software components. These models were used by the engineers to manually develop executable code that behaves according to the models. This workflow occasionally led to problems, as there was no coupling between the designed models and the code that was developed using these models. As a consequence, this led to inconsistencies between the behaviour as modelled by the state machine and the behaviour of the developed executable code.

One of the solutions adopted for simplifying the workflow of the engineers is the State Machine Modelling Tool (SMMT). SMMT is a proprietary modelling tool and specification language, developed by Canon Production Printing, which builds on the State-Chart Modelling (SCM) C++ and C# libraries used extensively at Canon Production Printing. It allows its user to model behaviour of software components using state machines. Furthermore, SMMT enables the generation of C# and C++ code from these SMMT models and its specification language.

In SMMT, each specification represents a single state machine that models the behaviour of a software component. To give a flavour of the language, we provide an informal introduction of the main concepts of the SMMT language using a running example (see also Fig. 1). The SMMT specification that is shown in this running example models a simple printer to which print jobs can be submitted. After the jobs are submitted, color correction (cc) and scaling (sc) actions are performed in parallel after which the job is printed and the state of the printer is set to idle again.

```
 1  State Machine printer                    22         Transitions
 2  namespace cpp.jordi.printer               23           on ev_applied_cc()
 3                                            24             go post_cc
 4  on events                                 25         SimpleState post_cc
 5    ev_submit_job( « ... » )                26         Transitions
 6    ev_applied_cc( « ... » )                27       entry CompositeState sc
 7    ev_applied_sc( « ... » )                28         Transitions
 8    ev_finish_job( « ... » )                29       entry SimpleState pre_sc
 9                                            30         Transitions
10  do events                                 31           on ev_applied_sc()
11    re_ready( « ... » )                     32             go post_sc
12                                            33         SimpleState post_sc
13    entry SimpleState idle                  34         Transitions
14      Transitions                           35       JointState joint_cc_sc
15        on ev_submit_job()                  36         Joins post_cc
16          go printing                       37               post_sc
17    ParallelState printing                  38         Exit Handlers
18      Transitions                           39           exit do re_ready()
19      entry CompositeState cc               40         Transitions
20        Transitions                         41           on ev_finish_job()
21      entry SimpleState pre_cc              42             go idle
```

(a) Textual Representation

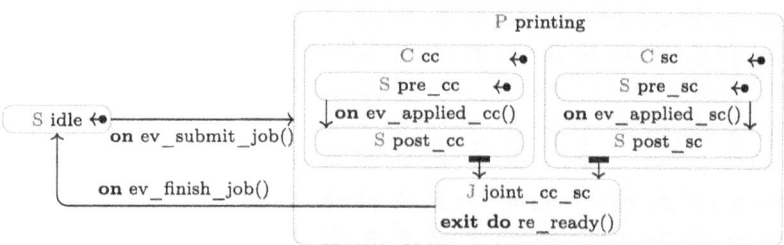

(b) Graphical Representation

Fig. 1. An SMMT specification consisting of a printer that applies color correction (cc) and scales (sc) the job before printing the job.

Each SMMT specification has a *name* and a *namespace* that are used to identify the SMMT specification, a list of events that are defined for the SMMT specification and a *region*. We next discuss the type of events that are supported by SMMT and what the region of an SMMT specification consists of.

SMMT distinguishes two types of events, namely *OnEvents* and *DoEvents*. *OnEvents* are events that are produced externally and may cause transitions of the SMMT specification to fire that are defined for that OnEvent. *DoEvents* are actions produced by the SMMT specification that serve as a response to a processed *OnEvent*. The running example defines the *OnEvents* ev_submit_job(), ev_applied_cc(), ev_applied_sc() and ev_finish_job(), as indicated by the on events keyword. It furthermore defines the *DoEvent* re_ready(), as indicated by the do events keyword.

The *region* of an SMMT specification is hierarchically structured and consists of at least one state. Each state of the SMMT specification consists of zero or more outgoing transitions, entry handlers and exit handlers. Some states are entry states, as indicated by the keyword entry. These are states that become active when the state machine moves to a configuration where its parent state is active.

The SMMT language supports four different type of states, namely: *SimpleStates*, *CompositeStates*, *ParallelStates* and *JointStates*. A *SimpleState* represents a state that has no children. A *CompositeState* defines multiple children, of which one is an entry state, and models a nested state machine. A *ParallelState* defines multiple children, which are all entry states, and models multiple state machines running in parallel. The parallel behaviour of the children of a *ParallelState* can be joined using a *JointState*.

Zero or more outgoing transitions can be defined for each state of an SMMT specification. Each transition consists of an *OnEvent* and a target state, though the latter can be omitted to make the transition internal. Furthermore, a transition may have a guard that restricts when the transition can fire and zero or more *BehavioralActions*, which typically consist of *DoEvents* that occur when the transition fires.

For each state of an SMMT specification zero or more entry and exit handlers can be defined. Entry and exit handlers model the behaviour that is performed when the state for which they are defined are entered and exited respectively by means of *BehavioralActions*. Entry handlers can be conditional based on the *OnEvent* that has led to the state of the entry handler.

In the running example (Fig. 1), the region is defined on lines 13–40. In the corresponding visualisation, states are represented by boxes with C, P and J indicating the state type. Entry states are denoted by the entry symbol (↪). Transitions are shown as arrows labelled with their *OnEvent*.

3 A Formal Semantics of SMMT

For the purpose of this paper, we focus on a subset of the SMMT language; we refer to [18] for details on our formalisation of the full SMMT language. Throughout this section and the next, Fig. 2 serves as a running example; it is a simplification of the running example of the previous section.

Abstract Syntax of SMMT. We focus on SMMT specifications that only contain states of type *SimpleState* or *CompositeState*, and transitions without guards or *BehavioralActions*. While this is a rather restricted fragment of SMMT, the definitions are representative of more complex language constructs.

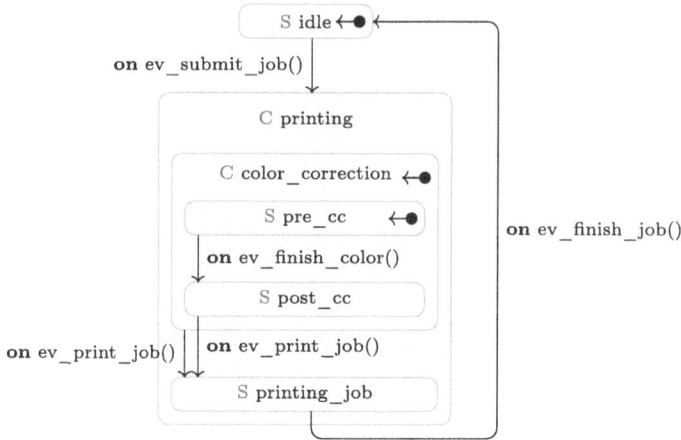

Fig. 2. An SMMT specification consisting of a printer that applies color correction before printing a job.

Definition 1 (SMMT Specification). *An SMMT specification is a tuple* $\mathtt{M} = \langle E, S_S, S_C, ES, \sqsubseteq, \mathcal{T} \rangle$ *where:*

- E *is the set of OnEvents;*
- S_S *is the set of SimpleStates and S_C is the set of CompositeStates; we assume $S_S \cap S_C = \emptyset$ and write S to abbreviate the set of states $S_S \cup S_C$;*
- $ES \subseteq S$ *is the set of entry states;*
- $\sqsubseteq \; \subseteq S \times S$ *is the child-of relation;*
- $\mathcal{T} : S \times E \rightharpoonup S$ *is the partial transition function.*

For the remainder of this section we fix an arbitrary SMMT specification $\mathtt{M} = \langle E, S_S, S_C, ES, \sqsubseteq, \mathcal{T} \rangle$. For states s, s', we say that s is a *child* of s', and s' is a *parent* of s iff $s \sqsubseteq s'$. The child-of relation $\sqsubseteq$ captures the hierarchy specified in the state machine. For instance, in Fig. 2, state color_correction is a child of printing, so color_correction $\sqsubseteq$ printing.

As a shorthand, we define the *entry* child-of relation $\sqsubseteq_{ES} = (ES \times S) \cap \sqsubseteq$. For $\sqsubseteq$ and $\sqsubseteq_{ES}$, we write $\sqsubseteq^+$ and $\sqsubseteq_{ES}{}^+$ to denote their transitive closure, and $\sqsubseteq^*$ and $\sqsubseteq_{ES}{}^*$ to denote their reflexive-transitive closure. Intuitively, the transitive closure captures the *descendants* of a state: for a state s', state s is its descendant iff $s \sqsubseteq^+ s'$. We say that state s is *younger* than state s' whenever $s \sqsubseteq^+ s'$. Those states of S that have no parent are referred to as *root states*; the set of all root states, denoted $\mathcal{R}(\mathtt{M})$, is defined as $\mathcal{R}(\mathtt{M}) = \{s \in S \mid \neg \exists_{s' \in S} : s \sqsubseteq s'\}$.

Definition 2. *We say that* $\mathtt{M}$ *is* valid *if, and only if:*

- $\mathtt{M}$ *has at least one state: $S \neq \emptyset$;*
- *SimpleStates have no children: $(S \times S_S) \cap \sqsubseteq \; = \emptyset$.*
- *States have at most one parent: for all $s, s', s'' \in S$, we have $s \sqsubseteq s'$ and $s \sqsubseteq s''$ implies $s' = s''$;*

- *Relation* $\sqsubset$ *is acyclic: for all* $s \in S$, $s \not\sqsubset^+ s$;
- M *has exactly one entry root state:* $|ES \cap \mathcal{R}(\mathtt{M})| = 1$;
- *CompositeStates have exactly one entry child state: for all* $s, s' \in S$ *and* $s'' \in S_C$, *we have* $s \sqsubset_{ES} s''$ *and* $s' \sqsubset_{ES} s''$ *implies* $s = s'$;

The validity conditions are essentially part of the (undocumented and not-enforced) static semantics of SMMT. Specifications that are not valid may not be reasonable. We exclude such specifications and henceforward focus on valid specifications only.

Operational Semantics. We provide an operational semantics for SMMT specifications by associating these specifications with a Labelled Transition System (LTS). This way, we can reason formally about the behaviour specified by an SMMT model.

The states of the LTS essentially consist of (specific) subsets of the states of the SMMT specification. These subsets are called *execution states*, and they reflect the hierarchy of states in the specification: the execution state associated with a state intuitively includes all its ancestors, but also all its entry descendants. They also indicate which states need to be considered when determining which transition(s) can fire. When M executes, exactly one of its root states must be in the execution state.

Definition 3 (Set of Execution States). *The* execution state *associated with some* $s \in S$, *denoted* $\mathsf{EXS}(s)$, *is the set* $\mathsf{EXS}(s) = \{s' \in S \mid s \sqsubset^* s' \vee s' \sqsubset_{ES}^* s\}$. *We define* $\mathsf{EXS}(\mathtt{M}) = \{\mathsf{EXS}(s) \subseteq S \mid s \in S\}$.

Recall that, by validity of M, there is exactly one entry root state and each *CompositeState* has exactly one entry child. From this, it follows that there exists exactly one *SimpleState* in the set of entry states ES, of which all ancestors are entry states, too. We call the execution state of this simple entry state the *initial execution state*, and denote it by $\mathsf{Init}(\mathtt{M})$.

Each state in an execution state EX may define, for a given *OnEvent* $e \in E$, which next state is reached. We say that e is *enabled* in a state $s \in EX$ iff $\mathcal{T}$ is defined for (s, e), and e is enabled for EX if there is a state $s \in EX$ for which e is enabled. If there are multiple states in the execution state capable of handling e, the transition specified by the youngest state takes priority. Note that there is always a youngest state in an execution state as all states in an execution state are ordered by $\sqsubset^+$. The notion of a prioritised transition function formalises which transitions, enabled in an execution state, take priority.

Definition 4 (Prioritised Transitions). *The prioritised transition function of* M *is a partial function* $\mathsf{PT}_\mathtt{M} : \mathsf{EXS}(\mathtt{M}) \times E \rightharpoonup S$, *defined as* $\mathsf{PT}_\mathtt{M}(EX, e) = s'$ *if* e *is enabled in* EX *and* $s' = \mathcal{T}(s)$ *for the youngest state* $s \in EX$ *for which* e *is enabled; and* $\mathsf{PT}_\mathtt{M}(EX, e)$ *is undefined otherwise.*

It may happen that an SMMT specification is offered an *OnEvent* which it cannot handle since it is in an execution state for which this event is not enabled.

In such a case, an internal software exception is thrown and the execution of the SMMT specification is terminated. We capture this using an explicit, designated *failure state* F in our operational semantics.

Definition 5 (Operational Semantics). *We associate a Labelled Transition System $\langle ST, s_0, L, \rightarrow \rangle$ to a SMMT specification* M, *where:*

- $ST = \mathsf{EXS}(\texttt{M}) \cup \{\texttt{F}\}$;
- $s_0 = \mathcal{I}(\texttt{M})$;
- $L = E \cup \{\mathit{FAIL}\}$;
- $\rightarrow\ \subseteq ST \times L \times ST$ *is the smallest relation satisfying:*
  - $EX \xrightarrow{e} \mathsf{EXS}(\mathsf{PT}_\texttt{M}(EX, e))$ *if e is enabled in EX;*
  - $EX \xrightarrow{e} F$ *if e is not enabled in EX;*
  - $F \xrightarrow{\mathit{FAIL}} F$.

Observe that an SMMT specification induces a deterministic LTS. The LTS of the SMMT specification of Fig. 2 is depicted in Fig. 3.

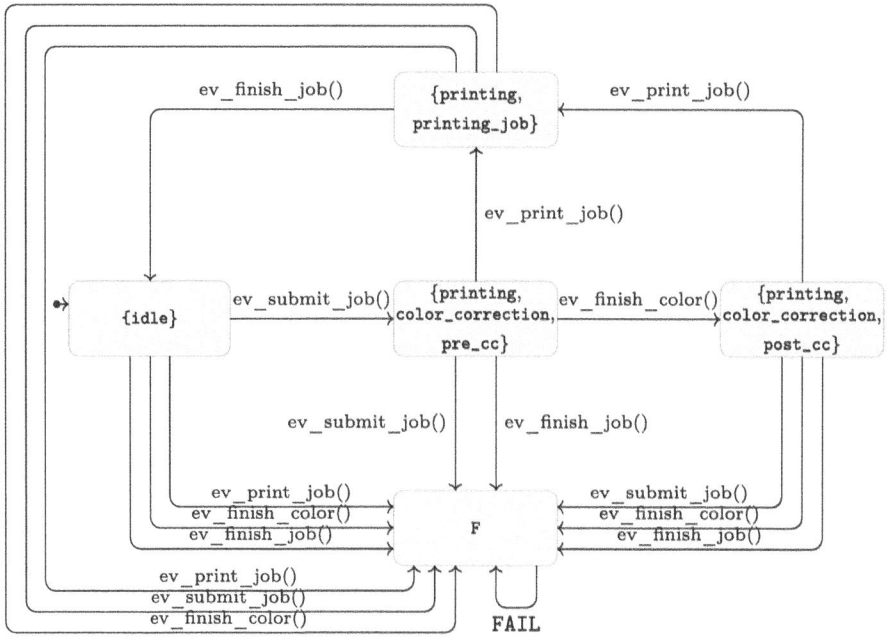

Fig. 3. The LTS of the SMMT specification of Fig. 2.

4 Translational Semantics in mCRL2

The mCRL2 language [11,12] is a process algebra extended with data; data is specified in abstract data types. The process algebraic constructs allow one to specify LTSs compositionally using constants, (parameterised) actions, recursion, and operators such as · (sequential composition), + (alternative composition), $\sum$ (alternative quantification), $||$ (parallel composition), *etc.*

For formalising the semantics of SMMT specifications, we only use processes in the *Linear Process Equation* (LPE) normal form. This is essentially a very restricted process term that uses only a few operators. The mCRL2 toolset [7] typically operates on this normal form: mCRL2 specifications are first converted to the LPE normal form, and state space generation and model checking tools only accept LPEs as input.

Definition 6 (Linear Process Equation). *A Linear Process Equation (LPE) is an mCRL2 process equation of the following shape:*

```
1 P(d: D)  =  sum e_1:E_1 .  c_1(d,e_1)  ->  a_1(f_1(d,e_1)) . P(g_1(d,e_1))
2           +  ...
3           +  sum e_n:E_n .  c_n(d,e_n)  ->  a_n(f_n(d,e_n)) . P(g_n(d,e_n))
```

where P *is the name of the process,* d *and* e_i *are vectors of variables,* D *and* E_i *are data types,* c_i *is a Boolean expression,* a_i *is an action,* f_i *is a vector of expressions providing the parameters of* a_i, g_i *is a vector of expressions representing the next state. The only variables allowed to occur freely in* c_i, f_i *and* g_i *are* d *and* e_i.

The semantics of an LPE is rather straightforward: each value d of the data type D represents a state, and for each index $i \in I$ and value e_i, if Boolean expression c_i evaluates to true for d and e_i, a parameterised action $a_i(v_i)$, where v_i is the value given by f_i(d,e_i), leads to a new state, whose value is given by g_i(d,e_i).

We use the abstract data types of mCRL2 to encode the static structure (*i.e.*, the abstract syntax of Definition 1), and all functions and computations needed for defining the operational semantics of SMMT. The operational semantics itself is described by an LPE which keeps track of the execution state of the specification.

A valid SMMT specification $M = \langle E, S_S, S_C, ES, \sqsubset, \mathcal{T} \rangle$ can be translated to an instance of structured sort Spec. Our presentation, depicted below, is somewhat simplified since we left out a few language constructs, but it reflects the main intuition behind the translation worked out in detail in [18].

```
 1  sort Spec  =  struct sm(OnEvents   : List(OnEvent),
 2                          SStates    : List(State),
 3                          CStates    : List(State),
 4                          EntryStates : List(State),
 5                          Children    : State -> List(State),
 6                          Transitions: State -> List(Transition)
 7                         );
 8       OnEvent    = struct e_1 | ... | e_n;
 9       State      = struct s_1 | ... | s_m;
10       Transition = struct tra(onEvent : OnEvent, target : State);
```

Structured sort Spec consists of a single constructor sm that represents an SMMT specification in mCRL2. It builds on a representation for the set of states $S = \{s_1, \ldots, s_m\}$, here represented by structured sort State, and a representation for the set of *OnEvents* $E = \{e_1, \ldots, e_n\}$, here represented by structured sort OnEvent.

Note that an instance of type Spec uses lists to store the data instead of sets. While mCRL2 does support sets, lists are more convenient when defining operations on them, as we can efficiently iterate over list instances; this is not possible for sets. We discuss the impact of different modelling styles in Sect. 6.

We furthermore remark that SMMT specifications can be translated fully automatically to mCRL2 in a straightforward manner: all that is needed is defining the six elements of the type Spec and defining the types OnEvent and State. This information can be extracted readily from the State Machine Modelling Tool. We give an example below.

Example 1. The SMMT specification depicted in Fig. 2 is modelled in mCRL2 by the instance sm(E,SS,CS,ES,Ch,T) of type Spec, where constants E, SS, CS, ES, Ch and T are defined as follows:

```
map  E: List(OnEvent);
     SS, CS: List(State);
     ES: List(State);
     Ch: State -> List(State);
     T: State -> List(Transition);
var  s: State;
eqn  E  = [ev_print_job, ev_finish_job, ev_finish_color, ev_submit_job];
     SS = [idle, pre_cc, post_cc, printing_job];
     CS = [printing, color_correction];
     ES = [idle, pre_cc, color_correction];
     Ch(idle)              = [];
     Ch(pre_cc)            = [];
     Ch(post_cc)           = [];
     Ch(printing_job)      = [];
     Ch(printing)          = [printing_job,color_correction];
     Ch(color_correction)  = [pre_cc,post_cc];
     T(idle)               = [tra(ev_submit_job, printing)];
     T(pre_cc)             = [tra(ev_finish_color, post_cc)];
     T(post_cc)            = [tra(ev_print_job, printing_job)];
     T(printing_job)       = [tra(ev_finish_job, idle)];
     T(printing)           = [];
     T(color_correction)   = [tra(ev_print_job, printing_job)];
```

Here, [] is the empty list and [pre_cc,post_cc] is a list of length two with head pre_cc.

Formalising the operational semantics of SMMT requires, among others, reasoning about the reflexive-transitive closures $\sqsubset^*$ and $\sqsubset_{ES}^*$. Both are needed to determine the execution states of an SMMT specification. In mCRL2, all computations on data are described using equations, which are interpreted as rewrite rules by tools that generate or analyse a state space. For instance, the function ESDescendants is a function with two arguments, which models the (strict) entry child descendants of a state (obtained by the $\sqsubset_{ES}^*$ relation) of a given specification spec, and is defined as a recursive function as follows:

```
map  ESDescendants  : Spec # State -> List(State);
     ESDescendants' : Spec # List(State) -> List(State);
var  s: State;
     spec: Spec;
     l: List(State);
eqn  ESDescendants(spec,s) = ESDescendants'(spec,Children(spec)(s));
```

```
7   ESDescendants'(spec,[])    = [];
8   ESDescendants'(spec,s|>1)  = if(s in EntryStates(spec),
9                                   s|>ESDescendants'(spec,Children(spec)(s
    )),
10                                  ESDescendants'(spec,1));
```

Here, $s|>1$ denotes a list with head s and tail 1. The $if(b,e_1,e_2)$ construct is an *if-then-else* which evaluates to e_1 in case b holds true and to e_2 otherwise.

State s that is passed as a parameter to ESDescendants is not included in the list that is constructed. To achieve this, we use an auxiliary function ESDescendants' which takes an alternative argument, *viz.*, the list of children of the state for which we are constructing the chain of descendants, and only includes states that are in that list (and their entry state children). The auxiliary function recursively processes this list and, based on whether the state at the head of this list is an entry state, decides to include that state and start processing its children, or skips the state and processes the remainder of the list.

In a similar vein, the (strict) ancestors of a state (obtained by the $\sqsubset^*$ relation), represented by Ancestors, can be computed. We ensure in our definition of the function Ancestors that the list of ancestors it yields is descending w.r.t. the relation $\sqsubset$. This can be achieved simply by recursively appending states at the end of the list. The function EXS(s) can then be formalised straightforwardly by defining a function ExState as follows:

```
1   map ExState : Spec # State -> List(State);
2   var spec: Spec;
3       s: State;
4   eqn ExState(spec,s) = (Ancestors(spec,s)) ++ (s|> ESDescendants(spec,s));
```

Note that since we guarantee, by construction, that both the list of ancestors and the list of descendants are descending w.r.t. $\sqsubset$, the list representing the execution state is also descending w.r.t. the relation $\sqsubset$.

The initial execution state Init(M) is, by definition, the execution state associated to the root entry state. Hence, we can simply introduce a function to return the root entry state; then the initial execution state is obtained by applying function ExState to this root entry state.

```
1   map EntryRoot  : Spec -> State;
2       EntryRoot' : Spec # List(State) -> State;
3   var spec: Spec;
4       s: State;
5       l: List(State);
6   eqn EntryRoot(spec) = EntryRoot'(spec,EntryStates(spec));
7       EntryRoot'(spec,s|>1) = if(Ancestors(spec,s) == [],
8                                  s, EntryRoot'(spec,1));
9
10  map InitExState : Spec -> List(State);
11  var spec: Spec;
12  eqn InitExState(spec) = ExState(spec,EntryRoot(spec));
```

For checking whether an *OnEvent* is enabled in a given execution state, we can inspect whether the event is enabled in some state in the execution state.

```
1   map Enabled  : Spec # List(State) # OnEvent -> Bool;
2       Enabled' : Spec # List(State) # OnEvent # List(Transition) -> Bool;
3   var spec: Spec;
4       e: OnEvent;
```

```
     s: State;
     l: List(State);
     t: Transition;
     lt: List(Transition);
 eqn Enabled(spec,[],e) = false;
     Enabled(spec,s|>l,e) = Enabled'(spec,s|>l,e,Transitions(spec)(s));
     Enabled'(spec,s|>l,e,[]) = Enabled(spec,l,e);
     Enabled'(spec,s|>l,e,t|>lt) = if(onEvent(t) == e, true,
                                     Enabled'(spec,s|>l,e,lt) );
```

The function `Priority`, modelling the function `PT`, is similar to the function `Enabled`. We can take advantage of the fact that our execution states are represented by lists that, by construction, reflect the $\sqsubset$ ordering. Thus, we can process the list representing the execution state and build a new list that contains all possible targets that can be reached by executing the *OnEvent* we are considering. The last state in the resulting list is the target we are after, as it must come from the *youngest* state in the execution state. We can obtain this target state by means of the `rhead` operation on the list. We omit further details, but refer to [18] for a possible formalisation and Sect. 6 for a discussion on the impact of different choices for modelling the semantics.

The operational semantics of an SMMT specification M in mCRL2 is now simply formalised by the process `SM(sp, InitExState(sp), false)`, where `sp` is the mCRL2 encoding of M, and `SM` is given by the following LPE:

```
 act event: OnEvent;
     FAIL;
 proc SM(spec: Spec, ex: List(State), fail: Bool) =
     sum e: OnEvent. (Enabled(spec,ex,e) ∧ ¬fail) ->
         event(e). SM(spec, ExState(PT(spec,EX,e)), fail)
   + sum e: OnEvent. (¬Enabled(spec,ex,e) ∧ ¬fail) ->
         event(e). SM(spec, ex, true)
   + fail -> FAIL. SM(spec, ex, fail);
```

5 Validation and Experiments

SMMT has been developed in JetBrains MPS [22], allowing the engineers to model the behaviour of software components both textually and graphically and allowing the engineers to automatically generate executable C# and C++ code from the state machines. The SMMT language was not designed with a focus on creating a formally well-defined language, and the main developers of the SMMT tool and language had moved to other projects when we started our efforts formalising the language.

Our semantics of SMMT, as explained in the previous sections, has been reverse-engineered by analysing models and the executables they generate, but also by talking to one of the original developers of the language. There is no guarantee, however, that our semantics is in line with the semantics intended by the developers. To validate our semantics, we therefore opted to compare the models that we obtained using the translation to mCRL2 to models that we extracted from the executables. The latter was done by instrumenting the code generator so that the executable essentially acts as a state space generator.

Table 1. Statistics for the 26 SMMT models (A–Z) used in our validation.

	A	B	C	D	E	F	G	H	I	J	K	L	M	N	O	P	Q	R	S	T	U	V	W	X	Y	Z
SimpleStates	48	16	17	20	14	13	9	9	6	32	26	12	49	14	14	12	4	2	9	17	27	22	30	5	5	14
CompositeStates	8	2	3	4	2	2	1	1	0	7	6	3	10	3	1	0	0	0	1	9	13	6	1	0	1	3
Parallel States	0	0	0	0	0	0	0	0	0	1	1	0	1	1	0	0	0	0	0	2	1	1	0	0	0	1
Transitions	129	28	56	67	30	27	18	18	7	67	59	31	133	15	25	14	20	8	32	34	80	40	72	18	13	15
Nesting depth	3	2	1	1	1	1	1	1	0	3	3	1	3	3	1	0	0	0	1	3	4	3	1	0	1	3

As input to our validation, we used 26 production-grade models. For reasons of confidentiality, we here identify these models with letters. Some of the statistics of these models are depicted in Table 1. The nesting depth, *i.e.*, the largest chain of successively younger states is at most four for these models, and in several cases even zero, indicating that all root states are *SimpleStates*. These are essentially flat models, *i.e.*, models without *CompositeStates*.

Of the models we assessed, models M, T and U violate one or more constraints that we have identified (for full details, see [18]). For instance, model U defined transitions from a state to multiple target states using the same *OnEvent*, violating the determinism requirement of SMMT. For all remaining models, except for model V, the labelled transition systems generated by our formalisation are strongly bisimilar to those generated by the instrumented executables. For model V, the non-bisimilarity is a consequence of an unfortunate disparity in the way the two editing modes of MPS can be used: we found that a guard as shown in the reflective editing mode of MPS, which directly modifies the abstract syntax tree, does not correspond to the guard shown in the regular editing mode, due to a missing parenthesiser for associativity of expression operators. Fixing this issue in the SMMT tool resolved the non-bisimilarity for model V.

Table 2 lists some characteristics of the sizes of the state spaces underlying each model, generated using our mCRL2 translation. These include statistics for models T and U that were modified so that they satisfy the validity constraints. For most models, the state space can be generated in a few seconds. There are a few exceptions: model K requires 41 min, model T requires 15 min, which is still reasonable, but models J and M required days (resp. 3 days and 20 days). While these numbers may look disappointing, we stress that there is room for making our translation more efficient for generating state spaces.

Table 2. Some statistics concerning the sizes of the generated state spaces.

#States	Models	#Transitions	Models
10–10^2	B – I, L, N, O – S, X – Z	10–10^2	I, Q, R, S, X, Y
10^2–10^3	A, V, W	10^2–10^3	B – H, L, N, P, W, Z
10^3–10^4	K, T, U	10^3–10^4	A, T, V
10^4–10^5	J	10^4–10^5	K, U
10^5–10^6	M	10^5–10^6	J
10^6–10^7	–	10^6–10^7	M

In addition to the above basic sanity checks we verified five generic requirements, expressed in the modal μ-calculus, for the SMMT models. These range from checking for deadlock freedom, *i.e.*, is it invariantly possible to execute an event and avoid reaching the fail state; to checking whether all states of the SMMT specification can become active (*i.e.*, part of an execution state) at some point. All properties we verified, save one, are violated by some model. The only property we found to hold true for all models is the requirement that all *DoEvents* can be produced during the execution of an SMMT model. The three models violating deadlock freedom (models N, P and Z) turn out to also model the successful termination of the component, which we did not account for in our formalisation. For model I, which fails three other requirements, discussions with the engineers revealed that this model indeed contained states and transitions that were not meant to be there.

6 Discussion

Both SMMT and OIL (which already had been formalised in mCRL2 [5,6]) are state-machine-like languages with a translation to mCRL2. A commonality in their translation is that they rely on the LPE format for specifying the transition relation and delegate most of the semantic issues and computations to the data language of mCRL2. In this regard, the translations are rather monolithic: they do not exploit the compositionality offered by process algebras such as mCRL2. This contrasts translations of languages such as Dezyne [2], which predominantly maps Dezyne language constructs to mCRL2 process algebraic operators. This difference is largely due to concepts in OIL and SMMT such as hierarchy (of states) and the associated prioritisation of transitions. These do not seem to have natural counterparts in process algebras such as mCRL2; indeed, it is non-trivial to add priority operators to such languages [8]. The different approaches in mapping a language to mCRL2 seem to translate to the effectiveness of the analysis capabilities of the mCRL2 toolset, with the monolithic translations performing poorer on average than the compositional approaches.

However, there is also a considerable difference in the approach taken in the formalisation of SMMT and OIL in how the translations to the mCRL2 data types are designed. This difference is based on the decision of where intermediate definitions of the operational semantics are resolved. As shown in Sect. 4, for the translation of SMMT to mCRL2 it was decided to have these fully resolved within mCRL2 by defining corresponding rewrite rules in mCRL2 such as those for functions ESDescendants and Enabled. For the translation from OIL to mCRL2 it was decided to have these resolved in the translation itself as much as possible. As an example, the mCRL2 specification produced by such a translation would not have rewrite rules for computing the initial execution state like is done with InitExState, including the rewrite rules for EntryRoot and Ancestors that are required for it. Instead, it would contain the initial execution state itself as the list [idle] wherever it is needed.

The main cause of this difference is the initial reason behind the creation of the translations. In case of SMMT, the translation to mCRL2 was made to test the correctness of the formal semantics by comparing it to the semantics implemented in SMMT. By creating a faithful representation of the definitions of the formal semantics of SMMT in mCRL2, one creates an executable version of the formal semantics, which can then be tested for a number of models. In the case of OIL, the focus was on the ability to do model checking on OIL specifications using the mCRL2 toolset [7]. In an attempt to make this efficient, the burden on the mCRL2 rewriter was lightened as much as possible by resolving as many formal definitions as possible in the translation to mCRL2 itself.

One benefit of defining the complete formal semantics in mCRL2 is that it makes the translation to mCRL2 relatively simple. The only model-specific part in the mCRL2 specifications produced by the translation from SMMT is the instance of Spec; the rest is generic. The close correspondence to the formal semantics also facilitates assessing the translation's correctness.

However, this approach may produce mCRL2 specifications that are less efficient to model check, since it places a greater burden on the mCRL2 rewriter. Note that the definitions in mCRL2 that we presented in Sect. 4 already implement the formal semantics of SMMT more efficiently compared to a more-or-less verbatim formalisation of the semantics. For instance, whereas the formal semantics defines an entry root state as the state in the *set* of entry states for which no parent *exists*, the definition of the entry root state in mCRL2 searches for the state in the *list* of entry states for which no parent is found by *repeated application* of the child relation. Since mCRL2 supports sets and quantifiers, a verbatim set-based formalisation of the semantics of the entry root state is possible and would be as follows:

```
map EntryRoot : Spec -> Set(State);
var spec: Spec;
eqn EntryRoot(spec) = EntryStates(spec)
                   * { s: State | ¬ exists s':State. s in Ch(spec)(s') };
```

Here, * is the set intersection operator of mCRL2. A significant drawback is that the mCRL2 rewriter is quite inefficient at processing expressions such as the above. Indeed, with an earlier definition of the semantics of SMMT in mCRL2 where sets and quantifiers were used, most models took hours to explore whereas they require a few minutes now; we believe that further optimisations of the rules formalising the semantics can speed up the exploration by orders of magnitude.

7 Conclusions

We formalised the syntax and semantics of the SMMT language for specifying state machines, developed by, and used at Canon Production Printing. Apart from a pen-and-paper semantics, we also provided an encoding of the semantics in the tool supported mCRL2 language. Our mCRL2 translation helped reveal (and fix) several issues in the implementation of SMMT that would have been hard to find otherwise. Moreover, using mCRL2, we have analysed a small set of generic properties (expressed in the modal μ-calculus) for a large number of models used to generate production code, and detect issues in one of them. This further stresses the case for combining Model-Driven Engineering and Formal Methods.

References

1. Abdelhalim, I., Schneider, S.A., Treharne, H.: An integrated framework for checking the behaviour of fUML models using CSP. Int. J. Softw. Tools Technol. Transf. **15**(4), 375–396 (2013). https://doi.org/10.1007/S10009-012-0243-0
2. van Beusekom, R., et al.: Formalising the Dezyne modelling language in mCRL2. In: Petrucci, L., Seceleanu, C., Cavalcanti, A. (eds.) AVoCS FMICS 2017. LNCS, vol. 10471, pp. 217–233. Springer, Cham (2017). https://doi.org/10.1007/978-3-319-67113-0_14
3. Bodeveix, J., Filali, M., Lawall, J., Muller, G.: Formal methods meet domain specific languages. In: Romijn, J., Smith, G., van de Pol, J. (eds.) IFM 2005. LNCS, vol. 3771, pp. 187–206. Springer, Heidelberg (2005). https://doi.org/10.1007/11589976_12
4. Bouwman, M., Luttik, B., van der Wal, D.: A formalisation of SysML state machines in mCRL2. In: Peters, K., Willemse, T.A.C. (eds.) FORTE 2021. LNCS, vol. 12719, pp. 42–59. Springer, Cham (2021). https://doi.org/10.1007/978-3-030-78089-0_3
5. Bunte, O., van Gool, L.C.M., Willemse, T.A.C.: Formal verification of OIL component specifications using mCRL2. In: ter Beek, M.H., Ničković, D. (eds.) FMICS 2020. LNCS, vol. 12327, pp. 231–251. Springer, Cham (2020). https://doi.org/10.1007/978-3-030-58298-2_10
6. Bunte, O., van Gool, L.C.M., Willemse, T.A.C.: Formal verification of OIL component specifications using mCRL2. Int. J. Softw. Tools Technol. Transf. **24**(3), 441–472 (2022)
7. Bunte, O., et al.: The mCRL2 toolset for analysing concurrent systems - improvements in expressivity and usability. In: Vojnar, T., Zhang, L. (eds.) TACAS 2019. LNCS, vol. 11428, pp. 21–39. Springer, Cham (2019). https://doi.org/10.1007/978-3-030-17465-1_2
8. Cleaveland, R., Lüttgen, G., Natarajan, V.: Priority and abstraction in process algebra. Inf. Comput. **205**(9), 1426–1458 (2007)
9. Cranen, S., et al.: An overview of the mCRL2 toolset and its recent advances. In: Piterman, N., Smolka, S.A. (eds.) TACAS 2013. LNCS, vol. 7795, pp. 199–213. Springer, Heidelberg (2013). https://doi.org/10.1007/978-3-642-36742-7_15
10. Denkers, J., Brunner, M., van Gool, L., Visser, E.: Configuration space exploration for digital printing systems. In: Calinescu, R., Păsăreanu, C.S. (eds.) SEFM 2021. LNCS, vol. 13085, pp. 423–442. Springer, Cham (2021). https://doi.org/10.1007/978-3-030-92124-8_24
11. Groote, J.F., Keiren, J.J.A., Luttik, B., de Vink, E.P., Willemse, T.A.C.: Modelling and analysing software in mCRL2. In: Arbab, F., Jongmans, S.S. (eds.) FACS 2019. LNCS, vol. 12018, pp. 25–48. Springer, Cham (2019). https://doi.org/10.1007/978-3-030-40914-2_2
12. Groote, J.F., Mousavi, M.R.: Modeling and Analysis of Communicating Systems. MIT Press, Cambridge (2014)
13. Hansen, H.H., Ketema, J., Luttik, B., Mousavi, M.R., van de Pol, J.: Towards model checking executable UML specifications in mCRL2. Innov. Syst. Softw. Eng. **6**(1–2), 83–90 (2010)

14. Hwong, Y., Keiren, J.J.A., Kusters, V.J.J., Leemans, S.J.J., Willemse, T.A.C.: Formalising and analysing the control software of the compact muon solenoid experiment at the large hadron collider. Sci. Comput. Program. **78**(12), 2435–2452 (2013)
15. Hwong, Y., Kusters, V.J.J., Willemse, T.A.C.: Analysing the control software of the compact muon solenoid experiment at the large hadron collider. In: Arbab, F., Sirjani, M. (eds.) FSEN 2011. LNCS, vol. 7141, pp. 174–189. Springer, Heidelberg (2011). https://doi.org/10.1007/978-3-642-29320-7_12
16. James, P., Moller, F., Pantekis, F.: OnTrack: reflecting on domain specific formal methods for railway designs. Sci. Comput. Program. **233**, 103057 (2024). https://doi.org/10.1016/j.scico.2023.103057. https://www.sciencedirect.com/science/article/pii/S0167642323001399
17. Kuske, S.: A formal semantics of UML state machines based on structured graph transformation. In: Gogolla, M., Kobryn, C. (eds.) UML 2001. LNCS, vol. 2185, pp. 241–256. Springer, Heidelberg (2001). https://doi.org/10.1007/3-540-45441-1_19
18. van Laarhoven, J.: Formalising the state machine modelling tool (SMMT). Master's thesis, Eindhoven University of Technology (2023)
19. Latella, D., Majzik, I., Massink, M.: Automatic verification of a behavioural subset of UML statechart diagrams using the SPIN model-checker. Formal Aspects Comput. **11**(6), 637–664 (1999)
20. Remenska, D., et al.: From UML to process algebra and back: an automated approach to model-checking software design artifacts of concurrent systems. In: Brat, G., Rungta, N., Venet, A. (eds.) NFM 2013. LNCS, vol. 7871, pp. 244–260. Springer, Heidelberg (2013). https://doi.org/10.1007/978-3-642-38088-4_17
21. Stoel, J., van der Storm, T., Vinju, J.J., Bosman, J.: Solving the bank with rebel: on the design of the rebel specification language and its application inside a bank. In: ITSLE@SPLASH, pp. 13–20. ACM (2016)
22. Voelter, M.: Language and IDE modularization and composition with MPS. In: Lämmel, R., Saraiva, J., Visser, J. (eds.) GTTSE 2011. LNCS, vol. 7680, pp. 383–430. Springer, Heidelberg (2011). https://doi.org/10.1007/978-3-642-35992-7_11
23. Vu, L.H., Haxthausen, A.E., Peleska, J.: A domain-specific language for generic interlocking models and their properties. In: Fantechi, A., Lecomte, T., Romanovsky, A. (eds.) RSSRail 2017. LNCS, vol. 10598, pp. 99–115. Springer, Cham (2017). https://doi.org/10.1007/978-3-319-68499-4_7
24. Wang, H., Zhong, D., Zhao, T., Ren, F.: Integrating model checking with SysML in complex system safety analysis. IEEE Access **7**, 16561–16571 (2019)

Fault Tree Inference Using Multi-objective Evolutionary Algorithms and Confusion Matrix-Based Metrics

Lisandro A. Jimenez-Roa[1(✉)], Nicolae Rusnac[2], Matthias Volk[3], and Mariëlle Stoelinga[1,4]

[1] Formal Methods and Tools, University of Twente, Enschede, The Netherlands
{l.jimenezroa,m.i.a.stoelinga}@utwente.nl
[2] Delft University of Technology, Delft, The Netherlands
N.Rusnac@student.tudelft.nl
[3] Formal System Analysis, Eindhoven University of Technology, Eindhoven, The Netherlands
m.volk@tue.nl
[4] Department of Software Science, Radboud University, Nijmegen, The Netherlands

Abstract. In the domain of reliability engineering and risk assessment, the development of fault tree (FT) models is pivotal for decision-making in complex systems. Traditional FT model development, relying on manual efforts and expert collaboration, is both time-consuming and error-prone. The era of Industry 4.0 introduces capabilities for automatically deriving FTs from inspection and monitoring data.

This paper presents `FT-MOEA-CM`, an extension of the `FT-MOEA` algorithm for inferring FT models from failure data using multi-objective optimization. `FT-MOEA-CM` enhances its predecessor by integrating confusion matrix-derived metrics and incorporating parallelization and caching mechanisms. Our evaluation on six FTs from diverse application areas showcases that `FT-MOEA-CM` exhibits (1) enhanced robustness, (2) faster convergence and (3) better scalability than `FT-MOEA`, suggesting its potential in efficiently inferring larger FT models.

Keywords: Fault tree analysis · multi-objective evolutionary algorithms · confusion matrix · model learning

1 Introduction

Fault Tree Analysis (FTA) [22,24] is a critical tool in reliability engineering and risk analysis, utilized extensively in industry for its ability to model complex systems and assess failure probabilities. Despite its creation in the 1960s and widespread application across a large range of industrial domains, the construction of fault trees remains a significant effort. Traditional methods involve

---

This research has been partially funded by NWO under the grant PrimaVera number NWA.1160.18.238, the Marie Sklodowska-Curie grant agreement No 101008233, and by the ERC Consolidator grant CAESAR number 864075.

© The Author(s), under exclusive license to Springer Nature Switzerland AG 2024
A. E. Haxthausen and W. Serwe (Eds.): FMICS 2024, LNCS 14952, pp. 80–96, 2024.
https://doi.org/10.1007/978-3-031-68150-9_5

manual, expert-driven development, a process that is not only laborious but also prone to errors and inconsistencies, especially in complex systems.

A promising approach is the automatic inference of fault tree (FT) models from failure data. Given a set of data points representing the status of components (operational/failed) and the corresponding overall system status, the aim is to automatically infer a compact FT model capturing the failure behaviour present in the data set. While first inference approaches date back to the 1970s [11], the recent surge of data collection allows new approaches for FT inference [7,8,15,27]. A recent algorithm for creating FT models from failure datasets is FT-MOEA [6], which employs both the *Elitist Non-Dominated Sorting Genetic Algorithm* (NSGA-II) [4] and the *Crowding-Distance* [12]. The former leverages multi-objective optimization and Pareto front concepts to infer FT models, while the latter serves as a diversity criterion, prioritizing diverse solutions over overcrowded ones.

However, FT-MOEA encounters challenges related to *robustness, scalability,* and *convergence speed*. Robustness pertains to its ability to consistently yield the same results. Scalability refers to the capacity to handle larger FTs, characterized by a greater number of *basic events* and *minimal cut sets* (MCS). Convergence speed concerns efficiency in completing the task.

These problems may stem from the limited features considered in FT-MOEA's optimisation process. Specifically, FT-MOEA incorporates only three features: error metrics based on accuracy and MCS, and the FT size, with the first two being correlated. Furthermore, computing MCSs for larger FTs is notably computationally expensive, which aggravates scalability and convergence speed concerns.

To address these challenges, this paper explores alternative features to guide the multi-objective optimization's convergence process, resulting in the development of the FT-MOEA-CM algorithm. This algorithm leverages 16 metrics derived from the well-established *confusion matrix (CM)* and eliminates the need for the computationally expensive MCS calculations.

Our methodology is structured into two phases: In a first phase, we perform *feature assessment* and identify the most informative and effective features for guiding the FT inference process. To achieve this, we conduct a *Principal Component Analysis* (PCA), a technique utilized for dimensionality reduction and feature selection. In a second phase, we perform an extensive *evaluation* of the new approach on six FTs from diverse application areas, and compare with FT-MOEA. In particular, we investigate how the inclusion of additional information in FT-MOEA-CM influences the robustness, scalability, and convergence speed of the FT inference process.

Contributions. The primary contributions of this work are as follows:

(i) Introduction of the FT-MOEA-CM algorithm, employing confusion matrix-based metrics for the automatic inference of FTs, which enhances robustness, scalability, and convergence speed over its predecessor FT-MOEA.
(ii) Improved performance through the integration of features like caching and parallelization, particularly beneficial for larger FT structures.

(iii) `FT-MOEA-CM` is available at https://gitlab.utwente.nl/fmt/fault-trees/ft-moea

Related Work. An early technique for *data-driven* FT inference is the `IFT` algorithm [11], utilizing Quinlan's ID3 algorithm to generate Decision Trees. The approach in [13] uses *text mining* techniques to enrich FTs with maintenance records as input data. Inspired by Causal Decision Trees, the `LIFT` algorithm [15] employs the *Mantel-Haenszel* test to identify dependencies between events, requiring not only basic event data but also intermediate event failure information. The `ILTA` [27] and `MILTA` [28] algorithms integrate *Knowledge Discovery in Datasets* (KDD), *Interpretable Logic Tree Analysis*, and *Bayesian probability rules*. The method in [10] constructs a *Bayesian Network* before converting it into an FT model, using *blacklists* and *whitelists* to identify absent or existing arcs. The `DDFTA` algorithm [8] derives FTs from failure data time series through binarization and Boolean equation simplification. The `DDFTAe` algorithm [16], an extension of `DDFTA`, addresses missing information in time series fault occurrence data. The `DDFTAnb` [18] algorithm extends the `DDFTA` to focus on *repairable FT* models using *naïve Bayes classification* and time series data. Evolutionary algorithm-based methods include `FT-EA` [9] and `FT-MOEA` [6], where the multi-objective cost function of `FT-MOEA` shows improvement over `FT-EA`'s one-dimensional cost function. The `SymLearn` tool chain [7] enhances scalability by leveraging symmetries and modules in failure datasets. [5] uses genetic algorithms to learn attack trees from sets of traces. The method in [26] generates FT models from sensor time series data, exemplified by a domestic heater case study, aiming to identify thresholds that differentiate *normal* from *error* conditions. The `ITCA` methodology [29] focuses on fault hierarchy causality through KDD and FTs, using causality analysis and NASA's turbofan dataset as an example. The methodology in [14] applies interpretable machine learning and causal analysis to derive *Petri Nets* from event logs, with potential application to FTs. The work in [19] proposes a method for learning *Dynamic* FTs from temporal *Truth Tables* and time series data. The study in [17] explores the integration of *collaborative data analytics* into deriving FT models, demonstrating enhanced accuracy in data-driven FT inference.

Outline. Section 2 introduces FTs and formally defines their inference. Section 3 details the `FT-MOEA-CM` methodology. Section 4 describes our experimental setup, and Sect. 5 presents our results from evaluating `FT-MOEA-CM` on six case studies. We conclude in Sect. 6 and present future work.

2 Preliminaries

2.1 Fault Trees

A *fault tree (FT)* models how failures occur and propagate in a system, and lead to a system failure [22,24]. Formally, a fault tree is a directed acyclic graph where the leaves, called *basic events (*BE*)*, correspond to (atomic) system components.

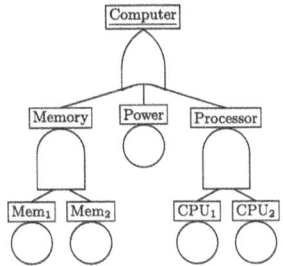

Fig. 1. Example FT.

Table 1. Example failure data set D.

	Mem$_1$	Mem$_2$	Power	CPU$_1$	CPU$_1$	Sys.
$\vec{b}_0$	0	0	0	0	1	0
$\vec{b}_1$	0	0	0	1	1	1
$\vec{b}_2$	0	0	1	0	0	1
$\vec{b}_3$	1	0	0	0	1	0
⋮	⋮	⋮	⋮	⋮	⋮	⋮

The intermediate nodes are equipped with logical *gates* modelling the failure propagation. A logical AND-gate fails, if all successor nodes fail, an OR-gate fails if at least one successor fails. An FT $\mathcal{F}$ fails if the dedicated root node fails. Figure 1 depicts an example FT modeling a computer. The root *Computer* is an OR-gate, *Memory* and *Processor* are AND-gates, circles indicate BE.

Definition 1 (Fault tree). *A fault tree (FT) is a rooted directed acyclic graph (V, E) assigning the type to nodes via function $Tp : V \to \{BE, AND, OR\}$ s.t. $Tp(v) = BE$ iff v is a leaf. The inputs of a node v, denoted $I(v)$, are the successors of v. All nodes $v \in V$ must be reachable from the root Top.*

All nodes of type BE are denoted by $\text{BEs} := \{v \in V \mid Tp(v) = BE\}$.

The *semantics* of an FT $\mathcal{F}$ are given by its *structure function* $f^{\mathcal{F}}$. Let $\vec{b} = \langle b_1, \ldots, b_{|\text{BEs}|} \rangle \in \{0,1\}^{|\text{BEs}|}$ be a *status vector* where $b_i = 1$ indicates that the i-th BE has failed, and $b_i = 0$ that it functions properly, respectively.

Definition 2 (Semantics of FT). *Let $\vec{b}$ be a status vector and $\mathcal{F}$ an FT. The structure function $f^{\mathcal{F}} : \{0,1\}^{|\text{BEs}|} \times V \to \{0,1\}$ returns the status of node v and is defined as*

$$f^{\mathcal{F}}(\vec{b}, v) := \begin{cases} b_i & \text{if } Tp(v) = BE \text{ and } v \text{ is the } i\text{-th BE}, \\ \bigwedge_{v' \in I(v)} f(\vec{b}, v') & \text{if } Tp(v) = AND, \\ \bigvee_{v' \in I(v)} f(\vec{b}, v') & \text{if } Tp(v) = OR. \end{cases}$$

We say FT $\mathcal{F}$ fails for $\vec{b}$ if $f^{\mathcal{F}}(\vec{b}, \text{Top}) = 1$. A status vector $\vec{b}$ can also be given as the set $C = \{b_i \in \vec{b} \mid b_i = 1\}$ of failed BE, and we write $f^{\mathcal{F}}(C)$ instead of $f^{\mathcal{F}}(\vec{b})$. C is as *minimal cut set (MCS)* if $f^{\mathcal{F}}(C) = 1$ and $\forall C' \subset C : f^{\mathcal{F}}(C') = 0$.

For the FT in Fig. 1, the set $C = \{\text{Mem}_1, \text{Mem}_2, \text{CPU}_1\}$ of failed BE leads to a failure of the overall FT: $f^{F}(C) = 1$. The FT has three MCS: $\{\text{Mem}_1, \text{Mem}_2\}$, $\{\text{Power}\}$ and $\{\text{CPU}_1, \text{CPU}_2\}$.

2.2 Failure Data Set

We assume the failure data is given in a format such that a data point represents the possible state of each component as well as the overall system state. Table 1 gives an example data set corresponding to the FT in Fig. 1. A row in the *failure data set* D corresponds to a status vector $\vec{b_k}$—giving the status of each (atomic) component—together with the overall system status $f^D(\vec{b_k})$. For instance, the first row (status vector $\vec{b_0}$) represents that only component CPU_2 has failed, and the system is still operational. The second row (status vector $\vec{b_1}$) represents the failure of components CPU_1 and CPU_2, leading to a system failure.

We assume the data set is *coherent*, i.e., a failed system stays failed for further component failures, and *noise-free*, i.e., the same status of components always yields the same system state.

2.3 Inference of Fault Tree Models

Fault tree inference finds a compact FT $\mathcal{F}_D$ matching a given failure data set D.

Problem statement. Given a failure data set $D = \left(\vec{b_k}, f(\vec{b_k}) \right)$, create a FT $\mathcal{F}_D$ that is both
1. *small*, i.e., the number of nodes F_D is minimal, and
2. *accurate*, i.e., the structure function $f^{\mathcal{F}_D}$ of the FT coincides with the given failure data set $f^D(\vec{b_k})$.

Our inference approach is guided by metrics based on the confusion matrix.

Table 2. List of 17 metrics evaluated to guide the inference process of FTs.

Metric name	Range	Comment
FT Size	$[2, \infty)$	Number of FT nodes $|\mathcal{F}_D| := |V|$
Precision, Specificity, Sensitivity, Negative predictive value, Accuracy, Threat score, Balanced accuracy, Negative likelihood ratio, Positive likelihood ratio, Diagnostic odds ratio, F1 Score, Fowlkes-Mallows Index	$[0, 1]$	Metrics that range between 0 and 1 (or 0 to infinity) are normalized to $[0, 1]$ with 0 being the optimum value
Matthews correlation coefficient, Informedness, Markedness, Kappa statistic	$[0, 2]$	Metrics that range between -1 and 1 are normalized to $[0, 2]$ with 0 being the optimum value

Confusion Matrix. The *confusion matrix* is a performance evaluation tool commonly used in machine learning classification tasks [23]. In binary classification, a 2×2 confusion matrix categorizes predictions into four outcomes: True Positives (TP), True Negatives (TN), False Positives (FP), and False Negatives (FN). In our setting TP and TN correspond to both the FT and the data giving the same result, i.e., $f^{\mathcal{F}_D}(\vec{b_k}) = f^D(\vec{b_k})$. FP and FN indicate that the outcome of the FT differs from the data, i.e., $f^{\mathcal{F}_D}(\vec{b_k}) \neq f^D(\vec{b_k})$.

To assess the FT's performance relative to input data D, we utilize 17 metrics outlined in Table 2. The first metric evaluates the FT's size via the number of nodes F_D, the remaining 16 metrics are derived from the confusion matrix. We normalize all confusion matrix-based metrics to the interval $[0, 1]$ such that 0 represents optimal values. Metrics ranging from -1 to 1, such as the *Matthews Correlation Coefficient* are scaled to the interval $[0, 2]$ to enhance the interpretability of simulation outcomes. Further details on the confusion matrix and associated metrics can be found in [3].

3 FT-MOEA-CM's Methodology

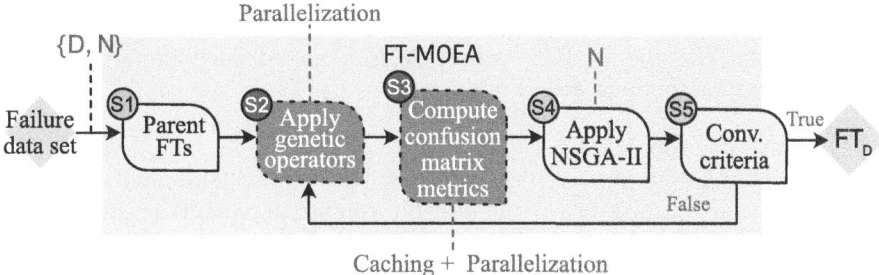

Fig. 2. FT-MOEA-CM methodology. Blue boxes indicate novel/improved steps. (Color figure online)

Figure 2 illustrates FT-MOEA-CM's FT inference process, which utilizes multi-objective evolutionary algorithms and metrics derived from the confusion matrix. The approach is based on the standard steps of genetic algorithms: each generation of FTs is mutated based on operators such as adding or removing gates. The resulting FTs are evaluated based on metrics and the best FTs are then used in the next generation. As FT-MOEA-CM is based on FT-MOEA, we direct the reader to [6] for detailed methodology information. Below, we outline each main step of the process.

S1.
- Input: The input includes the failure dataset D (Sect. 2.3) as well as FT-MOEA-CM's parameters, such as the maximum population size N.
- Process: The initial population consists of two *parent* FTs, one a single AND-gate and the other an OR-gate, each connecting to all BEs in D.
- Output: The parent FTs constitute the FT population.

S2.
- Input: The existing FT population.
- Process: Seven genetic operators (e.g., adding or removing gates, crossover of subtrees) are applied to alter the structure for each FT in the population (see [6] for details). We improve upon [6] by introducing *parallelization*, enabling the use of multiple system cores for FT generation.

S3.
- Output: An expanded FT population featuring new FTs.
- Input: The expanded FT population.
- Process: Each FT in the population is processed to calculate the 17 metrics listed in Table 2. *Caching* is used to avoid recalculating metrics for previously evaluated FTs, thus enhancing efficiency. *Parallelization* is implemented to further improve this process.
- Output: The enlarged FT population with corresponding metric values.

S4.
- Input: The enlarged FT population with corresponding metric values.
- Process: The *NSGA-II* algorithm [4] and *Crowding-Distance* [12] are utilized for multi-objective optimization to construct Pareto fronts of non-dominated FTs based on the metrics.
- Output: The top N FTs—where N is a user-defined parameter—are selected for the next generation.

S5.
- Input: The top N FTs.
- Process: Evaluate convergence criteria: (i) the maximum number of generations is reached, or (ii) the best FT candidate remains unchanged for a specified number of generations. If neither condition is fulfilled, the top N FTs are used as input for Step 2, and Steps 2 to 5 are repeated until one of the convergence criteria is met.
- Output: The inferred FT, $\mathcal{F}_D$, identified as the best FT candidate in the first Pareto front.

4 Experimental Evaluation

Case Studies. We evaluate our approach on six FTs stemming from various application areas. The *Data-driven Fault Tree (ddFT)* [8] was obtained from time series data. The *Mono-propellant Propulsion System (MPPS)* [24] is used for a small space flight vehicle. The *Covid-19* FT [2] is

Table 3. Overview of case studies.

Case study	|BEs|	|$\mathcal{F}$|	|D|	|$\mathcal{C}_D$|	All FTs
ddFT [8]	8	19	256	6	83 600
MPPS [24]	8	14	256	7	73 200
Covid-19 [2]	9	13	512	6	60 400
TS1 [7]	10	21	1024	16	127 200
GPT12BE	12	25	4096	13	139 200
GPT15BE	15	27	32 768	10	108 000

used in infection risk management. The *Truss System (TS1)* [7] models a symmetric truss bridge system. The two FTs *GPT12BE* and *GPT15BE* were generated with GPT-4 [20], representing larger FTs designed to test scalability. The prompts used for generation included examples of existing FTs, the number of nodes, and the number of gates. Table 3 outlines for each case study the number of Basic Events (|BEs|), FT Size (|$\mathcal{F}$|), failure dataset size (|D|), total number of MCSs (|$\mathcal{C}_D$|), and the number of all FTs across generations. The latter is further discussed in Sect. 5.1.

Implementation. The implementation of FT-MOEA-CM, available online[1], is complemented by a dedicated database server designed for storing and process-

---
[1] https://gitlab.utwente.nl/fmt/fault-trees/ft-moea.

ing data produced by `FT-MOEA-CM`. This server, developed in GO, employs a MySQL database and can be accessed online[2].

Generation of Failure Data Set. Access to real-life failure data is typically very limited. Instead, we evaluate our approach on synthetic failure data sets which are generated from realistic reliability models. We consider existing FTs from the literature as ground truth, see Table 3. For each FT, we generate a synthetic failure data set D by evaluating all the unique combinations of BEs in the respective FT, ensuring the completeness of the failure data set. Our data set allows us to compare the FT inferred from the data set with the ground-truth FT, and thereby evaluate the quality of the inferred FT.

Experimental Setup. Our case studies were executed five times on an E5-2683V4 CPU at 2.10 GHz, with 16 cores supporting 2 threads each on the EEMCS-HPC Cluster of the University of Twente. The evaluation comprises two primary sections: the first, elaborated in Sect. 5.1, concentrates on *feature assessment* through Principal Component Analysis to discern the most informative features from the confusion matrix for inferring FTs. Section 5.2 compares the efficacy of the confusion matrix-based metrics with the original `FT-MOEA` implementation, involving two configurations: `FT-MOEA-CM-All` includes all 17 features from Table 2, and `FT-MOEA-CM-Best` employs only the top 7 features identified in Sect. 5.1. The evaluation addresses robustness, convergence speed, and scalability. Lastly, we also evaluate `FT-MOEA-CM`'s features of parallelization and caching in Sect. 5.3.

5 Results

5.1 Feature Assessment

For Step 3 in the FT inference (cf. Fig. 2), we need to identify the most informative metrics listed in Table 2. We conduct this by performing *feature assessment* by evaluating the importance of different variables in a dataset. Here, the *features* are the *metrics* computed from the confusion matrix.

We use *Principal Component Analysis (PCA)*, a multivariate statistical technique that extracts information in the form of *principal components* [1], which are *orthogonal* vectors that maximize variance, capturing the most significant features. This technique is commonly used for dimensionality reduction and data analysis. We apply PCA using the Python `PCA` package [25]. This process was applied to all case studies listed in Table 3, compiling a *feature dataset* for each case study with the 17 metrics in Table 2.

Metrics were calculated for *every FT in each generation* to identify the most uncorrelated metrics. This is crucial as uncorrelated metrics enhance convergence in multi-objective evolutionary algorithms by improving diversity and preventing biased searches. The column titled "All FTs" in Table 3 specifies the total number of data samples available for PCA analysis in each case study.

---

[2] https://github.com/killB0x/ft-moea-cm-server.

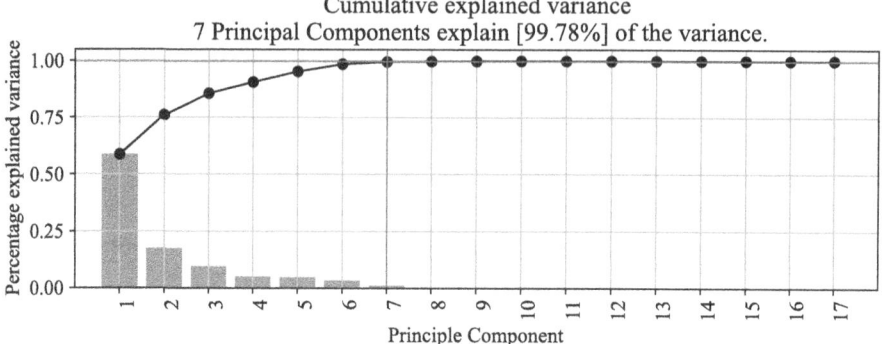

Fig. 3. Scree plot: cumulative explained variance per principal component.

Data pre-processing. To mitigate the potential dominance of any case study due to data volume discrepancies, random sampling is employed across all cases, ensuring uniformity by aligning dataset sizes with that of the smallest one (i.e., case Covid-19). Similarly, to avoid dominance of one feature over others due to magnitude disparities, we normalize each feature. This normalization involves subtracting the mean and scaling to unit variance, a process executed using the `StandardScaler` function from the `preprocessing` module in `scikit-learn` [21].

Principal Component Analysis. The analysis in this section is based on the *explained variance* and *loadings*. We refer the reader to the `PCA` package [25] documentation for further details. We examine the explained variance percentage of each principal component (PC), depicted in the scree plot in Fig. 3. This plot reveals that the first 7 out of 17 PCs account for 99.78% of the variance in the features dataset. This suggests that only these 7 PCs are highly informative.

The analysis of *loadings* reflects each feature's contribution magnitude to a particular PC and is crucial for identifying the most informative metrics for FT inference. Table 4 presents the loadings for each metric across the seven main PCs. A higher absolute loading value indicates a stronger contribution to the respective PC, and the loading's sign shows the correlation nature. This analysis reveals that the most informative metrics are **Matthews correlation coefficient, Speci-**

Table 4. Loading analysis per metric.

	PC	Feature	Loading	Type
1	PC1	Matthews correlation coef	0.296	best
2	PC2	Specificity	0.538	best
3	PC3	Negative predictive value	0.656	best
4	PC4	Precision	0.525	best
5	PC5	Diagnostic odds ratio	0.702	best
6	PC6	FT Size	0.791	best
7	PC7	Accuracy	0.873	best
8	PC2	Sensitivity	−0.370	weak
9	PC1	Threat Score	0.283	weak
10	PC4	Balanced accuracy	0.348	weak
11	PC1	F1 Score	0.283	weak
12	PC1	Fowlkew-Mallows Index	0.284	weak
13	PC4	Informedness	−0.393	weak
14	PC4	Markedness	0.348	weak
15	PC1	Kappa statistic	0.293	weak
16	PC2	Negative likelihood ratio	−0.315	weak
17	PC2	Positive likelihood ratio	0.487	weak

ficity, **Negative predictive value**, **Precision**, **Diagnostic odds ratio**, **FT size**, and **Accuracy**.

The *Matthews correlation coefficient* (0.296) has the highest loading on PC1. However, other features have similar loading on PC1, such as the *Threat Score* (0.296). This similarity may indicate a correlation between these metrics, so only the one with the highest loading is considered. For other PCs, such as PC6 and PC7, *FT Size* and *Accuracy* are respectively the highest contributors, indicating that these metrics are uncorrelated with the others.

Thus, the seven *best* metrics consistently contribute the most uniquely to their respective PCs and are minimally correlated across different case studies, whereas the *weak* features show higher correlations to one or more of the best features, and therefore left out of the analysis.

5.2 Comparing FT-MOEA and FT-MOEA-CM

The comparison between **FT-MOEA** and **FT-MOEA-CM** focuses on three key aspects: robustness, scalability, and convergence speed. Robustness is assessed by examining the variability in the output FT. Convergence speed is evaluated by analyzing the rate of convergence. Finally, scalability analysis involves studying case studies of various sizes.

Results Interpretation. Part of the comparative analysis includes box plots constructed from the outcomes of each experimental setup. In these setups, the algorithm is executed *five* times to generate distinct instances of the experiment, yielding five separate results for the same configuration. This repeated execution is crucial for accurately assessing the outcomes due to the stochastic nature of the optimization process, where genetic operators are randomly applied. By running the algorithm multiple times, we can effectively evaluate the impact of this randomness on the results.

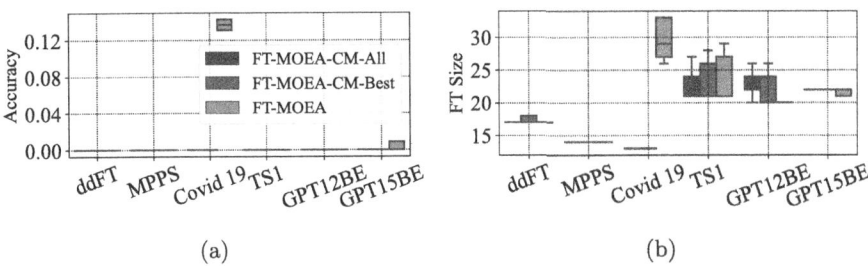

Fig. 4. Evaluating robustness for all case studies and algorithms. In (a), based on accuracy, **FT-MOEA-CM** reached global optima for all case studies, while **FT-MOEA** failed for *Covid 19* and *GPT15BE*. In (b) based on FT size.

Robustness. Robustness is assessed by analyzing the variability in the output FT upon convergence. An algorithm is considered robust if it consistently yields the same FT structure, though this criterion may not be universally applicable due to the potential existence of multiple optimal FT structures for the same failure data set.

Discussion. Robustness is evaluated by examining the variance in box plots for accuracy and FT size, where a variance close to zero suggests higher robustness. In Fig. 4(a), *accuracy* results for all case studies are presented using box plots to compare `FT-MOEA-CM-All`, `FT-MOEA-CM-Best`, and `FT-MOEA`. An accuracy of 0 is optimal. It is observed that `FT-MOEA-CM`'s configurations consistently achieved an Accuracy of 0.0 with zero variance, indicating they consistently reach the global optima across all case studies. In contrast, `FT-MOEA` failed to achieve the global optima in the Covid-19 and GPT15BE case studies.

Regarding *FT size*, Fig. 4(b) shows that results vary significantly among algorithms. For instance, in the TS1 case study, all algorithms yield varying FT sizes. For GPT12BE, `FT-MOEA` showed greater robustness compared to `FT-MOEA-CM-All` and `FT-MOEA-CM-Best`, whereas the opposite holds for Covid-19.

Conclusion. The results indicate that in terms of Accuracy, `FT-MOEA-CM-All` and `FT-MOEA-CM-Best` are more consistent compared to `FT-MOEA`, achieving the global optima for all case studies. However, regarding FT Size and the related FT structure, the consistency of the results varies.

Scalability. The scalability analysis assesses the algorithms' efficiency in managing more complex case studies. The complexity of a FT is linked to its number of elements (i.e., BEs and logic gates) and MCSs, indicating that a more complex FT represents a more challenging inference process.

Discussion. Table 3 presents the FT Size and the number of MCSs per case study, arranged from the one with the fewest BEs to that with the most. The underlying concept is that case studies with fewer BEs and MCSs should be simpler to manage. As indicated by the results in Fig. 4, `FT-MOEA-CM-All` and `FT-MOEA-CM-Best` consistently reached the global optima across all cases, while `FT-MOEA` did not in the Covid-19 and GPT15BE case studies. However, in the GPT12BE case, all three algorithms exhibited strong performance, especially `FT-MOEA`, which surpassed `FT-MOEA-CM-All` and `FT-MOEA-CM-Best`. Nevertheless, given that GPT12BE contains more BEs and MCSs than Covid-19, the reasons for `FT-MOEA`'s difficulties with the latter are not clear.

Figure 5 depicts the convergence over generations for each case study in terms of accuracy. It is observed that `FT-MOEA-CM`'s configurations converge more rapidly to the optimal accuracy compared to `FT-MOEA`. These findings suggest that `FT-MOEA-CM` may scale better than `FT-MOEA` due to its superior convergence profile, indicating enhanced capabilities to manage larger problems. Further research is necessary to examine this hypothesis more comprehensively.

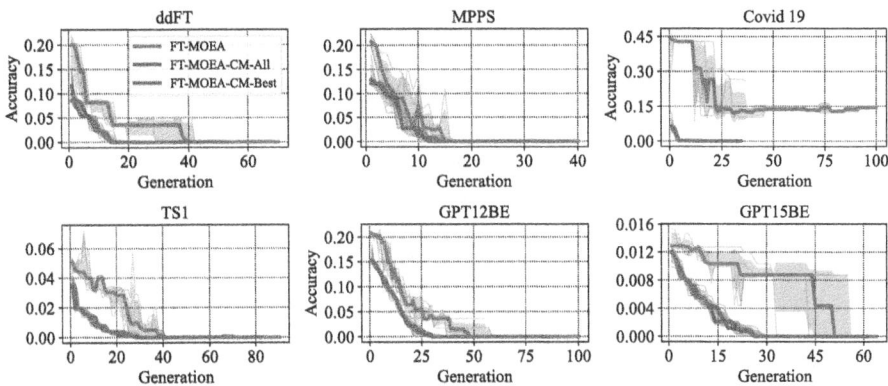

Fig. 5. Accuracy over generations for all case studies and algorithms.

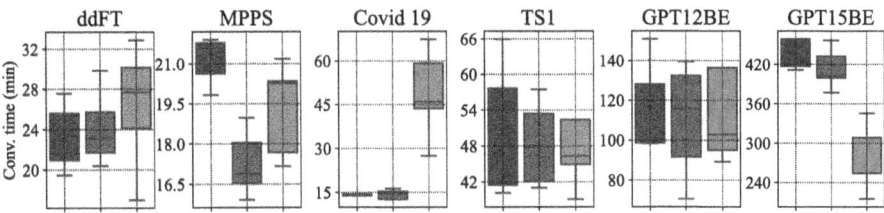

Fig. 6. Convergence time per case study and algorithm: `FT-MOEA-CM-All` (Blue box); `FT-MOEA-CM-Best` (Green box); `FT-MOEA` (Red box). (Color figure online)

Conclusion. Regarding scalability, our findings suggest that `FT-MOEA-CM` may be more scalable than `FT-MOEA`.

Convergence Speed. Convergence speed refers to the time required by an algorithm to automatically infer an FT from a failure data set.

Discussion. Figure 6 shows the convergence speed, measured in minutes. In specific case studies, such as ddFT, MPPS, and Covid-19, `FT-MOEA-CM` outpaced `FT-MOEA`. Notably, `FT-MOEA-CM-Best` demonstrated superior performance in the MPPS case study. For other cases, like TS1 and GPT12BE, the algorithms' convergence speeds were comparable. Nonetheless, in the GPT15BE case study, `FT-MOEA` converged faster but to a local optima.

A different perspective on the convergence process is illustrated in Fig. 7(a), focusing on FT Size across generations and Fig. 7(b), showing the computational time per generation. `FT-MOEA-CM` approaches larger FT sizes more rapidly (to attain global optima), then transitions to optimizing the FT structure by reducing FT Size, a pattern also identified in [6].

Conclusion. `FT-MOEA-CM` demonstrates higher convergence speed than `FT-MOEA`, evaluated based on both convergence time and convergence profile.

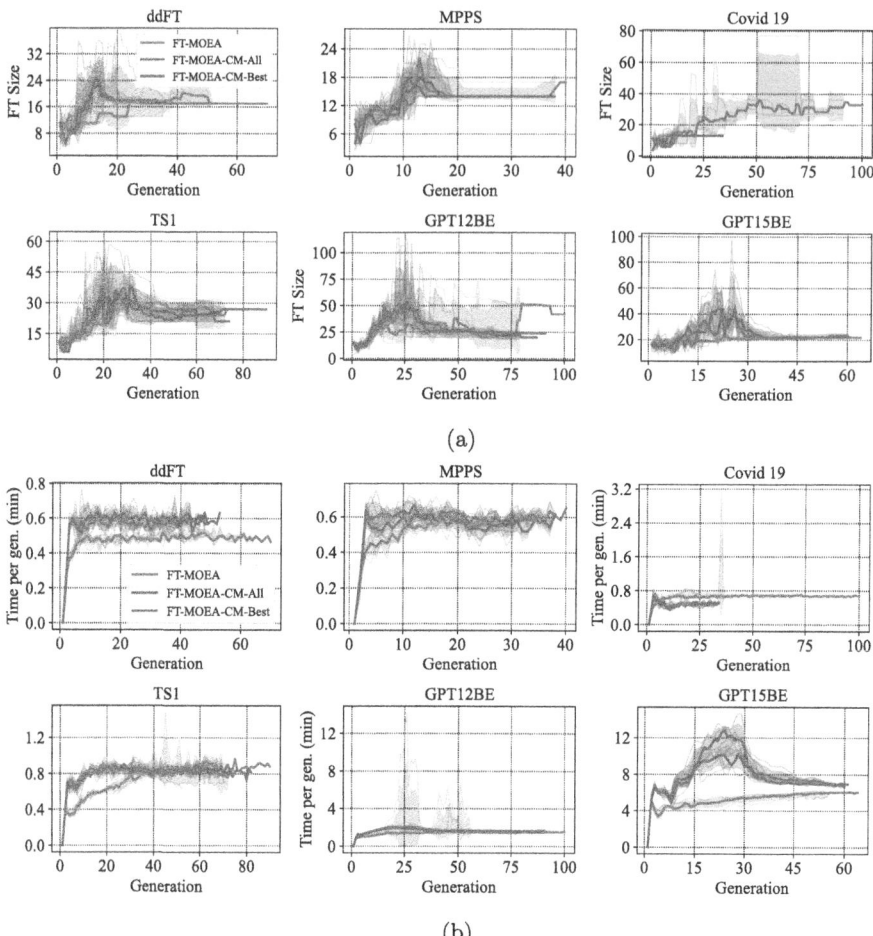

Fig. 7. Convergence across generations for all case studies and algorithms in function of (a) FT size and (b) computational time per generation.

Comparing FT-MOEA-CM-All and FT-MOEA-CM-Best. Both configurations yield the global optima in terms of robustness, yet exhibited less consistency in the TS1 and GPT12BE case studies. In terms of scalability, the two setups are on par. Their convergence speed is also similar, except in the MPPS case study, where FT-MOEA-CM-Best consistently outperformed. Importantly, FT-MOEA-CM-Best used only the top 7 features (identified through PCA in Sect. 5.1), compared to FT-MOEA-CM-All, which utilized all 17 features. This suggests that FT-MOEA-CM-Best provides a more efficient setup for FT-MOEA-CM.

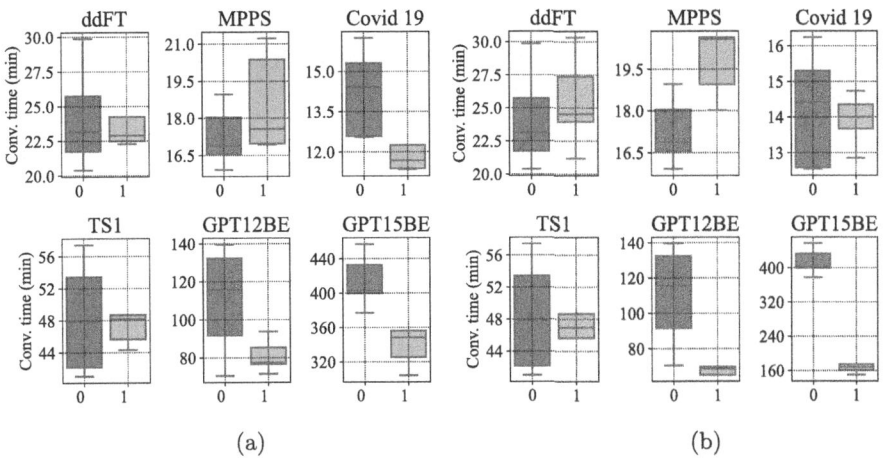

Fig. 8. Evaluation of (a) caching and (b) parallelization, where 0 (magenta box) and 1 (cyan box) indicate the feature "off" or "on", respectively. (Color figure online)

5.3 FT-MOEA-CM's Features: Parallelization and Caching

We evaluate the effects of parallelization and caching on FT-MOEA-CM-Best. Caching stores intermediate results to avoid redundant computations, thereby enhancing efficiency. Parallelization employs multiple processors to perform tasks concurrently, thus decreasing execution time by distributing the workload.

According to Fig. 8(a), caching benefits all case studies, excluding MPPS, by enabling quicker convergence. From Fig. 8(b), parallelization is shown to improve convergence speed by approximately 45% for larger case studies, namely GPT12BE and GPT15BE. While parallelization ensures enhanced consistency for TS1 and Covid-19, it negatively affects convergence time in ddFT and MPPS.

6 Conclusions

In this paper, we introduced FT-MOEA-CM, an extension of the FT-MOEA algorithm, specifically designed for inferring Fault Tree models from failure datasets using the NSGA-II and Crowding Sorting algorithms for multi-objective optimization.

A notable distinction of FT-MOEA-CM from its predecessor is the incorporation of features derived from the confusion matrix. We conducted a Principal Component Analysis on 17 available features, identifying 7 as the most important: **Matthews correlation coefficient, Specificity, Negative predictive value, Precision, Diagnostic odds ratio, FT size**, and **Accuracy**.

We compared FT-MOEA-CM with FT-MOEA across six case studies. The results showed that FT-MOEA-CM consistently achieve the global optima across all case studies, contrary to FT-MOEA. Although consistency in FT Size and related FT structure varies between algorithms, our findings suggest that FT-MOEA-CM may provide superior scalability relative to `FT-MOEA`. Moreover, `FT-MOEA-CM` demonstrated a higher convergence speed than `FT-MOEA`, as evaluated by both convergence time and convergence profile.

`FT-MOEA-CM`'s features, caching and parallelization, proved to improve convergence speed, with potential benefits to infer larger FTs.

Future Research. Possible directions for future work include:

- Addressing the scalability issue in computing the algorithm's confusion matrix metrics for exponentially growing datasets by using approximate evaluations with subsets of the failure dataset during initial algorithm generations.
- Exploring methods to facilitate convergence to Directed Acyclic Graphs (DAGs) instead of trees, using tree decomposition and Tree Width metrics to measure a graph's resemblance to a tree, applicable to specific DAG instances.
- Developing a benchmark for fair comparison of algorithms for automatic Fault Tree model inference to understand their comparative advantages and drawbacks, ensuring uniform and thorough evaluation.
- Extending our approach to handle missing information and noise, crucial for realistic scenarios where data may be incomplete or inaccurate.

References

1. Abdi, H., Williams, L.J.: Principal component analysis. Wiley Interdisc. Rev. Comput. Stat. **2**(4), 433–459 (2010)
2. Bakeli, T., Hafidi, A.A., et al.: COVID-19 infection risk management during construction activities: an approach based on fault tree analysis (FTA). J. Emerg. Manag. **18**(7), 161–176 (2020)
3. Božić, D., Runje, B., Lisjak, D., Kolar, D.: Metrics related to confusion matrix as tools for conformity assessment decisions. Appl. Sci. **13**(14), 8187 (2023)
4. Deb, K., Agrawal, S., Pratap, A., Meyarivan, T.: A fast and elitist multiobjective genetic algorithm: NSGA-II. IEEE Trans. Evol. Comput. **6**(2), 182–197 (2002). https://doi.org/10.1109/4235.996017
5. Dorfhuber, F., Eisentraut, J., Kretínský, J.: Learning attack trees by genetic algorithms. In: Ábrahám, E., Dubslaff, C., Tarifa, S.L.T. (eds.) ICTAC 2023. LNCS, vol. 14446, pp. 55–73. Springer, Cham (2023). https://doi.org/10.1007/978-3-031-47963-2_5
6. Jimenez-Roa, L.A., Heskes, T., Tinga, T., Stoelinga, M.: Automatic inference of fault tree models via multi-objective evolutionary algorithms. IEEE Trans. Dependable Secur. Comput. **20**(4), 3317–3327 (2023). https://doi.org/10.1109/TDSC.2022.3203805
7. Jimenez-Roa, L.A., Volk, M., Stoelinga, M.: Data-driven inference of fault tree models exploiting symmetry and modularization. In: Trapp, M., Saglietti, F., Spislander, M., Bitsch, F. (eds.) SAFECOMP 2022. LNCS, vol. 13414, pp. 46–61. Springer, Cham (2022). https://doi.org/10.1007/978-3-031-14835-4_4
8. Lazarova-Molnar, S., Niloofar, P., Barta, G.K.: Data-driven fault tree modeling for reliability assessment of cyber-physical systems. In: WSC, pp. 2719–2730. IEEE (2020). https://doi.org/10.1109/WSC48552.2020.9383882

9. Linard, A., Bucur, D., Stoelinga, M.: Fault trees from data: efficient learning with an evolutionary algorithm. In: Guan, N., Katoen, J.P., Sun, J. (eds.) SETTA 2019. LNCS, vol. 11951, pp. 19–37. Springer, Cham (2019). https://doi.org/10.1007/978-3-030-35540-1_2
10. Linard, A., Bueno, M.L., Bucur, D., Stoelinga, M.: Induction of fault trees through Bayesian networks. In: ESREL, pp. 910–917. Research Publishing (2019)
11. Madden, M.G., Nolan, P.J.: Generation of fault trees from simulated incipient fault case data. WIT Trans. Inf. Commun. Technol. **6** (1994)
12. Martí, L., Segredo, E., Pi, N.S., Hart, E.: Impact of selection methods on the diversity of many-objective Pareto set approximations. In: KES. Procedia Computer Science, vol. 112, pp. 844–853. Elsevier (2017). https://doi.org/10.1016/J.PROCS.2017.08.077
13. Mukherjee, S., Chakraborty, A.: Automated fault tree generation: bridging reliability with text mining. In: RAMS, pp. 83–88. IEEE (2007)
14. Nadim, K., Ragab, A., Ouali, M.: Data-driven dynamic causality analysis of industrial systems using interpretable machine learning and process mining. J. Intell. Manuf. **34**(1), 57–83 (2023). https://doi.org/10.1007/S10845-021-01903-Y
15. Nauta, M., Bucur, D., Stoelinga, M.: LIFT: learning fault trees from observational data. In: McIver, A., Horvath, A. (eds.) QEST 2018. LNCS, vol. 11024, pp. 306–322. Springer, Cham (2018). https://doi.org/10.1007/978-3-031-47963-2_5
16. Niloofar, P., Lazarova-Molnar, S.: Data-driven modelling of repairable fault trees from time series data with missing information. In: WSC, pp. 1–12. IEEE (2021). https://doi.org/10.1109/WSC52266.2021.9715375
17. Niloofar, P., Lazarova-Molnar, S.: Collaborative data-driven reliability analysis of multi-state fault trees. Proc. Inst. Mech. Eng. Part O: J. Risk Reliab. **237**(5), 886–896 (2023)
18. Niloofar, P., Lazarova-Molnar, S.: Data-driven extraction and analysis of repairable fault trees from time series data. Expert Syst. Appl. **215**, 119345 (2023). https://doi.org/10.1016/J.ESWA.2022.119345
19. Niloofar, P., Lazarova-Molnar, S.: Learning temporal truth tables of dynamic fault trees from time series data on faults. In: ICSRS, pp. 449–453. IEEE (2023). https://doi.org/10.1109/ICSRS59833.2023.10381460
20. OpenAI: GPT-4 technical report. CoRR abs/2303.08774 (2023). https://doi.org/10.48550/ARXIV.2303.08774
21. Pedregosa, F., et al.: Scikit-learn: machine learning in Python. J. Mach. Learn. Res. **12**, 2825–2830 (2011)
22. Ruijters, E., Stoelinga, M.: Fault tree analysis: a survey of the state-of-the-art in modeling, analysis and tools. Comput. Sci. Rev. **15**, 29–62 (2015). https://doi.org/10.1016/J.COSREV.2015.03.001
23. Sokolova, M., Lapalme, G.: A systematic analysis of performance measures for classification tasks. Inf. Process. Manag. **45**(4), 427–437 (2009). https://doi.org/10.1016/J.IPM.2009.03.002
24. Stamatelatos, M., Vesely, W., Dugan, J., Fragola, J., Minarick, J., Railsback, J.: Fault tree handbook with aerospace applications (2002)
25. Taskesen, E.: PCA: a Python package for principal component analysis (2020). https://erdogant.github.io/pca
26. Verkuil, B., Budde, C.E., Bucur, D.: Automated fault tree learning from continuous-valued sensor data: a case study on domestic heaters. Int. J. Prognostics Health Manag. **13**(2) (2022)

27. Waghen, K., Ouali, M.: Interpretable logic tree analysis: a data-driven fault tree methodology for causality analysis. Expert Syst. Appl. **136**, 376–391 (2019). https://doi.org/10.1016/J.ESWA.2019.06.042
28. Waghen, K., Ouali, M.: Multi-level interpretable logic tree analysis: a data-driven approach for hierarchical causality analysis. Expert Syst. Appl. **178**, 115035 (2021). https://doi.org/10.1016/J.ESWA.2021.115035
29. Waghen, K., Ouali, M.: A data-driven fault tree for a time causality analysis in an aging system. Algorithms **15**(6), 178 (2022). https://doi.org/10.3390/A15060178

Logika: The Sireum Verification Framework

Robby, John Hatcliff[✉], and Jason Belt

Kansas State University, Manhattan, KS 66506, USA
{robby,hatcliff,belt}@ksu.edu

Abstract. This paper gives an overview of Logika – a highly automated and interactive verification framework, that is designed for scalability and usability across a wide spectrum of users from beginners to experts in formal methods. To support the intuition of developers, it emphasizes programming constructs and idioms in both its contract-based specifications and integrated proof language. To integrate with developer workflows, verification feedback is provided directly within the industrial strength IntelliJ-based Sireum Integrated Verification Environment (IVE) and is expressed directly in terms of code features instead of lower-level SMT constraints or theorem prover languages. To support tailoring to different domains and properties, Logika includes multiple extensibility mechanisms to customize property specifications, verification rules, and proof tactics. To scale to large systems, Logika provides carefully engineered incremental verification and leverages modern hardware for (massive) parallelization on server-based platforms. To illustrate the wide range of Logika use cases for effective formal methods, we describe how Logika is being used to teach large classes of undergraduate students as well as to support industrial defense-related research projects. We present Logika performance experiments on both infrastructure and application code used on industry projects within the HAMR model-driven development tool chain for the AADL SAE standard architecture specification language.

1 Introduction

Several important qualities are needed for a code-level formal methods tool to be widely used, particularly in industry. Specifications and verification results must be presented in notations familiar to developers. The formal analysis must be scalable and predictable. The entire framework must be capable of handling the types of properties and code for which there are pressing needs for assurance. The tool capabilities must be integrated into widely used tooling and support use in realistic workflows.

Generally, the consensus is that, to be effective for conventional software developers, formal methods tools must be highly automated. Recent advances in Satisfiability Modulo Theory (SMT) solving have made significant industrial impacts in automated verification (e.g., [3,34]). Yet, some of the most impactful uses of formal methods for code-level verification (e.g., the CompCert compiler [24], the verified seL4 microkernel) were carried out in interactive theorem provers (ITP), which require a lot of manual interactions. These efforts have been undertaken by formal methods experts and applied to infrastructure code (as opposed to application code) that will be relied on and reused across many applications. Scaling was achieved using purpose-built abstraction layers to support verification, and reasoning techniques including resolution theorem proving and term rewriting.

We are intrigued by the tradeoffs and tensions between the approaches, and would like to understand if they could be reconciled (at least to some extent) in a single tool. More precisely, is it possible to build a highly automated SMT-based tool satisfying the effectiveness properties above, yet present *some* ITP techniques integrated with SMT-based code-level verification that "typical, but well-trained" developers might be able to use when SMT bogs down or when custom-built abstractions are useful for scaling?

SMT-based automated verification approaches are limited due to the inherent incompleteness when solving complex theories (e.g., quantified properties), which are required for reasoning about most interesting complex system properties. Counter example generation can help in such situations, but it is not always possible for SMT solvers to generate satisfying assignments, or it may take a long time to generate one (e.g., when reasoning about large bitvector integers/floating point numbers). This causes unpredictability issues from the user's perspective when applying SMT-based approaches. That is, when SMT solvers cannot discharge verification conditions (VCs), it is often difficult for users to understand what should be done to make progress. This problem is significantly exacerbated due to the challenge in providing SMT solving feedback to the users due to the sophisticated encoding of system VCs to the relatively low-level SMT queries. Most SMT solvers offer different strategies/heuristics that can be configured as solver-specific options, but it is a challenge to figure out the appropriate options to use for a given VC. Hints (e.g., as assertions) can be provided to help SMT-solving but it can be frustrating for users to figure out what hints to provide.

ITP tools fare better in this aspect because they are designed from the ground up for user interactions using a plethora of proof tactics (or even user-defined ones) systematically (i.e., predictable) for users to make progress. However, ITP tools require highly-trained and experienced experts in order to be successfully applied. Moreover, users are expected to model/translate the system to the ITP tool input language (often manually) and conduct the verification by term rewriting at that abstraction level (i.e., typically expensive, often prohibitively so, to employ). We desire to combine SMT-based automated verification with some aspects of ITP-style interactive reasoning in a single general verification framework. We would like the ITP-style aspects to work seamlessly with the SMT-based aspects and work at the *source code* level of abstraction, instead of requiring users to reason using a separate tool in terms of encodings in ITP input languages.

In this tool paper, we present an overview of the Logika verifier for Slang – a safety-critical subset of Scala. We describe how Logika aims to enable effective use of formal methods on real systems by addressing the challenges outlined above. Logika and Slang have been developed within a number of industry projects with Galois and Collins Aerospace with funding from the US Air Force Research Laboratory, US Army, and the Defense Advanced Research Projects Agency (DARPA). Slang and Logika are part of the larger Sireum framework that provides tools and infrastructure libraries for developing model/language analysis, transformation, and assurance capabilities. Most of Sireum is coded in Slang, which enables us to apply Logika to verify aspects of Sireum itself.

The contributions of this paper are as follows.

- We present the design goals and industrial usage context for Logika. A strategic theme for technology transition is the use of Slang as a verifiable intermediate language from which embedded C and Rust can be generated.
- We describe how we have embedded a rich contract language within Scala's syntactic features along with our decisions regarding which Scala features to include in Slang to enable Logika verification objectives while yielding a programming language capable of realistic system development.
- We illustrate how Logika verification is presented in IntelliJ – the most widely used integrated development environment (IDE) for Scala. This includes some of the themes that we emphasize in the Logika formal methods user experience (UX).
- We describe the significant engineering efforts including incremental verification, massive parallelization, and server-based architectural approaches that are used to achieve scalability of Logika verification.
- We describe Logika's novel approach for integrating highly automated SMT-based symbolic execution verification with an explicit and extensible proof language that supports theorem-prover-like verification directly within Slang. We illustrate this via Logika's rewriting tactics that provide built in support for proof term simplification based on Slang semantics.
- We summarize experimental results of Logika verification on different classes of code and specifications.

We also emphasize transitioning of formal methods into practice via education: Logika has been used for nine years to teach 2000+ undergraduate students at Kansas State University, and has been used for three years in both undergraduate and graduate courses at Aarhus University. The entire Sireum framework including Logika is publicly available under an open source license, accompanied by an extensive collection of teaching materials [40].

2 Design Goals and Background

Figure 1 presents the primary goals that drove the design of Logika. The goals collectively emphasize integrating specification and verification (both automated and manual proofs) directly with programming notations, activities, and tools.

The Slang dialect of Scala was designed "hand and glove" with Logika to achieve the goals of Fig. 1 while also supporting development for programming language and model processing as well as for embedded systems. Slang retains some of the expressive higher-level features of Scala (classes, traits, higher-order

> **G1 – Accessible:** Contract specifications, proof language, verification activities, and verification feedback should be presented using developer-friendly programming language syntax. The framework should ensure *continuity of user experience (UX)* by presenting information and interactions at the same level of abstraction across all specifications, development and verification activities, and verification reports, within the same IDE.
> **G2 – Usable:** Verification should respond with timely feedback, provide easy-to-access and understandable summaries of verification objectives and status.
> **G3 – Scalable:** Specification and verification should scale gracefully to large systems by leveraging modern compute architectures to support *massive server-based parallelization and distribution*, *optimized re-verification*, and *focused verification* (applying interactive verification only on immediately relevant artifacts).
> **G4 – Effective:** The framework should support implementation of real systems with contract notations that are rich enough to capture relevant properties ranging from abstract to full functional behavior specification.
> **G5 – Aligned with other quality assurance techniques:** Specification and verification should align with other quality assurance techniques such as testing.
> **G6 – Seamless integration of automated verification with manual proofs:** The framework should support highly automated verification and manual proof within the same tool environment, using programmer-oriented notations.
> **G7 – Extensible proof language:** The proof language should support the addition of new proof rules (whose soundness may be established externally) and new abstractions. This allows the proof language to be tailored to domain-specific reasoning principles, which supports easier use and greater scalability (multiple deduction steps associated with a particular domain can be encapsulated in a single derived rule).

Fig. 1. Logika Design Goals

functions) while restricting them to a form that enables more effective verification. A subset of Slang (called "Slang Embedded") is further restricted to constructs that can be translated to C and Rust appropriate for embedded systems. For a detailed overview of Slang features and design rationale, see [30].

Examples of Slang's restrictions of higher-level Scala features include: (a) a modified type system that strictly separates immutable and mutable ("yin-yang") types and (b) restrictions on mutable object aliasing, allowing aliasing to only be introduced in a single programming construct (i.e., method invocation) under certain object separation constraints. These customizations reduce developer reasoning effort and significantly simplify formal analyses. For example, verification can be done without explicitly modeling the object heap while limiting immutables to directed acyclic graph and mutables to tree structures (this does not preclude graph algorithms to be realized, e.g., [31]). Slang's *extension interfaces* (akin to those in the Bogor model checker [29]) allow Slang to interface to full Scala, Java, and C/Rust libraries, as well as achieving domain-specific customizations.

While Slang is a strict Scala subset, its programming language features are still rich enough to support large application development. The largest system implemented in Slang is Sireum itself (which includes Slang, Logika, and HAMR [15]). This allows for self-application of Sireum tooling to its own Slang codebase. At this point, the Sireum codebase consists of 35 (Maven) modules with close to 300k lines of code as 83.9% Slang, 10.4% Scala, and 5.7% Java. The Scala and Java code are extension bindings to reuse existing facilities such as for Slang contract/proof language embedding in Scala, Scala parsing, file/network accesses, process spawning, parallel collection, etc. The self-contained Sireum (fat) jar assembly, which includes all of its library dependencies, sits at 75Mb, while its size is only 29 Mb without library dependencies. This has some implications on our strategy for trustworthiness described later.

In addition to using Slang with standard JVM-based Scala/Java tools and ecosystems, the Slang Embedded subset can be transpiled to C without requiring garbage collection at runtime (i.e., objects are globally/stack-allocated). For additional assurance, the translated C code can be compiled using the CompCert verified C compiler [24]. We are developing transpilation of Slang Embedded code and contracts to Rust (with Verus [22]) as part of an ongoing DARPA PROVERS project led by Collins Aerospace.

The primary use of Slang and Logika on industrial research projects has been in the context of high-assurance model-based development at Collins Aerospace [8,11] and Galois [17,19]. Given an AADL [2] component-based system architecture model, the Sireum HAMR high assurance embedded system engineering framework generates AADL runtime services in Slang Embedded that can be deployed in various platforms, including the seL4 verified micro-kernel (via C) with formal evidence that architectural constraints are preserved, helping to guarantee safe/secure inter-component spatial and temporal separations [8]. The smallest HAMR AADL-based system – a building temperature control system, can be deployed on an STM32 board with only 192Kb SRAM. In collaboration with Collins Aerospace and seL4 developers, HAMR was used to build an experimental mission control subsystem running on seL4 for the Boeing CH-47 Chinook helicopter platform. In addition to supporting verification of thread component application code [19], Logika was used to verify key aspects of HAMR's AADL run-time libraries, including the inter-thread communication event queuing libraries. We recently developed SlangCheck [16,17] – a parallel/distributed Slang contract-based randomized testing framework for validating Slang/HAMR-based systems. Under the DARPA PROVERS Collins Aerospace INSPECTA project, we are prototyping an additional HAMR front-end for SysMLv2 [42], guided by HAMR's AADL semantics specification [18] and verification framework mechanized in Isabelle [14].

Regarding the primary developer-facing tooling, the Sireum Integrated Verification Environment (IVE) – a customized version of IntelliJ IDEA – integrates various Sireum tools such as the Slang front-end (providing, e.g., type checking, refactoring, etc.), the Proyek incremental/parallel build tool, and Logika, all running as microservices in a background Sireum server. HAMR is currently integrated in the Eclipse-based OSATE AADL development environment. Migration of HAMR to IVE will be ramped up as we transition to using SysMLv2. Sireum's server-based tooling architecture eases support for other environments in the future (e.g., VSCode).

Next, we highlight Logika features that meet the design goals above to a large extent. Section 4 describes Logika applications to HAMR, among others.

3 Features

Figure 2 shows a screenshot of Sireum IVE with an illustrative Slang example to drive the discussion throughout this section. The screenshot is actually four

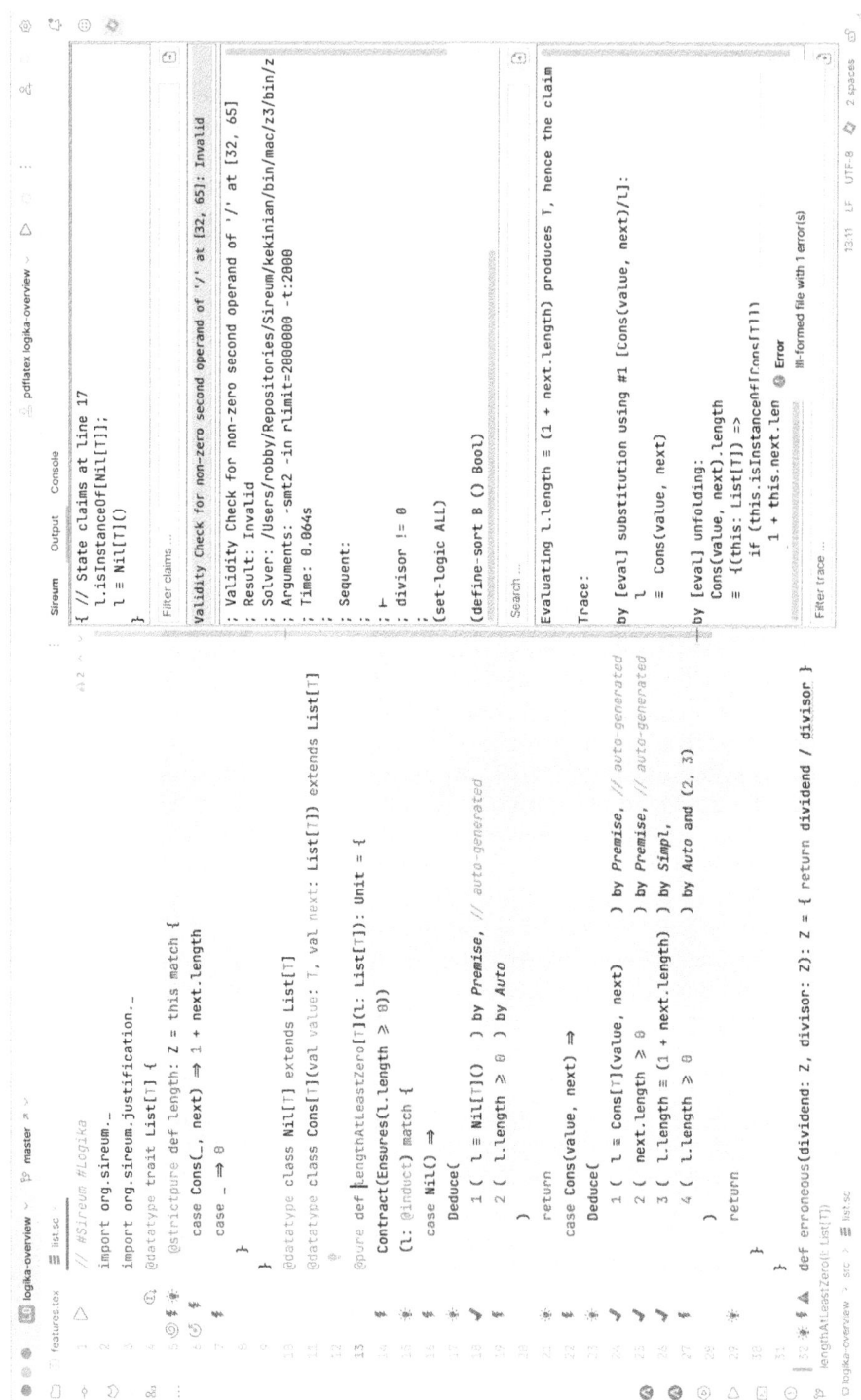

Fig. 2. An Illustrative Example in Sireum IVE

screenshots merged into one in order to save space, i.e., the merging of the three different kinds of Logika feedback based on user actions on the right-hand side of Fig. 2, which we will describe subsequently. The left-hand side is a customized IntelliJ Scala editor that understands Slang. `@datatype` denotes strictly immutable types (i.e., can only refer to other immutables). `@strictpure` methods cannot have side effects while `@pure` ones can make local/non-observational effects. `Z` is an arbirary-precision integer type. `lengthAtLeastZero` is in Slang's method theorem form (`@pure` with `Unit` return type), whose only value is its contract. Its postcondition `Contract Ensures` claims that `List#length` always returns a non-negative integer. *Proving* the claim requires a structural induction proof, which is *programmed* as `lengthAtLeastZero`'s implementation.

As can be observed, Slang contracts (line 14) and proof language (the `@induct` and `Deduce`s) are expressed purely in Scala, thus Scala's tooling ecosystem naturally works on them. For example, the Scala compiler checks for pattern matching exhaustivity, and all the excellent IntelliJ software engineering tooling (e.g., renaming variables) work in code, contracts, and proofs as is. These specification-level only constructs are erased in compilation targets so as not to affect runtime behaviors. `@induct match` denotes an induction scheme that Logika treats specially. That is, in addition to the inferred claims as results of successful pattern matching at lines 18 and 24 in Fig. 2, Logika infers the induction hypothesis at line 25. Each `Deduce` contains proof steps. Each proof step can be optionally uniquely labeled or positively numbered (can be unordered) but they have to be justified by applying previously proven lemmas/theorems or by using `@just` proof tactic methods such as `Premise`. These `@just` methods are declared at the Slang user-space level, in this case in the Slang runtime library written in Slang, but their implementation have to be provided as a plugin using Logika's extension facility described subsequently. The two `Deduce`s are actually optional in this simple proof because Logika can automatically prove it without them with just the `@induct match` structure, but they are kept for illustration's sake.

We next discuss Logika features, mixing its technical approaches with some accessibility/usability features interspersed (space constraints do not permit detailed exposition, thus we describe them at a high level, intuitively).

SMT-Based Automation: Logika uses symbolic execution (SymExe) [21] as its main verification engine with calls to SMT solvers to discharge VCs and check branch satisfiability to prune infeasible paths for reducing verification costs. Logika can use any SMT-LIB [41] compliant solver supporting quantification reasoning, but it ships with cvc4/5 [4,7] and Z3 [26] (as of this writing, cvc4 performs better than cvc5 on some queries, e.g., [35]).

Logika's engine implements both contract-based summarizing (state-merging at branch joints) and bounded loop/recursion unrolling SymExe that can be applied compositionally (former), interprocedurally (latter), or mixed based on user requests. Allowing interprocedural verification in some cases (e.g., when using refactored `@strictpure` helper methods used in contracts) helps reduce user specification burden. Users are sufficiently notified at the specific program location when bounds are exhausted as they affect the verification result soundness.

At its core, Logika's engine represents SymExe path conditions at a low level to simplify its implementation (akin to 3-address code in compilers). However, Logika's feedback is always expressed at the Slang source level. By default, Logika reports state claims that it infers to hold at each program point and offer them as ☀ editor gutter light bulb icon decorations shown in Fig. 2, which open a tool window on a click action to display the inferred Slang claim expressions (e.g., the top-right text area in Fig. 2 for line 17's lightbulb). Each claim can be copy-pasted directly as a valid claim in `Deduce` using `Premise`. The claim expressions are max-column-formatted for readability (user-configurable) and can be filtered via text search (as the user types). This feature is similar to ITP tool proof state claims display, which helps to ease transition between Logika automation and rewriting as proven claims are typically used to prove other/desired claims interactively. To some extent, the inferred claims also serve as human-readable evidence helping to confirm that Logika works as intended.

Similarly, SMT solver calls are represented using the ⚡ lightning editor gutter icon decorations to display SMT queries representing VCs and satisfiability checks. Any erroneous result is highlighted with a ▲ red exclaim triangle icon with a tooltip error message beside the lightning icon and an accompanying "red wavy" underlining on the offending expression (e.g., the `divisor` usage at line 32 in Fig. 2). Each query display is preambled with the SMT solvers used, their configured options, solving timing and results, and the Slang-level claim representation of the query (e.g., the middle-right text area for the lightning at line 32). The query can be searched in the tool window or ⎘ button click exported into a file and opened in an IntelliJ text editor tab. The IVE offers syntax highlighting for SMT query viewing/editing, and it recognizes Logika SMT query preamble for push-button launching the SMT solvers with the specific options listed there. Thus, users have the option to confirm the results of Logika SMT solver calls, or even play around with the query (for those rare SMT aficionados).

Moreover, Logika reports statement verification coverage by background highlighting code regions that have been analyzed (e.g., lines 5–8 and 14–30 in Fig. 2). As previously mentioned, Logika runs as a background service. Logika can be configured to verify files upon explicit key/menu action, on save, or as-you-type, with automatic cancellation of running verification process when a new one is requested. All feedback is communicated asynchronously once generated as Logika progresses, which the IVE renders when received so the user is kept up-to-date and can inspect feedback during an ongoing verification process.

Incremental/Focused Verification: One way that Logika addresses Goal **G3** is to trade off computing resources to optimize for user time by employing a stack of caching techniques throughout its verification pipeline phases. The smart caching enables it to conservatively skip analysis and reuse analysis results of un-impacted code upon changes across its server verification sessions (**G3**- *incremental verification*). In addition, it avoids processing irrelevant parts of the system under analysis for specific verification requests by maintaining a variety of dependence information and then only considering the current verification activity and the other elements on which it depends (**G3**- *focused verification*). For project-level dependences, Logika uses Sireum's Proyek build tool that provides incremental processing of Slang projects. Given a project, Proyek first builds the project's module (directed acyclic) dependency graph and processes the modules breadth-first starting from root modules. At each graph level, all Slang files are fingerprinted (by SHA3 secure hashing) and then parsed. Each syntax tree is cached by the file's fingerprint, which avoids parsing unmodified files in subsequent verification requests. After the Slang type outlining phase that fully resolves and type checks method and type signatures (including contracts), each module's resulting type hierarchy (including symbol table and type table) is fingerprinted and cached (note that unlike Scala, Slang method signatures have to be fully typed, to ease type outlining). Full type checking is focused based on the verification request, e.g., compositional verification of a method does not require type checking the entire system. Verification proceeds after type checking. Proyek's breadth-first traversal stops when all modules containing requested verification files have been processed.

During verification, Logika caches states after each transition resulting from statement symbolic execution, proof step deduction, etc., based on the type hierarchy fingerprint. Moreover, it caches each SMT query result based on its corresponding state path conditions. The IVE keeps track of individual elements of verification feedback (e.g., results of SMT queries) and associates each with the code-level verification coverage information (e.g., whether or not a particular line of code or expression traversed during symbolic execution). On cache hits, Logika skips state transitions and only sends the skipped code coverage report to the IVE. The IVE then simply "replays" the feedback associated with the coverage information. All the above brings about the magical perceived effect to the user that re-verification is incrementally very fast. For example, re-verifying an entire (reasonably-sized) file without modification is almost instantaneous on modern (laptop) hardware. Modifying a statement in a method and re-verifying it has the effect of the IVE replaying the feedback up to before the modified statement. Each Logika caching category can be turned off for users equipped with less capable hardware.

Parallelization: To address Goal **G3**, Logika offers multiple parallelization strategies to take advantage of the ever-increasing availability of high core count in modern CPUs. Proyek can parallelize processing of modules at the same breadth level. Type checking program units after type outlining is also suitable for parallelization. Verification of each contract case of a program unit is embarrassingly parallel, and it is ripe for a distributed approach in the future. Logika also offers a couple of local parallelization techniques that can be employed when analyzing a program unit. The first is branch parallelization, useful for analyzing pattern matching and if-then-else statements (more is better). The branch parallelization first executes all the branch conditions to compute each branch's entry state, then executes the branch body independently. To maximize branch parallelization, Logika does not merge method return points when checking method postconditions. That is, each return point checks the postconditions separately. This also simplifies the return points' path conditions (i.e., postcondition VCs), thus reducing SMT-solving complexity. Hence, having multiple return points as shown in Fig. 2 can be beneficial to reduce verification costs. Another local parallelization that Logika offers is SMT-solving parallelization. That is, Logika can be configured to use a suite of SMT solvers and/or the same solver with different solving options to use for each query. Recognizing the fact that a particular solver-option configuration may work better than others for a certain query (unfortunately, unpredictable), such a suite of solver calls can be parallelized. The fastest one that gives a conclusive result wins out and cancels the other calls.

Because Logika communicates feedback asynchronously as it progresses, users can visually observe Logika's parallelization in action in the IVE. For example, editor decorations on multiple method verifications progress in parallel. Similarly, decorations on branches appear in parallel. The fastest-winning SMT solver parallelization strategy is apparent in the feedback query preamble as shown in the middle right pane of Fig. 2, i.e., Logika lists only one solver-option configuration. If there is no conclusive result, Logika lists all the solvers and their corresponding options used along with their result and timing in the query preamble. All Logika parallelization is done using a parallel collection map-reduce computational pattern that is realized using a work-stealing fork/join implementation. Users can configure the number of cores (threads) that Logika should use if parallelization is enabled, as well as turning off any of the different strategies when running on resource challenged machines.

Extensibility: Our earlier work on the Bogor model checker was one of the first to emphasize extension interfaces in source code model checking tools. Bogor enabled tool builders to customize model checking algorithms and to add domain-specific modeling language extensions and semantics [13]. To support Goal **G7**, Logika's extension facility builds on Bogor concepts to provide a plugin architecture that enables parts of its verification submodules, such as its expression and statement SymExe engine to be customized and extended. This includes the previously discussed @just proof tactic method implementations. Logika can be configured to use an ordered list of plugins, each implementing one or more verification submodule API. Computationally, each submodule API kind is a partial function for querying whether the plugin wants to handle a specific verification task and then performing such task if the query is successful. For example, the @just API query accepts a proof step syntax tree that can be used to determine whether a plugin offers to handle it (e.g., based on the declared @just method fully qualified name and its signature). @just method handling API accepts the proof step tree, SymExe state, and previously deduced claims preceding it, and has access to all Logika configurations, type hierarchy, verification submodules, caching, etc. Each handler is expected to produce user-friendly feedback explicating the verification task result, which is denoted using the ✓ checkmark decoration in Fig. 2 (red colored for erroneous results). The API can optionally accept claims to focus on. For example, Auto by default uses all inferred/preceding proven claims to deduce the proof step claim via SMT solving if the claim has not already been inferred or previously proven (line 19 in Fig. 2). It also accepts claims to focus its reasoning using the and (...) syntax for reducing reasoning costs, e.g., to deduce the proof step claim at line 27 by only using proof step claims 2 (line 25) and 3 (line 26). Auto T (not shown) indicates that it should not use any of the preceding/inferred claims for its deduction.

Like Bogor specializations done by our group and others (e.g., [6,13]), customizations of Logika submodules are useful for applying it to various domains and/or for analyzing different kinds of properties. For example, SymExe optimizations can be introduced to optimize the engine to domain-specific abstract machines. In our case, we have specialized Logika SymExe submodules to support verification of secure conditional information flow, which we hope to present in the near future. Moreover, we are prototyping a temporal property reasoning approach for HAMR-based inter-component system traces (or their slices), by taking advantage of Logika's mixed compositional/interprocedural capability.

Rewriting System: Logika can potentially integrate with existing ITP tools by providing @just proof tactics that automatically export VCs to an ITP input language of interest. Avid ITP experts with vested experience can then work on proving the VCs at that level. Once proven, the proof tactics can confirm that the VCs have been proven using the specific ITP tools before accepting them. Based on availability of future opportunities, this can certainly be done to take advantages of existing decades-long ITP efforts. However, this unfortunately breaks Logika's continuity of UX principle (i.e., needing to work in two different tools, using two different program/specification representations, etc.). Therefore, as an example of supporting Goal **G6** (which emphasizes seamless integration of automatic verification with manual proof steps within the source code development environment), Logika provides a rewriting system that developers can use interactively similar to ITP tools. Logika adopts general aspects of Isabelle's rewriting system, including its bottom-up unification approach, conditional rewriting, etc. However, a key difference is that these concepts are realized at the Slang level of abstraction (instead of an encoding into a ITP representation), and the mechanism is presented to the developer via Logika's @just proof tactics. The Simpl proof tactic in Fig. 2 provides a simple illustration: the Logika simplifier rewrites the proof step claim at line 26 and reduces it to T (true), which is the accepting condition. Similar to Isabelle, Logika can generate human-readable rewriting traces, i.e., the bottom-right feedback text area in Fig. 2 holds trace information that provides evidence of successful verification ✓ at line 26. The traces can be filtered via a text search as the user types.

Another rewriting proof tactic is Rewrite as shown in Fig. 3. Rewrite takes an ordered rewrite set consisting of lemmas/theorems (e.g., zDistribute) and references to @abs methods to unfold (not shown), and a proven claim to be rewritten (e.g., 1 at lines 16 and 17). The RS rewrite set can be specified inline (line 16) or by defining a @rw val holding the rewrite set (line 10). Set union and difference work on RS, e.g., myRewriteSet ++ otherSet -- RS(m _), which can

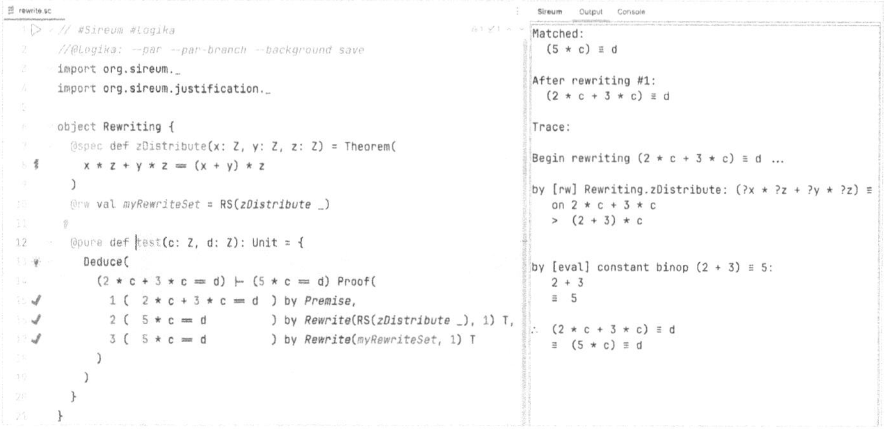

Fig. 3. Rewriting Example

also be stored in a @rw val or inlined. @abs methods are also strictly-pure, but they are not automatically unfolded when rewriting, unless specified in the rewrite set (similar to Isabelle's definition and fun distinction). For example, @strictpure List#length is automatically unfolded by Simpl in Fig. 2. The right textarea in Fig. 3 shows the evidence of ✔ for both lines 16 and 17 (i.e., they are the same). Note that the zDistribute specification-level theorem that is discharged by SMT-solving is used for rewriting; this provides a glimpse of the seamless interplay between Logika's automation and interaction possibilities.

One difference from Isabelle is that Logika is not a logical framework. That is, Slang as Logika's input language has fixed semantics. Thus, we leverage it to provide short-cuts for Slang semantics-based rewriting rules by realizing them as a Slang expression partial evaluator (instead of needing to pattern match against existing theorems and replace/substitute at each evaluation step). The evaluator works both top-down and bottom-up on expression trees. The feedback in Fig. 3 distinguishes when the rewriting system is used versus the evaluator ([rw] versus [eval], respectively). Simpl, actually, uses only the evaluator, while Rewrite uses both. Another difference is that Rewrite can be focused by labeling subexpressions of the argument claim, e.g., (e: @l) + f(x), which only rewrites e, leaving others unchanged.

Proof Engineering Support: In addition to benefiting from IntelliJ's software engineering tooling that naturally works on Slang code/contract/proof, the IVE offers additional Slang-specific tooling to support proof engineering. First, the @induct match proof structure in Fig. 2 was actually auto-generated. That is, one only needs to type 1: @induct and then ask the IVE to automatically generate the pattern match with all possible cases along with their inferred claims and induction hypotheses as Premises. That is, beside 1: @induct and lines 19, 26, and 27, lines 15–29 were automatically generated. Moreover, when adding proof steps, the user can ask the IVE to insert a proof step template (at the appro-

Table 1. Experiment Data (SMT validity checking configuration: `cvc4,-full-quant; z3;cvc5,-full-quant`; SMT satisfiability checking configuration: `z3`; SMT validity time/satisfiability time/resource limits: 2 sec./0.5 sec./2,000,000)

Example/ System	VNC -LoC	# of VCs	# of SATs	-P-B-S E(s)	-P-B-S V(s)	+P-B-S E(s)	+P-B-S V(s)	+P-B-S SpdUp	+P+B-S E(s)	+P+B-S V(s)	+P+B-S SpdUp	+P+B+S E(s)	+P+B+S V(s)	+P+B+S SpdUp
SlangRt	1664	1060	917	94.0	87.6	35.8	31.0	2.62×	37.2	32.3	2.53×	**21.3**	**16.5**	**4.41×**
OpSem-R	906	82	243	42.2	41.5	17.2	16.6	2.45×	**16.9**	**16.3**	**2.49×**	16.9	16.3	2.49×
Hamr-R	219	65	130	25.3	24.6	**11.4**	**10.7**	**2.22×**	**11.4**	**10.7**	**2.22×**	12.4	11.7	2.04×
TempCtrl	319	22	95	37.4	31.4	19.0	13.5	1.96×	**17.9**	**12.3**	**2.09×**	19.8	14.2	1.89×
Isolette	1179	64	266	91.9	85.5	27.2	21.4	3.37×	**26.1**	**20.3**	**3.51×**	35.8	30.0	2.57×
Hardens	683	16	28	21.3	14.8	**11.0**	**5.1**	**1.95×**	11.0	5.1	1.94×	11.2	5.2	1.91×
LMAadlQ	601	70	531	183.0	182.3	**33.6**	**33.0**	**5.44×**	40.9	40.2	4.48×	41.1	40.5	4.45×

priate place based on the location of the editor caret) with a unique (smallest fresh positive) numbering. For the example in Fig. 3, if the editor caret is at line 16 when the user asks the IVE for a regular proof step (there are other forms of proof step not presented here such as subproof, etc.), it will insert a new line after line 16 and put 4 (CLAIM) by Premise, which the user can edit. In addition, it is often the case the proof step numbering is out of order such as after the insertion above. The user can ask the IVE to reorder all the numbering, which also renumbers all their usages accordingly. Furthermore, IntelliJ can be used to reformat proofs because they are Scala. The IVE also offers proof reformatting to make sure the outermost parentheses between the proof step number/label and by are all at the same column on each Deduce, as shown in lines 15–17, to tidy up the proof to look more pleasant. The user can also ask the IVE to insert the current Logika configurations (e.g., SMT solver options, parallelization, background verification mode, etc.) at the top of the file (as shown in Fig. 3) or inlined at the editor caret as a special Sireum tool-option-setting `setOptions` method, e.g., `setOptions("Logika", "--interprocedural")`, which is recognized by Logika to perform inter-procedural verification from that point on.

Education and Training: We believe formal methods training is an important activity to support, and it should be done as early as possible in the education process. An earlier version of Logika and accompanying public online textbook and user's guide [39] have been used to teach undergraduate and graduate courses at our institution and by our collaborators at Aarhus University. We are committed to continually providing such support with the current version of Logika described in this paper. The current version's functionality subsumes that of the earlier version. Beyond the features that we have presented in this paper, it supports semi-manual reasoning about truth tables, propositional, predicate, and programming logics suitable for teaching beginning undergraduates. Custom proof tactics for such settings are provided to ease early student learning experience. The online textbook mentioned above [32] and other course materials have been converted to the current version of Logika and will be used for the first time in Fall 2024 courses. Our Aarhus collaborators have used Logika's automation presented here to teach graduate courses for the past year.

4 Assessment

This section demonstrates a variety of Logika applications on a collection of examples and (sub-) systems. Table 1 lists the examples/systems along with their verified number of non-comment lines of code/contract/proof (VNC-LoC), as well as their corresponding Logika performance timing. The experiment suite [37] includes SLANGRT – some of the Slang runtime library (e.g., option, either, array-based associated list, set, and map) that are pervasively used in Sireum, including by, for example, Logika and HAMR-generated AADL runtime services. The OPSEM-R example is a mechanization of both (inductive) specification and executable operational semantics of a small dynamically-typed expression language, with their refinement (galois connection) proofs. The HAMR-R example consists of some HAMR runtime services executable operational semantics with corresponding imperative implementations, along with their refinement proofs. This example is an initial prototype of our ongoing effort to directly verify that HAMR generated runtime services satisfy HAMR's high assurance AADL semantics. Both OPSEM-R and HAMR-R demonstrate the refinements of operational semantics specifications, down to their corresponding executable semantics, and finally their implementations, all codified in Slang and verified by Logika.

The suite also includes three HAMR-based systems: (a) TEMPCTRL – a building temperature control system, (b) ISOLETTE – a baby incubator system, and (c) Galois' HARDENS nuclear reactor trip system [36]. We previously used these systems to assess HAMR parallel/distributed contract-based unit [17] and system integration [16] testing frameworks based on SlangCheck, which offers a complementary validation approach. On each system, using Logika we verified contracts regarding: (a) AADL integration constraints (i.e., port data invariants are preserved by AADL component implementations), and (b) functional correctness of the application code for thread components, showing that application code conforms to component contracts for both periodic and sporadic (event triggered) components. TEMPCTRL has additional type invariants on temperature ranges. These contracts were automatically translated from GUMBO contracts [19] specified in their AADL architectural models, as part of HAMR AADL runtime services code generation, which helps in establishing traceability from high-level architectural design requirements.

For all of the above examples/systems, both implicit (i.e., absence of runtime errors such as indexing out of bounds) and explicitly-specified contracts are verified solely by using Logika automation. Additionally, each explicit contract claim is checked for satisfiability to ensure that it is not trivially false. The OPSEM-R example does require some deduction proof steps to connect operational semantic rules at their corresponding program point implementing them. Next, we focus our evaluation on Logika's scalability, as accessibility and usability are best appreciated first-hand in the IVE (i.e., proper evaluations require costly human case studies, which can be parts of future efforts once further matured; so far, we drove improvements on these aspects based on our self-applications and educational deployments). Table 1 gives Logika's performance when the different parallelization strategies are turned on (+) or off (-) on a 14-core Apple M3 Max 14-inch laptop with 128 GB RAM, representing a capable modern hardware for software development. Each timing data point is averaged over 20 runs, and each run was set without caching using Sireum's command-line interface (i.e., producing worst-case timing). In this experiment, Logika uses the same number of threads as the CPU cores to parallelize verification of **P**rogram units and their contract case, **B**ranches, and **S**MT suite calls using the default Logika SMT solver configuration (-**S**MT parallelization means the suite is called sequentially in order based on the listed solver-option configuration in Table 1 until a conclusive result is found or the list is exhausted). Note that the end-to-end running **E**lapsed time, in seconds (s), include JVM's cold boot up and (focused) Slang front-end processing of the entire Slang runtime library, which is 25.3 kilo-lines of code (kLoC). Additionally, the timing for the 3 HAMR-based systems also captures the processing of their entire Slang Embedded codebase (including their generated AADL runtime services, etc.): TEMPCTRL (13.4 kLoC), ISOLETTE (25.1 kLoC), and HARDENS (31.2 kLoC). The **V**erification time is only for the Logika phase after the Slang front-end processing. The **SpdUp** columns give comparative **E**lapsed speed-up of parallelization configurations compared without parallelization, with the best ones highlighted using a **bold** font (the speed-up is actually better when based on the **V**erification time, which works in favor for Logika's incremental approach via caching across verification sessions).

As can be observed from Table 1, parallelization is effective in reducing the end-to-end **E**lapsed time for the user. The effectiveness varies based on the characteristics of the verification requests and targets. The **P** parallelization generally gives greater improvements as the number of program unit/contract cases to be verified increases. Enabling **B** can provide additional speed-up when processing many branches with long bodies; one detrimental case is LMAADLQ where many of its branches consist of 2 and/or short-bodied branch cases. The **S** parallelization is more effective for more complex path conditions when many of the SMT solver-option configurations cannot give conclusive results, and it can be ineffective if the first listed solver-option can quickly discharge most (if not all) VCs. In many cases where the different parallelization strategies are ineffective, the overhead slowdown is quite low, thus, we believe the benefits outweigh the overhead risks (i.e., **+P+B+S** is the default Logika option in the IVE). It is perhaps worth noting that we previously deployed Logika on an (unfortunately more than a decade old) 80-core machine to achieve massive parallelization [38]. We are looking for opportunities to modernize our computing facility for conducting large-scale massive parallelization empirical studies, along with our envisioned distributed approach.

Finally, the LMAADLQ example contains a linked-list and linked-list-based map with lookup/update operations and some corresponding theorems about them (i.e., looking up a key k on a map updated with k and its value v produces v, and looking up a key k_1 on a map m updated with another key k_2 and its value v is the same as looking up k_1 on m). The example also includes a mechanization of AADL's event bounded/unbounded queueing dispatch executable operational semantics, parameterized by its full-queue policies (e.g., drop latest/earliest, error), with frame condition and well-formed-ness preservation theorems on queue operations. The LMAADLQ example demonstrates the interplay of Logika's automation and rewriting system. For this example, we used automation as much as possible and only resorted to specify proof annotations and/or use the rewriting system whenever SMT solving cannot discharge some VCs. Overall, there are 18 theorems, of which 9 (50%) are automatically discharged. Of the rest, 2 theorems (11.1%) require proof annotations without induction, and 7 theorems (38.9%) require inductions of which only 1 (5.6%) of them can be automatically verified without further proof annotations. Overall, there is a total of 20 induction cases (all with early `return` similar to Fig. 2), 5 (25%) of which can be proven automatically. The remaining 15 (75%) induction cases required proof annotations. There is a total number of 106 proof steps involved in the proof annotations. 62 (58.5%) `Premise`s are used to introduce inferred claims for using the rewriting systems, 13 of which (12.3% of proof steps) were generated by the IVE `@induct` expansion and the remaining 49 (46.2% of proof steps) were copy-pasted from inferred claims. `Auto`s were used whenever possible to build up claims for conditional rewriting/partial evaluation context (there are 10 of them, i.e., 9.4%). `Simpl` partial evaluation discharged 30 (28.3%) of the rest, and the remaining 4 (3.8%) used rewriting with a `RS`. There is one case where rewriting is followed by an `Auto`, illustrating that rewriting can intermediately help automation to make further progress, in addition to its more common usage patterns for final proof completion whenever SMT solving gives up/timed out.

Trustworthiness of Logika: At this point, Logika focuses on providing explanatory developer-friendly feedback, which can help to give some level of confidence of the correctness of the Logika implementation, since issues can be spotted based on the feedback. However, we also aspire to eventually provide a relatively small trusted computing base (TCB). It is cost prohibitive to develop Logika as a mechanically certified tool, especially due to its large dependencies. Instead, it is possible to enhance Logika as a certifying tool, i.e., by generating proof certificates that can be checked using a proof checker with much smaller TCB. We envision taking a similar approach to what we have done for Spark Ada 2014 in Coq [33], i.e., by first mechanizing Slang's semantics. It can then be shown that Logika SymExe and rewriting for a particular verification application is sound with respect to Slang's semantics. SMT solving with proof generation is still an active research effort (e.g., [5]), but such a capability that works on all SMT-LIB logics will help in reducing Logika's TCB.

5 Related Work

There have been much excellent work on automated program verification and ITP tools (e.g., [1,9,10,12,20,22,23,25,27,28]), so we summarize the comparative discussion here. In general, we believe Logika is uniquely positioned compared to other work in terms of its seamless integration of automated verification and rewriting capabilities that provides a continuous UX, immersion in

regular system development workflow even on large codebases (including on its own, over time), developer-oriented feedback, and other scalability, accessibility, and usability features described previously. As an emerging tool, however, the large body of other work gives maturity advantages with years of iterative feature-set and verified theorem/library additions/refinements, gaining confidence through usage, and for certified tools, smaller TCB. For example, Logika currently does not have an automatic termination analysis (i.e., it has to be manually elaborated), which we hope to offer in the future (the LMAADLQ example in [37] includes a termination analysis elaboration example using a program-level assertion). Also, Logika's proof language currently always requires claims to be explicitly specified. While this declarative proof style helps with proof readability, we also desire to support other ITP proof styles, e.g., allowing only the proof tactics to be specified without intermediate claims for speed-proving. Moreover, Logika can benefit from reusing existing bodies of established theorem libraries from various ITP tools by importing their theorem libraries to Slang.

As mentioned previously, Logika is very specific for Slang and is not a logical framework designed to ease direct embedding of other logics. However, we believe Logika's extensibility, like Bogor, can provide support for effective/efficient domain/property-specific applications by modeling the domain abstract machines using Slang's language extensions and by customizing Logika for handling those using first-class constructs with specialized algorithms for relevant property categories. Such an approach, however, should be treated using Logika as a back-end verifier, preferably with accompanying automatic translation, instead of something to be presented directly to the target domain audience (for UX's sake). For example, we are using this approach to also provide system property verifications at the architectural model abstraction level in HAMR.

6 Conclusion

The Logika verification framework is a part of the growing validation and verification (V&V) suite in the Sireum high assurance system engineering platform. We have presented Logika's design goals, features, and applications, with some discussions on future enhancements and further customized applications. Our application of Logika to Sireum itself, even at its beginning stage, has exposed unforeseeable issues, detected subtle/wide-reaching regressions, and brought invaluable insights driving further improvements, which we commit to continue. We believe Logika's seamless integration of SMT-based SymExe automation with rewriting approach, targeting a high-level mixed paradigms programming language supporting large application development and scaling to the regular software development workflows, is very effective and can be adopted in other contexts. We hope the descriptions of Logika's scalability, accessibility, and usability emphases help foster formal methods discussion and efforts in these aspects.

Acknowledgments. This work was primarily funded by a DARPA SBIR Phase 2 SIRFUR award, with some support from the DARPA CASE and PROVERS projects. The authors would like to express their sincere thanks to Todd Carpenter (Galois) and David Hardin (Collins Aerospace) for their continual strong support since the early development of Logika. We would also like to thank Stefan Hallerstede (Aarhus), Danielle Stewart (Galois), and Julie Thornton (KSU) for the numerous discussions and their invaluable feedback applying Logika in research and/or educational settings.

References

1. Ahrendt, W., Beckert, B., Bubel, R., Hähnle, R., Schmitt, P.H., Ulbrich, M. (eds.): Deductive Software Verification - The KeY Book - From Theory to Practice. LNCS, vol. 10001. Springer, Cham (2016). https://doi.org/10.1007/978-3-319-49812-6
2. Society of Automotive Engineers: Architecture analysis & design language (AADL). Aerospace Standard AS5506 (2004)
3. Backes, J., et al.: Semantic-based automated reasoning for AWS access policies using SMT. In: Formal Methods in Computer Aided Design (FMCAD), pp. 1–9. IEEE (2018)
4. Barbosa, H., et al.: cvc5: a versatile and industrial-strength SMT solver. In: Fisman, D., Rosu, G. (eds.) TACAS 2022. LNCS, vol. 13243, pp. 415–442. Springer, Cham (2022). https://doi.org/10.1007/978-3-030-99524-9_24
5. Barbosa, H., et al.: Generating and exploiting automated reasoning proof certificates. Commun. ACM **66**(10), 86–95 (2023)
6. Baresi, L., Ghezzi, C., Mottola, L.: Loupe: verifying publish-subscribe architectures with a magnifying lens. IEEE Trans. Softw. Eng. **37**, 228–246 (2011)
7. Barrett, C., et al.: CVC4. In: Gopalakrishnan, G., Qadeer, S. (eds.) Computer Aided Verification (CAV), pp. 171–177. Springer, Cham (2011). https://doi.org/10.1007/978-3-642-22110-1_14
8. Belt, J., et al.: Model-driven development for the seL4 microkernel using the HAMR framework. J. Syst. Archit. **134**, 102789 (2022)
9. Bertot, Y., Castéran, P.: Interactive Theorem Proving and Program Development: Coq'Art: The Calculus of Inductive Constructions. Springer, Cham (2013)
10. Boyer, R.S., Moore, J.S.: A theorem prover for a computational logic. In: Stickel, M.E. (ed.) CADE 1990. LNCS, vol. 449, pp. 1–15. Springer, Heidelberg (1990). https://doi.org/10.1007/3-540-52885-7_75
11. Cofer, D.D., et al.: Cyberassured systems engineering at scale. IEEE Secur. Priv. **20**(3), 52–64 (2022)
12. Dockins, R., Foltzer, A., Hendrix, J., Huffman, B., McNamee, D., Tomb, A.: Constructing semantic models of programs with the software analysis workbench. In: Blazy, S., Chechik, M. (eds.) VSTTE 2016. LNCS, vol. 9971, pp. 56–72. Springer, Cham (2016). https://doi.org/10.1007/978-3-319-48869-1_5
13. Dwyer, M.B., Robby, Deng, X., Hatcliff, J.: Space reductions for model checking quasi-cyclic systems. In: Alur, R., Lee, I. (eds.) EMSOFT 2003. LNCS, vol. 2855, pp. 173–189. Springer, Heidelberg (2003). https://doi.org/10.1007/978-3-540-45212-6_12
14. Hallerstede, S., Hatcliff, J.: A mechanized semantics for component-based systems in the HAMR AADL runtime. In: Cámara, J., Jongmans, S.S. (eds.) FACS 2023. LNCS, vol. 14485, pp. 45–64. Springer, Cham (2024). https://doi.org/10.1007/978-3-031-52183-6_3

15. Hatcliff, J., Belt, J., Robby, Carpenter, T.: HAMR: an AADL multi-platform code generation toolset. In: Margaria, T., Steffen, B. (eds.) ISoLA 2021. LNCS, vol. 13036, pp. 274–295. Springer, Cham (2021). https://doi.org/10.1007/978-3-030-89159-6_18
16. Hatcliff, J., Belt, J., Robby, Hardin, D.: Integrated contract-based unit and system testing for component-based systems. In: Benz, N., Gopinath, D., Shi, N. (eds.) NFM 2024. LNCS, vol. 14627, pp. 406–426. Springer, Cham (2024). https://doi.org/10.1007/978-3-031-60698-4_25
17. Hatcliff, J., Belt, J., Robby, Legg, J., Stewart, D., Carpenter, T.: Automated property-based testing from AADL component contracts. In: Cimatti, A., Titolo, L. (eds.) FMICS 2023. LNCS, vol. 14290, pp. 131–150. Springer, Cham (2023). https://doi.org/10.1007/978-3-031-43681-9_8
18. Hatcliff, J., Hugues, J., Stewart, D., Wrage, L.: Formalization of the AADL runtime services. In: Margaria, T., Steffen, B. (eds.) ISoLA 2022. LNCS, vol. 13702, pp. 105–134. Springer, Cham (2022). https://doi.org/10.1007/978-3-031-19756-7_7
19. Hatcliff, J., Stewart, D., Belt, J., Robby, Schwerdfeger, A.: An AADL contract language supporting integrated model- and code-level verification. In: Proceedings of the 2022 ACM Workshop on High Integrity Language Technology, HILT 2022 (2022)
20. Hoang, D., Moy, Y., Wallenburg, A., Chapman, R.: SPARK 2014 and GNATprove. Int. J. Softw. Tools Technol. Transfer **17**(6) (2015)
21. King, J.C.: Symbolic execution and program testing. Commun. ACM **19**(7), 385–394 (1976)
22. Lattuada, A., et al.: Verus: verifying Rust programs using linear ghost types. Proc. ACM Program. Lang. **7**(OOPSLA1), 286–315 (2023)
23. Leino, K.R.M.: Program Proofs. The MIT Press, Cambridge (2023)
24. Leroy, X., Blazy, S., Kästner, D., Schommer, B., Pister, M., Ferdinand, C.: CompCert-a formally verified optimizing compiler. In: ERTS 2016: Embedded Real Time Software and Systems, 8th European Congress (2016)
25. de Moura, L., Ullrich, S.: The lean 4 theorem prover and programming language. In: Platzer, A., Sutcliffe, G. (eds.) CADE 2021. LNCS, vol. 12699, pp. 625–635. Springer, Cham (2021). https://doi.org/10.1007/978-3-030-79876-5_37
26. de Moura, L., Bjørner, N.: Z3: an efficient SMT solver. In: Ramakrishnan, C.R., Rehof, J. (eds.) TACAS 2008. LNCS, vol. 4963, pp. 337–340. Springer, Heidelberg (2008). https://doi.org/10.1007/978-3-540-78800-3_24
27. Nipkow, T., Paulson, L.C., Wenzel, M.: Isabelle/HOL: A Proof Assistant for Higher-Order Logic, vol. 2283. Springer, Cham (2002)
28. Owre, S., Rushby, J.M., Shankar, N.: PVS: a prototype verification system. In: Kapur, D. (ed.) CADE 1992. LNCS, vol. 607, pp. 748–752. Springer, Heidelberg (1992). https://doi.org/10.1007/3-540-55602-8_217
29. Robby, Dwyer, M.B., Hatcliff, J.: Bogor: an extensible and highly-modular software model checking framework. In: 11th ACM SIGSOFT Symposium on Foundations of Software Engineering held jointly with 9th European Software Engineering Conference (ESEC/FSE), pp. 267–276. ACM (2003)
30. Robby, Hatcliff, J.: Slang: the Sireum programming language. In: Margaria, T., Steffen, B. (eds.) ISoLA 2021. LNCS, vol. 13036, pp. 253–273. Springer, Cham (2021). https://doi.org/10.1007/978-3-030-89159-6_17
31. Thiagarajan, H., Hatcliff, J., Robby: Awas: AADL information flow and error propagation analysis framework. Innov. Syst. Softw. Eng. **18**(4), 485–504 (2022)
32. Thorton, J.: Logical foundations of programming (online textbook for KSU CS 301). https://textbooks.cs.ksu.edu/cis301/index.html

33. Zhang, Z., Robby, Hatcliff, J., Moy, Y., Courtieu, P.: Focused certification of an industrial compilation and static verification toolchain. In: Cimatti, A., Sirjani, M. (eds.) SEFM 2017. LNCS, vol. 10469, pp. 17–34. Springer, Cham (2017). https://doi.org/10.1007/978-3-319-66197-1_2
34. How we built Cedar with automated reasoning and differential testing (2023). https://www.amazon.science/blog/how-we-built-cedar-with-automated-reasoning-and-differential-testing
35. cvc5 performance regression GitHub issues. https://github.com/cvc5/cvc5/issues/8736
36. Galois' HARDENS repository. https://github.com/GaloisInc/HARDENS
37. Logika overview case studies repository. https://github.com/santoslab/logika-overview-case-studies
38. Logika presentation at the 2022 Trusted Computing Center of Excellence Summit (TCCoE). https://doc.sireum.org/venues/presentations/logika/tccoe22/ (massive parallelization demo from an iPad starts at 22:33)
39. Logika v3. https://logika.v3.sireum.org/
40. Sireum. https://sireum.org/
41. SMT-LIB. https://smtlib.cs.uiowa.edu/
42. SysML v2. https://www.omgsysml.org/SysML-2.htm

Case Studies

Fuzzing an Industrial Proprietary Protocol

Eduard Baranov(✉), Axel Legay, and Martin Vivian

INGI, ICTEAM, UCLouvain, Ottignies-Louvain-la-Neuve, Belgium
{eduard.baranov,axel.legay,martin.vivian}@uclouvain.be

Abstract. For many proprietary systems source code and documentation are not available which makes them hard to test leaving only black-box approaches. In this work, we present an experience of fuzzing a protocol for drone control and the developed tool BinFuzz. BinFuzz is a man-in-the-middle stateful black-box protocol fuzzer. Listening to real communication as a man-in-the-middle, the fuzzer reconstructs states of the protocol as well as detects message types and their variable fields. The collected knowledge is used during the fuzzing to improve the quality of the generated inputs. For the application, we first test BinFuzz on an FTP protocol and then use it to fuzz the protocol for drone control.

Keywords: Protocol Fuzzing · Vulnerability Detection

1 Introduction

Software systems are moving towards distributed setup. Parts of a system can be placed in different locations or a system operation might utilize services provided by other companies. The Internet of Things is just one example. What makes the separate parts a single system is their interaction. In a distributed setup the interactions require one or several communication protocols for information transfer over a network. While many systems use one of the standard well-known protocols, proprietary protocols are common as well. In the latter case, documentation is often not up-to-date, not available, or does not exist at all.

One of the important aspects of system development is ensuring its correctness. Fuzzing is a well-known testing approach applicable to a black-box scenario where the knowledge of system internals is not required. The core idea of fuzzing is to generate a large number of inputs to the system and to monitor its behavior for unexpected results or crashes. A large number of fuzzing tools have been developed over the years, both in industry and in academia. A survey [12] lists about 50 black-box fuzzers that either appeared at a major conference or have many GitHub stars. Many systems have benefited from fuzzing and, according to Google, the number of bugs uncovered with fuzzers is immense [3,15] - only in Chromium tens of thousands of bugs have been found with fuzzing. However, the majority of the fuzzers focus on a single application rather than on communication protocols and interactions between different systems or parts of a system.

In this work, we have a task to test an industrial proprietary protocol for drone control. Only few details of this protocol have been given to us while source code and documentation were unavailable. In addition, traffic analysis uncovered several particularities of this protocol such as a lack of textual interpretation of the messages and no evident order of directions in a message sequence. As a result, none of the existing tools we tried to apply were capable of fuzzing the protocol. Therefore, we designed a new tool BinFuzz - a stateful man-in-the-middle (MITM) fuzzer that can be applied to a wide range of protocols including proprietary ones and, in particular, to the protocol for drone control. It combines a set of ideas for a more targeted input generation and can be used to test binary (non-text-based) protocols. BinFuzz operates in two phases: first it listens to the real communications and reconstructs an approximate protocol structure in the form of a Finite State Machine, and in the second stage it intercepts and mutates messages in the communication channel.

In this paper, we present challenges encountered in industrial protocol testing and present our solutions. We describe the ideas behind the BinFuzz tool and show its application to two protocols. First, we fuzz a faulty implementation of an FTP protocol to ensure that the tool is capable of finding bugs. Then we show the fuzzing of the protocol for drone control.

The rest of the paper is organized as follows. In Sect. 2 we list the challenges common to protocol fuzzing and particular to the protocol for drone control. In Sect. 3 we present the architecture of BinFuzz and how protocol learning and fuzzing are working. Section 4 shows the application of BinFuzz to two protocols and discusses the limitations. Related work is presented in Sect. 5. Section 6 concludes the paper.

2 Challenges

There are several challenges specific to protocol fuzzing in a black-box scenario. First of all, non-trivial protocols are stateful, and therefore the set of expected inputs changes over time during the execution and depends on the current state of the protocol. The fuzzer must be capable of reaching different states and selecting relevant inputs. Another challenge is to generate relevant inputs: message structures are usually fixed and might include a large number of different fields. If a detailed protocol specification is available, it is not complex to generate a valid input, however, this is rarely the case for proprietary protocols. In the latter case, the structure derivation is a complex task. For example, messages in the drone control protocol have 15 fields of different lengths in the header part. Moreover, valid messages may include information from previous messages, e.g. session ID is selected during the first steps of the communication and has to be included in all consequent messages.

An approach to overcome the aforementioned challenges has been proposed in [7]. The idea is to place a fuzzer between two communicating parties as MITM. First of all, this position allows the fuzzer to gather knowledge about a protocol by intercepting messages. Secondly, the fuzzer can modify messages in the network: instead of generating fuzzing inputs from scratch, it mutates real messages that are expected by the receiver. As a result, fuzzing can be performed without deriving full knowledge of the protocol, for example, session ID is included in the intercepted message and is included in the fuzzed input unless the corresponding field has been mutated. Several MITM fuzzers have been developed in recent years, however, they have their limitations. Some of them are stateless (e.g. [13,20]), and others support only text-based protocols (e.g. [7]) limiting their applicability. A common assumption in MITM fuzzers is an alternation of message direction, i.e. messages are always grouped in pairs with the first message always sent from the first communication party and the second message coming from another party.

The protocol for drone control that we have tested has a set of particularities adding additional challenges. First of all, messages do not have a text-based interpretation. Secondly, the protocol sends hundreds of messages per second adding a performance requirement to a fuzzer. Finally, it does not follow a request-response message sequence: it is common for the protocol to send multiple messages in one direction and then transfer a different number of messages in the opposite direction. In addition to that, the TCP protocol periodically transfers several messages in a single packet further complicating message ordering.

3 BinFuzz

The protocol for drone control due to its specifics cannot be fuzzed with existing tools. Therefore, for this work, we have developed a new tool BinFuzz. BinFuzz is a Man-in-the-Middle black-box fuzzer that can be applied to a large specter of protocols. A high-level architecture of the fuzzer is shown in Fig. 1. Its execution has two phases. At the first phase BinFuzz works as a passive listener: it records all the messages passing in the network in order to obtain some knowledge about the protocol. Alternatively, it can use previously collected communication traces. The communications are processed in order to extract different message types and to build a finite state machine (FSM) approximating the protocol behavior. The second step is active fuzzing: intercepted messages are mutated according to their type and current FSM state and are forwarded to the receiver. Throughout the fuzzing process, the FSM state is updated based on the messages going through the network. While it is possible to modify all the messages, we opted out to modify messages in one direction only, as it provides better control of the protocol state change. In the remainder of the paper, we call the communicating parties the client and the server, and the tool fuzzes messages from the client to the server.

BinFuzz has been forked from AutoFuzz [7] and implemented in Java. The tool is placed as a proxy server: a client has to be configured to communicate with the tool and the tool gets a server address as input. In the remainder of the section, we provide details about different parts of the tool.

3.1 Protocol Reconstruction Phase

During the first phase, shown on the left of Fig. 1, BinFuzz attempts to learn a protocol by listening to the network traffic or by scanning previously collected

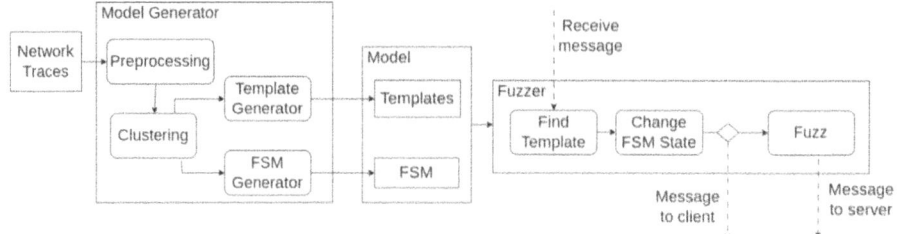

Fig. 1. BinFuzz Architecture.

data. The input to this phase is a set of traces; each trace is a sequence of messages and their directions. The output of this phase is a model of the protocol consisting of two parts: an FSM and a set of templates representing different message types. FSM transitions are labeled with templates.

The first step of model construction is message clustering. Messages to and from the server are clustered separately. At this step, all the messages in each direction from all the traces are taken and grouped according to their contents. The order of messages in the traces is not considered during the clustering. Messages are represented as hex strings and the similarity distance is based on the number of positions in which the messages have different values. Our approach is not limited to a particular clustering algorithm, in the implementation we used a Birch Leaf hierarchical clustering algorithm [31]. Hierarchy allows the user to adjust the number of clusters, as the number of message types is unknown in the black-box scenario, plus the ability of Birch to cluster incrementally is useful if the traces are not collected in advance.

In order to improve clustering results we use additional preprocessing. Some of the message fields can add noise to the clustering as their values may seem random. Examples of such fields are a millisecond part of a timestamp or a checksum. Moreover, these fields are usually located in a message header and likely in the same position in all message types. We use the Chi-Squared test to find positions in messages where the distribution of values across the whole message set is close to uniform. Such positions are ignored in the distance computation. The second heuristic is based on the idea that the message type is often encoded in its header or in the first bytes, for example, an FTP message starts with a command. Therefore, BinFuzz has the option to cluster according to the first n bytes of messages. With protocol knowledge, this bound can be set precisely, in black-box cases different values of n can be tried out.

Resulted clusters are used to build message templates and an FSM. The messages from traces are mapped to their respective clusters. Traces consisting of cluster sequences are used to construct an FSM. Transitions between states are labeled with cluster IDs. Note that messages to and from a server have been clustered separately, therefore the distinction between messages in different directions is maintained in the FSM. We use an open-source tool FlexFringe [28] to generate an FSM from the traces.

For each cluster, BinFuzz builds a template representing a message type. A template is a hex string with two special symbols: '-' and '+' representing variable parts of the message type. We call positions in the template with special symbols as a variable part of the template and all positions with standard hex symbols (i.e. from 0 to f) as a fixed part. Any message of the type corresponding to the template can have any values in the variable part while it is expected to coincide with the template's fixed part. For example, in FTP protocol a message type "USER" would have a template "5553455220------" where "5553455220" is a fixed part "USER" in hex and "------" is a variable part. Any message of this type is expected to start with "USER" followed by any symbols.

For the fuzzing, we consider two levels of variability for the variable part: strongly variable (denoted with "+") and weakly (denoted with "-") variable. The idea behind the separation is similar to the one for preprocessing described above. Strongly variable part positions have a close to uniform distribution of values in the cluster. An exhaustive fuzzing of fields such as milliseconds in timestamps or checksums rarely poses interest - all possible values can normally appear in real messages. During the fuzzing, the focus is given to the weakly variable parts.

The construction of templates is straightforward: if all messages in the cluster have the same value in a particular position then it is a fixed part, otherwise, we run the Chi-Squared test to distinguish between strongly and weakly variable parts. Note that while it is expected that positions labeled during the preprocessing become highly variable parts, the construction of templates has to recheck these positions. An example of a beginning of a template from the drone control protocol is "fe--0-0000+++++++++++++++++00...". The first byte "fe" indicates the beginning of a message and is the same for all messages. The next two bytes indicate message length; while messages could have different lengths, the distribution of values is not uniform. The part consisting of plus symbols corresponds to a checksum, the Chi-Squared test does not show a significant difference from the uniform distribution.

3.2 Fuzzing Phase

The second phase of BinFuzz shown in the right part of Fig. 1 is fuzzing. The tool continues to listen to network traffic and attempts to follow the protocol updating the state of the FSM accordingly. For this purpose, it searches for a corresponding template (i.e. cluster) for each message and then for an outgoing transition from the current FSM state labeled with the cluster. The metric for the template search is the proportion of the fixed part of the template coinciding with the message, the variable part of the template is ignored during the template search. If no template is found, the state is left unchanged.

In addition to the FSM state update, BinFuzz intercepts messages from the client, mutates them, and the server receives a modified version. For the mutations, we use the variable part of templates. A mutation function takes as an input an original message and a template and outputs a mutated message. We have implemented several mutation functions in our tool including:

- Random replace: with a predefined probability a value from the variable part of the template is changed to a new random value. We distinguish two probabilities for the mutation, for strongly and weakly variable parts.
- Random group replace: same as above but a group of several sequential hex digits is replaced. The maximal size of the group is a predefined parameter.
- 0/f replace: it replaces a value (or a group) with '0'(s) or 'f'(s).
- Random insert: it adds a random group of values at a random place of the message including at the beginning and the end of the message.
- Random delete: it deletes several values at a random place.
- Duplicate: it selects a group of hex digits and inserts several copies of the group at the end of the group. An alternative version duplicates the whole message in order to test the replayability of messages.

Other mutation functions can be easily added to BinFuzz. The mutated message is sent to the server. Logging at the server and client sides would allow the user to check if anything goes wrong. BinFuzz logs all the messages, their templates, and mutated versions allowing a reconstruction of the traces leading to an issue.

4 Protocol Fuzzing

As a first test to ensure that BinFuzz is capable of finding bugs, we used a faulty implementation of an FTP server. After that, we fuzzed the proprietary protocol for drone control. In this section, we present the fuzzing results.

4.1 FTP Protocol

FTP protocol [19], having dozens of implementations, is a classic case study for protocol fuzzers. Messages are text-based and have a simple structure: client messages start with a command of 3 or 4 symbols, followed by space and command arguments, and server replies start with a 3-digit code, followed by space and some text. Messages end with a new line ("/r/n" in the case of Windows).

Nevertheless, despite being quite simple, some of the implementations have vulnerabilities. We used a publicly available FTP server "Open and Compact FTP Server"[1] version 1.2 that is known to have several vulnerabilities. The goal of this test was to check that BinFuzz is capable of finding them.

We collected 166 communication traces using a Python script that represented a client: first, it attempts to connect to the server using one of the given credentials and then sends several commands randomly selected from a list. The collected traces have been given to BinFuzz as an input. During the first phase, BinFuzz builds a set of templates and an FSM of the protocol. Knowing that FTP commands are identified by at most 4 symbols and the server replies by 3 symbols, we set a header size to 8 (each byte is represented by 2 hex digits).

Examples of generated templates are shown in Table 1, where each row contains a cluster ID, a message direction, a template, and its length (the number

---
[1] https://sourceforge.net/projects/open-ftpd/files/open-ftpd/.

Table 1. A subset of templates for the FTP protocol. "+" and "-" symbols represent variable positions of the template. "S" represents messages sent to the server, "C" is for replies to the client. Several clusters with the same ID represent several versions of the cluster template for different message lengths.

ID	Dir	Size	Template
1000	S	24	5553455220-+-+-+-+-+0d0a
1000	S	26	5553455220-----+-+-+-+0d0a
1001	S	26	5041535320-+-+-+-+-+0d0a
1001	S	28	5041535320++++++++++++++0d0a
1002	S	30	4d4b4420++++++++++++++++++0d0a
...	...	...	...
1007	S	8	51554954
1008	S	42	5245545220-+-+-+-+---+-+---+-+2e7478740d0a
1009	S	42	44454c4520-+---+-------+-+-+-+2e7478740d0a
1010	S	12	4c4953540d0a
0	C	360	3232302d202a2a2a2a2a2a2a2a2a2a2a2a2a2a2a...
1	C	78	353330204c6f67696e206f722050617373776f7264...
1	C	54	353330204c6f67696e20696e636f72726563742e20...
...	...	...	...
5	C	86	3535302022-+-+-+-+---+-+---+-+2e7478742220...
6	C	110	323530204368616e67656420746f20646972656374...
6	C	68	323530204368616e67656420746f20646972656374...
7	C	126	313530204f70656e696e672062696e617279206d6f...
7	C	102	313530204f70656e696e672042696e617279206d6f...
8	C	50	3232362054726166666572420436f6d706c6574...

of hex digits). For clusters corresponding to client requests, the templates start with 6 or 8 hex digits followed by "20" representing a space symbol. This part represents a command and a space symbol. For example, cluster 1000 has templates for the "USER" command, cluster 1001 - for "PASS", and cluster 1007 is "QUIT". The next positions in the templates have either '-' or '+' representing variable parts of the template. These parts are fuzzed during the second phase. The substring "2e747874" in several clusters corresponds to ".txt" since all of the file operations in the collected traces used text files. All server replies start with a reply code followed by "20". Most of them are fixed messages, therefore almost all templates have no variable part. The only exception is the "file unavailable" message that includes the file name. All templates end with "/r/n" symbols.

A generated FSM for the FTP protocol is shown in Fig. 2. State 0 corresponds to the beginning of the protocol, and its outgoing transition is the first message which is a 220 "hello" message from the server. From the next state, there is an outgoing transition labeled with cluster 1000 - a USER command followed by either a reply "331" or "530". In the former case password is sent and it is either

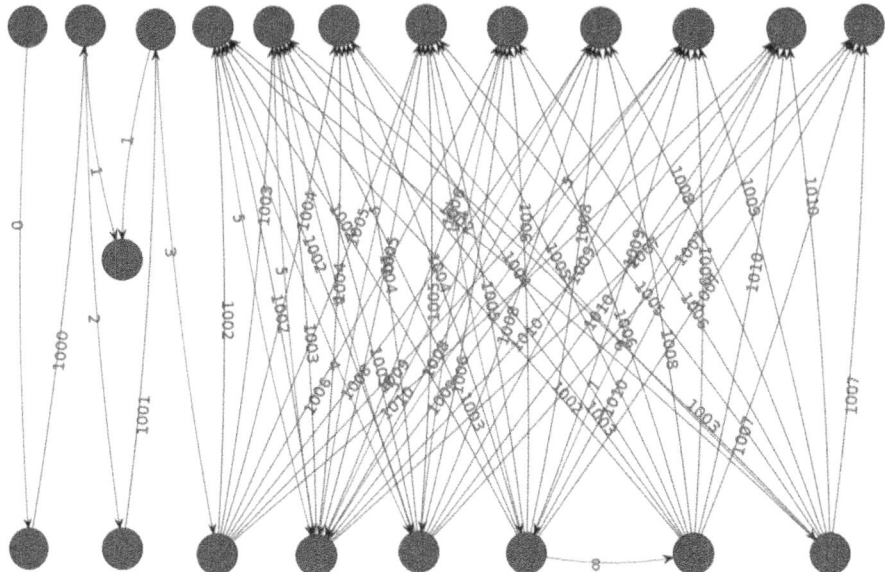

Fig. 2. FSM generated by BinFuzz for the FTP protocol. Blue transitions correspond to client messages and red transitions correspond to server replies. (Color figure online)

accepted or rejected. After the login procedure, the client can send any command and receive one of the possible responses. The FSM is almost bipartite: client requests (colored in blue) are followed by server replies (colored in red). The only exception is state 17, since during the data transfer the server sends two consecutive messages to open and close the data connection. There are 2 sink states without any outgoing transitions 3 and 20 representing wrong username or password and quit, respectively.

During the second phase, client commands have been mutated with different mutation functions. Multiple vulnerabilities have been quickly uncovered. Among them: the insertion of "/r", "/n" or a space symbol in the middle of the parameters could crash the server; the removal of the whole template variable part (i.e. sending a command without a parameter) could also result in the crash. These results show the effectiveness of the tool.

4.2 Proprietary Drone Control Protocol

We used BinFuzz to search for vulnerabilities in a proprietary protocol of an industrial company that is used to control unmanned aerial vehicles (UAVs). Limited knowledge of the protocol has been given that does not include either source code or documentation, therefore only the black-box approach is possible.

Protocol Description. Overall, the protocol involves three entities: a drone, a base station, and a server which are shown in Fig. 3. The drone runs software on

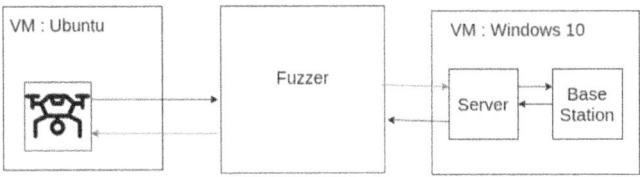

Fig. 3. Drone control system fuzzing setup.

an Ubuntu OS that includes components for network communication, navigation, control of the drone's modules such as engines, cameras, etc., and software for logging and telemetry. For the testing, we have been given a virtual machine with an installed drone emulator.

The base station serves as the primary interface through which users interact with the drone. A user can view the drone's position on a map, its telemetry data, such as speed and battery charge, and issue various commands such as take-off, landing, fly to a point, and other control operations. The base station is implemented as software running on a Windows 10 operating system.

The server is an intermediary component that transfers commands between the base station and the drone. It runs on Windows and in addition to the message relaying, the server is responsible for authentication and logging. In our case study, it is hosted on the same machine as the base station.

At the initialization step, both the base station and the drone establish a connection to the server that is further used to transfer the messages. There are multiple types of messages sent by the protocol including command messages issued by a user via the base station, telemetry messages with real-time information about the drone status, logging messages, and keep-alive messages to check the connection and to restart it in case of problems.

All messages have an identical structure. Each message has a start byte "fe" followed by a header, a payload, and ends with a byte "0a". Headers contain essential information such as message length, checksum, timestamp, and a service ID that is expected to receive the message. All fields of the header have fixed positions in the message. The payload comprises serialized objects.

As discussed in Sect. 2, the protocol has several specifics that make the fuzzing more complex. There is no general text-based interpretation of the messages. The messages are often sent in groups and we were not given any knowledge allowing us to find a relation of a message with one of the previous ones, i.e.. it is not possible to find request-response pairs. In addition, the protocol sends hundreds of messages every second, thus searching for related messages based on their timestamp is not possible either. For example, by attempting to decode text from messages, it is possible to find a supposedly logging message with a user command, yet the message transferring this command to the drone cannot be detected.

Trace Collection. BinFuzz inputs is a set of traces containing message sequences. BinFuzz has been placed on the network between the drone and the

Table 2. A subset of templates for drone protocol messages. "D" represents messages sent to the drone, and "S" is for messages to the base station.

ID	Dir	Size	Template
0	D	152	fe4c0000000+++++++-+++++++-000000000000101000008000...
1	D	152	fe4c0000000++++++++++++++++00000000000000101000008000...
2	D	136	fe44000000+-++++-++-+++++-+000000001000105000008000...
3	D	960	fee0010000+++++++++++++++++00000000530001010000002000...
...	...	...	...
1000	S	152	fe4c0000000++-+++++++-+++++00000000000000101000008000...
1001	S	152	fe4c0000000+++-+++++++-+++++00000000000000101000008000...
1002	S	136	fe44000000+++++++++++++++++000000006300009000002000...
1003	S	136	fe44000000+-++++-++-+++++-+000000001000009000008000...
1004	S	1180	fe--0-0000++++++++++++++++00000000630001010000002000...
1004	S	482	fe--0-0000++++++++++++++++00000000630001010000002000...
1004	S	3096	fe--0-0000++++++++++++++++00000000630001010000002000...
1005	S	634	fe----0000+++++--+++++++---+00000000--0-010100000-000...
...	...	...	...
1006	S	934	fe--010000+++++++++++++++++00000000630001010000002000...
1007	S	1392	fe--0-0000-++++++--+++++++-000000006300010100000002000...
1007	S	484	fe--0-0000-++++++--+++++++-000000006300010100000002000...
1007	S	452	fe--0-0000-++++++--+++++++-000000006300010100000002000...

server and recorded communications. At the beginning of each trace, we restarted the drone and the server. During the recording, a user issued several commands to the drone: in some traces, there are only 3–4 commands such as start or stop motors, while other traces contain longer lists of commands involving a flight to a destination. In total, we recorded 28 communication traces. The number of messages varies between 1500 and 5000, the total number of messages is 93000.

A quick exploration of messages showed the following statistics. The drone has been sending messages 3 times more often than the base station. Among all the messages there are only 104 different message lengths. 68% of messages are exactly 480 bytes long, 15% of messages have the length of either 68 or 76 bytes, 12% are longer than 6000 bytes, and the remaining messages have lengths between 170 and 750 bytes.

During the exploration of messages, we found out that some of the messages have been packed into a single TCP packet, moreover, a single packet could contain up to 8 messages. While it is possible to use these packed messages in the model construction, their utilization deteriorates the clustering results and the following FSM construction. Therefore, in order to obtain a better model of the protocol, we used the knowledge about the position of a message length field. This knowledge has been used only for the separation of messages: after the interception of a TCP packet a proxy server splits its payload into messages based on the message lengths. All other fuzzing steps have been performed in a black-box manner.

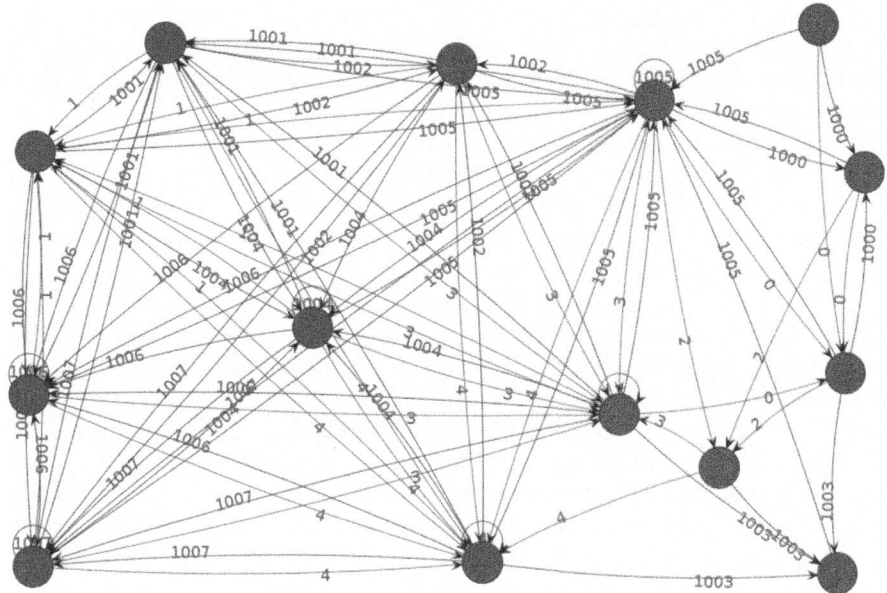

Fig. 4. FSM for the drone control protocol. (Color figure online)

BinFuzz Fuzzing. The first phase is protocol learning from communication traces. It starts with message clustering. Its results are affected by two parameters: header size i.e. length of a message part used in clustering and the number of clusters. Note that the header size parameter does not have to be the actual size of a message header since this value is unknown due to black-box fuzzing, but an expected length to encounter enough information to distinguish different message types. We used a trial-and-error approach to find a useful parameter value. For the drone protocol, setting up a small header size below 100 bytes resulted in unusable clusters: they either have identical templates (and therefore cannot be distinguished during fuzzing) or templates with almost empty variable parts, while 125 bytes or 250 hex digits yielded several distinct clusters with templates having both fixed and variable parts. For the number of clusters, the parameter is chosen to avoid, on one hand, clusters with identical templates and, on the other hand, clusters with few messages; for the drone protocol, it is achieved with 7 and 8 clusters for messages to and from the drone, respectively.

For each cluster, a template has been generated, some of them are shown in Table 2. An FSM generated by BinFuzz is shown in Fig. 4. Transitions are labeled with cluster IDs and the states they are connecting. Red transitions are for messages to the drone and the blue ones are for the messages from the drone. Unlike the FTP example, message direction does not alter after every single message, and it is not possible to separate states into sending messages only to or from the drone, respectively, but the majority of states have outgoing transitions for both message directions. Clustering and FSM construction have been run on a laptop with Intel Core i7-8650U CPU. Clustering of 93000 messages takes several seconds and the FSM construction takes about 3 min. However, the RAM consumption of the FlexFringe tool was above 20Gb thus limiting the number of messages to be used for the model reconstruction.

During the second phase, we fuzzed messages in both directions, first messages sent to the drone, and later we switched to fuzz messages towards the base station. The templates and the FSM have been reused in the second part. Independently from the fuzzing direction, all messages are intercepted and classified to one of the clusters in order to maintain the FSM state.

During the fuzzing, we kept the connection between the drone and the base station and periodically issued control commands. For the mutation, we tried all the mutation functions described in Sect. 3. We set up a 20% probability for messages to be passed unmodified. This way we can ensure that the protocol could periodically progress even if most of the fuzzed messages would be rejected. In addition, BinFuzz allows the user to stop and later restart fuzzing at any moment. Periodic pauses allowed us to check the recovery procedures of the protocol: if significant mutations of the messages prevent protocol execution, during the pause it is possible to validate that the protocol can resume its normal execution. BinFuzz logs intercepted messages, their clusters, and modified messages from the fuzzer. The drone software also writes the log including commands issued by the user and errors appearing in the application.

Fuzzing Results. We tested various mutation functions and observed their impact on the drone's behavior. The first finding is that neither the drone nor the base station checks the integrity of the messages. The message header includes a checksum, yet randomly modified messages have been processed. This discovery simplified the protocol fuzzing as various message modifications could be applied without an automatic message drop by a receiver. On the other hand, random inserts at the beginning or end of messages have no detectable effect on the protocol execution, from which we assume that the first and the last bytes of the message are checked and everything outside of the message is ignored.

Fuzzing with random insert and random delete shows that start and end bytes are checked as well as message length. Modification of the message size without changing the message length field leads to the message drop. The logs show that the drone considers itself disconnected from the base station and starts a recovery procedure returning him to the home location.

Random replacements yield more interesting results. The messages are not immediately dropped due to the wrong length or lack of start or end byte. However, the majority of commands are not executed. Even with a relatively low probability of mutation (each position in the weakly (strongly) variable part of templates can be mutated with 5% (1%) probability resulting in the expected number of mutated hex digits or groups of digits equal to 2.8) approximately 80% of the commands fail to execute. Contrary to the "disconnected" scenario, with random replacement the drone continues the flight. In its log, there are entries "Control Lost" and "Connection reestablished" appearing every second.

This leads to an issue reproducible on the emulator, that even being unable to execute any control command and acknowledging it the drone continues to maintain a connection and wait for the commands without returning to its home location. It is possible to maintain the drone in this state until its batteries are depleted.

Fuzzing messages towards the base station yields similar results. Messages' beginning and end bytes as well as message length are checked, but not the checksum. The data received from the drone is not checked either: the user interface of the base station sometimes shows drone speed being faster than the speed of light or instant teleportation to a remote location. However, this issue is not protocol-related, and, potentially, not important for the base station software.

Overall, the fuzzing showed the lack of message integrity checks on the protocol level, though the integrity checks on the TCP level, to some extent, cover this issue. In addition, the drone might need some tuning for the detection of cases when recovery procedures are required.

4.3 Limitations and Potential Extensions

The utilization of the MITM fuzzer allows the tester to use messages close to real ones without any knowledge of a protocol and its message structure. However, some of the mechanisms can prevent easy mutations. Any integrity checks of messages such as checksums would fail after a random mutation. In our use case, these checks have not been implemented, which simplified the fuzzing procedure. On the plus side, templates generated from real messages can provide insight into checksum field positions as such positions are expected to be highly variable. The beginnings of drone protocol templates have two groups of highly variable positions (the first group can be seen in Table 2): one of them is a checksum position, while the exploration of bytes next to the second one showed that it was a part of the timestamp. Having the position guessed it is possible to recompute and update the checksum after the mutation.

A related complication for which it is harder to find a workaround is encryption. In the case of encrypted messages, it is hard to build relevant templates for the encrypted parts of messages. If such messages include an unencrypted header, it might be possible to use this header for fuzzing: to build a model of the protocol and perform fuzzing, yet only random mutations of the encrypted part are possible. To the best of our knowledge, only one approach to deal with encryption exists: provide knowledge about the encryption algorithm and keys to the fuzzer, which would decrypt a message and later re-encrypt the mutated version. This approach has been implemented in SecFuzz [27].

There are some limitations in our implementation that we have encountered during protocol fuzzing. Currently, the number of clusters for messages has to be selected by the user. We consider some heuristics to provide an automated selection. To measure the clustering quality we need to check the generated templates. If there are templates that have (almost) no variable part, then there is a high chance of having too many clusters and their number shall be reduced (unless there is a constant message in the protocol that appears in multiple traces). Another heuristic is to check if there are almost identical templates and to merge them. If some templates have almost no fixed part but a big weakly variable part, the tool could attempt to split such templates into smaller clusters. Another limitation comes from comparing exact positions in the message when messages have different lengths. An extension of templates to support sequences of variable positions with non-constant length (e.g. instead of "----" with the length 4 use "-[4–8]" defining the length interval) might improve the generation of inputs. Finally, the FSM is constructed from real traces sending valid messages. Fuzzing might cause unexpected replies from the server that can potentially lead to an incorrect state. An interesting future direction for research is to build mechanisms for incorrect state detection and recovery.

5 Related Work

Fuzzing is a vulnerability discovery methodology [26] and its name was coined by Miller et al. in [16]. Over the years an immense number of fuzzers have been developed, a survey [12] mentioned more than 100 fuzzers. One of the most well-known fuzzer categorizations is the availability of the source code. White-box fuzzers (e.g. [6,10,18]) have full access to the source code, grey-box fuzzers (e.g. [22,30]) have partial knowledge about the internals of the system under test, and black-box fuzzers (e.g. [1,5]) can observe only inputs and outputs of the system. Another classification criterion is a type of system under test: many tools fuzz a single binary, and our use case was focused on the communication protocol.

Among the protocol fuzzers a big group consists of MITM fuzzers that can intercept and inject modified messages. This position provides an opportunity to obtain some information about the protocol from the exchanged messages. Moreover, real messages sent through the network can be used as a basis for input generation which has multiple benefits: (i) in case of insufficient knowledge about the message structure, mutations of a valid message would provide more meaningful inputs than ones generated from scratch; (ii) identifiers of the current message exchange such as session ID are present in the real message and, unless mutated, would be present in the fuzzer input. Protocol fuzzers can be classified into stateful and stateless. The latter processes each message separately reducing their effectiveness for complex protocols. ProxyFuzz [13] randomly mutates network traffic and, as a result, is inefficient for many protocols since the majority of packets become invalid. To avoid such inefficiency, many tools use templates for messages that allow smarter mutations. Polymorph [20] and mqtt_fuzzing [21] are stateless fuzzers that dissect messages with Tshark or Scapy. While these tools know message structures for a large number of protocols, their applicability to proprietary protocols cannot be guaranteed. SecFuzz [27] can perform fuzzing on encrypted messages, however it requires prior knowledge of the message structure, encryption keys, and encryption algorithm. PropFuzz [17] is another stateless fuzzer specialized in industrial protocols for Programmable Logic Controllers that use statistical computations to create message templates.

Stateful fuzzers use some kind of state automaton to model the protocol behavior. KiF [1] requires the automaton to be defined by the user. Restler [2] analyses API specification to infer the automaton. AutoFuzz [7] from which our fuzzer has been forked learns the automaton from network traffic. However, it is limited to text-based protocols compatible with socks5, thus it is unsuitable for our case study. Pulsar [5] is another fuzzer that uses intercepted network messages to infer protocol states, yet their current implementation does not support non-textual protocols. In AutoFuzz and Pulsar, a single transition of a state automaton represents a pair of messages: one message sent from a first communication party and a return message from another. The drone control protocol we were testing cannot be modeled in such a manner as there is no evident dependency in the number of consequent messages in one direction. FitM [11] attempts to build the FSM and message templates during the fuzzing thus limiting its effectiveness in case of complex message structure.

An example of a non-MITM fuzzer is Mutiny Fuzzing Framework [25] which is a network fuzzer that operates by replaying mutated PCAPs. This stateless fuzzer is limited to replaying collected traces. Authors of [4] test several implementations of a TLS protocol. Users have to provide a list of abstractions of the protocol messages and the fuzzer attempts to rebuild a state machine by sending different messages from this list. Another TLS protocol fuzzer TLS-Attacker [24] also relies on prior knowledge of the message structure.

Another related group of fuzzers checks web applications. Examples of tools for web applications are WFuzz [14], ffuf [9], and WebFuzz [23]. Their input can be considered as protocol messages, and are generated from a string in which parts indicated with the word "FUZZ" are modifiable. However, they can learn neither a state machine nor a structure of the input.

Mutation testing measuring test suite quality can also be applied to protocols. DaMAT [29] modifies the exchanged data at runtime to detect the test suite shortcomings, however it requires knowledge of message structure. The approach can be used to measure fuzzing quality as proposed in [8].

6 Conclusion

Testing of proprietary protocols is a complex task as usually their source code and documentation are not available leaving the testers with black-box techniques. Fuzzing results primarily depend on input quality, for protocols it is important for generated messages to not be rejected immediately due to incorrect structure or an unexpected message type. For the fuzzing of the drone control protocol, many common assumptions are not valid and, therefore, we have built BinFuzz that works as a stateful MITM fuzzer. The preliminary construction of the FSM and message templates allows it to improve the fuzzing quality and likelihood of finding vulnerabilities. The application of the tool showed several issues in the protocol. There are multiple directions for future research and improvement of BinFuzz that include the application of advanced automated techniques for protocol reengineering, the addition of details to the templates, and the addition of new heuristics for the detection of message fields such as checksums.

Acknowledgements. This work was supported by the Walloon Region of Belgium under the conventions n°8560 (DeepConstruct) and n°2110186 (Cyber Excellence).

References

1. Abdelnur, H.J., State, R., Festor, O.: KiF: a stateful SIP fuzzer. In: Proceedings of the 1st international Conference on Principles, Systems and Applications of IP Telecommunications, pp. 47–56 (2007)
2. Atlidakis, V., Godefroid, P., Polishchuk, M.: RESTler: stateful rest API fuzzing. In: 2019 IEEE/ACM 41st International Conference on Software Engineering (ICSE), pp. 748–758. IEEE (2019)
3. Chang, O.: Taking the next step: OSS-fuzz in 2023 (2023). https://security.googleblog.com/2023/02/taking-next-step-oss-fuzz-in-2023.html
4. De Ruiter, J., Poll, E.: Protocol state fuzzing of {TLS} implementations. In: 24th USENIX Security Symposium (USENIX Security 2015), pp. 193–206 (2015)
5. Gascon, H., Wressnegger, C., Yamaguchi, F., Arp, D., Rieck, K.: Pulsar: stateful black-box fuzzing of proprietary network protocols. In: Thuraisingham, B., Wang, X., Yegneswaran, V. (eds.) SecureComm 2015. LNICST, vol. 164, pp. 330–347. Springer, Cham (2015). https://doi.org/10.1007/978-3-319-28865-9_18
6. Godefroid, P., Levin, M.Y., Molnar, D.: Sage: whitebox fuzzing for security testing. Commun. ACM **55**(3), 40–44 (2012)
7. Gorbunov, S., Rosenbloom, A.: Autofuzz: automated network protocol fuzzing framework. Ijcsns **10**(8), 239 (2010)
8. Görz, P., et al.: Systematic assessment of fuzzers using mutation analysis. In: 32nd USENIX Security Symposium (USENIX Security 2023), pp. 4535–4552 (2023)
9. Hoikkala, J.: FFuF - fuzz faster u fool (2021). https://github.com/ffuf/ffuf
10. Kargén, U., Shahmehri, N.: Turning programs against each other: high coverage fuzz-testing using binary-code mutation and dynamic slicing. In: Proceedings of the 2015 10th Joint Meeting on Foundations of Software Engineering, pp. 782–792 (2015)
11. Maier, D., Bittner, O., Munier, M., Beier, J.: FitM: binary-only coverage-guided fuzzing for stateful network protocols. In: Workshop on Binary Analysis Research (BAR), vol. 35 (2022)
12. Manès, V.J., et al.: The art, science, and engineering of fuzzing: a survey. IEEE Trans. Softw. Eng. **47**(11), 2312–2331 (2019)
13. Marcos, R.: Proxyfuzz - mitm network fuzzer in Python (2007). https://www.darknet.org.uk/2007/06/proxyfuzz-mitm-network-fuzzer-in-python/
14. Mendez, X.: Wfuzz - the web fuzzer (2011). https://github.com/xmendez/wfuzz
15. Metzman, J., Arya, A., Szekeres, L.: Fuzzbench: Fuzzer benchmarking as a service (2020). https://security.googleblog.com/2020/03/fuzzbench-fuzzer-benchmarking-as-service.html
16. Miller, B.P., Fredriksen, L., So, B.: An empirical study of the reliability of UNIX utilities. Commun. ACM **33**(12), 32–44 (1990)
17. Niedermaier, M., Fischer, F., von Bodisco, A.: Propfuzz-an it-security fuzzing framework for proprietary ICS protocols. In: 2017 International Conference on Applied Electronics (AE), pp. 1–4. IEEE (2017)

18. Peng, H., Shoshitaishvili, Y., Payer, M.: T-fuzz: fuzzing by program transformation. In: 2018 IEEE Symposium on Security and Privacy (SP), pp. 697–710. IEEE (2018)
19. Postel, J., Reynolds, J.: RFC 959 - file transfer protocol (FTP) (1985). https://www.ietf.org/rfc/rfc959.txt
20. Ramos, S.H.: Polymorph: a real-time network packet manipulation framework. Exploit Database (2018)
21. Ramsauer, T.: mqtt_fuzzing (2018). https://github.com/ramsaut/mqtt_fuzzing
22. Rawat, S., Jain, V., Kumar, A., Cojocar, L., Giuffrida, C., Bos, H.: Vuzzer: application-aware evolutionary fuzzing. In: NDSS, vol. 17, pp. 1–14 (2017)
23. van Rooij, O., Charalambous, M.A., Kaizer, D., Papaevripides, M., Athanasopoulos, E.: webFuzz: grey-box fuzzing for web applications. In: Bertino, E., Shulman, H., Waidner, M. (eds.) ESORICS 2021, Part I. LNCS, vol. 12972, pp. 152–172. Springer, Cham (2021). https://doi.org/10.1007/978-3-030-88418-5_8
24. Somorovsky, J.: Systematic fuzzing and testing of TLS libraries. In: Proceedings of the 2016 ACM SIGSAC Conference on Computer and Communications Security, pp. 1492–1504 (2016)
25. Spadaro, J., Wyatt, L.: Mutiny fuzzing framework (2018). https://github.com/Cisco-Talos/mutiny-fuzzer
26. Sutton, M., Greene, A., Amini, P.: Fuzzing: brute force vulnerability discovery. Pearson Education (2007)
27. Tsankov, P., Dashti, M.T., Basin, D.: Secfuzz: fuzz-testing security protocols. In: 2012 7th International Workshop on Automation of Software Test (AST), pp. 1–7. IEEE (2012)
28. Verwer, S., Hammerschmidt, C.A.: Flexfringe: a passive automaton learning package. In: 2017 IEEE International Conference on Software Maintenance and Evolution (ICSME), pp. 638–642. IEEE (2017)
29. Viganò, E., Cornejo, O., Pastore, F., Briand, L.: DaMAT: a data-driven mutation analysis tool. In: 2023 IEEE/ACM 45th International Conference on Software Engineering: Companion Proceedings (ICSE-Companion), pp. 165–169. IEEE (2023)
30. Zalewski, M.: American fuzzy lop. http://lcamtuf.coredump.cx/afl/
31. Zhang, T., Ramakrishnan, R., Livny, M.: Birch: a new data clustering algorithm and its applications. Data Min. Knowl. Disc. **1**, 141–182 (1997)

Modelling and Analysis of DTLS: Power Consumption and Attacks

Lise Bech Gehlert[1], Malthe Peter Højen Jørgensen[1], Christoffer Brejnholm Koch[1], Tobias Møller[1], Signe Kirstine Rusbjerg[1], Tobias Worm Bøgedal[1], Danny Bøgsted Poulsen[1], René Rydhof Hansen[1(✉)], and Daniel Lux[2]

[1] Department of Computer Science, Aalborg University, Aalborg, Denmark
{lgehle20,mphj20,ckoch20,tmalle20,srusbj20}@student.aau.dk,
{tobiaswb,dannybpoulsen,rrh}@cs.aau.dk
[2] Seluxit a/s, Aalborg, Denmark
daniel@seluxit.com

Abstract. IoT devices are ubiquitous in modern society. These devices are often constrained by computational power, memory, and energy consumption. DTLS is a protocol that is widely used by IoT devices, including critical industrial IoT systems, as the transport layer for secure and authenticated communication. In this paper we create a formal model of DTLS in UPPAAL SMC and show how statistical model checking can be used to analyse, evaluate, and optimise energy consumption for the protocol. In particular we model and analyse different network scenarios, and show how energy consumption is highly dependent on the specific usage scenario. Based on this, we propose and analyse solutions to reduce energy consumption in common scenarios. Finally, we extend our model with an *active attacker* trying to drain as much energy as possible from the target system by (ab)using DTLS. Analysing and preventing such *Denial of Service* attacks is essential for critical systems.

1 Introduction

IoT devices are ubiquitous in the modern world and are an essential part of many industrial systems, including safety, security, and mission critical systems, e.g., large scale production plants and power plants. This also makes them favoured targets for sophisticated malicious actors such as cyber-criminals and nation state sponsored attackers, cf. the 2015 attack on the Ukrainian power grid. A threat environment like that combined with the typically strict resource constraints on IoT devices, the DTLS (Datagram Transport Layer Security) protocol is often chosen for communication between devices and servers as it provides essentially the same security and authentication guarantees as TLS and has seen substantial work on optimising (energy-)efficiency and making it suitable for (energy-)constrained devices.

However, the term "IoT device" covers a very wide spectrum of actual devices with varying and sometimes contradictory constraints and requirements. This is not least the case for a typical IoT/DTLS use case[1] where the IoT devices are operating behind a NAT (Network Address Translation) device and are expected to be suspended (or "sleeping") for extended periods of time in order to preserve (battery-)power. When the device "wakes up", it must then re-establish the DTLS connection, which is a potentially very costly operation in terms of energy. Adding the unpredictable nature of an attacker to the network, who may try and drain the resources of a device, and it becomes all but impossible to predict and optimise energy-consumption while preserving security.

With the above in mind, we argue that there is a strong need for a tool to model, evaluate, and optimise energy consumption (or other limited resources) for specific use cases, scenarios, and attackers, in order to choose the best trade-off between functionality, security, and resource consumption. In this paper we show how statistical model checking [16], using UPPAAL SMC, can be used as such a tool. In particular, we develop a formal model of DTLS taking energy consumption into account and use this as base for (formally) modelling different network configurations and usage scenarios; including the "tricky" case of a resource constrained IoT device operating behind a NAT as mentioned above. To the best of our knowledge, this is the first such formal model. Finally, we model an attacker trying to drain the IoT device for battery through DTLS interaction. Statistical model checking is then applied to derive performance characteristics, including energy consumption. Again, to the best of our knowledge, we believe this to be the first such model.

In summary, the main contributions of this paper are: *(1)* a novel formal model of DTLS 1.3 incorporating energy consumption using UPPAAL and timed automata; *(2)* a proposed heartbeat protocol to reduce energy consumption on session resumption; and *(3)* a method for modelling attackers and their impact on DTLS energy consumption.

The work in this paper is based on, and extends, the work described in [11].

2 Background

We briefly review the DTLS protocol (version 1.3), the UPPAAL model checker and its statistical model checking capabilities.

2.1 DTLS 1.3

The DTLS (Datagram Transport Layer Security) protocol can be seen as a UDP counterpart to the TCP-based TLS (Transport Layer Security) protocol. DTLS is used to obtain a secure and reliable connection on a UDP connection using datagrams. To achieve this on an inherently unreliable UDP connection, some TCP reliability features have to be ported to UDP, e.g., by implementing a simple time-out alongside retransmission if a message remains unanswered.

---

[1] This use case along with the others in this paper are simplified versions of actual scenarios encountered by Seluxit, our industrial partner.

Resource constrained IoT devices typically utilise UDP as the transport layer protocol, as UDP is significantly lighter than TCP, both in terms of power-consumption and network resources. Using UDP, devices do not have to maintain a constant connection between endpoints, and devices can enter power-efficient sleep states sooner, since the protocol does not handle lost packages or packages with errors. Since DTLS provides security over UDP, it is a suitable protocol for client-server IoT applications, in order to prevent eavesdropping, tampering, and message forgery: with the exception of order protection and non-replayability, DTLS 1.3 offers security guarantees equivalent to that of its counterpart TLS 1.3: confidentiality and integrity from AEAD encryption of data; forward secrecy; and length concealment [13].

To establish a connection using DTLS, a client initiates a handshake using a CLIENTHELLO (the full handshake is illustrated in Fig. 1). When the server receives this message, it replies with a HELLORETRYREQUEST alongside an appended cookie. From here the server awaits a new CLIENTHELLO that has the recently acquired cookie appended. This cookie exchange is done to limit harmful requests to the server, as most denial-of-service attacks are stopped when a retransmission is needed before the communication is fully established. When the server is convinced the client is not harmful, it proceeds to send a SERVERHELLO in conjunction with negotiation parameters. These negotiation parameters are used to find the most recent common version of DTLS, as DTLS 1.3 is backwards compatible with versions 1.2 and 1.0 (although version 1.0 is not recommended). The client then replies with a common version, and the server sends an acknowledgement to end the handshake and establish the communication. The handshake has to be performed every time the connection is closed and reopened. This is not very efficient, neither energy- nor time-wise, for either side, and therefore DTLS supports the feature known as *session resumption*. When session resumption is enabled, it allows a client to skip most of the handshake process by providing a Pre-Shared Key (PSK). This PSK can only be exchanged when a connection is established and therefore session resumption can only be used from the second session and onwards. Session resumption cryptographically ties the initial connection and any subsequent connections together. An example of session resumption is illustrated in Fig. 2.

2.2 UPPAAL

UPPAAL is a model checker for networks of timed automata. In this paper we use it to model the DTLS protocol and perform "sanity" checks of the model, ensuring that it complies with the specification. This model allows for simple simulations of several cases described in Sect. 5.

Timed automata are essentially an extension of finite automata with "clocks", designed to model systems where time is an important aspect, e.g., real-time systems. An example of a timed automaton specified in UPPAAL can be seen in Fig. 3 (adapted and simplified from [2]). This models an abstract device that requires two button presses within five time units of each other, i.e., a "double click", in order to turn on. To model this, the timed automaton uses three locations,

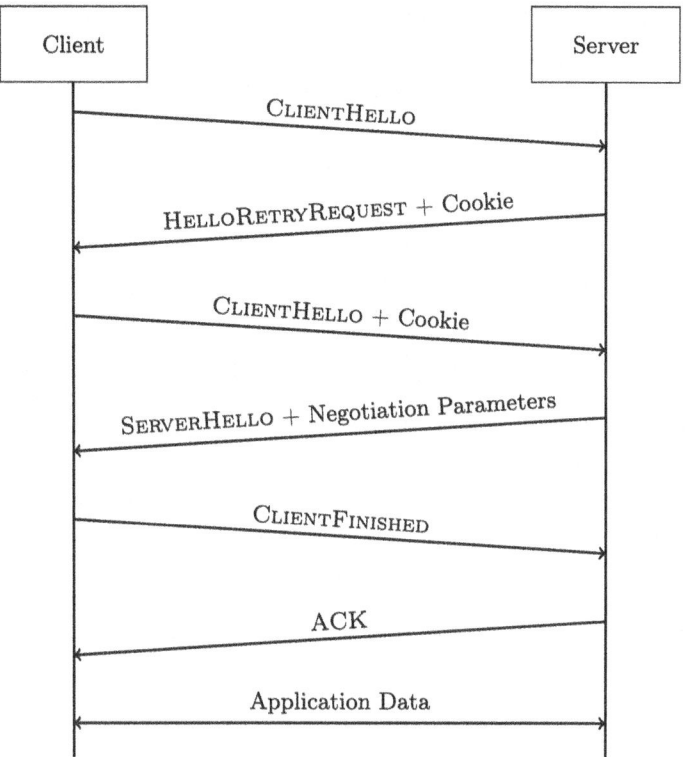

Fig. 1. Example of a full DTLS 1.3 handshake [11].

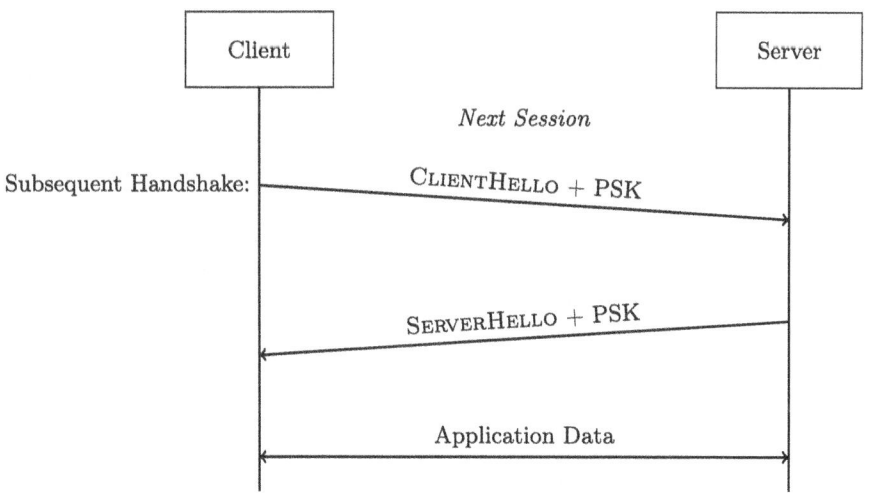

Fig. 2. Example of session resumption without cookie exchange [11].

named off, await and on. From the initial location (as indicated by the double circles) off, only an input-action (press?) is possible which occurs when the user presses the button. This action allows the system to move to location await while also setting the clock x to zero, thus starting the timer. From the await location there are now two possible actions: the input-action press? (another button press from the user) and the output-action timeout!. The last part of the model to be aware of is the *invariant* x <= 5 that enforces that in the await location, the clock x must be less than or equal to five. This invariant drives the timeout mechanism of the system: if the user does *not* press the button a second time (within five time units of the first press), the invariant becomes false and force an action. In this case, the only action that can be forced is the timeout! output action (since we can not force the user to press the button). However, the timeout! action can only be taken when the guard x==5 is satisfied, which in this case lines up with the timeout of the invariant. On the other hand, if the user presses the button a second time (within the time limit), the system moves on to the on location from which there is only one possible action, another button press from the user, which sends the system back to the initial location off.

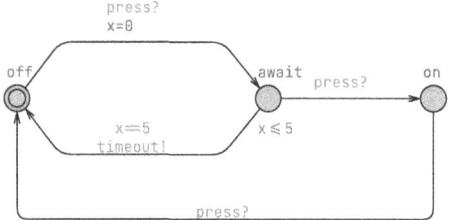

Fig. 3. UPPAAL model of a device requiring two presses to turn on (adapted from [2]).

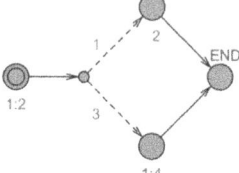

Fig. 4. An example of stochastic timed automata with rate of exponential [4].

2.3 UPPAAL SMC

UPPAAL SMC is an extension of UPPAAL that allows for models with *stochastic behaviour*, based on *stochastic timed automata* where the non-deterministic (discrete) choices are refined by probabilistic choices while time-delays are refined with a probability distribution.

Figure 4 (borrowed from [4]) shows an example timed automaton illustrating the probabilistic choice between locations, indicated by the dashed lines. It specifies that the upper location is selected with a probability of $\frac{1}{3+1} = \frac{1}{4}$ while the lower location is selected with a probability of $\frac{3}{1+3} = \frac{3}{4}$. Delays, in the different locations, are selected from an exponential distribution with a rate of $\frac{1}{2}$, 2 and $\frac{1}{4}$ respectively. We will not go into further detail here, but do explain special features as they are needed in the following. See [4] for a tutorial on UPPAAL SMC.

3 Modelling DTLS

Figure 5 illustrates the basic scenario that we wish to model and analyse: a user (e.g., a production plant manager) makes a data request to a server (e.g., to monitor production status) which then forwards the request to the relevant clients (e.g., sensors or plant control units). Our model abstracts away details of the user/server communication and focuses on the client/server communication over the DTLS 1.3 protocol.

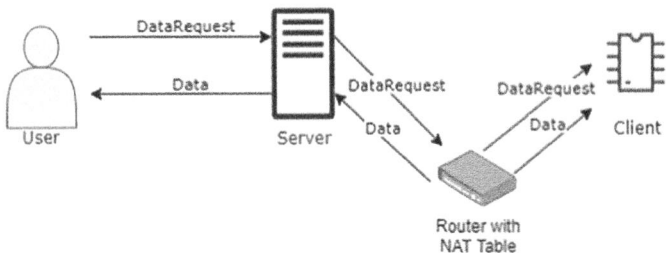

Fig. 5. Communication structure of the model.

An important feature of the client/server communication is that the client is assumed to be behind an Internet router that performs Network Address Translation (NAT). This makes it significantly more complicated and potentially costly for the client to contact the server because the cost of maintaining or re-establishing a connection must be taken into account.

Using UPPAAL 5.0, we have modelled the standard DTLS 1.3 protocol and two variants adding a "heartbeat" to the protocol to help reduce power consumption during suspend/resume cycles. The heartbeat protocols differ in that one is initiated by the client and the other by the server. All models are equipped with configurable parameters for easy setup of different scenarios and to evaluate how power consumption is affected and if/how it can be optimised.

In this paper, we only show illustrative excerpts of the UPPAAL models.[2]

3.1 Default DTLS 1.3 Protocol

The DTLS 1.3 model covers the basic protocol including session-resumption pre-shared keys (PSK) after the initial handshake as default. It comprises five automata: **User**, **Server**, **Client**, **Router** and **MaliciousUser**. The **Router** automaton simply ensures messages sent to the client are only received if the sender's IP-address is present within the router's NAT table. Communication does not go through the **Router**. The **User** automaton specifies that the user requests data from the server once every interval of 7200 s (this number is configurable via the **requestInterval** parameter).

---

[2] The full models are available at https://github.com/Goggon/DTLS_Paper_Models.

The first part of the server model can be seen in Fig. 6. It shows the cookie exchange of the protocol and a `WakeUp` call to the client. The locations marked with a U are *urgent locations*. While the state of the model contains at least one urgent location delay actions are not allowed. The `DoAction()` function seen in the Figure is described in a later section. A probabilistic choice is used to model the unreliability of the UDP protocol underlying DTLS, i.e., whether a packet is lost during transmission. This probability is a global parameter of the model, named `NDC` (short for "NoDropChance"), for easy exploration of various scenarios. Packet loss happens with a probability of $\frac{1}{NDC}$ meaning that higher values of `NDC` models a more reliable network. The `WakeUp[id]!` synchronization makes the client transition from being idle.

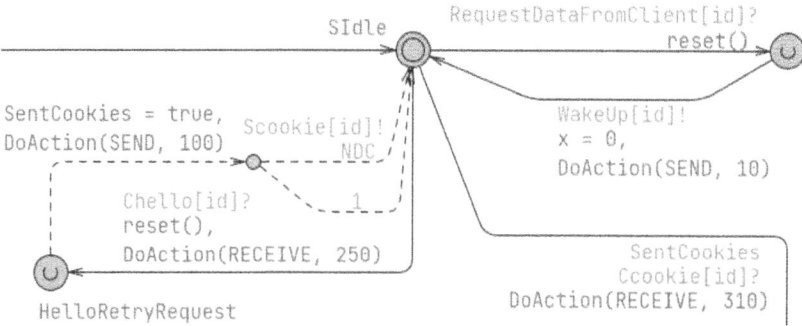

Fig. 6. Cookie exchange in DTLS handshake protocol.

The `WakeUp[id]!` broadcast models the server getting ahold of the client through undefined means. The DTLS protocol does not support such an action, but it is needed in case the server is ever dropped from the clients NAT-table since it would be impossible to reestablish the connection (from the server side) without it. We abstract away how such a `WakeUp` would work, but note that our heartbeat extension is intended to obviate it.

In Sect. 2.1 the necessity of the cookie exchange is explained in detail and the model takes the mentioned issues with DoS attacks into account. The server only allocates resources to the connection, if the client is willing to respond with a `ClientHello` with the same cookie attached. Experiments in Sect. 5.2 show the resilience of this implementation.

The server can respond with a `ServerHello`, either sending a full certificate to the client for the purpose of identification, or using a PSK to identify itself as seen in Fig. 7. If a PSK is used, a lot of power can be saved, but measures must be taken to ensure continuous safety with PSK. Additionally, before using PSK, a connection must first be established using a full certificate-based handshake.

In Fig. 8 the final part of the server model can be seen. The ACK messages include a request for data, where the server waits a set amount of time for a response, before re-requesting the data. Packages can be dropped and, as

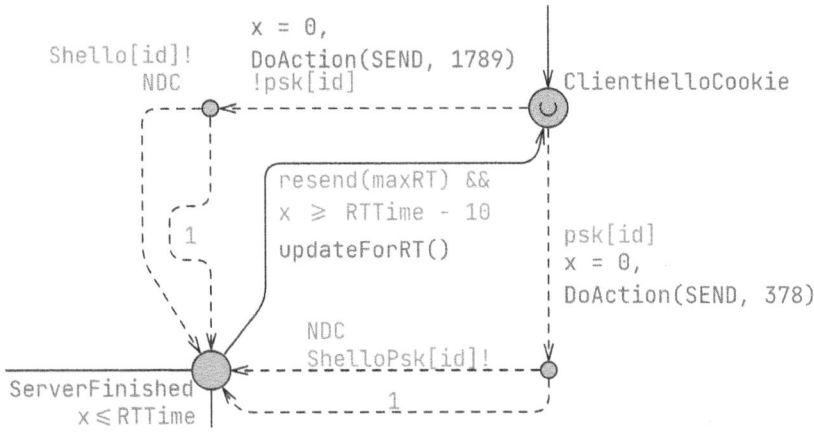

Fig. 7. Server hello.

mentioned above, DTLS is responsible for handling such drops in a meaningful manner. If the client has not responded to the request after a set amount of re-sends, the server drops the connection and release resources used towards it.

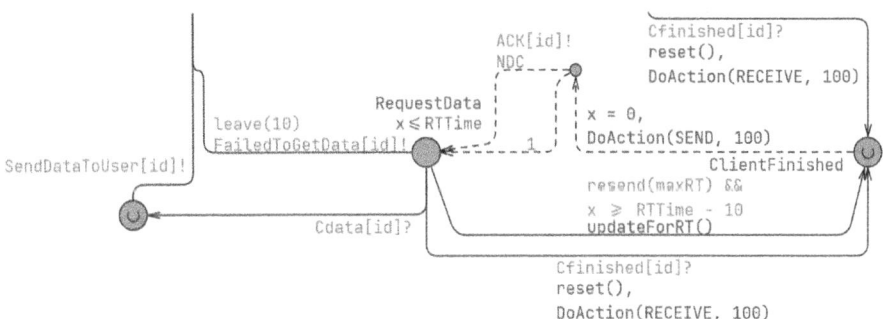

Fig. 8. Server request data.

The client model is very similar to the server model for the base protocol. The client receives messages from the server and responds in a similar way. A key difference is that the client only receives the message sent if the server is actively in the NAT table of the client's router. The server is dropped from this table after no more than 300 s.

To ensure that the basic implementation is correct, some symbolic queries were made for the model, e.g., to check if the model is able to reach certain desired states. As an example, consider the following query:

```
A[] Server.ServerFinished imply Server.sentCookies
```

This query states that if the server reaches the **ServerFinished** location, then it must have sent a cookie first. This query is expected to be true, as if it returns false, the model is out of order, and is thus incorrect. We will not go into further details with the sanity checks here, merely refer to [11].

Modelling Power Consumption. Power consumption is modelled as a per byte cost of sending/encrypting and receiving/decrypting messages. In the UPPAAL model, this is handled by the **DoAction()** function:

```
void DoAction(int action, int bytes){
  clientActionPowerConsumption =
    clientActionPowerConsumption +
  actionPower[action]*bytes;
  }

  //Actions
  double actionPower[3] = {0.000525, 0.0006, 0.5};
```

The actual power consumption numbers (seen in the **actionPower** array) are based on a detailed power consumption analysis performed by Tsoukaneri et al. in [14] and we refer to this for details.

3.2 DTLS 1.3 with Heartbeat Extension on Server

This model covers a server-side heartbeat extension to the default DTLS 1.3 protocol. The handshake is explained in full in Sect. 3.1 and here we focus only on the heartbeat.

The heartbeat extension is implemented on the server, as shown in Fig. 9. The server idles in the **ConnectedHB** location after the handshake is completed and send a heartbeat on a timer, which is a configurable parameter that should be adjusted to simulate the relevant environment. This is also the case for the probability of the server dropping the heartbeat message.

The user may request data from the server at this point making the server request data from the client. When awaiting data from the client the server stays in the **AwatingCdata** location, where an interesting issue is highlighted. Since the server is the system to end the handshake it does not expect an answer from the client after the final ACK message is sent. Therefore the server must be prepared to send another ACK, if the client did not receive the previous ACK and the client retransmits a **Cfinished**.

The client has to stay awake to ensure that the server heartbeats are received and not dropped by the router. In Fig. 10 the part of the client model when the client is connected is shown. Here the client model idles in the **Connected** location and wait to receive heartbeats from the server as well as data request. An important aspect is highlighted here, since the client must keep track of whether or not it receives the heartbeats sent from the server. If the server is dropped from the NAT table of the router, the client will not be able to receive

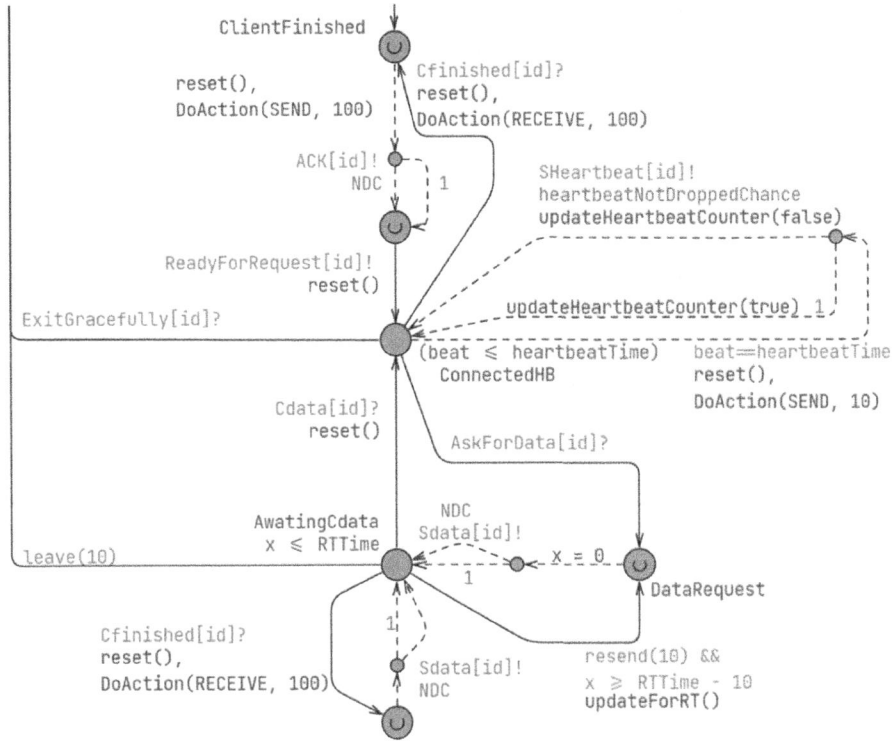

Fig. 9. Server connected - sending heartbeat.

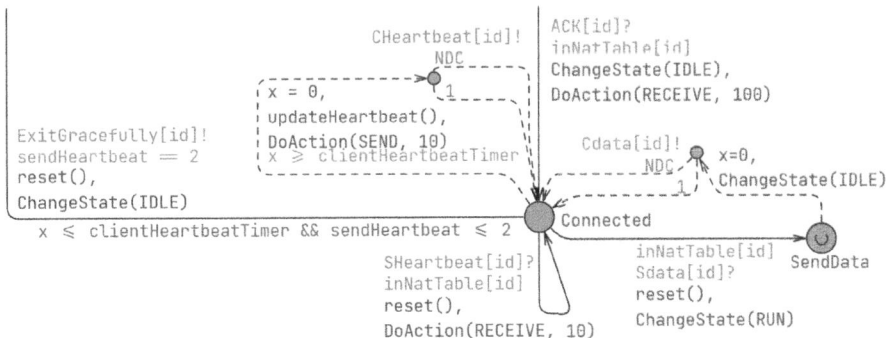

Fig. 10. Client await heartbeat.

them. Only the client will be able to re-establish the server in the NAT table and thus, if a heartbeat from the server has not been received for so long that the server is definitely dropped from the NAT table, the client sends a heartbeat of its own. This results in adding the server to the NAT table, and future heartbeats should be received. If this is not the case, the client attempts to send another heartbeat, before giving up on the connection and releasing the resources.

3.3 DTLS 1.3 with Heartbeat Extension on Client

The final model moves the responsibility of sending the heartbeat to the client. The overall structure of the model is very similar to the model with a heartbeat extension on the server. Moving the responsibility solves the issue of keeping track of lost heartbeats from the server. This was highlighted in Sect. 3.2 and happens because the server might be dropped from the router's NAT table. Moving heartbeat responsibility to the client facilitates the use of the clients ability to always reach the server, allowing the server to not track nor respond to heartbeats from the client.

Two issues may arise from this change: first, since the client may not know if the connection is down for some reason and the server cannot inform the client it does not receive heartbeats, this may lead to a dead connection. Second, the power consumption of the client may increase, since it has to do more work. In our experiments (see Sect. 5), we therefore focus on the server-side heartbeat and leave the client-side heartbeat for future work, e.g., modelling scenarios where clients are suspended more aggressively.

4 Modelling DTLS Under Attack

The models described in the previous section are well suited for analysing the energy consumption of the use of DTLS 1.3 in a wide spectrum of scenarios where the participants collaborate in good faith, i.e., no one is trying to abuse the protocol to drain energy. However, for a security protocol used in critical systems, it is important to also evaluate how it performs when the system is under attack. To this end, we have modelled a malicious actor, an attacker, inspired by the Dolev/Yao attacker [5]. The attacker can disguise itself as either the server or the client and continuously send messages to either the server or the client.

The attacker is a simple automaton with one location and a single transition that loops to this location. The attacker continuously sends heartbeats to the client, forcing the client to consume power by receiving and processing the message. This attacker can be modified to send any messages, and since disrupting service by draining energy is the motive, it does not need to send real messages.

The attacker can be modified to also send messages that the client or server expect to be encrypted, with the intent of them consuming energy by attempting to decrypt the messages. Other attacks against both server and client are explained and tested in Sect. 5. In this work we have focused on energy draining attacks, but it is straightforward to model attackers that target other elements of the protocol, e.g., authentication.

5 Experiments

In this section, we present the results of the two experiments that the model has been tested with. The first experiment is a basic comparison of the power consumption of the different cases, while the second experiment involves multiple tests of the power consumption of the scenarios where a malicious actor is present. We consider the server-side heartbeat the most realistic setup for the scenarios of interest in this work and therefore the focus of the experiments. However, to evaluate the expressiveness of our modelling approach and in anticipation of future experimentation with less typical scenarios, we have also modelled the client-side heartbeat.

All the experiments performed and reported on in this paper, were performed with a "NoDropChance" of 99, i.e., **NDC = 99**, meaning only a one in a hundred chance of dropping a packet (c.f., Sect. 3.1). The effect of varying this parameter is explored in more detail in [11].

5.1 Power Consumption Comparison

This experiment was conducted to compare the power consumption of the base case without any form of optimization to the power consumption of a scenario, called Case 5, which utilizes both the heartbeat protocol and session resumption during the day but only session resumption during night. This is done to reflect the activity of a IoT device, as it might have more requests during the day (here modelled as one message every 7200 s), while being quite limited at night (only one message during the entire night). This can easily be adapted to any specific case at hand. To get accurate power consumption results, the model was simulated for 24 h with a 12 h day and 12 h night. To average out bias in the results, the model was run 1000 times for each case. The results of the experiment can be seen in Fig. 11 and Table 1.

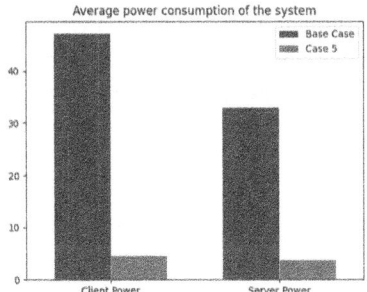

Table 1. Table of power consumption of the base case and Case 5.

	Client	Server
Base Case	47.2071 cJ	33.0076 cJ
Case 5	4.5847 cJ	3.8379 cJ

Fig. 11. Figure of power consumption of the base case and Case 5.

Looking at the results, we see that the power consumption of the base case is significantly higher than Case 5 for both the server and the client. This is to be expected, as the base case runs the full DTLS protocol with every message sent, while Case 5 only uses the full DTLS protocol once, and then uses session resumption to keep the connection alive. This results in a much lower power consumption for Case 5, as the full DTLS protocol is very costly in terms of power consumption. However, the simulation of Case 5 only has seven messages sent (six during the day and one during the night), whereas the base case has 12 messages sent. This was done to model a scenario that has little activity during the night with protocol taking advantage of this fact. If both cases had 12 messages exchanged, the power consumption of Case 5 would increase, but would still be significantly lower than the base case (roughly half), while a scenario with only one to two messages exchanged would result in the base case evening out if not outright being lower than Case 5 in power consumption. Case 4 has a higher power consumption than Case 5 (roughly 2.5 times as much), but still lower than the base case.

To further explore the power consumption of the cases, two extra cases were tested. These cases are based on Case 2 and Case 4 from [11] and we refer there for details and corresponding graphs. Case 2 simply runs using session resumption and heartbeat for the entire day, while Case 4 has the same setup as Case 5, but the message frequency continues during the night. Case 2 has similar performance to Case 5, but is outperformed by Case 5 if the message frequency is decreased. This is to be expected, as even with session resumption, the frequency of messages increases the power consumption.

5.2 Power Consumption with Malicious Actor

The experiment described here is based on scenarios where a malicious actor intrudes on the network, and tries to drain as much power as possible. This experiment is otherwise performed with the same parameters as the previous experiment. To test the robustness of the model, a few different scenarios are tested, where the malicious actor either disguises itself as the server or the client, and continuously sends messages to the other party. For the server side power consumption, the malicious actor sends a **CHello** message to the server repeatedly, while for the client side power consumption, the malicious actor sends a **SHeartbeat** message to the client.

Server Side Power Consumption. This test was conducted to showcase the importance of the cookie exchange in the DTLS protocol, as the server only allocates larger amounts of resources to the connection if the client is willing to respond with a **ClientHello** with the same cookie attached.

We tested two different scenarios with the attacker: the first where the client is able to send a cookie to continue each attack, and the second where the client does not respond with a **ClientHello** with the same cookie attached. The results of the experiment can be seen in Fig. 12 and Table 2.

The results show that the power consumption of the server is significantly lower when the server enforces a cookie exchange. The server will not allocate resources to the connection before the client expends further resources, thereby limiting attacks of that nature. This confirms the importance of the cookie exchange and the importance of dropping the connection and releasing resources if the exchange is not performed correctly.

Client Side Power Consumption. This experiment models a malicious user that continually sends the client a `SHeartbeat` message. The cost of receiving these heartbeats stack up, and the client eventually runs out of power. To remedy this, the client enters a "sleep" state in which it will not respond to any messages and only wakes up after a set amount of time. To evaluate the difference in power consumption, the client was tested with and without the sleep state, and both of these are compared with the basic Case 5 results from Sect. 5.1. The results of the experiment can be seen in Fig. 13 and Table 3.

The results show that the client has a significantly lower power consumption if it can enter the sleep state, thus validating this as a (partial) mitigation against power draining attacks.

6 Related Work

While the idea of using statistical model checking to model energy consumption in various contexts is well established, see e.g. [3,8,15], we believe that the application to DTLS and the inclusion of energy draining attacks is novel.

Prior work on DTLS has modelled and analysed the security of DTLS 1.3, including against DoS attacks [10,12], fuzz tested DTLS implementations [6,7], and has proposed more substantial changes to improve energy consumption of DTLS [1,9], although not in an adversarial context.

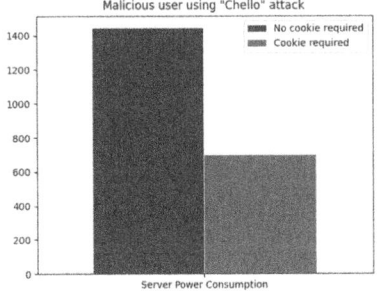

Fig. 12. Graph showcasing the importance of cookie exchange.

Table 2. Table showcasing the importance of cookie exchange.

No Cookie Required	Cookie Required
1443.03 cJ	696.01 cJ

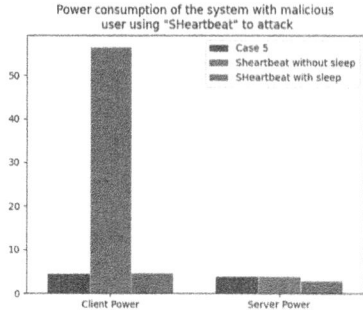

Fig. 13. Graph showcasing power consumption with a malicious user using Sheartbeat.

Table 3. Table showcasing power consumption with a malicious user using Sheartbeat.

	Client	Server
Case 5	4.5847 cJ	3.8379 cJ
Without Sleep	56.3966 cJ	3.9048 cJ
With Sleep	4.7211 cJ	2.9780 cJ

7 Conclusion

In this paper we have presented a novel formalisation of the DTLS 1.3 protocol using timed automata that enables simulation of energy consumption of the devices implementing the protocol. To the best of our knowledge, this is the first formal model of DTLS to do this. Furthermore, we have used the formalisation to propose and analyse energy preserving modifications, adding heartbeats, to DTLS for better session management. Finally, we have shown how attackers can be added to the model, in order to simulate and analyse the effect of attacks, especially regarding energy consumption. To the best of our knowledge, this is also the first formal model of DTLS to do this.

Acknowledgments. This work has been partially supported by both Innovation Fund Denmark and the Digital Research Centre Denmark (DIREC) through the bridge project *Secure Internet of Things* (SIoT); and also through the VILLUM Investigator grant S4OS (Scalable analysis and Synthesis of Safe, Secure and Optimal Strategies for Cyber-Physical Systems).

References

1. Banerjee, U., Juvekar, C., Fuller, S.H., Chandrakasan, A.P.: eeDTLS: energy-efficient datagram transport layer security for the internet of things. In: Proceedings of the IEEE Global Communications Conference (GLOBECOM 2017), pp. 1–6 (2017). https://doi.org/10.1109/GLOCOM.2017.8255053
2. Behrmann, G., David, A., Larsen, K.G.: A tutorial on UPPAAL. In: Bernardo, M., Corradini, F. (eds.) SFM-RT 2004. LNCS, vol. 3185, pp. 200–236. Springer, Cham (2004). https://doi.org/10.1007/978-3-540-30080-9_7
3. David, A., et al.: Statistical model checking for stochastic hybrid systems. In: Proceedings of the First International Workshop on Hybrid Systems and Biology (HSB 2012), pp. 122–136 (2012). https://doi.org/10.4204/EPTCS.92.9
4. David, A., Larsen, K.G., Legay, A., Mikucionis, M., Poulsen, D.B.: UPPAAL SMC tutorial. Int. J. Softw. Tools Technol. Transf. **17**(4), 397–415 (2015). https://doi.org/10.1007/S10009-014-0361-Y

5. Dolev, D., Yao, A.C.: On the security of public key protocols. In: Proceedings of the 22nd annual IEEE Symposium on the Foundations of Computer Science, pp. 350–357 (1981)
6. Fiterau-Brostean, P., Jonsson, B., Merget, R., de Ruiter, J., Sagonas, K., Somorovsky, J.: Analysis of DTLS implementations using protocol state fuzzing. In: 29th USENIX Security Symposium, (USENIX Security 2020), pp. 2523–2540 (2020)
7. Fiterau-Brostean, P., Jonsson, B., Sagonas, K., Tåquist, F.: DTLS-fuzzer: a DTLS protocol state fuzzer. In: 15th IEEE Conference on Software Testing, Verification and Validation (ICST 2022), pp. 456–458 (2022). https://doi.org/10.1109/ICST53961.2022.00051
8. Gamatié, A., Sassatelli, G., Mikucionis, M.: Modeling and analysis for energy-driven computing using statistical model-checking. In: Proceedings of the Design, Automation & Test in Europe Conference & Exhibition, (DATE 2021), pp. 980–985 (2021). https://doi.org/10.23919/DATE51398.2021.9474224
9. Haroon, A., Akram, S., Shah, M.A., Wahid, A.: E-lithe: a lightweight secure DTLS for IoT. In: 2017 IEEE 86th Vehicular Technology Conference (VTC-Fall) (2017). https://doi.org/10.1109/VTCFall.2017.8288362
10. Kim, J.Y., Holz, R., Hu, W., Jha, S.: Automated analysis of secure internet of things protocols. In: Proceedings of the 33rd Annual Computer Security Applications Conference (ACSAC 2017), pp. 238–249 (2017). https://doi.org/10.1145/3134600.3134624
11. Koch, C.B., Thesbjerg, K.L., Gehlert, L.B., Jørgensen, M.P.H., Rusbjerg, S.K., Møller, T.: IoT power consumption & DTLS modelling. Student report, Department Computer Science, Aalborg University (2024). https://github.com/Goggon/DTLS_Paper_Models
12. Maleh, Y., Ezzati, A., Belaïssaoui, M.: DoS attacks analysis and improvement in DTLS protocol for internet of things. In: Proceedings of the International Conference on Big Data and Advanced Wireless Technologies (BDAW 2016), pp. 54:1–54:7 (2016). https://doi.org/10.1145/3010089.3010139
13. Rescorla, E.: The transport layer security (TLS) protocol version 1.3. RFC 8446 (2018). https://doi.org/10.17487/RFC8446, https://www.rfc-editor.org/info/rfc8446
14. Tsoukaneri, G., Garcia, F., Marina, M.: Narrowband IoT device energy consumption characterization and optimizations. In: Proceedings of the International Conference on Embedded Wireless Systems and Networks (EWSN 2020), pp. 1–12. Junction Publishing (2020). https://ewsn2020.conf.citi-lab.fr/
15. Wognsen, E.R., Hansen, R.R., Larsen, K.G.: Battery-aware scheduling of mixed criticality systems. In: Margaria, T., Steffen, B. (eds.) ISoLA 2014. LNCS, vol. 8803, pp. 208–222. Springer, Cham (2014). https://doi.org/10.1007/978-3-662-45231-8_15
16. Younes, H.L.S.: Verification and planning for stochastic processes with asynchronous events. Ph.D. thesis, Carnegie Mellon (2005)

Verifying a Radio Telescope Pipeline Using HaliVer: Solving Nonlinear and Quantifier Challenges

Lars B. van den Haak[1]($^{\boxtimes}$), Anton Wijs[1], Marieke Huisman[2], and Mark van den Brand[1]

[1] Eindhoven University of Technology, Eindhoven, The Netherlands
{l.b.v.d.haak,a.j.wijs,m.g.j.v.d.brand}@tue.nl
[2] University of Twente, Enschede, The Netherlands
m.huisman@utwente.nl

Abstract. This paper describes a case study to verify memory safety of a radio telescope pipeline, which was targeted with the PADRE project of Astron, SURF and the Netherlands eScienceCenter. As performance is important for this application, the implementation of the radio telescope pipeline should run on a GPU device. Therefore, we encoded the radio telescope pipeline using the HALIDE scheduling language, which achieved a significant speedup. Next, we used the HALIVER tool to automatically generate formal pre- and postconditions, loop invariants and assertions, which the deductive verifier VERCORS can use to prove memory safety. We identified two challenges for the automatic generation of formal annotations for a tool such as VERCORS. The first challenge was related to the flattening of multi-dimensional arrays to single arrays and the second challenge concerns the use of many arrays in a program in combination with many quantifiers to specify read and write permissions. For both challenges, we propose solutions, and implemented these. Not every solution proved successful. We discuss the lessons learned and future plans to solve a core scalability issue for large optimised parallel programs.

Keywords: Formal Verification · Scheduling Language · Deductive Verification · Nonlinear Integer Arithmetic · Permission Quantifiers

1 Introduction

If advances in computational power are to be harnessed, code needs to be written for massively parallel hardware [12]. Optimising code to run in parallel is hard to do correctly as concurrency bugs can be easily introduced and are hard to detect. In addition, optimised code is often complicated and uses low-level intrinsics, making it harder to understand and reason about.

One solution to writing parallel optimised code comes from scheduling languages, such as the domain-specific language HALIDE [16]. HALIDE targets image and array processing code and allows one to write the *algorithm* part of a program separately from the applied *optimisations*. This makes it easier to try out different optimisations, and allows one to optimise for specific parallel hardware.

Often, formally *verifying* code with a deductive verifier comes at a steep cost in terms of required effort to formally specify pre- and postconditions, loop invariants and assertions, for instance using separation logic. This makes deductive verification less accessible to industry. With the tool HALIVER [20] we try to address this concern by combining HALIDE with the deductive verifier VERCORS [1]. This allows us to significantly reduce the required annotation effort for verifying optimised parallel code. When an optimisation is applied on an algorithm, the latter's pre- and postconditions, loop invariants and assertions are automatically altered to reflect the optimisation.

In this paper, we investigate how HALIVER can be used to verify the memory safety properties of an industrial case study related to an image pipeline of a radio telescope. We identify two key challenges in verifying this case study, which we suspect are common to optimised parallel code. We describe ways to overcome these challenges, but the proposed solutions run into the limitations of what deductive verifiers based on separation logic currently can handle. We discuss the lessons learned, and discuss a different encoding that we suspect would be better suited to these problems, so that the verifiers can deal with them.

The structure of the paper is as follows. In Sect. 2, we give a brief refresher on HALIDE, VERCORS and HALIVER. In Sect. 3, we introduce the case study. In Sect. 4, we discuss the challenges we encountered in verifying the case study, together with proposed solutions. Section 5 contains experiments, Sect. 6 discusses lessons learned and Sect. 7 considers related work. Finally, in Sect. 8, we draw conclusions.

2 Background

VERCORS. VERCORS[1] [1] is a deductive verifier that can verify the functional correctness of, possibly parallel, software. Its specification language uses permission-based separation logic [2], a combination of first-order logic and read-/write permissions. The latter are used for concurrency-related verification, to express which data can be accessed by a thread at which moment.

Programs written in a number of languages, such as JAVA and C, can be verified. VERCORS's verification engine relies on VIPER [14], which applies symbolic execution to analyse programs with persistent mutable state. VIPER in turn relies on the SMT solver Z3 [5].

We explain VERCORS annotations using an example C program given in Listing 1. Intended functional behaviour can be specified by means of pre- and postconditions, indicated by the keywords requires and ensures, respectively (Lines 2–3). The statement context P (Line 9) is an abbreviation for requires P;ensures P. Loop invariants (Lines 13–15) and assertions can be added to

---

[1] We only briefly touch upon the definitions here. For examples with more explanation, please refer to the online tutorial at https://vercors.ewi.utwente.nl/wiki/.

Listing 1. Example C program with annotations for VerCors.

```
1   // A side-effect free function taking a positive number and doubling it.
2   /*@ requires a > 0;
3       ensures \result == 2*a ∧ \result >0; @*/
4   int /*@ pure @*/ double(int a){ return a+a; }
5   // A predicate with write permission to array x.
6   /*@ resource f(int arr[], int len) = (arr ≠ null ∧ arr.length==len)
7       ∧ (∀ int i; 0≤i ∧ i<len;Perm(arr[i], 1\1)); @*/
8   // Fill array x with numbers 0..n−1.
9   /*@ context f(x, n);
10      ensures (∀ int j; 0≤j ∧ j<i; \unfolding f(x,n) \in x[j] == j);
11      decreases; @*/
12  void enumerate(int x[], int n){
13    /*@ loop_invariant 0 ≤ i ∧ i ≤ n;
14        loop_invariant f(x, n);
15        loop_invariant (∀ int j; 0≤j ∧ j<i; \unfolding f(x,n) \in x[j] == j);
16        decreases n-i; @*/
17    for(int i=0; i<n;i++){
18      //@ unfold f(x, n);
19      x[i] = i;
20      //@ fold f(x, n); }
21  }
22  // This ghost lemma proves that if we multiply positive numbers, the results is positive.
23  /*@ ghost
24      requires a≥0 ∧ b≥0;
25      ensures a*b ≥ 0;
26      decreases b;
27  void lemma_positive(int a, int b){
28    if(b>0) lemma_positive(a, b-1);
29  }@*/
```

the code to help VerCors in proving the pre- and postconditions. We refer to the pre- and postconditions, loop invariants and assertions together as the *annotations* of a code fragment.

With \result (Line 3) we can refer to the return value of a function. With (\let a = A;B) we introduce variable a with value A to be used in expression B.

A permission Perm(x, f) (Line 7) gives permission to memory location x, where f is a fractional, with 1\1 indicating permission to write and anything between 0\1 and 1\1 permission to read. A pure (Line 4) function is without side-effects, thus can be used in annotations. It has the keyword pure in the header, and its body is a single expression. In C files, annotations and other verification related definitions are given in special comments, like //@ or /*@...@*/ for multi-line comments.

VerCors can reason about a range of numbers using *quantifiers*. With (∀int i;C;B) (Line 10 & 15) you can indicate that expression B holds for all values of i for which expression C hold. This can also be used to range over expressions which contain permissions. (Line 7).

VerCors can prove termination of loops and recursive functions. Whenever the clause decreases r (Line 16 & 26) is added, VerCors will try to prove that the function or loop terminates, by showing that recursive calls or the loop body will strictly decrease the value of r, that r has a lower bound and only

Listing 2. HALIDE example which multiplies two input buffers and sums the rows.

```
1   void mulSum(Buffer<int,2> a,
2     Buffer<int,2> b, Func &out, int n){
3     Func mul, sum; Var x, y; RDom r(0, n);
4     mul(x, y) = a(x, y)*b(x, y);
5     sum(y) = 0;
6     sum(y) = sum(y) + mul(r, y);
7     out(x, y) = Tuple(mul(x,y), sum(y));
8
9     // Schedule
10    out.parallel(x).reorder(y,x);
11    sum.compute_at(out, x);
12    mul.compute_root();
13  }
```

Listing 3. Resulting loop-nest of Listing 2

```
1   produce mul:
2     for y:
3       for x:
4         mul(...) = ...
5   consume mul:
6     produce out:
7       parallel x:
8         produce sum:
9           for y:
10            sum(...) = ...
11          for y:
12            for r:
13              sum(...) = ...
14        consume sum:
15          for y:
16            out(...) = ...
```

terminating functions are called. Stating `decreases` (Line 11) checks that a non-recursive function terminates.

A *predicate* definition is indicated by the keyword `resource` (Lines 6–7) and is used to store conditions and permissions to memory locations. You create a predicate *instance* with `fold` (Line 20) where the permission needed for the predicate is removed from the program state and the conditions of the predicate need to hold. With `unfold` (Line 18) the reverse happens; the information of the instance is added back to the program state. With \unfolding ...\in ... (Line 10 & 15) you can temporally unfold the predicate such that it can be used in an annotation. To extend the program state with helper code and variables, you can introduce `ghost` (Line 23) code. This exists only for the purpose of verification and extends the program state with a *ghost state*. A verification *lemma* (Line 23–29) is a helper function which proves a certain property and can be called to assert this property. Such a lemma lives in the ghost state.

HALIDE. HALIDE is a DSL embedded in C++, tailored for image processing pipelines and array computations [16,17].[2] HALIDE separates the *algorithm*, defining what you want to calculate, from the *schedule*, defining how the calculation should be performed. Typically, when optimising code for a specific architecture, the code becomes much more complex and loses portability. By separating the schedule, the code expressing the functionality is not altered.

We explain HALIDE using the example from Listing 2. HALIDE uses a functional style, which allows algorithms to be compact and loop-free. Multidimensional arrays are represented as functions where each variable implicitly defines a complete dimension. The keyword `Func` (Line 3) denotes a HALIDE function and `Var` (Line 3) a variable. In the example, `mul(x, y)` implicitly defines a two-dimensional array. With `Buffer<T,D>` (Line 1–2) you can supply an input *buffer* of type T and D dimensions. Each function can have several *definitions*,

---

[2] A HALIDE tutorial can be found here: https://halide-lang.org/tutorials/.

which are calculated in order. E.g. the first definition of sum is on Line 5 and the second on Line 6. The result of a function can be single valued (Line 4 & 5) or can have multiple values stored as Tuple (Line 7).

Each dimension of a function implicitly defines a loop. For example, the function mul would be calculated as for(int y=...){for(int x=...){mul(x,y)= a (x,y)*b(x,y);}}. A *reduction domain* RDom r(min, extent) (Line 3) defines another loop to be executed for a definition with minimum min and extent number of iterations. For instance, the second definition of sum would result in for(int y=...){for(int r=0;r<n;r++){sum(y)= sum(y)+mul(r,y);}}.

The resulting function, along with all its dependencies, is called a *pipeline*. The HALIDE compiler translates the HALIDE pipeline into the *intermediate representation* (IR), which shows the loop structure that is implicitly defined. We call this structure a *loop-nest*. This representation also explicitly states when functions are produced or only used with produce and consume nodes.

A HALIDE *schedule* (Line 10–12) defines how the loop-nest is structured and controls how it is executed, therefore expressing possible optimisations. We can schedule a dimension, and thus the associated loop, to be parallel (Line 10). We can reorder (Line 10) the order of the dimensions. With f.compute_at(g, x) (Line 11) we define that function f should be computed at the loop from dimension x for function g. With f.compute_root (Line 12) we indicate f as computed at the root of the program. The example program with its schedule leads to the loop-nest structure of Listing 3. The schedule directive split(x, x_in, x_out, n) splits the dimension x into x_in and x_out, where x_in has size n. The directive unroll(x) marks the loop associated with x to be unrolled. Finally, the directive gpu(bx, tx) marks the function to be computed on the GPU, taking the dimension bx as thread blocks and tx as threads.

HALIVER. HALIVER [20] is a tool built into the HALIDE compiler and a tutorial can be found at [19]. HALIVER adds the ability to annotate to HALIDE code. The tool then transforms these annotations and attaches them to the generated optimised C code, which can then in turn be verified using VERCORS. HALIVER automatically generates the necessary permission annotations. These steps result in a significant reduction in annotation effort. VERCORS can then prove that a program has only safe memory accesses, does not contain data races, and is functionally correct up to the level of the annotations provided.

Annotations can be added as *pipeline annotations*, which specify the pre- and postconditions of the entire pipeline. With *intermediate* annotations specific functions can be annotated, such as f.ensures(E), which specifies that after f is calculated, condition E holds. Intermediate annotations help prove the pipeline pre- and postconditions, much like loop-invariants do in a C program.

3 Case Study Description

The case study used in this paper concerns a pre-processing pipeline for the Low Frequency Array (LOFAR) radio telescope used in astronomy. The PADRE project[3] of ASTRON, the Netherlands eScience Center and SURF aimed to improve this processing pipeline. Specifically, part of the DP3 (the Default Preprocessing Pipeline) for LOFAR[4] was optimized and ported to the GPU. For this case study, we investigate how this part can be ported to HALIDE and what lessons we learned trying to verify data-race freedom using the HALIVER tool.

First, we discuss the DDECAL algorithm, which is the specific algorithm ported in the PADRE project, and which we port as well in this case study.

3.1 DDECAL

The direction-dependent calibration algorithm (DDECAL) [6] calibrates radio telescope data to compensate for different errors. It tries to find the distortion of an antenna by transforming the signal to observations and comparing these with the expected sky mode. It does this by solving the following equation.

$$\mathcal{V}_i = \mathcal{J}_i \mathcal{M}_i \tag{1}$$

For each antenna i, this equation tries to find a solution for matrix $\mathcal{J}_i$, whilst fixing $\mathcal{V}_i$ and $\mathcal{M}_i$. Here $\mathcal{V}_i$ represents the observed *visibility* matrix, i.e. the expected sky model. The $\mathcal{M}_i$ matrix represents the actual measurement of two antennas. Lastly, the $\mathcal{J}_i$ matrix models how a certain antenna warps the visibility because of instrumental effects and propagation effects, such as ionospheric distortions [8]. Each of these matrices have 2×2 complex matrices as elements. For the complete details see [6], but for this paper it is enough to know that we are trying to solve a linear equation involving matrices.

Various ways to solve Eq. 1 are implemented in DDECAL. The PADRE project ported the version called `Iterative Diagonal Solver`. In Listing 4, the structure of this algorithm is given. The goal of this algorithm is to find better approximations of the $\mathcal{J}$ matrices, represented by `solutions` and `next_solutions`. It performs a while loop, which stops when `solutions` and `next_solutions` are sufficiently close, determined by the function `assign_solution`. In the algorithm there are *channel blocks* and *directions*, which are ways to group measurements of certain radio frequencies and time intervals. The expected sky model is represented by *visibilities* (`vis`, $\mathcal{V}$), the measurements are represented by `model` ($\mathcal{M}$), and both are grouped by channel blocks and directions.

In the original CPU implementation, the loop over channel blocks was parallelised. Since there are typical in the order of 10^1 number of channel blocks, this is not a fit for GPU parallelism. The PADRE project chose to parallelise the loops over the visibilities, since there are typically in the order of 10^5 visibilities, meaning there is enough parallelism for GPUs available. More specifically, they converted the `add_or_substract_direction`, `solve_direction` and `step` functions to CUDA kernels.

---
[3] https://research-software-directory.org/projects/the-petaflop-aartfaac-data-reduction-engine-padre.
[4] https://git.astron.nl/RD/DP3/.

Listing 4. Structure of the `Iterative Diagonal Solver` algorithm in DDECAL. The M^H indicates a Hermitian transpose and M_{ij} is used to index a matrix.

```
1   def ddecal(vis, solutions, model):
2      while (not has_converged):
3         foreach cb in channel_block:
4            foreach d in directions[cb]:
5               vis[cb] = subtract_direction(vis[cb], solutions, d, model[cb])
6            foreach d in directions[cb]:
7               vis_temp[cb] = add_direction(vis[cb], solutions, d)
8               next_solutions = solve_direction(vis_temp[cb], d, solutions)
9         next_solutions = step(solutions, next_solutions)
10        (has_converged, solutions) = assign_solutions(solutions, next_solutions)
11
12  def add/subtract_direction(vis, solutions, d, model):
13     foreach v in vis:
14        v = v {+/-} solutions[si_v,d,ant1_v] * model_v * solutions[si_v,d,ant2_v]^H
15     return vis
16
17  def solve_direction(vis, solutions, d, model):
18     foreach v in vis:
19        numerator[si_v,ant1_v] += v * solutions[si_v,d,ant2_v] * model_v^H
20        numerator[si_v,ant2_v] += v^H * solutions[si_v,d,ant1_v] * model_v
21        denominator[0,si_v,ant1_v] += norm(solutions[si_v,d,ant2_v] * model_v^H)
22        denominator[1,si_v,ant2_v] += norm(solutions[si_v,d,ant1_v] * model_v)
23     foreach a in ant:
24        foreach s in si:
25           next_solutions[s,d,a]_00 = numerator[s,ant]_00 / denominator[0,s,ant]
26           next_solutions[s,d,a]_11 = numerator[s,ant]_11 / denominator[1,s,ant]
27     return next_solutions
28
29  def step(solutions, next_solutions):
30     foreach cb in channel_block:
31        foreach d in directions[cb]:
32           foreach a in ant:
33              foreach s in si:
34                 next_solutions[s,d,a] = solutions[s,d,a] * (1-step_size)
35                                       + next_solutions[s,d,a] * step_size
36     return next_solutions
```

3.2 HALIDE Implementation

Most computations inside the converted functions reason about complex numbered 2×2 matrices. HALIDE does not have direct support for this, but this can be modeled via meta-programming in C++ using tuples. Therefore, we create extra modules for complex numbers and matrices. For complex numbers, we add support for +, -, *, complex *conjugation* and taking the *norm*. For matrices we add support for +, -, *matrix multiplication* and *conjugate transposition*.

Additionally, in HALIDE, each tuple value is stored separately as an array. In the original implementation the matrices and complex numbers are stored as a single multi-dimensional array. So we created methods to switch between tuple and multi-dimensional array representations.

In Listing 5, the `add_or_subtract_direction` code is found, which shows that we can use the meta-programming to arrive at relatively simple HALIDE

Table 1. Running time of HALIDE implementation of DDECAL algorithm compared to the base version and Padre implementation.

	Platform	Time (s)	Speed up vs base	Speed up per platform
Base	CPU	15.67	1.0	1.0
Halide		**3.20**	4.9	4.9
Padre	GPU	2.40	6.5	1.0
Halide		**0.86**	18.2	2.8

Listing 5. The add_or_subtract_direction function written in HALIDE.

```
Func add_or_subtract_direction(bool add, Func vis_in){
    Func vis_out("vis_out");

    MatrixDiag solution_1 = solutions(solution_index(v), antenna_1(v));
    MatrixDiag solution_2 = solutions(solution_index(v), antenna_2(v));
    Matrix contribution = solution_1 * Matrix(model(v)) * HermTranspose(solution_2);

    if(add){
        vis_out(v) = Matrix(vis_in(v)) + contribution;
    } else {
        vis_out(v) = Matrix(vis_in(v)) - contribution;
    }
    return vis_out;
}
```

code.[5] We have also made a separate version for the solve_direction and step functions, so we can verify smaller functions first.

We compared the HALIDE implementation with the base and PADRE implementation, see Table 1 for the results. We ran the benchmarks on a Intel® Core™ i7-11800H @ 2.30 GHz × 16 computer with a NVIDIA RTX A2000 used as GPU. As you can see HALIDE allows for a significant speedup. With HALIDE we could test many different optimisations and for our GPU setup it was advantageous to compute the functions subtract and add directly per visibility at the solve_direction function, essentially performing kernel fusion, and leading to the achieved speedup.

4 Verification Challenges and Solutions

We used HALIVER for checking for memory-safety, such that no data-races occur and no unsafe memory locations are accessed. This led to some interesting verification challenges, for which we propose solutions in this paper.

---

[5] The complete implementation in HALIDE together with optimization schedules can be found at https://github.com/sakehl/padre-casestudy together with the original code.

4.1 Tuple Support

Before addressing the verification challenges, we first made sure that HALIVER can support tuples. Tuples are essential for this case study to model complex numbers, matrices, and operations on these constructs, and allow HALIVER to store them as structures of arrays, rather than arrays of structures. A function without tuples is compiled to a single array in C code, which stores all its values. For a function with tuples, a separate array in C code should be created for each element of the tuple. Extending HALIVER to support this was relatively straightforward. Array references are named correctly, and for each separate array that is generated, read and write permissions are generated and distributed accordingly. So the normal process of generating and transforming annotations is applied to each individual tuple value.

4.2 Verifying Flattened Multidimensional Arrays

In the original HALIVER paper [20] the bounds of buffers passed as input need to be concrete integer values. Otherwise, *nonlinear* integer arithmetic is required and a deductive verifier relying on an SMT solver, such as VERCORS, cannot solve nonlinear integer arithmetic, as this is undecidable in general [7].

The nonlinear arithmetic emerges when a multi-dimensional HALIDE function is flattened to an array. The function `f(x, y)= ...` is a typical HALIDE function of two dimensions. When HALIDE compiles this function towards the C back-end, the compiler *flattens* this to an array like `f[(y-y.min)*x.extent +(x-x.min)]`, where `x.extent` and `x.min` are equal to the size and minimal value of the x dimension, respectively. This array has length `x.extent*y.extent`. When verifying this code, it is checked that the access to `f` is within bounds. If VERCORS tries to verify this, without any additional information, this will fail. To be precise, the expression `(y-y.min)*x.extent` contains nonlinear integer arithmetic.

Proving Safe Nonlinear Access. Fortunately, we can use VERCORS to prove certain information, using verification *lemmas*. For the nonlinear case, we want to prove the following mathematical property:

$$\text{Given that: } a \geq 0 \land b > 0 \land a < a_{max}$$
$$\text{We prove that: } a * b \leq (a_{max} - 1) * b$$

We want to prove this, without using nonlinear integer arithmetic. To do so, we perform an induction proof on b using only linear logic. For the base case $b := 1$, $a * b \leq (a_{max} - 1) * b$ is trivially true due to the pre-conditions.

For the induction case, we take $a * b \leq (a_{max} - 1) * b$ as the induction hypothesis. We want to prove this holds for $b + 1$.

$$a * b \leq (a_{max} - 1) * b \text{ (Induction hypothesis)}$$
$$a * b + a \leq (a_{max} - 1) * b + a \text{ (Add } a \text{ to both sides)}$$
$$a * (b + 1) \leq (a_{max} - 1) * b + a_{max} - 1 \text{ (Since } a <= a_{max} - 1)$$
$$a * (b + 1) \leq (a_{max} - 1) * (b + 1)$$

This nonlinearity can be proven by induction, without using nonlinear logic.

To prove the nonlinear array access of the previous section: (y-y.min)*x.extent +(x-x.min)<x.extent*y.extent, we fill in $a := $ y-y.min, $b := $ x.extent, $a_{max} := $ y.extent to arrive at the information:

$$(\text{y-y.min})*\text{x.extent} \leq (\text{y.extent-1})*\text{x.extent}$$
$$(\text{y-y.min})*\text{x.extent} + \text{x.extent} \leq \text{y.extent}*\text{x.extent}$$
$$(\text{y-y.min})*\text{x.extent} + (\text{x-x.min}) < \text{y.extent}*\text{x.extent}$$

In Listing 6, we show how we prove these lemmas in VERCORS. Note that we made the lemma for accessing arrays more general, by allowing a different stride for each dimension. In that case, a flattened 2-dimensional array is accessed with f[(y-y.min)*y.stride +(x-x.min)*x.stride]. Lemmas for higher dimensional arrays follow the same proof structure, and are included in the code for the case study.

Listing 6. Lemmas encoded in VERCORS that help prove that nonlinear array accesses are within bounds.

```
1   requires a ≥ 0;
2   requires b > 0;
3   requires a < max a;
4   ensures a*b ≤ (max_a-1)*b;
5   ensures \result;
6   decreases b;
7   pure bool lemma_nonlinear(int a, int b, int max_a) =
8     b>1 ? lemma_nonlinear(a, b-1, max_a) : true;
9
10  requires x-x.min ≥ 0 ∧ x-x.min < x.extent;
11  requires y-y.min ≥ 0 ∧ y-y.min < y.extent;
12  requires x.stride > 0;
13  requires y.stride ≥ x.extent * x.stride;
14
15  ensures 0 ≤ (x-x.min)*x.stride + (y-y.min)*y.stride;
16  ensures (x-x.min)*x.stride + (y-y.min)*y.stride < y.stride*y.extent;
17  ensures \result;
18  decreases;
19  pure bool lemma_2d_access(
20    int x, int x.min, int x.stride, int x.extent,
21    int y, int y.min, int y.stride, int y.extent) =
22    lemma_nonlinear(x-x.min, x.stride, x.extent) ∧
23    lemma_nonlinear(y-y.min, y.stride, y.extent);
```

Supplying Nonlinear Information. We cannot globally specify that the nonlinear access of a flattened array is safe. VERCORS needs this information to be given at the appropriate times for each specific instance of nonlinearity. To call the lemma, we need the exact dimensions of the functions, but these depend on the schedule and the bound inferencing compiler pass of HALIDE. Therefore, we add the information for the lemma in the intermediate representation of HALIDE, during the flattening pass of the HALIDE compiler. Then, during code generation, the appropriate lemma is called just before the array is accessed in the ghost state.

We have chosen to make the lemmas of Listing 6 to be *pure* functions, so they can be used inside annotations. This is needed because VERCORS also needs to prove that an array access inside an annotation respects the bounds of the array. Thus we extended the HALIVER tool to automatically insert the lemmas just before a flattened array is accessed in the code.

4.3 Dealing with Quantifiers

Our next challenge arose when we tried to verify memory safety of the function `solve_direction`. Even with concrete bounds, verification failed. The cause for this was related to insufficient permissions for memory accesses, but repeated attempts to verify memory safety led to VERCORS non-deterministically pointing to different lines in the source code. A manual inspection of the specification, however, showed that sufficient permission had been given for these accesses.

Quantifiers. The cause of the failed verification attempt was that multiple permission quantifiers were used, which specified permission for each array member. When specifying multiple memory locations of the same type with quantifiers, each location is compared to the other locations to see if they do not overlap [15]. This check is automatically added by the VIPER infrastructure and is inherent to separation logic. Conversely, if there are multiple quantifiers, these checks blow up in size. In Subsect. 5.1, we add a micro-benchmark that explicitly shows this blow up in verification time which ultimately leads to verification failures. However, in our case study, we know that memory locations do not overlap. Therefore, we investigated ways to circumvent these checks.

Predicates. Predicates can be used to *hide* (quantified) permissions, and create a new type of *resource* per predicate. When quantifiers are completely hidden, checks for overlapping memory do not need to happen. However, if the code includes a write to a location and this write can happen in parallel, the involved write permission must be precisely divided over the parallel threads. Because of this, we cannot hide the complete quantified permission. To address this problem, we wrap a specific array location in a unique predicate inside the quantifier. Thus, we encode the permissions in two types of predicates, see Listing 7.

Type 1 (for writing): Predicates inside quantifiers: for each array, every location is wrapped in a predicate specific to that array. In Listing 7, f_r is an example. Predicates need to prove that an array access is inside of bounds for each context, thus this extra information is also folded inside the predicate.

Listing 7. Wrapping predicate of two dimensional function f(x,y), after it is flattened to an array. Predicate f_r (Type 1) captures permission to only 1 element of the array, whilst array_2d_all (Type 2) captures permission towards all elements.

```
resource f_r(int x, int x_min, int x_extent, int x_stride,
             int y, int y_min, int y_extent, int y_stride,
             int[] f) =
  (f ≠ null ∧ f.length == x_stride*y_stride ∧
  x-min_x ≥ 0 ∧ x-min_x<extent_x ∧
  y-min_y ≥ 0 ∧ y-min_y<extent_y ∧
  stride_x > 0 ∧ stride_y ≥ extent_x*stride_x ∧
  lemma_2d_access(x, x_min, x_stride, x_extent,y, y_min, y_stride, y_extent)
  ) ** (\let int i = (x-x_min)*x_stride + (y-y_min)*y_stride;
  (0 ≤ i ∧ i < f.length) **
  Perm(f[i], write)
  );

resource array_2d_all(int[] data) = data ≠ null ** (∀ i; 0 ≤ i ∧ i < data.length;
        Perm(f[i], write));
```

Type 2 (for reading): Predicates containing quantifiers: the quantified permission of the whole array is folded inside the predicate. In Listing 7, array_2 d_all is an example.

In the intermediate representation (IR) of HALIDE, the compiler keeps track when an array, corresponding to a function, is realized and when it is only used. Under a *produce* node, the array can be written to. In a *consume* node, the array can only be read. Thus in a produce node of a function, we use predicates of type 1 for that function. In a consume of a function we use predicate type 2. Similarly, buffers given as input are read- or write-only, so write-only buffers get predicate type 1 and read-only buffers get predicate type 2.

To use these predicates, they need to be *unfolded* and *folded*, to take them in and out of scope. Since the HALIVER tool lives inside the HALIDE compiler, we can place these precisely whenever a memory load or store happens. Furthermore, when a new array is allocated, we immediately fold the permission to remove it from scope. Lastly, the annotations can also contain references towards these array values. Thus use the \unfolding ...\in ... syntax of VerCors to unfold and fold the specific predicate in the annotations when needed.

5 Experiments

In this section, we report about our verification efforts for the *PADRE* case study with HALIVER. Since verification of the complete DDECAL algorithm encoded in HALIDE failed, we tried to verify specific parts of the algorithm. With HALIVER we generated several versions of the sub_direction, solve_direction and step PADRE functions, which we then tried to verify w.r.t. memory safety using VERCORS. We show that our efforts allow some problems with non-linearity to be solvable. However, the predicate approach turned out not to help for this case study, which we further investigated with some micro-benchmarks that provided useful insights for future research. In Table 2, we show the results for all the versions we considered.

Table 2. Verification results for `sub_direction` and `solve_direction` produced by HALIVER. We use abbreviations for versions with concrete bounds (CB), nonconcrete bounds (NCB), lemmas (L) and predicates (P).

Version	Time (s)	Result	Version	Time (s)	Result	Version	Time (s)	Result
CB	180	**Pass**	CB	57	**Pass**	CB	547	Fail
NCB	534	Fail	NCB	96	Fail	NCB	671	Fail
NCB-L	693	**Pass**	CB-P	70	**Pass**	CB-P	950	Fail
NCB-L-P	248	Fail	NCB-L-P	180	**Pass**	NCB-L-P	1202	Fail

(a) `sub_direction`　　　　　(b) `step`　　　　　(c) `solve_direction`

Nonlinear Arithmetic. We were able to verify `sub_direction` and `step` with concrete bounds (CB) with the regular HALIVER approach. However, when we did not have concrete bounds (NCB), we were not able to verify these files due to nonlinear arithmetic. For the versions indicated with L we have added the nonlinear arithmetic lemmas mentioned in Sect. 4.2. These versions do indeed verify, showing this approach is viable for proving flattened multidimensional arrays memory safe.

Using Predicates. As can be seen in Table 2, we are unable to verify the function `solve_direction`. When looking at verification failures for all the versions, we see that VERCORS non-deterministically fails at some code line. When inspecting a specific failure instance, and removing everything in the program that is not related to that failure, the program *does* verify. This leads us to believe that the annotations are correct, but with our current encoding and problem domain, we run into the limits of deductive verifiers based on separation logic. We suspect this stems from the fact that many arrays are in scope for which permissions need to be managed. The HALIDE implementation of the `solve_direction` function has six arrays as input, one as output, and allocates 28 intermediate arrays. For comparison, `step` and `sub_direction` have the same amount of input and output arrays, but allocate two and zero intermediate arrays, respectively.

5.1 Micro-benchmarks

We applied VERCORS to some micro-benchmarks in a controlled setting to see how the verification time is influenced when the number of arrays is increased.[6] In

---

[6] An example program can be found at https://github.com/sakehl/padre-casestudy/blob/main/verification_goals/Quant/data/quant9.pvl.

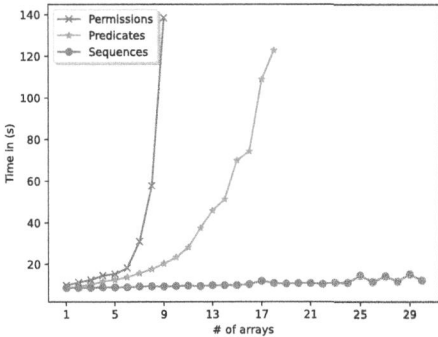

Fig. 1. The verification time of VERCORS for micro-benchmarks containing arrays, using different encoding methods.

Fig. 1, the results can be found. When encoding the arrays regularly without hiding the quantified permissions, the verification time seems to increase quadratically up to nine arrays and beyond that VERCORS cannot verify these problems anymore. This issue is fundamental to how the VIPER infrastructure [14] encodes separation logic in SMT solvers.[7] In turn, VERCORS relies on VIPER to prove these problems. In the same figure we also plot how the verification performs if we, instead, use predicates to hide the permissions. We see that this performs better, but beyond eighteen arrays a similar problem occurs.

Based on these results, we implemented a version of HALIVER which hides predicates instead, as described in Sect. 4.3. As not all the arrays used in `sub_direction` are in scope at the same time, we wanted to investigate if this solved our issues. However, as Table 2 shows, the versions that use predicates (P) actually do not help in solving the verification problems. Thus we were unable to prove the memory safety of `solve_direction`.

Lastly, we also encoded the micro-benchmark program in the internal language of VERCORS called PVL. This language allows the use of *sequences*, which are lists providing input that cannot be written to, i.e., they represent immutable arrays. This approach does not seem to exhibit a scalability problem. We discuss this observation further in Sect. 6.

6 Lessons Learned

Nonlinear Arithmetic. In this paper, we show that deductive verifiers based on SMT solvers can be used to prove nonlinear properties, using only linear arithmetic logic. This allows us to supplement the needed nonlinear logic at exact program points when needed. This is feasible when the nonlinear occurrence is either predictable, as is the case when flattening multi-dimensional arrays, or

---

[7] We confirmed this here github.com/viperproject/silicon/issues/831. Although some heuristics could be applied, the scaling issue stands.

occurs at only a few points in the program. When this is not the case, it will take a lot of effort to annotate the programs.

Quantified Permissions and Scalability. As the experiments in Sect. 5 show, with the current encoding we are unable to verify the complex optimised parallel code output of HALIDE for our case study. For smaller parts of the code, the generated annotations from HALIVER are sufficient, but for larger problems we run into the boundaries of what deductive verification tools and SMT solvers currently can handle. This problem domain of verifying highly optimised code is particularly difficult. For instance, a typical optimisation technique for GPUs is to fuse two functions together to improve memory locality. However, for verification, decomposing the program in separate functions is typically better. Similarly, in our case study, we have many different arrays in scope, since data is stored as a structure of arrays which is generally better for performance than storing the data in a single array of structures. On the other hand, an array of structures is probably better suited for verification.

However, we expect that deductive verifiers based on separation logic can solve these kinds of problems when the correct encoding is used. The strength of separation logic is that we can reason about programs without considering all the possible interleavings of a parallel program. However, if we have too *many* memory locations on which we specify read or write permissions, the verification time will explode. We argue that treating every memory location as a place where a possible data race can occur is an over-estimation that hurts verification time. We think that we can use the knowledge that certain *inputs* of the program are never written to reduce the number of memory locations that need to be reasoned about. In the internal language of VERCORS, called PVL, this is easily expressed by using *sequences*, which are immutable arrays. Something like this is not currently possible for C files, since arrays are always translated to mutable arrays. As shown in Fig. 1, an encoding using sequences does not seem to lead to a blow up in verification time.

As a solution, we envisage a way to indicate that an array is never mutated, using a custom annotation or the **const** type specifier. In this case the array should be translated to a sequence. In the programs HALIDE generates, it is often the case that an array is first completely produced, and after that is only read from. In such cases, it would be helpful if we can indicate that a value is read-only from a certain point in the program. We expect that this solution will also reduce the annotation effort, since we will no longer need to specify permission annotations for such arrays. However, we would need additional program analyses or guarantees that the array is never actually modified. These should check for no explicit writes, but also that no function calls can modify the array.

7 Related Work

Several approaches to solving non-linear arithmetic with approximating methods exist [3,9–11]. For example, in [9] they discuss how to over-approximate nonlinear integer arithmetic using reals by altering the verification conditions sent to the SMT solver. This approach is interesting and we plan to investigate whether we can use this tool in combination with the VIPER infrastructure, which ultimately sends the verification conditions to the SMT solver that VERCORS uses. These methods lead to new cases of non-linear arithmetic to be solved, however sometimes they also lead to original programs not being able to be verified anymore. It can be argued that it is crucial to fine-tune these methods for specific domains. In the HALIVER context, we know exactly when we should apply our lemmas for nonlinear arithmetic, so we expect that the approach of [9] would be too coarse to apply.

Liu et al. [13] propose an approach inspired by scheduling languages, with proof obligations generated when a program is optimised, for automatic verification using Coq. The used programs can be parallelised in an external C program, but the approach does not inherently support parallelism.

ALPINIST [18] is a tool related to HALIVER. It automatically optimises PVL code, along with its annotations, for verification with VERCORS. It allows the specification of intended behaviour, but it does not separate algorithms from schedules, forcing the user to reason about the technical details of parallelisation.

The work of Clément and Cohen [4] is similar to HALIVER in that it tries to prove that the compilation process of the HALIDE compiler is correct. In their work they try to prove that the original HALIDE program refines to the generated code using equivalence reasoning. Their approach works for *affine* HALIDE programs, but the case study we consider in this paper is not affine since inputs are indexed with other inputs, see for example line 5 of Listing 5.

8 Conclusion

We ported the DDECAL algorithm to HALIDE, achieving significant speedup over both the original parallel CPU code and the GPU code ported by the PADRE project. For the CPU schedule of HALIDE we tried to verify the code with respect to memory safety and data-race freedom using HALIVER. For this no annotation effort was required. We were not able to verify the entire program, but several parts of the program were verified for memory safety properties. We identified two challenges, and although we did not overcome them completely, we gained insight for good directions for verifying parallel optimised C programs.

References

1. Blom, S., Darabi, S., Huisman, M., Oortwijn, W.: The VerCors tool set: verification of parallel and concurrent software. In: Polikarpova, N., Schneider, S. (eds.) IFM 2017. LNCS, vol. 10510, pp. 102–110. Springer, Cham (2017). https://doi.org/10.1007/978-3-319-66845-1_7
2. Bornat, R., Calcagno, C., O'Hearn, P., Parkinson, M.: Permission accounting in separation logic. In: POPL, pp. 259–270 (2005)
3. Cimatti, A., Griggio, A., Irfan, A., Roveri, M., Sebastiani, R.: Experimenting on solving nonlinear integer arithmetic with incremental linearization. In: Beyersdorff, O., Wintersteiger, C. (eds.) SAT 2018. LNCS, vol. 10929, pp. 383–398. Springer, Cham (2018). https://doi.org/10.1007/978-3-319-94144-8_23

4. Clément, B., Cohen, A.: End-to-end translation validation for the halide language. Proc. ACM Program. Lang. **6**(OOPSLA1), 1–30 (2022). https://doi.org/10.1145/3527328
5. de Moura, L., Bjørner, N.: Z3: an efficient SMT solver. In: Ramakrishnan, C.R., Rehof, J. (eds.) TACAS 2008. LNCS, vol. 4963, pp. 337–340. Springer, Heidelberg (2008). https://doi.org/10.1007/978-3-540-78800-3_24
6. Gan, H., et al.: Assessing the impact of two independent direction-dependent calibration algorithms on the LOFAR 21 cm signal power spectrum - and applications to an observation of a field flanking the north celestial pole. Astron. Astrophys. **669**, A20 (2023). https://doi.org/10.1051/0004-6361/202244316
7. Gödel, K.: Über formal unentscheidbare Sätze der principia mathematica und verwandter Systeme I. Monatshefte Math. Phys. **38**, 173–198 (1931)
8. Hamaker, J.P., Bregman, J.D., Sault, R.J.: Understanding radio polarimetry. I. Mathematical foundations. Astron. Astrophys. Suppl. Ser. **117**(1), 137–147 (1996). https://doi.org/10.1051/aas:1996146
9. Hozzová, P., Bendík, J., Nutz, A., Rodeh, Y.: Overapproximation of non-linear integer arithmetic for smart contract verification. In: EPiC Series in Computing, vol. 94, pp. 257–269. EasyChair (2023). https://doi.org/10.29007/h4p7
10. Jovanović, D.: Solving nonlinear integer arithmetic with MCSAT. In: Bouajjani, A., Monniaux, D. (eds.) VMCAI 2017. LNCS, vol. 10145, pp. 330–346. Springer, Cham (2017). https://doi.org/10.1007/978-3-319-52234-0_18
11. Kremer, G., Corzilius, F., Ábrahám, E.: A generalised branch-and-bound approach and its application in SAT modulo nonlinear integer arithmetic. In: Gerdt, V., Koepf, W., Seiler, W., Vorozhtsov, E. (eds.) CASC 2016. LNCS, vol. 9890, pp. 315–335. Springer, Cham (2016). https://doi.org/10.1007/978-3-319-45641-6_21
12. Leiserson, C.E., et al.: There's plenty of room at the top: what will drive computer performance after Moore's law? Sci. (New York, N.Y.) **368**(6495) (2020). https://doi.org/10.1126/science.aam9744
13. Liu, A., Bernstein, G.L., Chlipala, A., Ragan-Kelley, J.: Verified tensor-program optimization via high-level scheduling rewrites. Proc. ACM on Program. Lang. **6**(POPL), 55:1–55:28 (2022). https://doi.org/10.1145/3498717
14. Müller, P., Schwerhoff, M., Summers, A.: Viper - a verification infrastructure for permission-based reasoning. In: Jobstmann, B., Leino, K. (eds.) VMCAI 2016. LNCS, vol. 9583, pp. 41–62. Springer, Heidelberg (2016). https://doi.org/10.1007/978-3-662-49122-5_2
15. Müller, P., Schwerhoff, M., Summers, A.J.: Automatic verification of iterated separating conjunctions using symbolic execution. In: Chaudhuri, S., Farzan, A. (eds.) CAV 2016. LNCS, vol. 9779, pp. 405–425. Springe, Cham (2016). https://doi.org/10.1007/978-3-319-41528-4_22
16. Ragan-Kelley, J., et al.: Halide: decoupling algorithms from schedules for high-performance image processing. Commun. ACM **61**(1), 106–115 (2017). https://doi.org/10.1145/3150211
17. Ragan-Kelley, J., Barnes, C., Adams, A., Paris, S., Durand, F., Amarasinghe, S.: Halide: a language and compiler for optizing parallelism, locality, and recomputation in image processing pipelines. SIGPLAN Not. **48**(6), 519–530 (2013). https://doi.org/10.1145/2499370.2462176
18. Sakar, Ö., Safari, M., Huisman, M., Wijs, A.: Alpinist: an annotation-aware GPU program optimizer. In: Fisman, D., Rosu, G. (eds.) TACAS 2022. LNCS, vol. 13244, pp. 332–332. Springer, Cham (2022). https://doi.org/10.1007/978-3-030-99527-0_18

19. van den Haak, L.B.: Artifact for: HaliVer: deductive verification and scheduling languages join forces. Zenodo (2023). https://doi.org/10.5281/zenodo.10047853
20. van den Haak, L.B., Wijs, A., Huisman, M., van den Brand, M.: HaliVer: deductive verification and scheduling languages join forces. In: Finkbeiner, B., Kovács, L. (eds.) TACAS 2024. LNCS, vol. 14572, pp. 71–89. Springer, Cham (2024). https://doi.org/10.1007/978-3-031-57256-2_4

Reconstructing the High-Level Structure of Legacy Code via Software Model Checking: An Experience Report

Roberto Cavada[1], Alessandro Cimatti[1], Alberto Griggio[1(✉)], Stefano Tonetta[1], Federico Bonafini[2], Matteo Campidelli[2], and Andrea Zasa[2]

[1] Fondazione Bruno Kessler, Trento, Italy
griggio@fbk.eu
[2] Innova Engineering, Tione, Italy

Abstract. The high-level structure of control software of reactive systems in many embedded applications can be described in terms of (extended) state machines. The extraction of such state machines from the code itself can be a valuable form of documentation, e.g. to allow developers to familiarise with legacy implementations, or to validate that the actual implementation is consistent with the high-level specifications. In this paper, we present a tool for the automatic extraction of high-level state machines from legacy code using software model checking techniques. The tool works by slicing and abstracting the code under analysis guided by user feedback, and reconstructs the target state machine via a sequence of reachability queries. We demonstrate the usefulness of the tool by applying it for understanding the high-level structure of the code of a legacy controller for an advanced domestic heat pump system, and showing how the extracted information uncovered some unexpected behaviours of the software.

1 Introduction

Legacy software poses significant challenges for software developers, particularly in terms of costs for maintenance and integration. Analyzing and understanding such legacy code is often difficult due to its complex structure, lack of documentation, and the potential for unforeseen behaviors.

In the case of embedded control software, the control logic usually relies on a high-level control structure, which can be formalized as an (extended) state machine. However, while structure would provide a useful conceptual framework to understand the control logic, it may not be readily apparent from the code itself.

The work is financed by the Autonomous Province of Trento in scope of L.P. No. 6/1999 with determination. No. 592 of 09/08/2021. – Ref.: 2021-AG12-00783. - project NPDCR (Nuova Pompa di Calore Residenziale - New residential heat pump).

© The Author(s), under exclusive license to Springer Nature Switzerland AG 2024
A. E. Haxthausen and W. Serwe (Eds.): FMICS 2024, LNCS 14952, pp. 170–181, 2024.
https://doi.org/10.1007/978-3-031-68150-9_10

In this paper, we report on the experience of applying model checking techniques to automatically extract high-level state machines directly from the codebase of industrial control software. We present a tool that works by slicing and abstracting the code under analysis guided by user feedback, and reconstructing the target state machine via a sequence of reachability queries. We demonstrate the utility of the approach on a case study that includes a legacy controller for an advanced domestic heat pump system and illustrate the effectiveness and usefulness of our tool in extracting the main FSM of the controller, showing how the extracted information uncovered some unexpected (and potentially problematic) behaviours of the legacy software, confirmed by the domain engineers.

Related Work. The problem of reengineering or migrating legacy software systems has been widely studied in the literature [2]. Many approaches propose the usage of formal methods for automating the analysis, either by means of transformations to extract a formal specification [12] or deductive techniques to prove properties in a modular way [1]. However, as highlighted by [1], one of the main challenges in post-hoc verification is writing the specifications. In this work, we focus on more lightweight formal techniques to extract models using software model checking.

Many works proposed to extract formal models from legacy systems with the purpose to understand the code or to use such models in the migration. Some works, such as [11] and [10], focus on the generation of timed automata from recordings of the system execution. Other approaches infer structured data models from low-level programs [3]. We instead focus on the extraction of the high-level state machine of a control software.

The extraction of state machines for model checking or for conformance testing is quite standard in software engineering (see, e.g., [5] or [9]). Our method is based on the common notion of predicate abstraction [7], where the abstract graph is built from a partitioning of the state space based on a set of predicates. We report on the experience of using such abstraction to understand the control structure of embedded code.

Outline. The rest of the paper is organized as follows: in Sect. 2, we describe the overall methodology to extract the state machine; in Sect. 3, we detail the tool support; in Sect. 4, we report on the application of the methodology on an industrial control software for a domestic heat pump system; finally, in Sect. 5, we draw some conclusions and directions for future work.

2 Methodology

In this section, we describe the overall methodology we adopt to extract high-level FSMs from code. We begin by outlining in Sect. 2.1 the assumptions under which we operate, regarding the structure of the code under analysis, the way the state machine is represented, and the model of execution. We then describe the main FSM reconstruction algorithm in Sect. 2.2. Finally, we describe how we apply abstraction in order to reduce the computational cost of the analysis in Sect. 2.3.

2.1 Operating Assumptions

As stated above, our methodology is aimed specifically at software controllers in embedded applications. These controllers are typically characterized by a recurring operational cycle divided into three phases:

1. Input Acquisition: the system collects inputs from the environment, e.g. through sensors or internal data streams.
2. Control (Step Function Execution): this phase is where the core logic of the controller executes. Our methodology assumes that the controller's logic is encapsulated in a "step" function, which is called every cycle. The step function assesses the input data and updates the system's state accordingly. This function utilizes global variables to maintain state information across cycles.
3. Output/Actuation Generation: following the processing in the control phase, this final phase involves the system responding via outputs or actuations that influence the external environment or internal operations.

In this context, the reconstruction of the high-level state machine (henceforth simply called the target FSM), is based on the following assumptions:

- Persistent State Storage: the methodology assumes that the state of the system is persistent and stored in global variables between executions of the step function.
- State Encoding through Global Variables: we assume that the state of the FSM is encoded using a combination of known predicates over the global variables. These predicates define the conditions under which transitions occur between different states. For instance, a predicate might check if a temperature value, stored in a global variable, exceeds a certain threshold.
- Definition and Transition Identification: the primary goal is to identify all possible transitions between states within the FSM. A transition, in this context, is defined by a single execution of the step function.

2.2 Main FSM Extraction Algorithm

Our FSM reconstruction algorithm is based on (software) model checking. More specifically, we reduce the problem to a series of reachability checks, for each pair of FSM states a and b (expressed as a combination of truth values of the predicates defining the states, as defined above). For each pair a, b, the process involves the following steps:

1. Assuming state a: we begin by setting the system to assume it is in state a. All the global variables of the code are assigned a non-deterministic value, and constrained to satisfy the predicates associated with state a.
2. Executing the step function: under the assumption that the system starts in state a, the step function of the controller is executed. This function processes the inputs and updates the system's state by modifying global variables according to the embedded logic.

```
Extract-FSM(program, step-function, predicates):
 1.  fsm := ∅
 2.  for each a ∈ predicates:
 3.      for each b ∈ predicates:
 4.          instructions := []
 5.          for each global variable v in program:
 6.              instructions.append(havoc v)
 7.          instructions.append(assume a)
 8.          instructions.append(call step-function)
 9.          instructions.append(assert ¬b)
10.          new-program := Program(instructions)
11.          res := ModelCheck(new-program)
12.          if res = unsafe:
13.              fsm.add-edge(a → b)
14.  return fsm
```

Fig. 1. FSM extraction algorithm.

3. Asserting not state b: after execution of the step function, the model checker asserts that state b has not been reached. If the model checker finds that reaching state b is possible from state a, this indicates a potential transition under the given inputs and conditions.
4. Adding FSM edges: if the assertion that state b is not reached fails, an edge from a to b is added to the FSM diagram.

The pseudo-code of the algorithm above is reported in Algorithm 1.

2.3 Code Abstractions

In the context of software model checking, abstraction is a fundamental technique used to reduce the state space that needs to be explored during the FSM reconstruction. By abstracting the program state, we simplify the model of the system by focusing only on the aspects that are critical to the behavior under investigation. This involves creating a simplified model of the program that retains essential properties relevant to the FSM but reduces the complexity involved in the model checking process.

Our methodology integrates several abstraction techniques, including (static) program slicing, the abstraction of program state with user-provided constraints, and approximation of function behaviour via user-defined stubs. Importantly, we do not force such abstractions to provide an overapproximation of the original program behaviour, like is typically done in verification contexts. As our main goal is to produce artifacts that can aid developers in understanding and exploring the code behaviour, it might make sense in certain cases to consider also program underapproximations, restricting the behaviour of the code to specific scenarios and/or environment conditions, e.g. in order to analyze only some specific "views" of the target FSM. For example, in the case of a heat pump, the controller might feature different operating modes according to the season (e.g. winter vs summer), so that analysing the various modes separately (by considering different underapproximations of the controller) might result in more informative FSMs than a single global analysis.

3 The fsm-explorer Tool

We have implemented the methodology outlined above in a tool called fsm-explorer. The tool is written in Python, and relies on Kratos2 [8] for reachability checking. Kratos2 is a tool for verifying imperative programs, working on an intermediate verification language called K2, with semantics based on first-order logic and Satisfiability Modulo Theories (SMT). Kratos2 allows specifications of things like reachability and liveness properties. It integrates several state-of-the-art verification engines based on SAT and SMT. It also provides utilities such as a flexible Python API (which is what our FSM-explorer tool uses), a customizable C front end, counterexample generation, support for simulation and symbolic execution, and translation into multiple formalisms for low level verification.

fsm-explorer operates on C programs whose structure is assumed to satisfy the constraints described in Sect. 2.1. In terms of language constructs, it supports a fairly-large subset of C, including pointers and bit-precise floating-point arithmetic,[1] but no recursion or indirect calls via function pointers. The tool operates in two phases, namely *configuration* and *analysis*. In the configuration phase, the user is required to define the inputs for the FSM extraction algorithm, including the definition of the predicates used to represent the machine state, the step function implementing its transitions, and the desired abstractions to apply to the code. The actual FSM reconstruction is then performed in the subsequent analysis phase, where the algorithm of Fig. 1 is executed using Kratos2 as verification backend, producing the target FSM as result. In the rest of the section, we shall describe the two steps in more detail.

3.1 Configuration

The tool configuration is controlled via a configuration file, in Yaml syntax, defining the predicates to use as FSM state, the step function implementing its transition (i.e. the analysis entry point), and the abstractions to apply to the program functions and variables. fsm-explorer assists the user in creating the configuration, via an interactive and iterative procedure based on an automatic exploration of the program source code.

FSM State. The first element of a configuration is the definition of the predicates encoding the state of the target FSM. fsm-explorer assumes that such state is defined by a combination of values of global variables of the program. To start

---

[1] It should be said however that the use of such features might have a non-negligible impact on performance and scalability in practice.

exploring the FSM, the user must indicate which variables are used to track its state. The user must provide the names of one or more global variables in the program. In addition, for each state variable, the user is required to define its domain of possible values, which must always be finite. This domain can be specified as a list of valid values, a continuous range of values, or any combination of the two. The space of the machine states is then defined as the Cartesian product of the domains of all state variables.

Entry Point. In addition to the valid domain of state variables, the user must also provide the entry point to the FSM. This can be any program function, including the main function. Specifying an entry point other than the main entry point helps eliminate code during analysis that is not vital to the behavior of the FSM. This will contribute to speed of execution and simplicity for the user.

Variable Abstraction. By default, all global variables that are not part of the FSM state are assigned a nondeterministic value before executing the step function in the EXTRACT-FSM algorithm (represented by the **havoc** instructions in Fig. 1, lines 5–6). fsm-explorer allows also to specify additional constraints that must be satisfied by such nondeterministic assignments, in order to reduce the search space, either to improve the precision of the abstraction by ruling out combinations of values that do not make sense for the program (e.g., by constraining variables corresponding to sensor measurements from the environment to ranges that are physically plausible), or to focus the analysis on some specific behaviours of the code (c.f. the example of a controller operating with multiple modes as mentioned in Sect. 2.3). Additional constraints can be defined in the configuration, by specifying either a range of possible values for individual global variables, or arbitrary boolean expressions that are assumed to be true before executing the step function in the EXTRACT-FSM algorithm. Additionally, it is also possible to mark some variables as *ignored*: in this case, such variables are completely removed from the generated program, replacing all the conditionals in which they occur with nondeterministic choices, and all assignments to variables which depend on them with havoc instructions.

Function Abstraction. The second form of abstraction supported by fsm-explorer is at the level of functions. For each function that is (syntactically) reachable from the defined entry point, the user must specify in the configuration file whether the function should be treated precisely by the analysis (i.e. its body should be *expanded*), or whether it should be *abstracted*, i.e. replaced with a simple stub. In the latter case, the specific behaviour of the stub can be defined by imposing additional constraints on the returned values and side effects of the function, similarly to the case of global variables. By default, an abstracted function returns a nondeterministic value and havocs all global variables that are possibly modified by its body and the body of its callees. This set is determined by recursively traversing the function body and collecting all the global variables that are potentially written (if pointers are present, a conservative overapproximation of such set is computed). Also in the case of functions, it is possible to mark them to be *ignored* to ensure that they are completely removed from the generated program (in this case, no side effect is applied, and return values are replaced with nondeterministic values).

User Interaction. fsm-explorer supports the user in the definition of the analysis configuration, using an interactive and iterative approach that gradually increases the functions and variables that are considered. Initially, only the entry point function needs to be specified. When executed in configuration mode, then, fsm-explorer analyses the program and the partial configuration specified so far, extending it with new global variables and functions that are (syntactically) reachable from the functions that are marked as expanded. The user is then asked to classify the newly-discovered variables and functions according to the criteria above: for variables, this amounts to specifying whether they are part of the FSM state (and in such case, their domain must be provided) or whether they should be abstracted (possibly with constraints on their values) or ignored; in the case of functions, instead, the possible classifications are expand, abstract (and in this case, additional constraints can be provided), or ignore. The configuration procedure then terminates when a fixpoint is reached in the configuration (i.e., no more new variables or functions are discovered).

3.2 Analysis

In the analysis phase, fsm-explorer extracts the target FSM by applying the algorithm of Fig. 1, using Kratos2 to answer the reachability queries, and the configuration generated in the previous phase to perform the desired progam abstractions. The tool exploits the Python API of Kratos2 to automatically generate the target programs for verification and to run the reachability algorithms (based on symbolic model checking). The output FSM is then saved in dot format [6], a graph description language that is widely used for visualizing network structures. The dot format provides a clear, visual representation of the FSM, with nodes representing the states and directed edges depicting the transitions between them, which can be easily interpreted by developers and other stakeholders.

4 Analysis of a Legacy Heat Pump Controller

The fsm-explorer tool introduced in the previous section has been applied to the analysis of a legacy software controller for heat pump systems made by Innova, an Italian company developing and producing innovative solutions for heating, ventilation and air conditioning. The case study has been carried out within a larger collaboration between the center for Digital Industry at FBK and Innova Engineering (the R&D branch of Innova) with the goal of integrating formal- and model-based techinques in an industrial setting in the domain of heating systems with heat pumps.

The control system is designed for air-to-water (ATW) heat pumps for residential and light commercial applications. It is built around a 32-bit microcontroller unit (MCU) that operates on bare-metal architecture, programmed directly in C. This setup ensures no overhead from an operating system and minimum resource usage, allowing cost savings and space reduction that are of key importance for the target markets of the products that use the solution. This approach, however, complicates the system's programming and maintenance, as it excludes the advanced debugging, modularity and flexibility that could be made readily available with the use of a multitasking OS and/or higher level programming languages. The primary functions of the MCU within the heat pump control system focus on optimizing the refrigerant cycle and managing the hydronic functions. The MCU's tasks are split into controlling the compressor, fan and EEV (Electronic Expansion Valve) for refrigerant cycle optimization, and managing pumps and valves for efficient water distribution to space heating and cooling terminals and/or DHW (Domestic Hot Water) storages. More in detail the MCU directly controls the inverter compressor and associated fan and EEV to maintain the optimal working point of the refrigerant cycle. By dynamically adjusting the speed of the compressor and the operation of the fan based mainly on pressure and temperature measurements, the MCU ensures that the refrigerant is cycled through the system at the ideal pressure and temperature. This aims to maximize the efficiency of the heat exchange process, thus improving the overall energy efficiency of the system. Moreover, in addition to managing the refrigeration cycle, the MCU also controls the hydronic components of the system - namely, the pumps and valves. This manages water flow through the plant and distribution system of the building. The control system is engineered to support both monoblock heat pumps, which feature direct hydronic connections to the external unit, and traditional split systems, where the external and internal units are separate. This dual compatibility is achieved through configurable parameters and flexible hardware configuration on the control boards. Communication within the system is realized through Controller Area Network (CAN) and RS-485 buses, ensuring reliable data transfer between the MCU and other components like the inverter compressor driver, which is a separate component managed via serial communication. In a similar way, the main MCU is connected to the user control panel, which enables unit control and advanced parameter access for system tuning. User interaction is managed through a local display interface for direct access to system settings, functional modes, and parameter adjustments. Remote configuration is also enabled via serial transmission, providing equal priority and functionality to adjustments made either locally or remotely.

From the implementation point of view, the full MCU consists of multiple subsystems, implementing various different state machines. The state of the various subsystems are stored in statically allocated global data structures, with low-level access to the memory and hardware devices (e.g. reading from sensors and user inputs, and controlling actuators and the user interface) encapsulated in getter and setter functions, clearly separated from the control functions imple-

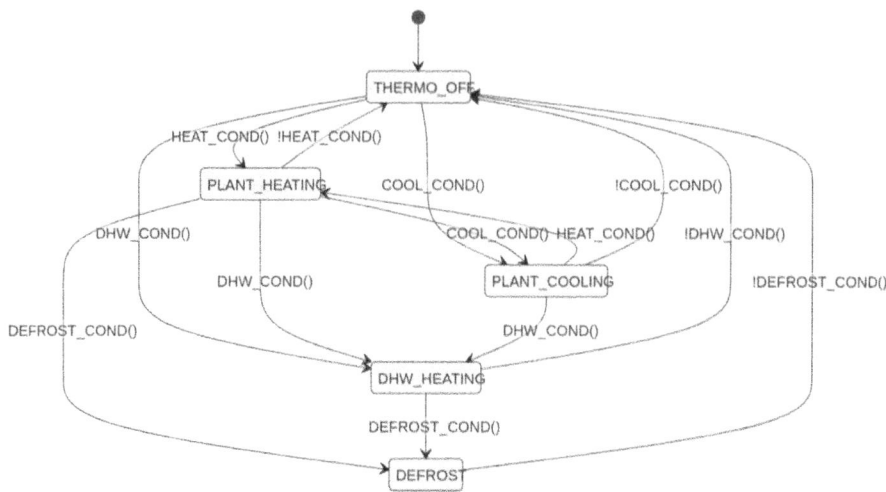

Fig. 2. Nominal high-level FSM of the heat pump obtained from the MCU documentation.

menting the state machines. Overall, the code base of the MCU consists of 30 header files and 30 source files, for a total of approximately 20000 lines of code and about 300 global variables.

For this case study, we focused on the main FSM of the pump. The machine consists of the following states:

THERMO_OFF, corresponding to the unit being stopped (either in standby or caused by an alarm condition);
PLANT_HEATING, corresponding to the unit heating plant water;
PLANT_COOLING, when the unit is cooling plant water;
DHW_HEATING, corresponding to heating of domestic hot water;
DEFROST, when the unit is in a defrost cycle.

The nominal FSM, derived from the documentation of the code, is shown in Fig. 2. In order to validate our proposed toolchain, we set up an experiment to extract the same FSM automatically with fsm-explorer.[2] Note that manually reconstructing such FSM via code inspection is nontrivial, since the (legacy) MCU code has lost most of its original structure due to various evolutions, updates, additions and removals of features over time; in its current version, the code makes heavy use of gotos for control flow and global variables for temporary storage of data shared among subsystems, and it moreover contains a significant amount of dead code.

For the FSM reconstruction, we configured fsm-explorer to abstract all low-level access functions (replacing memory and I/O operations with access to global

---

[2] Note however that we are only interested in discovering the states of the machine and the transitions among them, without synthesizing the conditions that enable the transitions.

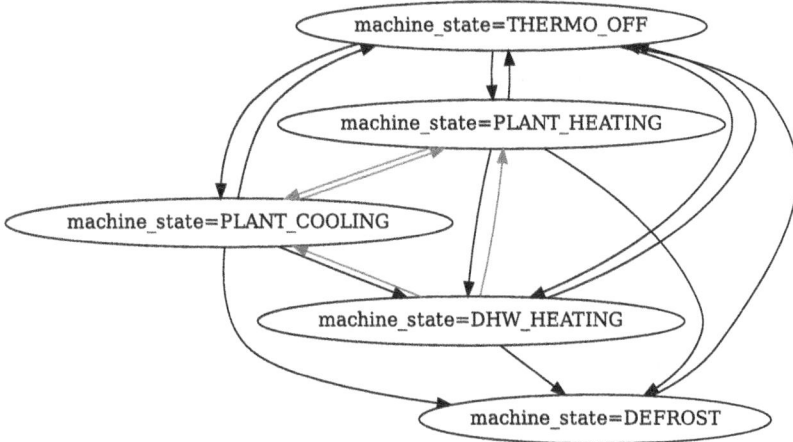

Fig. 3. FSM of the heat pump generated by fsm-explorer. Red edges (manually colored) correspond to possible but unexpected transitions, not present in the nominal FSM. (Color figure online)

variables) and to track precisely only the variables storing the state of the pump. Additional user-provided assumptions were injected to ensure that values for inputs were within legal ranges, and to forbid some invalid combination of values for state variables that are not part of the target FSM state, but which can affect the enabled transitions. Finally, all the code not reachable from the step function of the pump (Sys_Arbiter) was automatically sliced away. The size of the program after such abstractions reduced to about 2100 lines of code with approximately 100 global variables. We executed fsm-explorer to produce the FSM shown in Fig. 3. The execution took less than 20 s on an average Linux laptop, using the default verification engine of Kratos2, based on IC3 with implicit predicate abstraction [4]. Comparing the machine of Fig. 3 with the expected one of Fig. 2, we notice three additional transitions in the automatically-extracted one (the corresponding edges have been colored in red for readability). All the transitions show unexpected behaviours of the MCU, which could potentially result in erroneous operations of the system. A closer inspection of the produced execution traces (of the abstracted code) by the domain experts suggested that the conditions for triggering the unexpected transitions should not occur in practice in the full system, due to additional global constraints emerging from the interaction among the various components of the MCU. However, the engineers confirmed that the unwanted transitions are definitely possible when considering the pump subsystem in isolation. Such local violations of the specification are considered problematic, and constituted additional evidence in favor of the ongoing redesign of the MCU controller using a model-based approach.

5 Conclusions

We have presented fsm-explorer, a tool aimed at reconstructing high-level Finite State Machines of legacy code through model checking, and we have explored its application in analyzing a legacy controller for heat pump systems. Our investigation has demonstrated the effectiveness of the tool in identifying some undesired behaviors within the code that were not initially evident from mere code inspection. Regarding future work, we plan to enhance fsm-explorer by extending its applicability to more general execution models, particularly for scenarios where the system may experience transient states that should not be included in the generated FSM. We also intend to generalize the current implementation, to allow e.g. to specify the machine state using arbitrary predicates instead of simple assignments to finite-state variables, and to define global constraints to encode assumptions on the operating environment of the code under analysis. Additionally, we aim to refine the methodology to extract detailed conditions for state transitions (e.g. based on a specified set of predicates or variables of interest), so as to improve its utility and precision in complex legacy system analyses.

References

1. Beckert, B., Bormer, T., Grahl, D.: Deductive verification of legacy code. In: Margaria, T., Steffen, B. (eds.) ISoLA 2016. LNCS, vol. 9952, pp. 749–765. Springe, Cham (2016). https://doi.org/10.1007/978-3-319-47166-2_53
2. Bisbal, J., Lawless, D., Bing, W., Grimson, J.: Legacy information systems: issues and directions. IEEE Softw. **16**(5), 103–111 (1999)
3. Ceccato, M., Dean, T.R., Tonella, P., Marchignoli, D.: Data model reverse engineering in migrating a legacy system to java. In: WCRE, pp. 177–186. IEEE Computer Society (2008)
4. Cimatti, A., Griggio, A., Mover, S., Tonetta, S.: Infinite-state invariant checking with IC3 and predicate abstraction. Formal Methods Syst. Des. **49**(3), 190–218 (2016)
5. Corbett, J.C., et al.: Bandera: extracting finite-state models from Java source code. In: ICSE, pp. 439–448. ACM (2000)
6. Gansner, E.R., North, S.C.: An open graph visualization system and its applications to software engineering. Softw. - Pract. Exp. **30**(11), 1203–1233 (2000)
7. Graf, S., Saïdi, H.: Construction of abstract state graphs with PVS. In: Grumberg, O. (ed.) CAV 1997. LNCS, vol. 1254, pp. 72–83. Springer, Heidelberg (1997). https://doi.org/10.1007/3-540-63166-6_10
8. Griggio, A., Jonás, M.: Kratos2: an SMT-based model checker for imperative programs. In: Enea, C., Lal, A. (eds.) CAV 2023. LNCS, vol. 13966, pp. 423–436. Springer, Cham (2023). https://doi.org/10.1007/978-3-031-37709-9_20
9. Habibi, A., Moinudeen, H., Tahar, S.: Generating finite state machines from SystemC. In: DATE Designers' Forum, pp. 76–81. European Design and Automation Association, Leuven (2006)
10. Huselius, J., Andersson, J., Hansson, H., Punnekkat, S.: Automatic generation and validation of models of legacy software. In: RTCSA, pp. 342–349. IEEE Computer Society (2006)

11. Sifakis, J., Tripakis, S., Yovine, S.: Building models of real-time systems from application software. Proc. IEEE **91**(1), 100–111 (2003)
12. Ward, M.P., Bennett, K.H.: Formal methods for legacy systems. J. Softw. Maintenance Res. Pract. **7**(3), 203–219 (1995)

Formal Analysis and Monitoring of Legacy Safety-Critical Interlocking Systems with the Use of Certified Industrial Tools

Dalay Almeida[✉], Florian Jamain, and Thierry Lecomte

CLEARSY, Aix-en-Provence, France
{dalay.almeida,florian.jamain,thierry.lecomte}@CLEARSY.com

Abstract. Although Formal Methods have been used for decades in the development of industrial critical systems, there are still many products that do not use this technology. The use of Formal Methods in such a context is generally highly recommended, but not mandatory, as other technologies may be used as support to certify the safety of the systems. Relay-based railway interlocking systems, for instance, are legacy systems used in the majority of railway installations and whose safety has been attested through their use for decades. Their maintenance, however, requires analysis to avoid losing their safety features. In previous papers, we have presented the CLEARSY Safety Platform (CSSP) and how it can be used to analyse and replace these legacy interlocking systems in a safety-proved manner using certified industrial tools. In this paper, we extend this discussion to present how the CSSP can be used to monitor the legacy relay-based RIS to improve their safety during their execution. The strategy is to describe the system safety properties using logic and then implement it in the CSSP, which in turn is responsible for monitoring the system components to ensure its correct functioning and raise flags when an unsafe state is found. The benefits of using our approach in industry are discussed as we present how it can be applied in two industrial case studies.

Keywords: System Monitoring · Formal Specification · B-method · Relay-based Railway Interlocking Systems · CLEARSY Safety Platform

1 Introduction

Although the railway standards strongly recommend formal specification methodologies for the development of critical systems, there are still many products that do not use this technology. This may not always be a problem, as there are other manners to demonstrate the safety of a system. As an example, many legacy systems have been used for decades, which confer them a certain level of confidence, like in relay-based Railway Interlocking Systems (RIS). In previous papers [10, 15], we have discussed the difficulties of analysing these legacy systems and we proposed certified industrial tools (the CLEARSY Safety Platform - CSSP) and a methodology to replace these RIS with computer-based systems created based on a formal development strategy using B-method. As a result, it is possible to generate safety-proved systems with the same behaviour as the legacy RIS.

Although the CLEARSY Safety Platform has presented some important results in the replacement of the relay-based RIS technology and logic with a smaller, cost-effective and safety-proved solution, it is important to consider that the industry still uses relay-based technology in the majority of RIS installations [24] as they are necessary in determined cases, notably in the connection between the computer-based systems and the railway equipment (train presence detection, signals, turnouts). So, replacing relay-based technology may not always be a solution. In such cases, the analysis of the safety of these systems remains a challenge as manual analysis cannot be trusted [13]. In this context, the industry needs a solution to analyse and monitor relay-based RIS to guarantee their safety without aiming at completely replacing them with new technology.

This paper presents an approach to apply CSSP in the analysis and monitoring of relay-based RIS. Based on a strategy for describing the behaviour of artificial intelligence [21], we propose describing the relay-based RIS expected behaviour in Propositional Logic. This behaviour can be extracted from the documentation of these systems, like the electrical circuit diagrams that represent their structure. As Propositional Logic is one of the bases of the B-method [1], the RIS logical description can be used in the formal specification necessary for the development strategy of the CSSP, as B is the main foundation of the CSSP system specification. Once this specification is proved and implemented, it is possible to connect the relay-based RIS components to the CSSP board inputs as a way to analyse if their states correspond to the expected behaviour. An approach to creating the monitor system using the certified tools and the benefits of using the CSSP monitor are discussed. Furthermore, two industrial cases are discussed and used as examples to present how important safety properties can be analysed and monitored with our approach. These case studies are based on the examples provided by the French National Railway Company (SNCF), discussed in previous works [3,10].

Previously, we have proposed using propositional logic as the basis for specifying and implementing relay-based RIS as computer-based systems through a formal development strategy [8,10]. Although this work has some similarities with these previous strategies, it proposes an alternative to those that do not want to replace the existing relay-based systems, allowing monitoring of legacy systems based on a formal strategy. Nonetheless, this work also does not invalidate our previous results on replacing legacy systems. The solution presented in this article is a complementary solution to be used in cases where the relay-based technology cannot be replaced and it does not diminish the importance of the previously proposed solutions.

The literature is scarce regarding the analysis of relay-based RIS when compared with computer-based strategies. Some works have proposed using formal methods to analyse these relay-based Railway Interlocking Systems [2,5,11, 12,19,22,23,25,26], and we have analysed these works in previous publications

[3,8–10]. The methodology we present in this paper stands out from the ones presented in the literature by proposing a different approach: instead of specifying the system to be implemented, our strategy is to analyse and constantly monitor existing systems with the use of certified tools based on a formal specification of their safety properties through a logical description of the system's expected behaviour. By using our methodology, it is possible to provide formal means to analyse and monitor legacy relay-based systems based on Formal Methods and industrial tools with the highest level of safety certification (SIL4 [6]).

This paper is organised as follows. The Sects. 2 and 3 present some background of our work, providing some details about relay-based RIS and the CLEARSY Safety Platform, respectively. While Sect. 4 is devoted to presenting how the system safety properties may be logically modelled, Sect. 5 presents our strategy for modelling and implementing the CSSP monitor. Some case studies are discussed in Sect. 6, followed by a discussion about the benefits of industrial use of our approach in Sect. 7. A conclusion is provided in Sect. 8.

2 Relay-Based RIS

Relay-based Railway Interlocking Systems are the implementation of interlocking systems using electrical circuits and components. A component is electrified (activated) when it is connected to the positive and negative source poles in a way that the electricity can flow through it. The most important component is the relay, which is composed of an electromagnet and one or more metallic contacts. When electrified, the relay produces an electromagnetic field that closes and opens contacts, controlling the electricity flow to other components. While monostables relays contain one coil that can pull or push contacts against gravity, bistable relays contain two coils that pull vertically-positioned contacts.

Table 1. Relay-based diagrams electrical components

Symbol	Description
	Monostable and bistable relays (coils), respectively.
	A monostable and a bistable contacts, respectively.
	Energy sources.
	A lever, a button, a junction and a capacitor, respectively.
	Blocks for timed activation and deactivation, respectively.

There are many different types of components. Some of them are depicted in Table 1. Each component has a different behaviour. As in this paper we focus on the activation/deactivation of components, we opted to focus on monostable relays, which is one of the most abundant components in the RIS electrical circuits. A more curious reader may be interested on reading our previous works in order to better understand the behaviour of other components [8,10]. As our approach is based on the activation/deactivation of components, it can be applied to any type of electric component, thus, the function and behaviour of the components do not affect our methodology.

3 The CLEARSY Safety Platform (CSSP)

The B-method [1] has been industrially used for decades in the development of safety-critical systems [4]. It is strongly recommended by the industry standard for SIL4 software development [15]. By using the Atelier B [7,14], a certified industrial tool to support the development, analysis and proof of systems, the industry has the necessary means to develop SIL3/SIL4 systems through a formal development strategy. However, regarding safety computers to run these applications, the market is limited: one may use PLCs (Programable Logic Computers) or SIL3/SIL4-ready boards. Both of them bring a series of limitations that may hinder the development of systems [15].

In this context, the CLEARSY Safety Platform combines redundant hardware with proven software developed with B to create a solution for the development and implementation of SIL4 systems to be applied in critical environments. While producing our own hardware can significantly reduce costs, the use of Atelier B provides more freedom and control on software development compared to other solutions in the market [15]. The design of the CSSP was created to ease the certification process as each part of the hardware and development approach was designed to create and implement safety-critical systems.

The starting point of the development process is the B formal model which specifies the safety function to implement. This model is divided into an Abstract Machine, the abstract model based on logic, and an Implementation, the concrete refinement of the Abstract Machine. This implementable model is then translated by Atelier B using two different chains: a translation to C followed by a standard C compilation (gcc), and a translation to MIPS Assembly and then to the binary code. The software obtained is uploaded to the execution platform to be executed in parallel by two micro-controllers. The results obtained from both instances are compared to detect possible divergent behaviours. Besides, several other automatic safety analyses are provided within the IDE and the micro-controllers. The safety board design is presented in Fig. 1. More information about the CLEARSY Safety Platform can be found at [15–18]. In this paper, we use the CSSP development kit containing: a physical version of the safety board and a CSSP version of Atelier B, which, in turn, contains the development interface (IDE), proof tools, translators and compilers, an interface for the communication with the safety board and a safety board simulator that can be used when the physical version is not available.

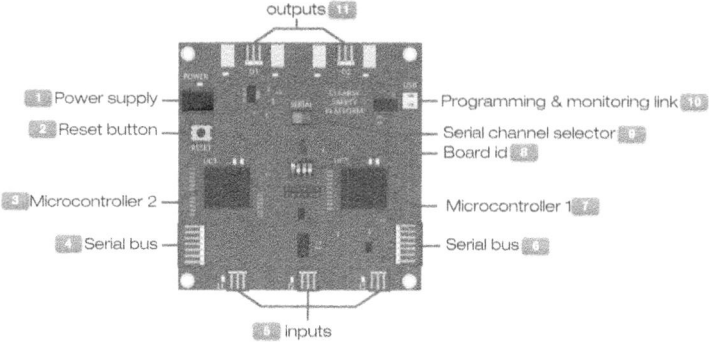

Fig. 1. The CLEARSY Safety Platform Starter Kit 0 (SK0) - documentation available at https://github.com/CLEARSY/CSSP-Programming-Handbook

4 Logical Description of the RIS Behaviour

To use the CSSP as a tool to monitor Relay-based Railway Interlocking Systems, it is necessary to model the properties of these systems in the subset of the B language used by the tool. Besides, this formal model must be connected to the system to be analysed. In this section, we discuss an approach to model the relay-based Railway Interlocking Systems properties using propositional logic. We have already explored a similar strategy in previous work [10] to translate relay-based RIS to a software-based version of it. In this paper, however, this strategy is updated to provide a way to monitor relay-based RIS safety properties during the system execution instead of modelling the whole RIS. This section focuses on explaining how the relation between electrical components may be logically described so it can be implemented as a RIS monitor.

The approach discussed in this section is based on the logical description of system intelligence as discussed in [21]. The objective is to describe how the system must react to certain states by defining logical relations between the states of the components. In this context, one may use an implication ($=>$),

    (A = TRUE) => (B = TRUE)

to model that: if a component A is activated ($TRUE$), a component B must also be activated. In this context, we use the Boolean values $TRUE$ and $FALSE$ to represent the activated and deactivated states of a component. This may be used, for instance, to state that if a train is detected in a certain portion of the tracks, the signals around it must be closed so no other train may enter the same portion of the tracks.

Similarly, one may use a bi-implication ($<=>$) to represent RIS safety properties. In this case, the notation to be used is the following:

    (A = TRUE) <=> (B = TRUE)

In this context the state of both A and B are linked, meaning that one may never be updated without the other also being updated. This is important to represent components whose states follow the same rules, like signals that must always present the same information. Conversely, one may define that two components may never reach a specific state by using a negation (*not*) of a conjunction (&):

not((A = TRUE) & (B = TRUE))

It is important to consider that more than two components may be involved in a safety property. For instance, two components may be responsible for the activation of a third one. In this context, conjunctions and disjunctions (*or*) may be used to add conditions. For instance, if a component C must be activated when the components A and B are activated, one may model it as:

(A = TRUE & B = TRUE) => (C = TRUE)

However, if only one between A and B must be true for the activation of C, one may model it as:

(A = TRUE or B = TRUE) => (C = TRUE)

Some examples of how the relation between component states can be logically described are presented in Fig. 2.

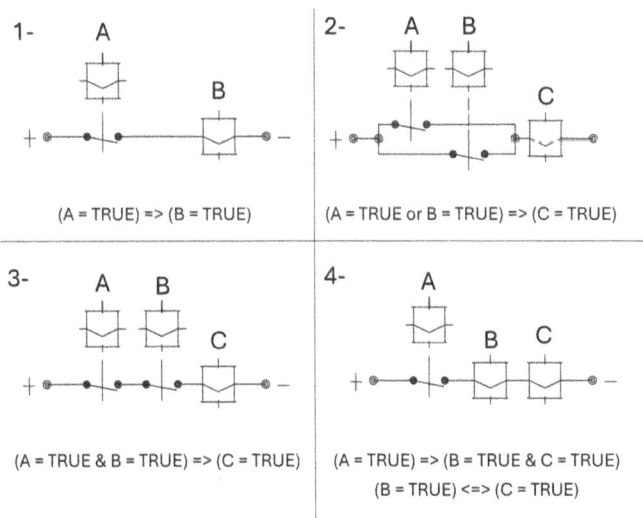

Fig. 2. Examples of logical description of some relay-based RIS configurations

Nonetheless, although formally modelling a complete relay diagram has been an interesting way to develop a safety-proved computer-based version of it, it does not respond to our need to monitor the existing relay-based ones. To do so, we may focus on the safety aspects of the system instead of modelling every component presented in a diagram. In this context, knowing the components and their function is essential to this task. For instance, in the example of Fig. 3, the output *EF11* is responsible for permitting a signal related to a turnout to turn green. To send this information, the system must guarantee that no other train is using the turnout. The component *PG 911* is the pedal that detects train presence in this portion of the track and this component deactivation indicates that the track is occupied. Guaranteeing that the signal will not turn green if the track is occupied is a safety-related condition that may be written as:

(PG_911 = FALSE) => (EF11 = FALSE)

This example is used in the remainder of this paper to illustrate the approach.

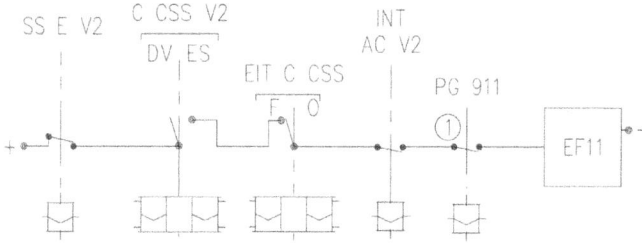

Fig. 3. Example of a component EF11 (output) whose activation depends on the activation of a relay PG 911

The information about the function of the components and their system safety conditions is generally described in documents that are delivered with the system and/or during maintenance. So, we believe that this material can be used as a basis to describe the safety conditions in propositional logic. To use this logic in the B-method subset language used in the CSSP, one may apply the notation accepted by the tools. The next section describes how the RIS logical description can be specified in the CSSP tools to monitor relay-based RIS.

5 Creation and Use of the RIS CSSP Monitor

Once the safety properties of the system to be monitored are logically modelled, one may specify and refine them using the CSSP development kit. The states of the components considered in the logic are attached to the CSSP inputs. The core of this methodology is to physically connect the relay-based RIS components to the CSSP inputs. The CSSP may then constantly analyse the states of the components according to the logically modelled safety properties and then output boolean information about the correctness of the system. This Section details all the steps regarding the development and use of the CSSP monitor.

The CSSP development approach divides the specification into an abstract machine and an implementation, respectively from the most abstract to the most concrete level of abstraction. The Atelier B has the tools to prove that the implementation is a correct refinement of the abstract machine. In our strategy for building a CSSP monitor, we focus on creating an abstract machine that contains the logic defined in propositional logic and an implementation that refines this logic. As we deal with the states of electrical inputs and outputs, instead of using the usual true and false boolean values, in our strategy we use IO_ON and IO_OFF to indicate the activation and deactivation of the inputs and outputs. In the CSSP model, these values belong to a basic type called uint8_t.

In order to formally specify the RIS monitor, one must focus on updating an output according to the modelled logic. In B, one may use the notation $a : (l)$ to update a variable a according to a logical expression l. For instance, to specify the example mentioned in the previous section, one may write:

```
board_0_O1 :( board_0_O1 : uint8_t &
    (((board_0_I1 = IO_OFF) => board_0_I3 = IO_OFF) <=>
     (board_0_O1 = IO_ON)))
```

which updates the output variable board_0_O1 according to the CSSP established output type uint8_t, with the value IO_ON (activated) if the implication (board_0_I1 = IO_OFF) => board_0_I3 = IO_ON is true for the inputs board_0_I1 and board_0_I3. These board inputs must then be physically connected to the components *PG 911* and *EF11*, respectively.

In this context, the strategy to specify the safety properties modelled in propositional logic is to follow the steps:

1. Update an output that indicates whether the monitored system is behaving correctly using the notation, $a : (l)$
2. Type the output in the l part of the notation,
3. Condition the output value according to the defined logic using a bi-implication. This last step is also in the l part of the notation.

So, one may use the pattern

```
board_0_O1 :( board_0_O1 : uint8_t & (( <logic> ) <=>
    ( board_0_O1 = IO_ON )))
```

to specify any safety condition in <logic> by replacing the variables of the propositional logic defined in the previous section by the board inputs and then output on board_0_O1 whether the safety property is met or not. Figure 2 may then be updated to present how the logic of some components configurations may be specified into the <logic> part of the pattern, as depicted in Fig. 4. The renaming of the variables in the logic with the board inputs is important as the components are to be connected to these inputs at a later moment in our approach. The state of the output may also be updated during the system specification: it is a developer's choice whether the output is activated or not when the safety property is not met. The purpose of the output value (activating other components or being read by a computer) plays an important part in this decision.

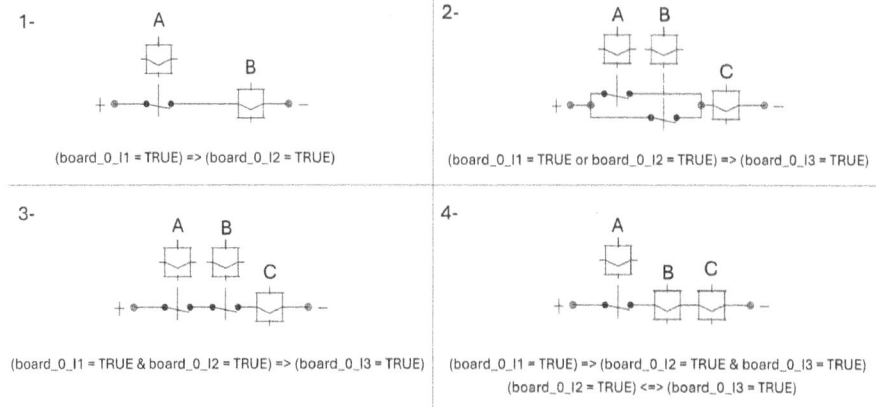

Fig. 4. Examples of CSSP specification of some relay-based RIS configurations, renaming the components with the board inputs, where A, B and C are attached to the board inputs board_0_I1, board_0_I2 and board_0_I3, respectively

Once the abstract machine is specified with the safety properties to be monitored, one may implement it using the B-method strategy. When implementing this logic, the notation to be used is closer to those of programming languages. The Atelier B either automatically proves or provides the tools to prove that the implementation is coherent with the specification. A possible implementation of the logic used as an example throughout the paper initially creates variables that receive the states of the inputs and initialises the output of the board as IO_OFF:

```
VAR i1, i2 IN
    i1 :( i1 : uint8_t );
    i2 :( i2 : uint8_t );

    i1 <-- get_board_0_I1;
    i2 <-- get_board_0_I2;

    board_0_O1 := IO_OFF;
```

Then, the logic can be implemented using conditions:

```
IF i1 = IO_OFF THEN
    IF i3 = IO_OFF THEN
        board_0_O1 := IO_ON
```

```
        END
    ELSE
        board_0_01 := IO_ON
    END
```

The Atelier B is capable of automatically proving that this implementation is a valid refinement of the abstract machine.

Once the abstract machine and the implementation are defined, one may run the automatic compilation tool existing in Atelier B. By connecting the board to the computer, the tool can automatically translate and compile the specified system and upload it to the board, which may then execute it. Once the system is executing, one may connect it to the RIS electrical circuit to receive the states of the components and analyse them according to the specified logic (see Fig. 5). As the RIS runs, the electrification of the wires activates the board inputs that are read by the implemented system. The monitor analyses if these inputs follow the modelled logic and then outputs the result of it. This output may then be read by a computer or it may trigger a light that may be used in the tracks to guide the train drivers. The use of lights to indicate signalling problems is already a normal practice in railway signalling. Some light panels contain this type of "system error" light in a pattern that is already known by the drivers [20].

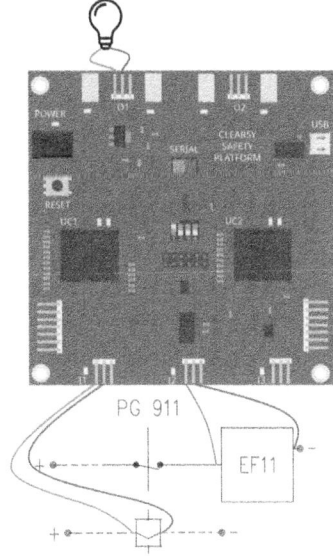

Fig. 5. Example of connection between the RIS and the CSSP board

There are many different ways of implementing each propositional logic pattern we have presented as examples in this paper. As the implementation of the specification is closer to programming and as the consistency of the implementation regarding the specification is completely proven, we are not presenting how each pattern may be implemented. The choice of how to implement the conditions to comply with the modelled logic is a matter of the developer's choices. Nonetheless, in the next section, we discuss some examples and provide their specification elsewhere, which may be satisfactory to the more curious readers.

6 Case Studies

In this paper, we apply our CSSP monitor strategy in two previously studied industrial case studies: the Temporary Reversed Direction Installation (ITCS - Installations Temporaires de Contre Sens) [10] and the Signalling Light Panel [3] examples, both used by the French National Railway Company. They exemplify how the CSSP monitor can be used to analyse the safety of the system according to logically specified safety properties. The case studies specification, implementation and the CSSP academic tools are available elsewhere[1].

6.1 Temporary Reversed Direction Installation

The ITCS is a system that controls the signals related to a turnout. The railway tracks are divided into portions called Control Areas. In a two-way portion of the tracks, when one of the tracks is blocked, the trains must pass through the opposite-way tracks (see Fig. 6), which may cause a collision. The signals must guarantee that only one train may access this "dangerous zone" at a time. The ITCS is responsible for the communication between the two involved control areas, informing whether the signals may go green according to the train's presence and safety conditions. In this case study, we model and analyse the system in Control Area A. While the component *KIT C 911* is responsible for controlling the signal on the left, the component *EF11* is responsible for informing Control Area C whether its signal may turn green or not. The activation of each of these components generates permission to enter the dangerous zone, so the system may guarantee that these components are never activated at the same time.

By analysing the relay diagram and the documentation about it (not provided in this paper due to confidentiality reasons), there are many safety properties we can model. The most obvious is that the components *KIT C 911* and *EF11* must never be activated at the same time:

```
not((KIT_C_911 = TRUE) & (EF11 = TRUE))
```

Another safety property modelled in the relay diagram is the one used as an example throughout this paper. Nonetheless, we may extend the safety condition to consider both light signals. When the pedal *PG 911* detects a train in the dangerous area, the signals around it must be closed so no train has permission to enter. Thus, we can model this condition as:

```
(PG_911 = FALSE) => (KIT_C_911 = FALSE & EF11 = FALSE)
```

---

[1] https://zenodo.org/records/11094051.

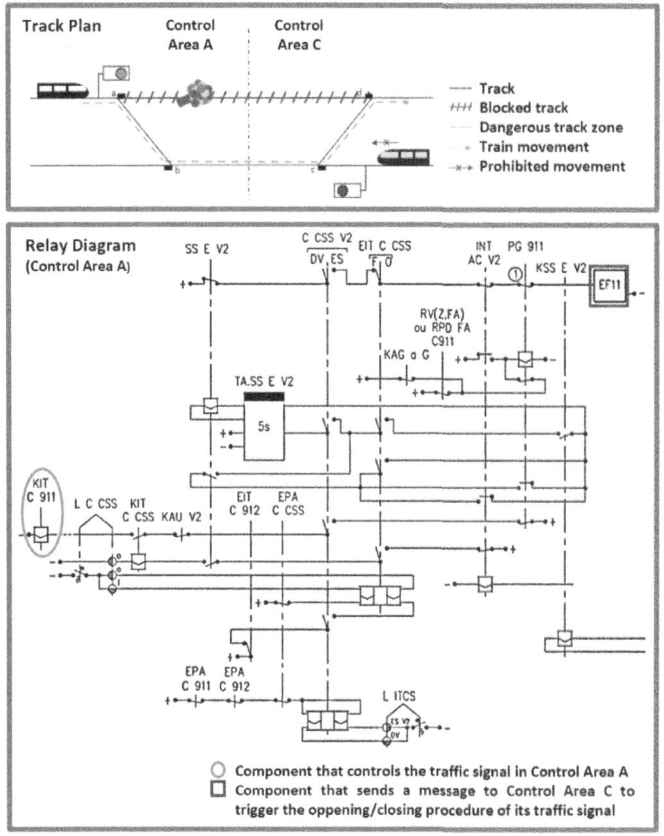

Fig. 6. The track plan and the relay diagram of the ITCS example

6.2 Signalling Light Panel

The control of a signal panel must meet many safety properties. Figure 7 depicts one example of a relay-based schema of such a control system. There are many different types of signal panels with different types of lights. In our case study, our panel has five lights that are used to communicate four types of information. The lights VL, A and S are, respectively, the green, yellow and red lights. The functions of these lights follow the pattern: green for movement authorisation, yellow for attention and red to stop. A pair of yellow lights is represented by R in the diagram and it has the function of informing the train driver to limit its velocity to 30 km/h.

When analysing the control of signal panels, it is important to understand that when a problem is found, the system must seek a safer state. In a light panel, the safest state is always the red light, i.e., when the train has no permission to move. In this context, the relay $RPCS$ has the task of turning off all other

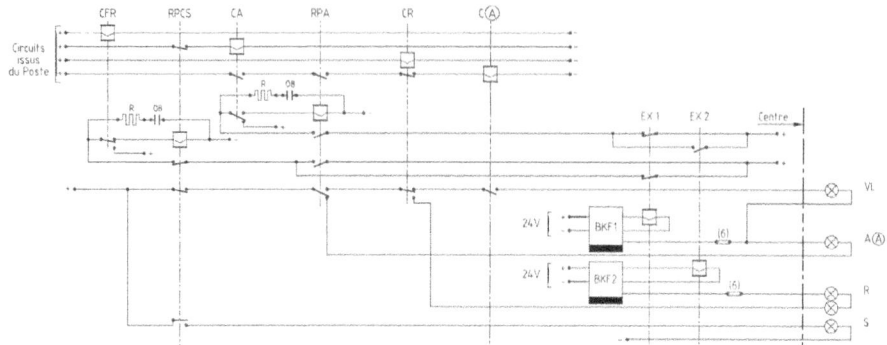

Fig. 7. Relay diagram of the signal panel case study

lights and turning only the red one on when a problem is found. If this relay is deactivated, the red light must be on:

(RPCS = FALSE) => (S = TRUE)

Similarly, the relay *RPA* is responsible for activating the yellow light when the green light is not available as the former is already safer than the latter. This scenario occurs when the system does not detect a problem dangerous enough to trigger the red light (*RPCS* is on), but still it requires some attention from the driver. In this context, we may define the following safety property:

(RPCS = TRUE & RPA = FALSE) => (A = TRUE)

A last important safety property is focused directly on the lights: if the green and all yellow lights are off, the red light must be on. This verification is redundant as the analysis involving the relays *RPCS* and *RPA* already analyses the state of the red light when the other cannot be turned on by the relays. Nonetheless, monitoring the system regarding this safety property is still important as a dysfunctional analysis to avoid false positives due to component failures or short circuits. This safety property can be monitored by connecting the CSSP board to all lights and make the following verification:

(VL = FALSE & A = FALSE & R = FALSE) => (S = TRUE)

This is an example that can be easily specified, implemented and executed with the industrial version of the CSSP board. However, as the academic version of the CSSP (available for research purposes) contains only three inputs, this analysis requires a new approach: the conjunction between the states of *VL*, *A* and *R* is calculated in one CSSP board *CSSP-1* that sends the resulting boolean value to another CSSP board *CSSP-2* (connection between the output of *CSSP-1* and the input of *CSSP-2*) that may then receive the state of *S* and calculate the implication. As the strategy discussed in this paper is focused on industrial purposes, the application of the monitoring of this safety property does not require such a specific approach. Thus, this example is not available to the reader of this paper. Nonetheless, it serves as a reminder that the industrial CSSP board has twenty-four inputs or outputs, which is more than enough to be used to monitor such industrial examples. Thus, one single CSSP board can be responsible for analysing several safety properties at the same time by addressing the correct inputs and outputs when specifying the safety properties logic.

7 Discussion

The case studies presented in this paper exemplify many safety properties that can be analysed and monitored using our CSSP strategy. Once the CSSP board is attached to the system to be monitored, it is possible to constantly analyse the system execution based on the components states. When the monitor detects that a safety property is not met, it raises a flag that may trigger a signal light to the driver and/or that may be read by computers connected to a control centre responsible for triggering a repair team. In this section, we present how detected problems in different safety properties may be interpreted and how the CSSP monitor can be applied to benefit the industry.

Our initial concern is to formally analyse existing systems without aiming at replacing them with computer-based systems. The documentation of these systems is generally focused on the safety properties that they must meet, so an analysis of these properties is the most essential task in our process. By using the CSSP, it is possible to support the in-loco tests that are performed during the maintenance of the legacy relay-based RIS. In this context, it is possible to provide a formal analysis of the system's safety properties by using the certified safety board and development approach to create a monitoring application. In this context, although we are dealing with a legacy system that was not conceived with Formal Methods, one is still capable of ensuring it follows the defined safety properties using Formal Methods.

Another way of using the CSSP Monitor follows the same principle, however, instead of analysing the system during in-loco tests, one may use the CSSP to constantly monitor the system regarding these safety properties. In this context, it is possible to obtain a constant analysis of the system regarding the defined safety properties. If the monitor is connected to a "defect" light, it can signal to the train driver that the system is defective when the safety conditions are not met, and then the driver may take standard precautions. When the monitor is connected to a computer, it may be used to inform the concerned engineers that the system needs maintenance as it is not behaving properly. For instance, if, for some reason, the outputs *KIT C 911* and *EF11* of the ETCS example are activated at the same time, it may turn on the "defect" light of the signals. As a result, the driver may be immediately informed that the information presented in this signal may not be trusted. Then, as the CSSP is connected to a computer that sends the output information to a control centre, the engineers may send people to analyse the system and find the defects. In this context, the CSSP monitor may not only avoid a dangerous situation but also provide the necessary information for engineers to take action and repair the system.

Nonetheless, it is important to observe that safety problems may not only be created during the conception or maintenance phases. The engineering behind relay-based RIS is constantly concerned about dysfunctional problems that may affect the system. This is the main reason why the components must be highly certified to endure stress and time. As a way to create a second layer of protection, the CSSP analysis may also be used to provide a constant dysfunctional analysis of the system, raising a flag when components with linked behaviours are not working properly. As an example, the pedal *PG 911* is responsible for controlling the state of the output *EF11* through one of its contacts. In a case where the mechanical parts of the relay fail, the CSSP is capable of detecting the inconsistency between the states of the relay and the component *EF11* according to the defined safety property.

Although we use real industrial examples as case studies, the approach presented in this paper has not yet been used in an industrial context. Monitoring systems based on our formal approach is still an idea that may become a product shortly. The proposed specification of the safety properties is based on the documentation of the system, which may vary according to the company. Some examples of documentation are: the relay diagrams, the system requirements specification and the Domain-Specific Languages (DSLs) used to model the systems. To specify the safety properties of our case studies, we used as a basis the relay diagrams and other documents that detail the components and their function in the system. Other case studies from other contexts may need different approaches. Nonetheless, in such a railway context, a document that specifies the system requirements is commonly available. The specification of the system properties in propositional logic, their translation into B and the refinement of the specification must be made manually, as it depends on the knowledge about the system safety. The automation of the approach relies on the automatic proof, implementation and execution of the monitor using the CSSP board.

8 Conclusion

This paper presents an approach to using the CLEARSY Safety Platform to monitor existing relay-based Railway Interlocking Systems. Differently from our previous works, instead of proposing the transformation of such legacy systems into computer-based ones, we propose the use of the certified CSSP tools and development methodology to formally analyse and monitor the RIS regarding safety properties. Our solution may be used to improve the quality of legacy manually analysed relay-based systems by allowing their formal analysis and monitoring based on Formal Methods. Besides, the monitor may be used to provide constant safety and dysfunctional analysis to guide the drivers and trigger repair teams with minimal delays. Two industrial case studies are presented to exemplify how our approach may be used in an industrial context.

In the future, we aim to study how the CSSP may be applied in other contexts to analyse and/or rebuild safety-related systems. We are now aiming at applying it to analyse systems related to the safety aspects of electricity production.

Besides, we aim to improve our methodology to be able to analyse and monitor safety-critical computer-based systems as well. As an industrial product, we are in discussion with many industrial and academic partners from other areas to discover new applications of such a flexible and useful tool in systems different from those where we are applying them right now. Future publications may result from these partnerships.

References

1. Abrial, J.R., Lee, M., Neilson, D., Scharbach, P., Sørensen, I.: The B-method. In: Prehn, S., Toetenel, H. (eds.) VDM 1991. LNCS, vol. 552, pp. 398–405. Springer, Heidelber (1991). https://doi.org/10.1007/BFb0020001
2. Amendola, A., Becchi, A., et al.: NORMA: a tool for the analysis of relay-based railway interlocking systems. In: Fisman, D., Rosu, G. (eds.) TACAS 2022. LNCS, vol. 13243, pp. 125–142. Springer, Cham (2022). https://doi.org/10.1007/978-3-030-99524-9_7
3. Bezerra, P.E.R., Oliveira, M.V.M., Lecomte, T., de Almeida Pereira, D.I.: CSP specification and verification of a relay-based railway interlocking system. In: Barbosa, H., Zohar, Y. (eds.) SBMF 2023. LNCS, vol. 14414, pp. 36–54. Springer, Cham (2023). https://doi.org/10.1007/978-3-031-49342-3_3
4. Butler, M., et al.: The first twenty-five years of industrial use of the B-method. In: ter Beek, M.H., Ničković, D. (eds.) FMICS 2020. LNCS, vol. 12327, pp. 189–209. Springer, Cham (2020). https://doi.org/10.1007/978-3-030-58298-2_8
5. Cavada, R., Cimatti, A., Mover, S., Sessa, M., Cadavero, G., Scaglione, G.: Analysis of relay interlocking systems via SMT-based model checking of switched multi-domain Kirchhoff networks. In: 2018 Formal Methods in Computer Aided Design (FMCAD), pp. 1–9. IEEE (2018)
6. Cenelec, E.N.: 50128-railway applications-communication, signalling and processing systems-software for railway control and protection systems. Book EN, 50128 (2012)
7. ClearSy. Atelier B User Manual, version 4.0. ClearSy System Engineering, Parc de la Duranne - 320 av. Archimède - Les Pléïades III Bat A - 13857 AIX EN PROVENCE CEDEX 3 - France
8. de Almeida Pereira, D.I.: Analysis and formal specification of relay-based railway interlocking systems. Ph.D. thesis, Centrale Lille Institut (2020)
9. de Almeida Pereira, D.I., Debbech, S., Perin, M., Bon, P., Collart-Dutilleul, S.: Formal specification of environmental aspects of a railway interlocking system based on a conceptual model. In: Laender, A., Pernici, B., Lim, E.P., de Oliveira, J. (eds.) ER 2019. LNCS, vol. 11788, pp. 338–351. Springer, Cham (2019). https://doi.org/10.1007/978-3-030-33223-5_28
10. de Almeida Pereira, D.I., Deharbe, D., Perin, M., Bon, P.: B-specification of relay-based railway interlocking systems based on the propositional logic of the system state evolution. In: Collart-Dutilleul, S., Lecomte, T., Romanovsky, A. (eds.) RSSRail 2019. LNCS, vol. 11495, pp. 242–258. Springer, Heidelberg (2019). https://doi.org/10.1007/978-3-030-18744-6_16
11. Ghosh, S., Das, A., Basak, N., Dasgupta, P., Katiyar, A.: Formal methods for validation and test point prioritization in railway signaling logic. IEEE Trans. Intell. Transp. Syst. **18**(3), 678–689 (2016)

12. Haxthausen, A.E., Kjær, A.A., Le Bliguet, M.: Formal development of a tool for automated modelling and verification of relay interlocking systems. In: Butler, M., Schulte, W. (eds.) FM 2011. LNCS, vol. 6664, pp. 118–132. Springer, Heidelberg (2011). https://doi.org/10.1007/978-3-642-21437-0_11
13. Haxthausen, A.E., Le Bliguet, M., Kjær, A.A.: Modelling and verification of relay interlocking systems. In: Choppy, C., Sokolsky, O. (eds.) Monterey Workshop 2008. LNCS, vol. 6028, pp. 141–153. Springer, Heidelberg (2008). https://doi.org/10.1007/978-3-642-12566-9_8
14. Lecomte, T.: Atelier B. In: Formal Methods Applied to Complex Systems: Implementation of the B Method, pp. 35–46 (2014)
15. Lecomte, T.: Programming the CLEARSY safety platform with B. In: Raschke, A., Méry, D., Houdek, F. (eds.) ABZ 2020. LNCS, vol. 12071, pp. 124–138. Springer, Cham (2020). https://doi.org/10.1007/978-3-030-48077-6_9
16. Lecomte, T., Deharbe, D., Fournier, P., Oliveira, M.: The CLEARSY safety platform: 5 years of research, development and deployment. Sci. Comput. Program. **199**, 102524 (2020)
17. Lecomte, T., et al.: Low cost high integrity platform. arXiv preprint arXiv:2005.07191 (2020)
18. Lecomte, T., Lavaud, B., Sabatier, D., Burdy, L.: A safety flasher developed with the CLEARSY safety platform. In: ter Beek, M.H., Ničković, D. (eds.) FMICS 2020. LNCS, vol. 12327, pp. 210–227. Springer, Cham (2020). https://doi.org/10.1007/978-3-030-58298-2_9
19. Mirabadi, A., Yazdi, M.: Automatic generation and verification of railway interlocking control tables using FSM and NUSMV. Transp. Probl. **4**, 103–110 (2009)
20. Rétiveau, R.: La signalisation ferroviaire. Presse de l'école nationale des Ponts et Chaussées (1987)
21. Russell, S., Norvig, P.: Artificial Intelligence: A Modern Approach, 3rd edn. Prentice Hall (2010)
22. She, X., Sha, Y., Chen, Q., Yang, J.: The application of graphic theory on railway yard interlocking control system. In: 2007 IEEE Intelligent Vehicles Symposium, pp. 883–887. IEEE (2007)
23. Sun, P., Collart-Dutilleul, S., Bon, P.: A model pattern of railway interlocking system by petri nets. In: 2015 International Conference on Models and Technologies for Intelligent Transportation Systems (MT-ITS), pp. 442–449. IEEE (2015)
24. Theeg, G., Vlasenko, S.: Railway Signalling & Interlocking: International Compendium (2019)
25. Van Eijk, P.H.J.: Verifying relay circuits using state machines. Logic Group Preprint Ser. **173** (1997)
26. Winter, K.: Model checking railway interlocking systems. Austral. Comput. Sci. Comm. **24**(1), 303–310 (2002)

Neural Networks

Unifying Syntactic and Semantic Abstractions for Deep Neural Networks

Sanaa Siddiqui[1]([✉]) [iD], Diganta Mukhopadhyay[2] [iD], Mohammad Afzal[2,3] [iD], Hrishikesh Karmarkar[2] [iD], and Kumar Madhukar[1] [iD]

[1] Indian Institute of Technology Delhi, New Delhi, India
{sanaasiddiqui,madhukar}@cse.iitd.ac.in
[2] TCS Research, Pune, India
{diganta.m,afzal.2,hrishi.karmarkar}@tcs.com
[3] Indian Institute of Technology Bombay, Mumbai, India

Abstract. Deep Neural Networks (DNNs) are being trained and trusted for performing fairly complex tasks, even in safety-critical applications such as autonomous driving, medical diagnosis, and air traffic control. However, these real-world applications tend to rely on very large DNNs to achieve the desired accuracy, making it a challenge for them to be executed in resource-constrained and real-time settings. The size of these networks is also a bottleneck in proving their trustworthiness through formal verification or explanation, limiting the deployability of these networks in safety-critical domains. Therefore, it is imperative to be able to compress these networks while maintaining a strong formal connection while preserving desirable safety properties. Several *syntactic* abstraction techniques have been proposed that produce an abstract network with a formal guarantee that safety properties will be preserved. These, however, do not take the *semantic* behaviour of the network into account and thus produce suboptimally large networks. On the other hand, compression and *semantic* abstraction techniques have been proposed that achieve a significant reduction in network size but only weakly preserve a limited set of safety properties. In this paper, we propose to combine the semantic and syntactic approaches into a single framework to get the best of both worlds. This allows us to guide the abstraction using global semantic information while still providing concrete soundness guarantees based on syntactic constraints. Our experiments on standard neural network benchmarks show that this can produce smaller abstract networks than existing methods while preserving safety properties.

Keywords: DNN Abstraction · Formal Verification · DNN Compression

1 Introduction

Advances in Deep Neural Networks (DNNs) have enabled the scalable solution of several previously intractable problems such as image recognition and natural language processing. Due to this, DNNs have increasingly assumed a central role across various domains. These include several safety-critical domains like healthcare [15], where they contribute significantly to medical diagnosis and predictive analysis [31], and autonomous vehicles, where DNNs serve as the backbone for sophisticated perception systems, supporting tasks such as object recognition and decision making [3].

However, given the enormous size and the substantial resource requirements of these DNNs in terms of CPU, memory and power, their implementation on embedded devices and real-time systems is often infeasible. This issue becomes especially apparent when integrating DNNs into embedded and real-time systems for performing safety-critical tasks, such as obstacle recognition in autonomous vehicles. Furthermore, DNNs are well known to be vulnerable to adversarial [5, 6, 23, 27, 33, 45] and backdoor attacks [9], and are also difficult to interpret. While a number of formal analysis techniques have been proposed to build trust on the reliability of DNNs in safety-critical settings, including verification [20, 25, 43, 47, 53] and formal explainability [2, 32], the size of the DNNs continues to be the limiting factor for the scalability of these techniques [20]. To tackle both these issues, it is imperative to reduce the size of the DNNs involved while maintaining a strong formal connection to the original network, and preserving desirable safety properties.

A typical approach within formal methods to reduce the complexity of any object while maintaining a strong formal connection with the original object is *abstraction*. For DNNs, structural abstraction based on the *syntax* (the local weights and biases at each neuron of the DNN) forms the basis of several techniques [13, 20, 35, 54] that work by converting a large *concrete* DNN $\mathcal{N}$ into a smaller *abstract* DNN $\mathcal{N}'$ via *merging* groups of neurons in $\mathcal{N}$ into single neurons in $\mathcal{N}'$. Each such merge is done in a way that ensures that there are *concrete*, formal soundness guarantees linking the behavior of $\mathcal{N}$ and $\mathcal{N}'$, thus maintaining safety-critical properties. In particular, one can verify properties on $\mathcal{N}'$, and using the concrete soundness guarantees, lift the result to $\mathcal{N}$ and argue about its reliability. However, while these techniques have been shown to extend the scalability of neural network verification techniques, they do not take the *semantic* behavior of the network into account, thereby producing sub-optimally large $\mathcal{N}'$. [20]. In fact, in [20], $\mathcal{N}'$ produced was sometimes observed to be larger than the original $\mathcal{N}$. This sub-optimality with respect to size prevents these techniques from being useful for compressing DNNs for deployment in safety-critical resource-constrained environments.

On the other hand, neural network compression techniques [11] and semantic abstraction techniques [1, 7] take into account the global *semantic* behavior of the network, and are able to achieve a significant reduction in size. However, heuristic based compression techniques [11] do not formally maintain any connection with $\mathcal{N}$, while semantic abstraction [1, 7] techniques only provide some limited kinds of formal connections with $\mathcal{N}$. In particular, the guarantees provided by clustering based methods like [1] are limited to lifting specific bound propagation based proofs from $\mathcal{N}'$ to $\mathcal{N}$, and those provided by linear combination based methods like [7] only bound the difference in behavior of $\mathcal{N}'$ and $\mathcal{N}$ on a finite subset of the input space. Thus, without strong formal guarantees connecting the behaviors of $\mathcal{N}'$ and $\mathcal{N}$, $\mathcal{N}'$ may not preserve desired safety properties.

In this work, we combine the syntactic and semantic approaches into a single framework for generating an abstract network. By splitting and labeling the neurons *inc* and *dec* and restricting ourselves to merges involving only similarly labeled neurons, as described in [20], we provide a concrete formal link between the behavior of $\mathcal{N}$ and $\mathcal{N}'$ via syntactic constraints. At the same time, to take into account the global semantic behavior, we introduce a semantic closeness metric between two neurons in the same layer. Using this metric, we construct a tree of merge operations that captures the relative contribution of each merge to the quality of the abstraction. We propose a CEGAR framework where the refinement procedure uses this tree as a guide to choose an optimal set of merge operations that produces a small size $\mathcal{N}'$. In the resulting refined network, groups of neurons that remain merged are semantically closer than neurons that get unmerged. Thus, combining both syntactic and semantic approaches, our framework is able to find an $\mathcal{N}'$ that preserves desired safety properties and is of a smaller size. To demonstrate the usefulness of this framework we set up experiments verifying the ACASXu [25,36] networks, and find that we are able to produce smaller networks than existing works that are still strong enough to verify the property.

2 Background

2.1 Notation

We restrict ourselves to fully-connected, feed-forward neural networks with *ReLU* activation function. Neurons in our network are denoted as $n_{(i,l)}$, where i signifies the neuron number in layer l. The function taking a given input x to the value of $n_{(i,l)}$ is represented by $v_{(i,l)}(x)$, The function $o_{(i,l)}$ takes a list of input vectors $[x_1 \cdots x_N]$ and returns a vector with $[v_{(i,l)}(x_1) \cdots v_{(i,l)}(x_N)]$ for a particular neuron $n_{(i,l)}$.

2.2 Formal Analysis of Neural Networks

Several techniques and methods have been studied to improve the reliability and trustworthiness of DNNs deployed in safety-critical settings via formal analysis. This includes verifying DNNs with respect to a given safety property [1,7,13,20,25,35,43,54], providing formal explanations of the behavior of DNNs [2,32], and defending against backdoor attacks [38]. To provide the formal guarantees behind the analyses performed, all of these techniques rely on making *neural network queries*.

These neural network queries are of the form $(P, \mathcal{N}, Q)$ and ask: if for all inputs x to $\mathcal{N}$ for which the formula P holds, the formula Q also holds for the output $\mathcal{N}(x)$. While there are several tools that can handle such queries, like Marabou [25,26,48], $\alpha, \beta - CROWN$ [40,41,47,49–53] and NeuralSAT [16], scalability remains an issue, and so reducing the size of $\mathcal{N}$ is desirable.

2.3 Semantic Compressions and Abstractions with Empirical Guarantees

Several techniques utilize semantic information, typically extracted via simulation of the DNNs, to obtain a smaller $\mathcal{N}'$. Neural network compression techniques [11], produce small $\mathcal{N}'$, but the behavior of $\mathcal{N}'$ in connection to $\mathcal{N}$ is only characterized empirically. Similarly, some semantic abstraction techniques [7] provide bi-simulation guarantees bounding the difference in the behavior of $\mathcal{N}'$ and $\mathcal{N}$ on a finite set of input points, typically a subset of the training dataset. Since these techniques characterize the behavior of $\mathcal{N}'$ only on a finite set of input points, the trust obtained on the connection between $\mathcal{N}$ and $\mathcal{N}'$ is only of an empirical nature. Other techniques, like [1], use bi-simulation to lift interval bound propagation performed on $\mathcal{N}'$ to get sound bounds on $\mathcal{N}$. While this does provide a sound proof, interval bounds are typically not strong enough to prove many interesting and practically relevant neural network queries.

2.4 Strong Formal Connections Between $\mathcal{N}$ and $\mathcal{N}'$

Structural abstraction techniques, including [20], provide the following strong formal connection between the behavior of $\mathcal{N}$ and $\mathcal{N}'$: $\forall x, \mathcal{N}'(x) \geq \mathcal{N}(x)$. Any general neural network query can be converted to a query of the form $(P, \mathcal{N}, y < c)$ for some c by encoding the postcondition as extra layers in $\mathcal{N}$ [20,25,39]. Therefore, this notion of formal connection allows one to abstract the larger $\mathcal{N}$ to a smaller $\mathcal{N}'$, dispatch the easier query $(P, \mathcal{N}', y < c)$ using a solver call, and argue that the original query holds [13,20,54]. This immediately makes such an $\mathcal{N}'$ useful for accelerating several formal analysis techniques (Sect. 2.2). Therefore, in this work, we focus on developing a framework that produces abstract networks that maintain this formal connection.

2.5 Syntactic Neural Network Splitting and Merging

In order to ensure soundness guarantees when transforming $\mathcal{N}$ into $\mathcal{N}'$, we adopt a modification of the four-way split approach proposed in [20]. In this approach, a two-way split is used instead [8,28,29], partitioning neurons in $\mathcal{N}$ into duplicate copies labeled with either *inc* or *dec*. This partitioning is done in a way that ensures that any increase (decrease) in the value of a neuron labeled *inc* (*dec*) only results in an increase in the output value. This can be done because it is not necessary to perform *pos-neg* splitting to soundly obtain an *inc-dec* split, as seen in [8,28,29]. Then, following [20], a sound abstraction can be obtained by *merging* all similarly labeled neurons as follows: if the neurons have the label *inc* (*dec*), replace incoming edges from the same previous layer neuron with a single edge with the maximum (minimum) of the original edge weights. Outgoing edges to the same next layer neuron are replaced with a single edge with the sum of the weights for both the *inc* and *dec* cases.

For example, consider the network and property in Fig. 1. For this example, all the neurons in the output and middle layer get classified as *inc*. Thus, they are all merged together, leading to the network in Fig. 2.

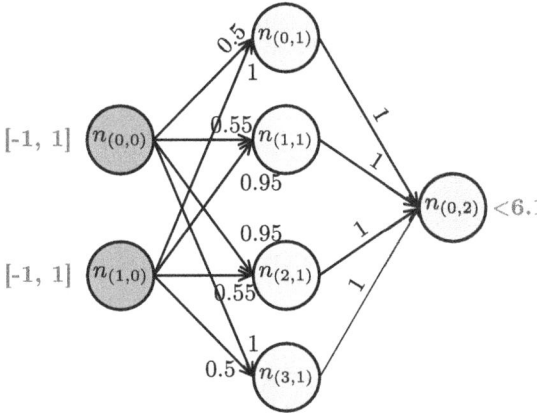

Fig. 1. Original Network and Property

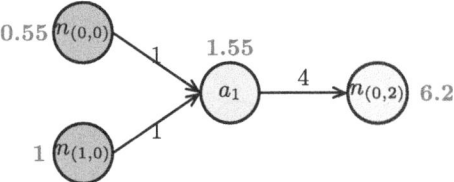

Fig. 2. Fully Abstracted Network

Note that this process only considers the syntactic structure of the network, no semantic information is used.

2.6 Syntactic Refinement

The fully merged network obtained in Sect. 2.5 may not be sufficiently strong to be able to dispatch, that is, there may be spurious counterexamples. In such situations, a common approach to obtaining a better-quality $\mathcal{N}'$ is to perform refinement steps based on a spurious counterexamples β [13,20,54]. In existing techniques, this is typically done by restoring a single neuron coming from $\mathcal{N}$ that had been merged with other neurons in $\mathcal{N}'$. The neuron chosen is typically one whose contribution to β is estimated to be the highest.

These techniques, however, do not consider any semantic behavior to guide their refinement. As such, the refinement process tends to produce a large number of restored neurons that are not merged with any other neurons. A proliferation of these *singleton* neurons lead to $\mathcal{N}'$ having a larger size. At the same time, a large group of neurons remains merged in $\mathcal{N}'$, which affects the quality of $\mathcal{N}'$.

We can see this in our example. Say the fully merged network in Fig. 2 we get a β given by the values in **bold**. Then, in the next refinement step, the neuron $n_{(3,1)}$ gets restored, giving us the network in Fig. 3. Again, the β obtained is shown in **bold**, and the next refinement step restores $n_{(0,1)}$ leading to Fig. 4. We see that in the resultant network, two semantically dissimilar neurons, $n_{(1,1)}$ and $n_{(2,1)}$, remain merged, while the merges between the similar pairs of neurons $n_{(3,1)}$, $n_{(2,1)}$ and $n_{(1,1)}$, $n_{(0,1)}$ have been un-done. Indeed, the network in Fig. 4 still admits spurious counterexamples, as seen by the values in **bold**, and we end up refining all the way to the original network.

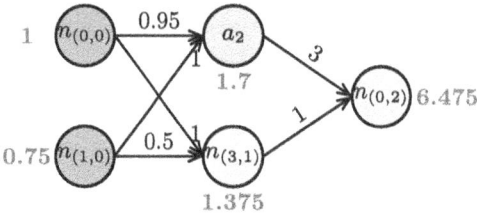

Fig. 3. Refine Step 1: Culprit Neuron is 3

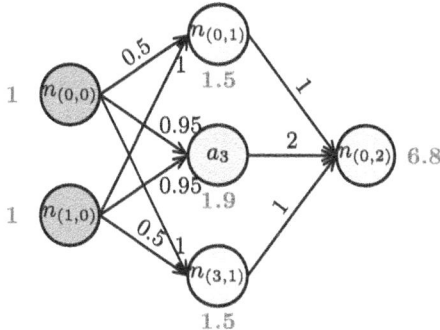

Fig. 4. Refine Step 2: Culprit Neuron is 0

3 Methodology

In this work, we aim to utilize information from the semantic behavior of $\mathcal{N}$ to better control and guide the refinement process, producing a smaller $\mathcal{N}'$ while retaining the strong formal connection to $\mathcal{N}$.

In particular, we define a *semantic closeness metric* that captures how close the semantic behavior of two neurons is (Sect. 3.1). We utilize this semantic closeness metric to arrange the merge operations into a tree where the lower quality merges involving semantically far neurons appear higher and can be refined with higher priority (Sect. 3.2).

Using this tree, we build a framework where refinement can be done by making cuts of this tree while still providing concrete soundness guarantees (Sect. 3.3). We show that the merges retained in this refinement process are optimal with respect to the semantic information (Sect. 3.4). This allows us to avoid restoring a large number of singleton neurons (see Sect. 2.5) and lets us retain merge operations of higher quality.

Using these components, we propose a general CEGAR [12,20] loop-based framework (Sect. 3.5) that combines syntactic merge operations with semantic behavior. This framework is able to produce an $\mathcal{N}'$ strong enough to not have any spurious counterexamples while having a much smaller size.

3.1 Semantic Closeness Factor

To guide the semantic abstraction process, we define a *semantic closeness metric* $\mathcal{C}$: $\mathcal{C}(n_{(i_1,l)}, n_{(i_2,l)})$ is a function that takes two neurons $n_{(i_1,l)}$ and $n_{(i_2,l)}$ in the same layer l, and returns a real number that captures how close the behaviors of $n_{(i_1,l)}$ and $n_{(i_2,l)}$ are from a semantic point of view. The number returned by $\mathcal{C}$ should be smaller for neurons whose semantic behavior is closer. Intuitively, this metric would characterize the semantic behavior of the neurons in layer l relative to each other and prioritize certain merges over others.

Depending on the application, the precise definition of this metric may be chosen in various ways. We note that our framework is agnostic to the particular choice of semantic metric, and the concrete soundness guarantee holds for any such choice. Inspired by [1], we chose the semantic closeness metric to be the difference between the functions computed by the two neurons: $||v_{(i_1,l)} - v_{(i_2,l)}||_2$, where $||\cdot||_2$ is the L_2 norm on the space of continuous functions on the input region $P \subset \mathbb{R}^i \to \mathbb{R}$. Generally, inputs to DNNs are bounded, and therefore so is P. Since $v_{(i_1,l)}$ and $v_{(i_2,l)}$ are neuron evaluations, they are Lipschitz continuous [46], which ensures that the L_2 norm is well defined.

However, since computing $||v_{(i_1,l)} - v_{(i_2,l)}||_2$ precisely is not feasible, we estimate it using a sample set of inputs X: $||o_{(i_1,l)}(X) - o_{(i_2,l)}(X)||_2$. In general, this X may be chosen in different ways, and our framework is agnostic to the sampling strategy used. In our experiments, we use a uniform sampling of the input region where P holds. Since the input region is usually an interval, such sampling is quite straightforward to do.

3.2 Tree of Merges

We use $\mathcal{C}$ to create a tree structure to prioritize merges where leaf nodes represent the original neurons and non-leaf nodes represent merge operations. In particular, each non-leaf node m_i represents an operation merging all the neurons corresponding to the leaf nodes that are descendants of m_i. For instance, the top half of Fig. 5 shows a tree where m_4 merges $n_{(0,1)}$ and $n_{(1,1)}$, while m_6 merges $n_{(0,1)}$, $n_{(1,1)}$, $n_{(2,1)}$ and $n_{(3,1)}$.

The construction of the tree follows a bottom-up approach, where we start with individual neurons and greedily perform the merge operation involving the most similar groups of neurons, delaying the merging of dissimilar ones. This is detailed in Algorithm 1[1]:

We start with an initial structure consisting only of leaf nodes corresponding to original neurons (line 1). At this stage, no merge operation has yet been done, and each node is a potential candidate for a merge, stored in *Cand* at line 2.

Now, as long as we have at least two candidates that we can merge, we keep greedily merging them in the loop, starting at line 11. To do this, we find which two candidate nodes m_i and m_j are most semantically similar in line 12, and introduce an operation merging them in lines 13–15.

We measure how semantically close a pair of candidates m_1 and m_2 are by looking at the maximum semantic distance between a neuron merged as a part of m_1's process and that merged as a part of m_2's process. This is done recursively by the *PairwiseMax* function in lines 3–10.

The resulting tree captures an optimal ordering of merge operations. That is, as we progress up the tree, the maximum value of $\mathcal{C}$ between any two neurons involved in a merge increases and the imprecision introduced by the merge operation increases. This is formalized in Sect. 3.4.

Algorithm 1. Building the Tree

Input: Neurons $\{n_{(i_1,l)}, \cdots, n_{(i_r,l)}\}$ with *inc-dec* label, Closeness metric $\mathcal{C}$
1: Initialize G with nodes $\{n_{(i_1,l)}, \cdots, n_{(i_r,l)}\}$ and no edges.
2: Initialize $Cand = \{n_{(i_1,l)}, \cdots, n_{(i_r,l)}\}$
3: **function** PAIRWISEMAX(m_1, m_2)
4:   **if** m_1 or m_2 has children **then**
5:     Without loss of generality, say m_1 has children c_1 and c_2.
6:     **return** $\max(PairwiseMax(c_1, m_2), PairwiseMax(c_2, m_2))$
7:   **else**
8:     m_1 and m_2 are neurons, **return** $\mathcal{C}(m_1, m_2)$.
9:   **end if**
10: **end function**
11: **while** $|Cand| > 1$ **do**
12:   $m_{j_1}, m_{j_2} = \arg\min_{m_1, m_2 \in Cand} \text{PairwiseMax}(m_1, m_2)$
13:   Add new node m_{j_3} to T
14:   Make m_{j_1}, m_{j_2} children of m_{j_3} in T
15:   Remove m_{j_1}, m_{j_2} from $Cand$ and add m_{j_3} to $Cand$.
16: **end while**
17: G now is a tree, call it T
Output: Tree of merges T

As an example, consider the middle layer in Fig. 1. Here, $n_{(0,1)}$ and $n_{(1,1)}$ are semantically closest. Thus, in the tree (top half of Fig. 5), we first merge these two to get the node m_4, representing the merge group $\{n_{(0,1)}, n_{(1,1)}\}$. At this

---

[1] For our choice of $\mathcal{C}$, (Sect. 3.1), Algorithm 1 reduces to hierarchial clustering [24], allowing us to leverage existing efficient implementations. Nonetheless, the general algorithm presented here will work for any choice of $\mathcal{C}$.

point, we have three choices for the next merge operation: m_4 and $n_{(2,1)}$, m_4 and $n_{(3,1)}$, or $n_{(2,1)}$ and $n_{(3,1)}$. Since $n_{(2,1)}$ and $n_{(3,1)}$ are semantically closer to each other than $n_{(0,1)}$ or $n_{(1,1)}$, the algorithm merges $n_{(2,1)}$ and $n_{(3,1)}$ to get m_5. This produces the merge group $\{n_{(2,1)}, n_{(3,1)}\}$, which has elements that are semantically closer than the groups $\{n_{(0,1)}, n_{(1,1)} n_{(2,1)}\}$ or $\{n_{(0,1)}, n_{(1,1)}, n_{(3,1)}\}$ obtained from following the other two choices. Finally, m_4 and m_5 get merged to m_6, giving us the complete tree.

3.3 Tree-Cuts and Refinement

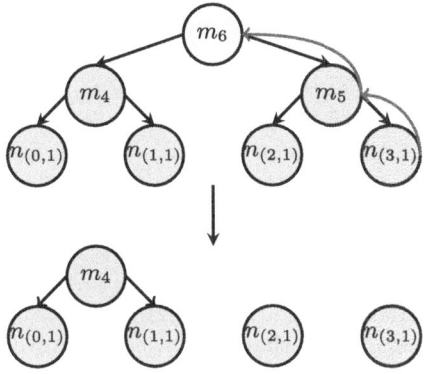

Fig. 5. Trees and Cuts

In our abstraction refinement loop, we start with the fully merged network. Then, whenever we get a spurious counterexamples β, we wish to refine the network. That is, we wish to choose which neurons should remain merged. Intuitively, this choice should be guided by two factors: optimizing with respect to the semantic behavior of the network and attempting to eliminate β. The tree produced in the previous Sect. 3.2 captures the semantic behavior, and we use it to guide the refinement process as follows: Any cut of the tree produces a set of trees. Then, the groups of neurons that we choose to keep merged correspond to the leaf nodes of these trees. Therefore, finding a refinement reduces to finding cuts in the tree. To attempt to eliminate β, we identify a *culprit neuron* γ that contributes most to the spurious output on β. The intuition is that γ should not be merged with any other neuron, as any over-approximation of the behavior of γ has a high chance of introducing β. Thus, we do refinement in two steps. Firstly, we find the culprit neuron γ. Then, we find a cut in the tree that ensures that γ is not merged with any other neuron.

Finding γ. Many possible strategies may be used to identify the culprit neuron γ, and our framework is agnostic to the specific strategy chosen. In our experiments, the strategy we chose is based on the *gradient-guided refinement* described in [7]. For each potential gamma, we calculated the following score and chose γ with the largest score:

$$\|v_\gamma^*(\beta) - v_\gamma(\beta)\|_2 \cdot \left|\frac{\delta y(\beta)}{\delta v_\gamma}\right|$$

Here, $v_\gamma(\beta)$ is the value at the neuron γ for input β in the original $\mathcal{N}$, while $v_\gamma^*(\beta)$ is the value of the neuron that γ has been merged into within our current $\mathcal{N}'$. $\frac{\delta y(\beta)}{\delta v_\gamma}$ is the partial derivative of the output y of $\mathcal{N}$ with respect to the value at γ for the input β.

Cutting the Tree. We wish to find a cut in the tree where γ is not merged with any other neuron, while also making sure that as many neurons remain merged as possible (therefore minimizing the increase in size of $\mathcal{N}'$). To do this, we delete precisely those nodes that are dependent on γ, starting from the parent of γ and moving up the tree following the parent links.

In our example, the culprit neuron is $n_{(3,1)}$. Thus, we traverse the tree following the blue edges in Fig. 5, undoing m_5 and m_6. This produces three trees, corresponding to leaving $n_{(0,1)}$ and $n_{(1,1)}$ merged while undoing the merge of $n_{(2,1)}$ and $n_{(3,1)}$. Therefore, we get the $\mathcal{N}'$ shown in Fig. 6. Note that in contrast to the refinement process followed by [20] (Sect. 2.5), we retain merges of neurons that are semantically close ($n_{(0,1)}$ and $n_{(1,1)}$), avoid proliferation of singletons, and achieve a smaller $\mathcal{N}'$ that is sufficient to prove the property in fewer iterations.

Once we have cut the tree and decided on which neurons to leave merged, the actual merge operation is the exact same as that followed by [20] (Sect. 2.5). Therefore, we are able to retain concrete soundness guarantees.

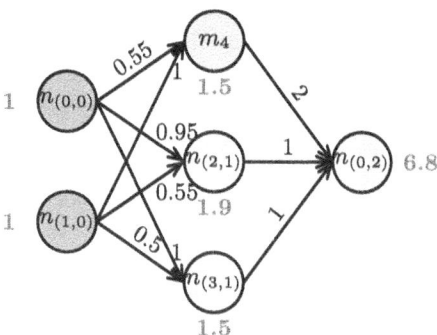

Fig. 6. Refining by our method: Culprit Neuron is 3

3.4 Optimality of Tree

Notation: Given a (sub)tree T of merge operations, we say a neuron $n_{(i,l)} \in T$ if and only if T has a leaf node corresponding to $n_{(i,l)}$. That is, $n_{(i,l)} \in T$ if and only if the merge operations forming T involve $n_{(i,l)}$ at any point.

The tree T produced in Sect. 3.2 captures an optimal ordering of merge operations with respect to the semantic information in the following sense:

Lemma 1. *Let T_1 and T_2 be two sub-trees of T. Then, we have:*

$$\max_{\substack{n_{(i_1,l)} \in T_1 \\ n_{(i'_1,l)} \in T_1}} \mathcal{C}(n_{(i_1,l)}, n_{(i'_1,l)}) \leq \max_{\substack{n_{(i_1,l)} \in T_1 \\ n_{(i_2,l)} \in T_2}} \mathcal{C}(n_{(i_1,l)}, n_{(i_2,l)})$$

Proof. This fact can be easily proved via induction on the combined size of T_1 and T_2. If a violation to the inequality exists, there may be two cases. In the first case, we have $n_{(i_1,l)}, n_{(i'_1,l)} \in T'_1$ where T'_1 is a strict sub-tree of T_1. But T'_1 and T_2 would then form a violation of the induction hypothesis. The other case directly violates the pairwise maximum condition used in the construction of the tree in Algorithm 1 line 3 in Sect. 3.2.

Intuitively, the lemma shows that for any cut in the tree, the maximum difference in the semantic behavior of neurons that have been left merged is less than the maximum difference in the semantic behavior of neurons that have been unmerged. In particular, this implies that, after each refinement step, the groups of neurons that remain merged together are optimal with respect to the semantic behavior of the network.

However, note that our semantic closeness metric fails to say anything about the value produced at the output layer of the network for any given input. Thus, although we have optimality with respect to semantic behavior, we are unable to predict the result that making a cut would have on the output for the given spurious counterexamples. Attempting to make such a prediction or provide some guarantees on the output of the network for a given spurious input, would nonetheless be an interesting direction for future work.

3.5 CEGAR [12,20] Loop Framework

We combine the pieces discussed so far into a CEGAR [12,20] loop. We start with the fully merged network. Then, utilizing spurious counterexamples, we iteratively refine the network until we have obtained an $\mathcal{N}'$ where there is no spurious counterexamples. This loop is parametrized by:

– The definition of the semantic closeness factor $\mathcal{C}$.
– The strategy for selecting the culprit neuron γ.

We note that while we have provided specific strategies for each of these, our framework is flexible enough so that, depending on the application, these pieces may be swapped out or modified to achieve better performance. We intend to study other strategies for each of these pieces in the future.

4 Experiments

We have implemented our method in python[2] utilizing the NumPy library for linear algebra operations and the SciPy library for an implementation of hierarchial clustering [24]. We have used a linkage-matrix-based data structure similar to the one used in SciPy to store the tree and have precomputed and cached several operations that may need to be repeated every refinement iteration. This allows us to quickly perform the merge and split operations and calculate the scores (Sect. 3.3), without having to do (relatively) expensive tree traversal operations in each iteration of the abstraction refinement loop.

Using this implementation, we have performed a set of experiments demonstrating the effectiveness of our abstraction technique for verification of neural network queries on the ACASXu [25,36] set of networks, using both the original safety properties from [25] and the ϵ-robustness properties introduced in [20]. To do so, we set up a CEGAR [12,20] loop (Sect. 3.5) using our abstraction technique, using the NeuralSAT [16] solver as the underlying solver to dispatch the verification queries on $\mathcal{N}'$. We compare our abstraction framework with the existing CEGAR [12,20] framework proposed in [20][3] setting a timeout of 200 s for each instance in the benchmark and for both our technique and the existing work. The experiments were run on a machine running on Intel(R) Core(TM) i7-6700 CPU with 8 CPUs running at 3.40 GHz, having 16 GB of RAM, and running Ubuntu 22.04 LTS.

If the $\mathcal{N}'$ produced has multiple neurons with the exact same set of incoming edges in the same layer, these neurons compute the same function and are redundant. Therefore, as an added optimization step in our method, we safely *re-merge* them by summing up the weights of the outgoing edges. Note that this does not change the behavior of $\mathcal{N}'$.

Tables 1 and 2 summarizes the results on these benchmarks. We find that using our framework, we are able to perform better than the existing CEGAR [12,20] approach on the original safety properties, verifying more networks to be safe, while we do not loose performance on the robustness properties.

Table 1. Summary of ACASXu [25,36] on original safety properties

Method	No. Safe	No. Unsafe	No. Timeout	Average Size
Ours	121	43	16	335.3
Existing [20]	118	43	19	536.0

---

[2] The entirety of the code, networks and datasets utilized in our evaluation are available on https://github.com/digumx/unified-merges.

[3] We have used a faithful re-implementation of this framework that follows exactly the procedure in the paper, with the only two distinctions being that we are using a two-class classification as seen in [8,28,29], and that the call to verify the $\mathcal{N}'$ obtained in each iteration is sent to an instance of the NeuralSAT [16] solver as opposed to Marabou [25,26,48].

Table 2. Summary of ACASXu [25,36] on robustness properties

Method	Percentage Verified	Average Size
Ours	100%	27.9
Existing [20]	100%	31.5

For each framework, we collected the final $\mathcal{N}'$ at the end of the CEGAR [12,20] iterations, for which either the property can be proved to be safe, or the solver is able to find an actual counterexample, or the solver times out. Figure 7 shows a scatter plot comparing the sizes of these final $\mathcal{N}'$ obtained by our framework and by existing work [20] for each instance in the benchmark. A point below the red diagonal line represents an instance for which we obtain a smaller final $\mathcal{N}'$ than the existing work; therefore, points below the line

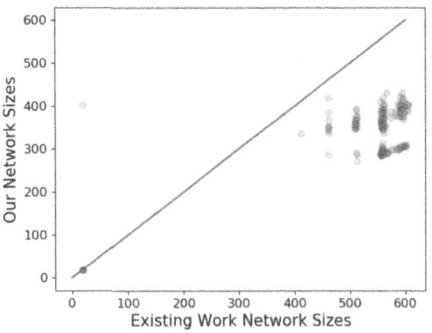

Fig. 7. Scatter plot of network sizes produced by our framework vs existing work [20] on ACASXu [25,36]

represent instances for which we perform better. The average sizes of these $\mathcal{N}'$ over all instances are reported in the 'Average Size' columns in Tables 1 and 2.

It is apparent from Fig. 7, Table 1, and Table 2 that, compared to the existing techniques, we explore smaller $\mathcal{N}'$ that are effective at proving or disproving the property in question. This shows that using semantic information to guide the CEGAR process can effectively find more efficient abstractions than the existing technique.

Note that in our experiments, we found that the time taken by both our CEGAR approach and the existing CEGAR approach [20] was more than what the NeuralSAT [16] solver takes for the ACASXu [25,36] benchmarks. However, while we would expect the solver call times to exponentially scale with network size, the overheads from the abstraction procedure will not scale exponentially. Thus, for larger and larger benchmarks, being able to find smaller $\mathcal{N}'$ will produce a significant difference in times. Furthermore, we believe that a verified $\mathcal{N}'$ is useful beyond verifying a single property - it may be used for other related queries or may be useful as a safely deployable compressed network.

Additionally, we find that the final solver times on the $\mathcal{N}'$ are actually comparable with the times obtained on the original un-abstracted $\mathcal{N}$. In general, it has been observed both by our experiments and in [20] that the effort needed to verify a network is dependent on more than just network size. In fact, in [20], they are able to achieve smaller solver times on larger networks. While it is true that in general the worst-case performance of neural network solvers will almost certainly remain exponential in the size of the network [25], other factors on which the performance of neural network solvers may depend remain an interesting direction of future work.

5 Related Work

In general, methodologies for verifying neural networks generally fall into two main categories: sound and complete methods [10,17,19,21,25,26,30,34,47,50,51], and sound and incomplete methods [18,22,42–44,53]. Sound and complete methods aim to explore the entire state space to verify the properties of neural networks. In contrast, sound and incomplete methods employ an overapproximation of the state space, sacrificing completeness for scalability and efficiency.

An instance of a sound and complete methodology is Reluplex, which extends the simplex algorithm [14] to handle ReLU constraints. Initially, it focuses on finding an assignment that satisfies the linear constraints, subsequently incorporating non-linear constraints to validate their satisfaction. In [19] the authors introduce triangular over-approximation, infer neuron phase fixtures, learn conflict clauses and safe neuron phase fixtures to aid in pruning the search space, which is similar to classical SMT solving approaches. Another complete technique is NeuralSAT [16], which performs exhaustive theory propagation and conflict clause learning similar to DPLL(T) used in classical SMT solving. However, these methods often encounter scalability issues due to their exhaustive exploration of the entire state space.

On the other hand, alternative techniques like [43,53], which propagates linear upper and lower bound constraints, exhibit better scalability at the cost of overapproximation. [50] optimizes the bounds of [53] using gradient descent. [47] incorporates ReLU split constraints into the CROWN bound propagation process, allowing integration into the branch and bound (BaB) framework [4,37,52]. This combined implementation makes the $\alpha, \beta - CROWN$ [40,41,47,49–53] framework sound and complete.

6 Conclusion and Future Work

This paper puts forth a framework to combine syntactic and semantic approaches for DNN abstraction. While this opens several directions for future work, an immediate question that can be asked is about achieving "optimal refinement". In the abstract network, it would be ideal to not have neurons that can be merged back without introducing spurious counterexamples. This implies that we should have added the minimum number of neurons necessary to prevent spurious counterexamples. It would be interesting to explore if there is a refinement path guaranteed to do such a *minimal* refinement. It would also be interesting to explore if other methods of finding abstractions beyond the merge and unmerge operations described here and in other existing works [1,13,20,54] produce optimal abstract networks.

Exploring alternative measures for the semantic closeness factor $\mathcal{C}$ is another intriguing prospect. Note that our framework allows one to seamlessly experiment with any $\mathcal{C}$. Our current $\mathcal{C}$ does capture optimality with respect to the I/O behavior of the neurons, but we are not able to guarantee minimization of the over-approximation at the output layer. It would help to identify better metrics for the semantic closeness factor that minimize over-approximation at the output neuron.

In our experiments, we noticed that the time needed to verify a specific property of a network is not solely determined by the network's size. It is possible that a larger network can be verified quickly, while a smaller one may take longer or even fail to be verified altogether. Obtaining a more accurate measure of the effort required to verify a network would provide a better optimization target for abstraction used in the context of verification.

Acknowledgments. This project was partly funded by IRD, IIT Delhi under the Multi-Institutional Faculty Interdisciplinary Research Programme (MFIRP) Scheme, Project No. MI02571G, jointly between Indian Institute of Technology Delhi and Hebrew University of Jerusalem. This work was also partially supported by the CSE Research Acceleration Fund of IIT Delhi. The authors would also like to thank Guy Katz, a faculty member in School of Computer Science and Engineering at Hebrew University of Jerusalem, for his valuable inputs and feedback

References

1. Ashok, P., Hashemi, V., Křetínský, J., Mohr, S.: DeepAbstract: neural network abstraction for accelerating verification. In: Hung, D.V., Sokolsky, O. (eds.) Automated Technology for Verification and Analysis. ATVA 2020. LNCS, vol. 12302, pp. 92–107. Springer, Cham (2020). https://doi.org/10.1007/978-3-030-59152-6_5
2. Bassan, S., Katz, G.: Towards formal XAI: formally approximate minimal explanations of neural networks. In: Sankaranarayanan, S., Sharygina, N. (eds.) Tools and Algorithms for the Construction and Analysis of Systems. TACAS 2023. LNCS, vol. 13993, pp. 187–207. Springer, Cham (2023). https://doi.org/10.1007/978-3-031-30823-9_10
3. Bojarski, M., et al.: End to end learning for self-driving cars. CoRR **abs/1604.07316** (2016)
4. Bunel, R., Lu, J., Turkaslan, I., Torr, P.H.S., Kohli, P., Kumar, M.P.: Branch and bound for piecewise linear neural network verification. J. Mach. Learn. Res. **21**, 42:1–42:39 (2020)
5. Carlini, N., Katz, G., Barrett, C., Dill, D.L.: Provably minimally-distorted adversarial examples (2018)
6. Carlini, N., Wagner, D.A.: Towards evaluating the robustness of neural networks. In: 2017 IEEE Symposium on Security and Privacy, SP 2017, San Jose, CA, USA, 22–26 May 2017, pp. 39–57. IEEE Computer Society (2017)
7. Chau, C., Kretínský, J., Mohr, S.: Syntactic vs semantic linear abstraction and refinement of neural networks. In: André, É., Sun, J. (eds.) Automated Technology for Verification and Analysis. ATVA 2023. LNCS, vol. 14215, pp. 401–421. Springer, Cham (2023). https://doi.org/10.1007/978-3-031-45329-8_19

8. Chauhan, A., Afzal, M., Karmarkar, H., Elboher, Y., Madhukar, K., Katz, G.: Efficiently finding adversarial examples with dnn preprocessing (2022)
9. Chen, X., Liu, C., Li, B., Lu, K., Song, D.: Targeted backdoor attacks on deep learning systems using data poisoning. CoRR **abs/1712.05526** (2017)
10. Cheng, C., Nührenberg, G., Ruess, H.: Maximum resilience of artificial neural networks. CoRR **abs/1705.01040** (2017)
11. Cheng, Y., Wang, D., Zhou, P., Zhang, T.: A survey of model compression and acceleration for deep neural networks. CoRR **abs/1710.09282** (2017)
12. Clarke, E.M., Grumberg, O., Jha, S., Lu, Y., Veith, H.: Counterexample-guided abstraction refinement for symbolic model checking. J. ACM **50**(5), 752–794 (2003)
13. Cohen, E., Elboher, Y.Y., Barrett, C.W., Katz, G.: Tighter abstract queries in neural network verification. In: Piskac, R., Voronkov, A. (eds.) LPAR 2023: Proceedings of 24th International Conference on Logic for Programming, Artificial Intelligence and Reasoning, Manizales, Colombia, 4–9th June 2023. EPiC Series in Computing, vol. 94, pp. 124–143. EasyChair (2023)
14. Dantzig, G.B.: Linear Programming and Extensions. RAND Corporation, Santa Monica, CA (1963). https://doi.org/10.7249/R366
15. Djavanshir, G.R., Chen, X., Yang, W.: A review of artificial intelligence's neural networks (deep learning) applications in medical diagnosis and prediction. IT Professional **23**(3), 58–62 (2021)
16. Duong, H., Nguyen, T., Dwyer, M.: A DPLL(T) framework for verifying deep neural networks (2024)
17. Dutta, S., Jha, S., Sankaranarayanan, S., Tiwari, A.: Output range analysis for deep feedforward neural networks. in: Dutle, A., Muñoz, C., Narkawicz, A. (eds.) NASA Formal Methods. NFM 2018. LNCS, vol. 10811, pp. 121–138. Springer, Cham (2018). https://doi.org/10.1007/978-3-319-77935-5_9
18. Dvijotham, K., Stanforth, R., Gowal, S., Mann, T.A., Kohli, P.: A dual approach to scalable verification of deep networks. In: Globerson, A., Silva, R. (eds.) Proceedings of the Thirty-Fourth Conference on Uncertainty in Artificial Intelligence, UAI 2018, Monterey, California, USA, 6–10 August 2018, pp. 550–559. AUAI Press (2018)
19. Ehlers, R.: Formal verification of piece-wise linear feed-forward neural networks. In: D'Souza, D., Narayan Kumar, K. (eds.) Automated Technology for Verification and Analysis. ATVA 2017. LNCS, vol. 10482, pp. 269–286. Springer, Cham (2017). https://doi.org/10.1007/978-3-319-68167-2_19
20. Elboher, Y.Y., Gottschlich, J., Katz, G.: An abstraction-based framework for neural network verification. In: Lahiri, S., Wang, C. (eds.) Computer Aided Verification. CAV 2020. LNCS, vol. 12224, pp. 43–65. Springer, Cham (2020). https://doi.org/10.1007/978-3-030-53288-8_3
21. Fischetti, M., Jo, J.: Deep neural networks and mixed integer linear optimization. Constraints Int. J. **23**(3), 296–309 (2018)
22. Gehr, T., Mirman, M., Drachsler-Cohen, D., Tsankov, P., Chaudhuri, S., Vechev, M.T.: AI2: safety and robustness certification of neural networks with abstract interpretation. In: 2018 IEEE Symposium on Security and Privacy, SP 2018, Proceedings, 21–23 May 2018, San Francisco, California, USA, pp. 3–18. IEEE Computer Society (2018)
23. Goodfellow, I.J., Shlens, J., Szegedy, C.: Explaining and harnessing adversarial examples. In: Bengio, Y., LeCun, Y. (eds.) 3rd International Conference on Learning Representations, ICLR 2015, San Diego, CA, USA, 7–9 May 2015, Conference Track Proceedings (2015)

24. Ward Jr, J.H.: Hierarchical grouping to optimize an objective function. J. Am. Stat. Assoc. **58**(301), 236–244 (1963)
25. Katz, G., Barrett, C., Dill, D.L., Julian, K., Kochenderfer, M.J.: Reluplex: an efficient SMT solver for verifying deep neural networks. In: Majumdar, R., Kunčak, V. (eds.) Computer Aided Verification. CAV 2017. LNCS, vol. 10426, pp. 97–117. Springer, Cham (2017). https://doi.org/10.1007/978-3-319-63387-9_5
26. Katz, G., et al.: The marabou framework for verification and analysis of deep neural networks. In: Dillig, I., Tasiran, S. (eds.) Computer Aided Verification. CAV 2019. LNCS, vol. 11561, pp. 443–452. Springer, Cham (2019). https://doi.org/10.1007/978-3-030-25540-4_26
27. Kurakin, A., Goodfellow, I.J., Bengio, S.: Adversarial examples in the physical world. In: 5th International Conference on Learning Representations, ICLR 2017, Toulon, France, 24–26 April 2017, Workshop Track Proceedings. OpenReview.net (2017)
28. Liu, J., Xing, Y., Shi, X., Song, F., Xu, Z., Ming, Z.: Abstraction and refinement: towards scalable and exact verification of neural networks (2022)
29. Liu, J., Xing, Y., Shi, X., Song, F., Xu, Z., Ming, Z.: Abstraction and refinement: towards scalable and exact verification of neural networks. ACM Trans. Softw. Eng. Methodol. (2024). https://doi.org/10.1145/3644387
30. Lomuscio, A., Maganti, L.: An approach to reachability analysis for feed-forward relu neural networks. CoRR **abs/1706.07351** (2017). http://arxiv.org/abs/1706.07351
31. Mangal, A., Kalia, S., Rajgopal, H., Rangarajan, K., Namboodiri, V.P., Banerjee, S., Arora, C.: Covidaid: COVID-19 detection using chest x-ray. CoRR **abs/2004.09803** (2020)
32. Marques-Silva, J., Ignatiev, A.: Delivering trustworthy AI through formal XAI. In: Thirty-Sixth AAAI Conference on Artificial Intelligence, AAAI 2022, Thirty-Fourth Conference on Innovative Applications of Artificial Intelligence, IAAI 2022, The Twelveth Symposium on Educational Advances in Artificial Intelligence, EAAI 2022 Virtual Event, February 22–1 March 2022, pp. 12342–12350. AAAI Press (2022)
33. Moosavi-Dezfooli, S., Fawzi, A., Frossard, P.: Deepfool: a simple and accurate method to fool deep neural networks. In: 2016 IEEE Conference on Computer Vision and Pattern Recognition, CVPR 2016, Las Vegas, NV, USA, 27–30 June 2016, pp. 2574–2582. IEEE Computer Society (2016)
34. Neider, D., Johnson, T.T.: Track C1: safety verification of deep neural networks (DNNs). In: Steffen, B. (eds.) Bridging the Gap Between AI and Reality. AISoLA 2023. LNCS, vol. 14380, pp. 217–224. Springer, Cham (2024). https://doi.org/10.1007/978-3-031-46002-9_12
35. Ostrovsky, M., Barrett, C., Katz, G.: An abstraction-refinement approach to verifying convolutional neural networks. In: Bouajjani, A., Holík, L., Wu, Z. (eds.) Automated Technology for Verification and Analysis. ATVA 2022. LNCS, vol 13505. Springer, Cham (2022). https://doi.org/10.1007/978-3-031-19992-9_25
Ostrovsky, M., Barrett, C., Katz, G.: An abstraction-refinement approach to verifying convolutional neural networks. In: Bouajjani, A., Holík, L., Wu, Z. (eds.) Automated Technology for Verification and Analysis. ATVA 2022. LNCS, vol. 13505, pp. 391–396. Springer, Cham (2022). https://doi.org/10.1007/978-3-031-19992-9_25
36. Owen, M.P., Panken, A., Moss, R., Alvarez, L., Leeper, C.: ACAS XU: integrated collision avoidance and detect and avoid capability for UAS. In: 2019 IEEE/AIAA

38th Digital Avionics Systems Conference (DASC), pp. 1–10 (2019). https://doi.org/10.1109/DASC43569.2019.9081758
37. Palma, A.D., et al.: Improved branch and bound for neural network verification via lagrangian decomposition. CoRR **abs/2104.06718** (2021)
38. Pham, L.H., Sun, J.: Verifying neural networks against backdoor attacks. In: Shoham, S., Vizel, Y. (eds.) Computer Aided Verification. CAV 2022. LNCS, vol. 13371, pp. 171–192. Springer, Cham (2022). https://doi.org/10.1007/978-3-031-13185-1_9
39. Ruan, W., Huang, X., Kwiatkowska, M.: Reachability analysis of deep neural networks with provable guarantees. In: Lang, J. (ed.) Proceedings of the Twenty-Seventh International Joint Conference on Artificial Intelligence, IJCAI 2018, 13–19 July 2018, Stockholm, Sweden, pp. 2651–2659. ijcai.org (2018)
40. Salman, H., Yang, G., Zhang, H., Hsieh, C.J., Zhang, P.: A convex relaxation barrier to tight robustness verification of neural networks. Adv. Neural Inf. Process. Syst. **32**, 9835–9846 (2019)
41. Shi, Z., Jin, Q., Kolter, J.Z., Jana, S., Hsieh, C.J., Zhang, H.: Formal verification for neural networks with general nonlinearities via branch-and-bound. In: 2nd Workshop on Formal Verification of Machine Learning (WFVML 2023) (2023)
42. Singh, G., Gehr, T., Mirman, M., Püschel, M., Vechev, M.T.: Fast and effective robustness certification. In: Bengio, S., Wallach, H.M., Larochelle, H., Grauman, K., Cesa-Bianchi, N., Garnett, R. (eds.) Advances in Neural Information Processing Systems 31: Annual Conference on Neural Information Processing Systems 2018, NeurIPS 2018, 3–8 December 2018, Montréal, Canada, pp. 10825–10836 (2018)
43. Singh, G., Gehr, T., Püschel, M., Vechev, M.T.: An abstract domain for certifying neural networks. Proc. ACM Program. Lang. **3**(POPL) 41, 1–41:30 (2019)
44. Singh, G., Gehr, T., Püschel, M., Vechev, M.T.: Boosting robustness certification of neural networks. In: 7th International Conference on Learning Representations, ICLR 2019, New Orleans, LA, USA, 6–9 May 2019. OpenReview.net (2019)
45. Szegedy, C., et al.: Intriguing properties of neural networks. In: Bengio, Y., LeCun, Y. (eds.) 2nd International Conference on Learning Representations, ICLR 2014, Banff, AB, Canada, 14–16 April 2014, Conference Track Proceedings (2014)
46. Virmaux, A., Scaman, K.: Lipschitz regularity of deep neural networks: analysis and efficient estimation. In: Bengio, S., Wallach, H.M., Larochelle, H., Grauman, K., Cesa-Bianchi, N., Garnett, R. (eds.) Advances in Neural Information Processing Systems 31: Annual Conference on Neural Information Processing Systems 2018, NeurIPS 2018, 3–8 December 2018, Montréal, Canada, pp. 3839–3848 (2018). https://proceedings.neurips.cc/paper/2018/hash/d54e99a6c03704e95e6965532dec148b-Abstract.html
47. Wang, S., et al.: Beta-crown: Efficient bound propagation with per-neuron split constraints for neural network robustness verification. In: Ranzato, M., Beygelzimer, A., Dauphin, Y.N., Liang, P., Vaughan, J.W. (eds.) Advances in Neural Information Processing Systems 34: Annual Conference on Neural Information Processing Systems 2021, NeurIPS 2021, 6–14 December 2021, virtual, pp. 29909–29921 (2021)
48. Wu, H., et al.: Marabou 2.0: a versatile formal analyzer of neural networks. CoRR **abs/2401.14461** (2024)
49. Xu, K., et al.: Automatic perturbation analysis for scalable certified robustness and beyond. In: Larochelle, H., Ranzato, M., Hadsell, R., Balcan, M., Lin, H. (eds.) Advances in Neural Information Processing Systems 33: Annual Conference on Neural Information Processing Systems 2020, NeurIPS 2020, 6–12 December 2020, virtual (2020)

50. Xu, K., et al.: Fast and complete: enabling complete neural network verification with rapid and massively parallel incomplete verifiers. CoRR **abs/2011.13824** (2020)
51. Zhang, H., et al.: General cutting planes for bound-propagation-based neural network verification. Adv. Neural Inf. Process. Syst. (2022)
52. Zhang, H., Wang, S., Xu, K., Wang, Y., Jana, S., Hsieh, C.J., Kolter, Z.: A branch and bound framework for stronger adversarial attacks of ReLU networks. In: Proceedings of the 39th International Conference on Machine Learning, vol. 162, pp. 26591–26604 (2022)
53. Zhang, H., Weng, T., Chen, P., Hsieh, C., Daniel, L.: Efficient neural network robustness certification with general activation functions. In: Bengio, S., Wallach, H.M., Larochelle, H., Grauman, K., Cesa-Bianchi, N., Garnett, R. (eds.) Advances in Neural Information Processing Systems 31: Annual Conference on Neural Information Processing Systems 2018, NeurIPS 2018, 3–8 December 2018, Montréal, Canada, pp. 4944–4953 (2018)
54. Zhao, Z., Zhang, Y., Chen, G., Song, F., Chen, T., Liu, J.: CLEVEREST: accelerating CEGAR-based Neural network verification via adversarial attacks. In: Singh, G., Urban, C. (eds.) Static Analysis. SAS 2022. LNCS, vol. 13790, pp. 449–473. Springer, Cham (2022). https://doi.org/10.1007/978-3-031-22308-2_20

Multimodal Model Predictive Runtime Verification for Safety of Autonomous Cyber-Physical Systems

Alexis Aurandt(✉), Phillip H. Jones, Kristin Yvonne Rozier, and Tichakorn Wongpiromsarn

Iowa State University, Ames, USA
{aurandt,phjones,kyrozier,nok}@iastate.edu

Abstract. Autonomous cyber-physical systems must be able to operate safely in a wide range of complex environments. To ensure safety without limiting mitigation options, these systems require detection of safety violations by mitigation trigger deadlines. As a result of these system's complex environments, multimodal prediction is often required. For example, an autonomous vehicle (AV) operates in complex traffic scenes that result in any given vehicle having the ability to exhibit several plausible future behavior modes (e.g., stop, merge, turn, etc.); therefore, to ensure collision avoidance, an AV must be able to predict the possible multimodal behaviors of nearby vehicles. In previous work, model predictive runtime verification (MPRV) successfully detected future violations by a given deadline, but MPRV only considers a single mode of prediction (i.e., unimodal prediction). We design multimodal model predictive runtime verification (MMPRV) to extend MPRV to consider multiple modes of prediction, and we introduce Predictive Mission-Time Linear Temporal Logic (PMLTL) as an extension of MLTL to support the evaluation of probabilistic multimodal predictions. We examine the correctness and real-time feasibility of MMPRV through two AV case studies where MMPRV utilizes (1) a physics-based multimodal predictor on the F1Tenth autonomous racing vehicle and (2) current state-of-the-art deep neural network multimodal predictors trained and evaluated on the Argoverse motion forecasting dataset. We found that the ability to meet real-time requirements was a challenge for the latter, especially when targeting an embedded computing platform.

1 Introduction

Autonomous cyber-physical systems such as autonomous vehicles (AVs), unmanned aerial systems (UAS), and robots are considered safety-critical due to their regular and close interaction with humans. Runtime verification (RV) offers an approach to monitor these systems for safety violations in a real-time online manner [9,24]. On-board RV can both detect safety violations and trigger mitigation actions to ensure safety, but the most effective mitigation strategies could require fault detection of future violations

---

Supported by NSF:CPS Award 2038903. Reproducibility artifacts and additional details available at http://temporallogic.org/research/MMPRV.

to prevent unsafe states [46,63,65,66]. For example, if it takes an AV three seconds to come to a complete stop, then the AV must apply the brakes three seconds before a complete stop is required to mitigate an impending crash. Due to the complexity of these systems' environments, multiple modes of future behavior are plausible [27,44]. For example, a human driver can display different behaviors given a specific traffic scene (e.g., stop, slow down, swerve, merge, turn, etc.). Therefore, for RV to be effective in such systems, it must be able to support multimodal predictions.

Predictive runtime verification [46,66] employs model predictors to detect future specification violations. In previous work, some utilize the given knowledge of a system to produce a model predictor [16,22,46,65], while others learn a system model by statistical learning [6–8,47,63] or machine learning [23,38,42], but all of these works focus solely on unimodal prediction. While the complete set of a system's reachable states is infeasible to directly compute in real-time, some have also looked at variations of reachability analysis that compute the reachability offline or over-approximate the reachability online in real-time [1,3,10,12,15,17,55,64]. Overall, reachability analysis produces over-conservative results, potentially leading to numerous false positives; therefore, multimodal prediction has become increasingly popular as it reduces the complete set to a handful of the most plausible future behaviors, but to the best of our knowledge, multimodality has not been considered in predictive runtime monitors. Therefore, we introduce Multimodal Model Predictive Runtime Verification (MMPRV), which evaluates a safety specification by a deadline d given K finite sequences of future states.

MMPRV is a direct extension of Model Predictive Runtime Verification (MPRV) [65] and leverages MPRV's definition of deadline and unique utilization of maximum observed data and minimum predicted data to make an on-deadline evaluation. The MPRV framework was deployed on the R2U2 (Realizable, Responsive, Unobtrusive Unit) RV engine [29,50,51,53] and was the first predictive RV framework to provide memory and real-time guarantees. We also deploy MMPRV on the R2U2 RV engine as it is one of the few RV engines that can operate in real-time [19]. Additionally, R2U2 has a strong history of being deployed on real-time, resource-constrained, mission-critical systems [5,13,20,26,33] and has recently undergone changes for added user usability and further reduction of memory requirements [29,30].

R2U2 natively encodes specifications expressed in Mission-time Linear Temporal Logic (MLTL), but we introduce Predictive MLTL (PMLTL) as an extension of MLTL with the addition of four important features: (1) semantics that utilize maximum observed data and minimum predicted data to evaluate a specification by a deadline d, (2) ability to reason over K finite sequences of future states (i.e., supports multimodality), (3) supports the evaluation of a *sequence* of probabilistic atomic propositions, and (4) allows user-defined probabilistic inference techniques. No existing logic supports even two of these features. Several extensions of Signal Temporal Logic (STL) [43] reason about probabilistic signals by quantifying the probability of satisfying an atomic predicate (C2TL [28], StTL [34], StSTL [36], STL-U [42], PrSTL [52], and ProbSTL [59]), but they all make strong assumptions on the underlying probabilistic inference. There is a single extension of Metric Temporal Logic (MTL) [4] called P-MTL [58] that allows the probabilistic inference technique to be determined by the user. Additionally,

STL-U is the only aforementioned extension that can also reason about a *sequence* of probabilistic atomic predicates.

We design MMPRV to allow for *any* user-defined model predictor, extending its applicability to a wide range of systems. To this extent, we minimize MMPRV's memory requirements for deployability to resource-constrained, real-time systems. We examine the correctness and real-time feasibility of MMPRV through two case studies that employ (1) a physics-based Monte Carlo (MC) multimodal predictor and (2) state-of-the-art (SOTA) deep neural network (DNN) multimodal predictors. We illustrate that MMPRV determines the verdict of a PMLTL specification φ by a deadline d utilizing K finite sequences of future states produced by these predictors. In the first case study, we target an embedded computing platform (i.e., NVIDIA® Jetson Xavier NX) and observe that our implementation is feasible in real-time with a 20 Hz control loop, but we do not achieve SOTA accuracy through this approach. In the second case study, we examine the real-time feasibility of SOTA DNNs, but none of these DNNs meet the real-time requirements of a 10 Hz control loop on the NVIDIA® Jetson Xavier NX and instead require the computing capabilities of a desktop GPU.

Our contributions include (1) syntax and semantics of PMLTL (Sect. 3.1), (2) the MMPRV algorithm and proofs of correctness (Sect. 3.2), (3) memory requirements for MMPRV (Sect. 3.3), and (4) application and real-time feasibility of MMPRV utilizing a physics-based MC multimodal predictor on the F1Tenth autonomous racing vehicle (Sect. 4.1) and (5) utilizing SOTA DNN multimodal predictors trained and evaluated on the Argoverse dataset (Sect. 4.2).

2 Preliminaries

2.1 Mission-Time Linear Temporal Logic (MLTL) [35,50]

MLTL is a variant of LTL over finite traces with temporal intervals that are bounded, closed, and discrete. MLTL expresses the most commonly utilized fragments of MTL [4] and STL [43].

Definition 1 *(MLTL Syntax).* The syntax of an MLTL formula φ over a set of atomic propositions $\mathcal{AP}$ is recursively defined as:

$$\varphi ::= \text{true} \mid \text{false} \mid p \mid \neg \psi \mid \psi \wedge \xi \mid \psi \vee \xi \mid \Box_I \psi \mid \Diamond_I \psi \mid \psi \, \mathcal{U}_I \, \xi \mid \psi \, \mathcal{R}_I \, \xi$$

where $p \in \mathcal{AP}$ is an atom, ψ and ξ are MLTL formulas, and I is a closed interval $[lb, ub]$ where lb and ub denote the lower and upper bound, respectively, such that $lb \leq ub$ and $lb, ub \in \mathbb{N}_0$.

Definition 2 *(Finite Trace).* A finite trace, denoted by π, is a finite sequence of sets of atomic propositions. The ith set is denoted by $\pi(i)$ and contains the atomic propositions that are satisfied at the ith time step. $|\pi|$ denotes the length of π (where $|\pi| < \infty$), and $\pi[lb, ub]$ denotes the trace segment $\pi(lb), \pi(lb+1), ..., \pi(ub)$.

Definition 3 *(MLTL Semantics).* We recursively define $\pi, i \models \varphi$ (finite trace π starting from time index $i \geq 0$ satisfies, or "models" MLTL formula φ) as

- $\pi, i \models \text{true}$
- $\pi, i \models p$ for $p \in \mathcal{AP}$ iff $p \in \pi(i)$
- $\pi, i \models \neg\psi$ iff $\pi, i \not\models \psi$
- $\pi, i \models \psi \wedge \xi$ iff $\pi, i \models \psi$ and $\pi, i \models \xi$
- $\pi, i \models \psi \, \mathcal{U}_{[lb,ub]} \, \xi$ iff $|\pi| \geq i + lb$ and $\exists j \in [i+lb, i+ub]$ such that $\pi, j \models \xi$ and $\forall k < j$ where $k \in [i+lb, i+ub]$ we have $\pi, k \models \psi$

Given two MLTL formulas ψ and ξ, they are semantically equivalent (denoted by $\psi \equiv \xi$) if and only if $\pi \models \psi \Leftrightarrow \pi \models \xi$ for all traces π. To complete the MLTL semantics, we define $\text{false} \equiv \neg\text{true}$, $\psi \vee \xi \equiv \neg(\neg\psi \wedge \neg\xi)$, $\neg(\psi \, \mathcal{U}_I \, \xi) \equiv (\neg\psi \, \mathcal{R}_I \, \neg\xi)$, and $\neg\Diamond_I \psi \equiv \Box_I \neg\psi$. MLTL also keeps the standard operator equivalences from LTL, including $\Diamond_I \psi \equiv (\text{true} \, \mathcal{U}_I \, \psi)$, and $\Box_I \psi \equiv (\text{false} \, \mathcal{R}_I \, \psi)$. Notably, MLTL discards the next ($\mathcal{X}$) operator since $\mathcal{X}\psi \equiv \Box_{[1,1]}\psi$.

2.2 Abstract Syntax Tree Architecture

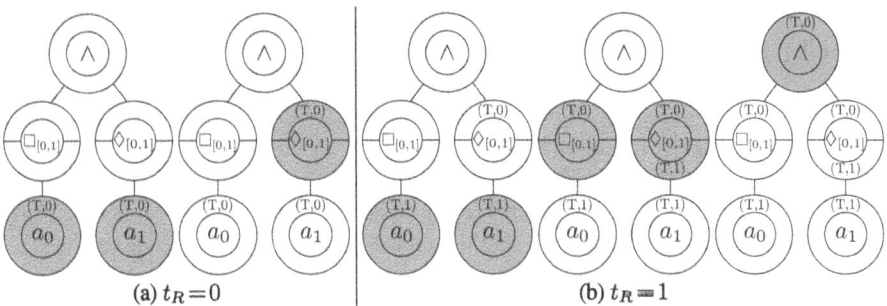

Fig. 1. Abstract syntax tree evaluation of $\varphi = \Box_{[0,1]}a_0 \wedge \Diamond_{[0,1]}a_1$ where $a_0, a_1 \in \mathcal{AP}$. The highlighted nodes are the nodes currently being updated at each step as verdicts are propagated upwards through the tree. Results are shown for the current timestamp $t_R = 0$ and $t_R = 1$.

R2U2 is a stream-based RV engine that reevaluates MLTL formulas for each time index i. These MLTL formulas are represented by decomposing them into subformula nodes in an Abstract Syntax Tree (AST). R2U2 determines the evaluation of each subformula node from the bottom-up and propagates the verdict to the parent node(s). Each node of the AST computes and stores verdict-timestamp tuples $T_\psi = (v, \tau)$ for its subformula ψ, where $v \in \{\text{true}, \text{false}\}$ and $\tau \in \mathbb{N}_0$. Each node stores the verdict-timestamp tuples in a shared connection queue (SCQ); the SCQ is a circular buffer that overwrites verdict-timestamp tuples in a circular manner. Figure 1 demonstrates an example of how R2U2 evaluates over an AST.

Propogation Delay. To compute the SCQ size of each node in the AST, the propagation delay of each subformula must first be computed.

Definition 4 *(Propagation Delay [33])*. The propagation delay of an MLTL formula φ is the time between when a set of propositions $\pi(i)$ arrives and when the verdict of $\pi, i \models \varphi$ is determinable. The best-case propagation delay ($\varphi.bpd$) is its minimum time delay, and the worst-case propagation delay ($\varphi.wpd$) is its maximum time delay.

Definition 5 *(Propagation Delay Semantics [33])*. Let ψ and ξ be MLTL subformulas of MLTL formula φ where the best- and worst-case propagation delay for an MLTL formula φ is structurally defined as follows:

- $\varphi \in \mathcal{AP} : \begin{cases} \varphi.wpd = 0 \\ \varphi.bpd = 0 \end{cases}$
  $\varphi = \neg \psi : \begin{cases} \varphi.wpd = \psi.wpd \\ \varphi.bpd = \psi.bpd \end{cases}$

- $\varphi = \psi \vee \xi \text{ or } \varphi = \psi \wedge \xi : \begin{cases} \varphi.wpd = max(\psi.wpd, \xi.wpd) \\ \varphi.bpd = min(\psi.bpd, \xi.bpd) \end{cases}$

- $\varphi = \square_{[lb,ub]} \psi \text{ or } \varphi = \Diamond_{[lb,ub]} \psi : \begin{cases} \varphi.wpd = \psi.wpd + ub \\ \varphi.bpd = \psi.bpd + lb \end{cases}$

- $\varphi = \psi\, \mathcal{U}_{[lb,ub]}\, \xi \text{ or } \varphi = \psi\, \mathcal{R}_{[lb,ub]}\, \xi : \begin{cases} \varphi.wpd = max(\psi.wpd, \xi.wpd) + ub \\ \varphi.bpd = min(\psi.bpd, \xi.bpd) + lb \end{cases}$

SCQ Memory Size. To promote deployability to resource-constrained platforms, R2U2 minimizes the size requirement for its SCQs. The minimum SCQ size of an AST node g is determined by the worst-case propagation delay of its sibling nodes and its own best-case propagation delay. A node g must store verdict-timestamp tuples in its SCQ until all of its siblings have the same timestamp τ for these tuples to be consumed by their parent node. Therefore, the size of node g's SCQ corresponds to the maximum timestamp mismatch between node g and its siblings. If we let $\mathbb{S}_g$ be the set of all of g's sibling nodes, then the size of g's SCQ is given by the following [33,65]:

$$SCQ_{size}(g) = max(max\{s.wpd | s \in \mathbb{S}_g\} - g.bpd, 0) + 1 \qquad (1)$$

2.3 Model Predictive Runtime Verification (MPRV) [65]

MPRV strives to produce the most accurate evaluation of a specification φ possible by a mitigation trigger deadline d to allow for effective mitigation triggering. Since observed data is often more accurate than predicted data, MPRV utilizes maximum observed data (i.e., observed data for time steps up to and including the current timestamp) and minimal predicted data (i.e., predicted data only after the current timestamp) to make an on-deadline evaluation.

Definition 6 *(Deadline)*. Given an MLTL formula φ and trace π starting from time index $i \geq 0$, the deadline $d \in \mathbb{Z}$ is the number of time steps measured relative to i by which the verdict of φ must be determined such that $0 \leq i + d \leq M$, where M denotes the timestamp at the end of the mission (i.e., φ cannot be evaluated before the mission begins or after it ends).

Definition 7 *(Finite Trace with Prediction).* Trace $\hat{\pi}$ is a finite trace (following from Definition 2) that has an observed and predicted segment such that the segment $\hat{\pi}[0, |\pi| - 1] = \pi$ where π is derived from observed data and $|\pi| \leq i + d$, and the segment $\hat{\pi}[|\pi|, |\hat{\pi}| - 1]$ is populated using prediction to determine the verdict of a MLTL specification φ for time index i by deadline d.

Definition 8 *(MLTL Semantics with Deadline).* MLTL semantics with deadline d is an extension of the MLTL Semantics in Definition 3. Given a finite trace π, time index i, and deadline d to produce a finite trace with prediction $\hat{\pi}$ (following from Definition 7), we recursively define $\pi, i, d \models \varphi$ (trace π starting from time index $i \geq 0$ satisfies, or "models" MLTL formula φ by deadline d) as

- $\pi, i, d \models$ true
- $\pi, i, d \models p$ for $p \in \mathcal{AP}$ iff $\hat{\pi}, i \models p$ such that $p \in \hat{\pi}(i)$
- $\pi, i, d \models \neg \psi$ iff $\pi, i, d \not\models \psi$
- $\pi, i, d \models \psi \wedge \xi$ iff $\pi, i, d \models \psi$ and $\pi, i, d \models \xi$
- $\pi, i, d \models \psi \, \mathcal{U}_{[lb,ub]} \, \xi$ iff $|\hat{\pi}| \geq i + lb$ and $\exists j \in [i + lb, i + ub]$ such that $\pi, j, d \models \xi$ and $\forall k < j$ where $k \in [i + lb, i + ub]$ we have $\pi, k, d \models \psi$

Definition 9 *(Prediction Horizon).* The prediction horizon H_p is the length of the predicted segment of $\hat{\pi}$ (i.e., $H_p = |\hat{\pi}| - |\pi|$). Given an MLTL formula φ, the maximum prediction horizon is denoted by $max(H_p)$ and is bounded such that $max(H_p) = \varphi.wpd - d$.

To prevent overwriting original SCQ data with any predicted data, we determine $max(H_p)$ at design time and add $max(H_p)$ extra entries to each SCQ given by the following equation:

$$SCQ_{size}(g) = max(max\{s.wpd \mid s \in \mathbb{S}_g\} - g.bpd, 0) + max(H_p) + 1 \quad (2)$$

Note that we improve on these memory requirements in Sect. 3.3.

3 Multimodal Model Predictive Runtime Verification (MMPRV)

MMPRV extends MPRV [65] to support multimodal prediction and to reason over a finite sequence of sets of probabilistic atomic propositions (i.e., atomic propositions with associated probability). To determine the verdict of a PMLTL formula φ by a deadline d (Definition 6) such that $\pi, i, d \models \varphi$, either the verdict must be determinable by the trace $\pi[0, i + d]$ (i.e., observed data only) or prediction must be utilized by populating K finite traces with prediction $\hat{\pi}_0, \hat{\pi}_1, ..., \hat{\pi}_{K-2}, \hat{\pi}_{K-1}$ (Definition 10 below). In other words, if the verdict of $\pi, i, d \models \varphi$ is unknown at the current timestamp $t_R = i + d$, then MMPRV must receive predicted values to determine the verdict of φ by deadline d. If MMPRV reveals that φ does not hold (i.e., the specification was violated), the result can trigger an appropriate mitigation action.

Definition 10 *(K Finite Traces with Prediction).* Let $K \in \mathbb{N}$ be the number of predicted finite traces (following from Definition 2) denoted by $\hat{\pi}_0, \hat{\pi}_1, ..., \hat{\pi}_{K-2}, \hat{\pi}_{K-1}$ where $\hat{\pi}_j$

is the jth predicted trace. Each trace has an observed and a predicted segment. Every trace has the identical observed segment such that $\forall j \in [0, K-1]$ we have $\hat{\pi}_j[0, |\pi| - 1] = \pi$ where π is derived from observed data and $|\pi| \leq i + d$. We populate each trace segment $\hat{\pi}_j[|\pi|, |\hat{\pi}| - 1]$ (where $j \in [0, K-1]$) using a different mode of prediction to make an evaluation decision by d.

Consider an autonomous vehicle (AV) where the specification violation of $\varphi = \Box_{[0,3]} a$ (where a is an atomic proposition) indicates a collision and the appropriate mitigation action is coming to a complete stop. Let's assume that the mitigation trigger deadline for the AV to brake and come to a complete stop is $d = -4$ (i.e., the verdict must be determined four time steps before time index i). Therefore, for this AV to ensure safety, it must be able to determine the verdict of $\pi, i, -4 \models \varphi$. At the current

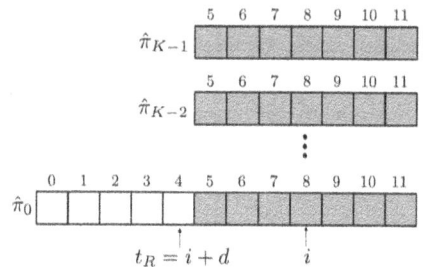

Fig. 2. K finite traces with prediction evaluating $\pi, 8, -4 \models \Box_{[0.3]} a$. White boxes indicate observed data and gray boxes are predicted data.

timestamp $t_R = 4$, as illustrated in Fig. 2, MMPRV must determine the verdict of $\pi, 8, -4 \models \varphi$ (i.e., $t_R = i + d = 8 + (-4) = 4$). Following from Definition 9, the $max(H_p) = \varphi.wpd - d = 3 - (-4) = 7$; therefore, MMPRV will obtain up to seven predicted values of a for all K traces such that MMPRV will incrementally obtain predicted values for $\hat{\pi}_j(t_R + 1), \hat{\pi}_j(t_R + 2), ..., \hat{\pi}_j(t_R + max(H_p))$ $\forall j \in [0, K-1]$ until φ evaluates to true or false. In Fig. 2, this means we incrementally populate $\hat{\pi}_j(5), \hat{\pi}_j(6), ..., \hat{\pi}_j(11)$ $\forall j \in [0, K-1]$ with predicted values of a until the verdict of $\pi, 8, -4 \models \varphi$ is known. At the next timestamp ($t_R = 5$), these predictions are no longer relevant; therefore, MMPRV will obtain new predicted values for $\hat{\pi}_j(6), \hat{\pi}_j(7), ..., \hat{\pi}_j(12)$ $\forall j \in [0, K-1]$ until the verdict of $\pi, 9, -4 \models \varphi$ is determinable.

3.1 Predictive Mission-Time Linear Temporal Logic (PMLTL)

PMLTL is an extension of MLTL (Definition 3) that evaluates a specification φ utilizing K finite traces with prediction $\hat{\pi}_0, \hat{\pi}_1, ..., \hat{\pi}_{K-2}, \hat{\pi}_{K-1}$ (Definition 10) to determine the verdict of φ by a deadline d. (Note that unimodal prediction is still supported within PMLTL when $K = 1$.) Predictions often have an associated probability, and while it is often safe to assume that the observed segment of a trace $\hat{\pi}$ (i.e., π) has a probability of 1.0 because it has been physically observed, observed data can also have an associated uncertainty (e.g., sensor error). As a result, PMLTL introduces the probability operator P_δ, which allows specification and evaluation over sequences of sets of probabilistic atomic propositions. To this extent, a PMLTL specification can quantity the amount of uncertainty that is deemed acceptable by the user. For example, $P_{0.95}(\Box_{[0,3]}a)$ is a PMLTL formula that expresses "the probability of a being globally true from 0 to 3 is greater than or equal to 95%". PMLTL also supports the evaluation of observed and predicted traces without the consideration of probability.

Definition 11 *(PMLTL Syntax).* The syntax of PMLTL is an extension of the MLTL syntax defined in Definition 1. The syntax of a PMLTL formula φ over K sets of atomic propositions $\mathcal{AP}$ is recursively defined as:

$$\varphi ::= \text{true} \mid \text{false} \mid p \mid \neg\psi \mid \psi \wedge \xi \mid \psi \vee \xi \mid \Box_I \psi \mid \Diamond_I \psi \mid \psi \mathcal{U}_I \xi \mid \psi \mathcal{R}_I \xi \mid P_\delta \psi$$

where $K \in \mathbb{N}$, $p \in \mathcal{AP}$, ψ and ξ are PMLTL formulas, $\delta \in [0,1]$ is the desired probability, and I is a closed interval $[lb, ub]$ where lb and ub denote the lower and upper bound, respectively, such that $lb \leq ub$ and $lb, ub \in \mathbb{N}_0$.

Definition 12 *(Probability Space of K Finite Traces).* Given a time index i, K finite traces of prediction $\hat{\pi}_0, \hat{\pi}_1, ..., \hat{\pi}_{K-2}, \hat{\pi}_{K-1}$, and an atomic proposition $p \in \mathcal{AP}$, let the sample space $\Omega_i = \{p \in \hat{\pi}_0(i), p \notin \hat{\pi}_0(i), p \in \hat{\pi}_1(i), p \notin \hat{\pi}_1(i), ..., p \in \hat{\pi}_{K-2}(i), p \notin \hat{\pi}_{K-2}(i), p \in \hat{\pi}_{K-1}(i), p \notin \hat{\pi}_{K-1}(i)\}$. Let the σ-algebra $\mathcal{F}_i = 2^{\Omega_i}$ (i.e., the powerset of Ω_i) be a collection of events. Let the probability measure $\mathbb{P}_i$ assign a probability $\mathbb{P}_i(A)$ to every event A in $\mathcal{F}_i$ such that $\mathbb{P}_i : \mathcal{F}_i \mapsto [0,1]$ where $\mathbb{P}_i(\Omega_i) = 1$ and $\mathbb{P}_i(A) = \sum_{\omega \in A} \mathbb{P}_i(\{\omega\}) \leq 1^1$. Note that the complement of an event $A \in \mathcal{F}_i$ is denoted as $A^c = \Omega_i \backslash A$ such that $\mathbb{P}_i(A^c) = 1 - \mathbb{P}_i(A)$. Then, $(\Omega_i, \mathcal{F}_i, \mathbb{P}_i)$ defines the probability space of K finite traces at time index i for $p \in \mathcal{AP}$.

Definition 13 *(PMLTL Semantics).* PMLTL semantics are an extension of the MLTL semantics with deadline in Definition 8. Given a finite trace π, time index i, and deadline d to produce K finite traces with prediction $\hat{\pi}_0, \hat{\pi}_1, ..., \hat{\pi}_{K-2}, \hat{\pi}_{K-1}$ (following from Definition 10) and a probability space $(\Omega_i, \mathcal{F}_i, \mathbb{P}_i)$ for each $p \in \mathcal{AP}$ (as defined in Definition 12)[2], we recursively define $\pi, i, d \models \varphi$ (trace π starting from time index $i \geq 0$ satisfies, or "models" PMLTL formula φ by deadline d according to K predictions) as

- $\pi, i, d \models \text{true}$
- $\pi, i, d \models p$ for $p \in \mathcal{AP}$ iff $\forall j \in [0, K-1]$ we have $p \in \hat{\pi}_j(i)$
- $\pi, i, d \models \neg\psi$ iff $\pi, i, d \not\models \psi$
- $\pi, i, d \models \psi \wedge \xi$ iff $\pi, i, d \models \psi$ and $\pi, i, d \models \xi$
- $\pi, i, d \models \psi \mathcal{U}_{[lb, ub]} \xi$ iff $\forall j \in [0, K-1]$ we have $|\hat{\pi}_j| \geq i + lb$ and $\exists j \in [i+lb, i+ub]$ such that $\pi, j, d \models \xi$ and $\forall k < j$ where $k \in [i+lb, i+ub]$ we have $\pi, k, d \models \psi$
- $\pi, i, d \models P_\delta \psi$ iff $\Pr(\pi, i, d \models \psi) \geq \delta$ where $\Pr(\pi, i, d \models \psi)$ (the probability of $\pi, i, d \models \psi$) is defined recursively as follows:
  - $\Pr(\pi, i, d \models \text{true}) = 1$
  - $\Pr(\pi, i, d \models p) = \mathbb{P}_i(A)$ for $p \in \mathcal{AP}$, A is an independent event, and $A \in \mathcal{F}_i$ s.t. $A = \bigcup_{j=0}^{K-1} \{\omega \in \Omega_i \mid \omega \equiv p \in \hat{\pi}_j(i)\}$
  - $\Pr(\pi, i, d \models \neg\psi) = 1 - \Pr(\pi, i, d \models \psi)$

---

[1] For all $\omega \in \Omega_i$, $\mathbb{P}_i(\{\omega\})$ is defined by the user's choice of probabilistic inference (e.g., Markov chain, Bayesian inference, normal distribution, etc.) but must follow the properties defined in Definition 12.

[2] The probability space $(\Omega_i, \mathcal{F}_i, \mathbb{P}_i)$ is only required if $p \in \mathcal{AP}$ is an operand of P_δ.

- $\Pr(\pi, i, d \models \psi \wedge \xi) = \Pr(\pi, i, d \models \psi) * \Pr(\pi, i, d \models \xi)$
- $\Pr(\pi, i, d \models \psi \mathcal{U}_{[lb,ub]} \xi) = \Pr\left(\bigvee_{m=i+lb}^{i+ub}((\bigwedge_{k=i+lb}^{m-1} \pi, k, d \models \psi) \wedge \pi, m, d \models \xi)\right)$

Given two PMLTL formulas ψ and ξ, they are semantically equivalent (denoted by $\psi \equiv \xi$) if and only if $\pi, i, d \models \psi \Leftrightarrow \pi, i, d_j \models \xi$ for all possible K finite traces with prediction $\hat{\pi}_0, \hat{\pi}_1, ..., \hat{\pi}_{K-2}, \hat{\pi}_{K-1}$. PMLTL keeps the standard operator equivalences from MLTL with the addition that these equivalences also apply to $P_\delta \psi$ (i.e., $P_\delta(\text{false}) \equiv P_\delta(\neg\text{true})$, $P_\delta(\psi \vee \xi) \equiv P_\delta(\neg(\neg\psi \wedge \neg\xi))$, $P_\delta(\neg(\psi \mathcal{U}_I \xi)) \equiv P_\delta(\neg\psi \mathcal{R}_I \neg\xi)$, $P_\delta(\neg\Diamond_I \psi) \equiv P_\delta(\Box_I \neg\psi)$, $P_\delta(\Diamond_I \psi) \equiv P_\delta(\text{true } \mathcal{U}_I \psi)$, and $P_\delta(\Box_I \psi) \equiv P_\delta(\text{false } \mathcal{R}_I \psi)$). Figure 3 illustrates a few examples of determining the probability of φ (i.e., $\Pr(\pi, i, d \models \varphi)$).

	Time index i				
	0	1	2	3	4
$a_0 \in \hat{\pi}_0(i)$	true	true	false	true	false
$\mathbb{P}_i(\{a_0 \in \hat{\pi}_0(i)\})$	0.40	0.45	0.90	0.80	0.85
$\mathbb{P}_i(\{a_0 \notin \hat{\pi}_0(i)\})$	0.00	0.00	0.00	0.00	0.00
$a_0 \in \hat{\pi}_1(i)$	false	true	true	false	true
$\mathbb{P}_i(\{a_0 \in \hat{\pi}_1(i)\})$	0.60	0.55	0.10	0.20	0.15
$\mathbb{P}_i(\{a_0 \notin \hat{\pi}_1(i)\})$	0.00	0.00	0.00	0.00	0.00
$\Pr(\pi,i,d \models a_0)$	0.40	1.00	0.10	0.80	0.15

	Time index i				
	0	1	2	3	4
$a_1 \in \hat{\pi}_0(i)$	true	false	false	true	true
$\mathbb{P}_i(\{a_1 \in \hat{\pi}_0(i)\})$	0.95	0.35	0.20	0.90	0.85
$\mathbb{P}_i(\{a_1 \notin \hat{\pi}_0(i)\})$	0.05	0.65	0.80	0.10	0.15
$\Pr(\pi,i,d \models a_1)$	0.95	0.65	0.80	0.90	0.85

	Time index i				
	0	1	2	3	4
$\Pr(\pi,i,d \models a_0 \vee a_1)$	0.97	1.00	0.82	0.98	0.8725
$\Pr(\pi,i,d \models \Box_{[0,1]} a_0)$	0.40	0.10	0.08	0.12	–
$\Pr(\pi,i,d \models \Diamond_{[0,1]} a_1)$	0.9825	0.93	0.98	0.985	–
$\Pr(\pi,i,d \models \Box_{[0,1]} a_0 \wedge \Diamond_{[0,1]} a_1)$	0.393	0.093	0.0784	0.1182	–
$\Pr(a_0 \mathcal{U}_{[0,1]} a_1)$	0.963	0.93	0.818	0.968	–

Fig. 3. Determining the probability of φ (i.e., $\Pr(\pi, i, d \models \varphi)$) where $a_0, a_1 \in \mathcal{AP}$

3.2 MMPRV Algorithm

Algorithm 1 defines the MMPRV algorithm for the R2U2 engine. Offline, the Configuration Compiler for Property Organization (C2PO) [29] compiles PMLTL formula(s) for input into R2U2 by decomposing these formula(s) into an AST (Sect. 2.2). The AST is a list of nodes in topological order (i.e., child nodes appear before their parent nodes); therefore, evaluating the AST at a specific timestamp means sequentially evaluating each of its nodes (lines 1–2 and 11–12 of Algorithm 1). Algorithm 1 first evaluates the AST based on observed data only (lines 1–2). If the latest time index for a PMLTL formula φ produced by the AST (i.e., the latest $T_\varphi.\tau$ found by reading the root node $\varphi.Queue$) is less than the current timestamp t_R minus the deadline d (i.e., the verdict of $\pi, t_R - d, d \models \varphi$ is unknown), then prediction is required (line 3).

Algorithm 1: MMPRV Algorithm

Input: Current timestamp: t_R; Deadline: d; Prediction modes: K; Finite trace: $\pi[0, t_R]$;
AST representing PMLTL formula φ: φ_{AST}

1 **foreach** Node $g \in \varphi_{AST}$ **do** // Update φ_{AST} for current time stamp t_R
2 $\quad$ $Node\_step([\pi], t_R, g)$; // Algorithm 2
3 **if** $read(\varphi.Queue).\tau < t_R - d$ **then** // Prediction required
4 $\quad$ **foreach** Node $g \in \varphi_{AST}$ **do** // store original AST state
5 $\quad\quad$ Store Node g's metadata; // e.g., read/write pointers
6 $\quad$ **foreach** $j \in [0, K-1]$ **do** $\hat{\pi}_j \leftarrow \pi$; // initialize $\hat{\pi}_j, \forall j \in [0, K-1]$ with π
7 $\quad$ $t \leftarrow t_R$; // initialize t with current timestamp
8 $\quad$ **while** $read(\varphi.Queue).\tau < t_R - d$ **do** // if prediction is needed, loop
9 $\quad\quad$ $t \leftarrow t + 1$; // look into next prediction step
10 $\quad\quad$ **foreach** $j \in [0, K-1]$ **do** $\hat{\pi}_j(t) \leftarrow model\_predict(t, j)$; // update $\hat{\pi}_j(t)$
11 $\quad\quad$ **foreach** Node $g \in \varphi_{AST}$ **do**
12 $\quad\quad\quad$ $Node\_step([\hat{\pi}_0, \hat{\pi}_1, ..., \hat{\pi}_{K-1}], t, g)$; // Algorithm 2
13 $\quad$ **foreach** Node $g \in \varphi_{AST}$ **do** // restore original AST state
14 $\quad\quad$ Store Node g's metadata; // e.g., read/write pointers

---

Algorithm 2: $Node\_step$: Evaluate a node g in φ_{AST} for one timestamp

1 **function** $Node\_step([\pi_0, \pi_1, ..., \pi_{K-1}], i, g)$ **is**
$\quad$ **Input:** Array of finite traces: $[\pi_0, \pi_1, ..., \pi_{K-1}]$; Time index: i; Node: g
2 $\quad$ **if** g is a descendant of $\mathcal{P}_\delta$ operator **then**
3 $\quad\quad$ **if** g is an $\mathcal{AP}$ operator **then** // record the value of the atomic proposition
4 $\quad\quad\quad$ $p \leftarrow 0$
5 $\quad\quad\quad$ **for** $j \leftarrow 0$ to $K - 1$ **do** // evaluate $Pr(g)$ based on K finite traces
6 $\quad\quad\quad\quad$ **if** $g \in \pi_j(i)$ **then** $p \leftarrow p + get\_Pr(g \in \pi_j(i))$;
7 $\quad\quad\quad\quad$ **else** $p \leftarrow p + get\_Pr(g \notin \pi_j(i))$;
8 $\quad\quad\quad$ $g.Queue.write((p, i))$; // write $T_g = (p, \tau)$
9 $\quad\quad$ **else**
10 $\quad\quad\quad$ $(p, \tau) \leftarrow$ evaluate Node g; // Algorithms 4, 5, and 6
11 $\quad\quad\quad$ $g.Queue.write((p, \tau))$; // write $T_g = (p, \tau)$
12 $\quad$ **else**
13 $\quad\quad$ **if** g is an $\mathcal{AP}$ operator **then** // record the value of the atomic proposition
14 $\quad\quad\quad$ **for** $j \leftarrow 0$ to $K - 1$ **do** // evaluate g based on K finite traces
15 $\quad\quad\quad\quad$ **if** $g \in \pi_j(i)$ **then continue**;
16 $\quad\quad\quad\quad$ **else** $g.Queue.write((false, i))$ **return**; // write $T_g = (v, \tau)$
17 $\quad\quad\quad$ $g.Queue.write((true, i))$; // write $T_g = (v, \tau)$
18 $\quad\quad$ **else**
19 $\quad\quad\quad$ $(v, \tau) \leftarrow$ evaluate Node g; // Algorithm 3 and Algorithms 3-6 from [33]
20 $\quad\quad\quad$ $g.Queue.write((v, \tau))$; // write $T_g = (v, \tau)$

MMPRV provides predictions based on maximum observed data; therefore, to retain observed data in the SCQ that may still be relevant for future evaluations, we size each node according to Eq. 3 in Sect. 3.3. While the observed data is never overwritten, a node's metadata (e.g., its read and write pointers) will change as nodes are evaluated based on predicted data (lines 11–12). Therefore, we store each node's metadata before prediction starts (lines 4–5) and restore it after prediction ends (lines 13–14) to ensure that predicted data is never unintentionally reused at the next execution of Algorithm 1. To support multimodal prediction during the prediction phase (lines 3–14), there are K finite traces with prediction (Definition 10) initialized with observed data (line 6) and populated with predicted data generated by a user-defined $model\_predict$ function (line 10) until $\pi, t_R - d, d \models \varphi$ evaluates to true or false (line 8).

Each node of the AST contains a write pointer to store tuples within its SCQ and read pointer(s) for its children's SCQ(s). R2U2's read and write SCQ operations are defined in [33]. With the addition of MMPRV, the write operation must never write past $t_R - d$ when utilizing prediction to ensure maximum observed data is utilized for all future verdicts. Previously, each node's SCQ stored verdict-timestamp tuples (i.e., $T_\psi = (v, \tau)$ as discussed in Sect. 2.2), but with the addition of the probability operator P_δ, descendants of the probability operator (i.e., probabilistic operators) will now store a probability-timestamp tuple $T_\psi = (p, \tau)$ where $p \in [0.0, 1.0]$. Additionally, the worst-case propagation delay for probabilistic operators follows Definition 5, but the best-case propagation delay is equivalent to the worse-case as the entire interval $[lb, ub]$ is required for evaluation (i.e., cannot evaluate early based on partial information).

Theorem 1 (Correctness of MMPRV Algorithm). *Given the current timestamp t_R, deadline d, number of prediction modes K, trace $\pi[0, t_R]$, the AST representing the PMLTL formula φ (φ_{AST}), and a model predictor function (model_predict), the MMPRV algorithm (Algorithm 1) utilizes maximum observed data and minimum predicted data to populate K finite traces with prediction in order to evaluate $\pi, i, d \models \varphi$ such that $\forall i \; T_\varphi.v = $ true iff $\pi, i, d \models \varphi$.*

Proof. MMPRV makes evaluations utilizing all observed data values from π before prediction is even considered (lines 1–2). After this initial evaluation on observed data, if $T_\varphi.\tau \geq t_R - d$, then all deadlines have been met and MMPRV terminates guaranteeing to have determined the verdict of $\pi, i, d \models \varphi$ based on observed data only. But if $T_\varphi.\tau < t_R - d$ (line 3), then MMPRV takes maximum observed data (line 6) augmented incrementally with K modes of minimum prediction data until MMPRV produces the tuple such that $T_\varphi.\tau = t_R - d$ (lines 8–12); therefore, MMPRV only terminates when the verdict of $\pi, t_R - d, d \models \varphi$ is determinable. □

Algorithm 3: Probability Operator: $P_\delta \psi$

1 At each new input T_ψ:
2 **return** $(T_\psi.p >= \delta, T_\psi.\tau)$

Algorithm 4: Probabilistic Negation Operator: $Pr(\pi, i, d \models \neg \psi)$

1 At each new input T_ψ:
2 **return** $(1 - T_\psi.p, T_\psi.\tau)$

Algorithm 5: Probabilistic And Operator: $Pr(\pi, i, d \models \psi \wedge \xi)$

1 At each new input (T_ψ, T_ξ) s.t. $T_\psi.\tau = T_\xi.\tau$:
2 **return** $(T_\psi.p * T_\xi.p, T_\psi.\tau)$

Algorithm 6: Probabilistic Until Operator: $Pr(\pi, i, d \models \psi \, \mathcal{U}_{[lb, ub]} \, \xi)$

1 At each new input (T_ψ, T_ξ) s.t. $T_\psi.\tau = T_\xi.\tau$:
2 **if** $T_\psi.\tau - ub \geq 0$ **then**   // check if $i \geq 0$
3 $\quad p_{temp} = T_\xi.p$ // initialize p_{temp} to $Pr(\pi, i+ub, d \models \xi)$ s.t. $T_\xi.\tau = i+ub$
4 $\quad$ **for** $t \leftarrow 1$ **to** $ub - lb$ **do**   // iterate backwards through ψ and ξ's SCQs
5 $\quad\quad p_{temp} = p_{temp} * read(\psi.Queue, \psi.rd\_ptr - t).p$
6 $\quad\quad p_{temp} = (1 - [(1 - read(\xi.Queue, \xi.rd\_ptr - t).p) * (1 - p_{temp})]$
7 $\quad$ **return** $(p_{temp}, T_\psi.\tau - ub)$ // return probability-timestamp tuple

---

The correctness of Algorithms 2, 3, 4, and 5 follows directly from Definition 13.

Theorem 2 (Correctness of the Probabilistic Until Operator). *Algorithm 6 correctly implements $\varphi = Pr(\pi, i, d \models \psi \, \mathcal{U}_{[lb, ub]} \, \xi)$ such that for all $i \geq 0$ Algorithm 6 returns the tuple $T_\varphi = \left(\Pr\left(\bigvee_{j=i+lb}^{i+ub}((\bigwedge_{k=i+lb}^{j-1} \pi, k, d \models \psi) \wedge \pi, j, d \models \xi)\right), i\right)$.*

Proof. To evaluate the probability of $\pi, i, d \models \psi \, \mathcal{U}_{[lb,ub]} \, \xi$, the probability values for the children ψ and ξ for the entire interval $[i+lb, i+ub]$ where $lb \leq ub$ are required (i.e., cannot evaluate early based on partial information). When $T_\psi.\tau - ub \geq 0$ (line 2), the probability-timestamp tuple of the Until operator can be calculated for $i = T_\psi.\tau - ub$ such that $i \geq 0$ as the children SCQs are guaranteed to have stored from $[T_\psi.\tau - ub + lb, T_\psi.\tau]$ or $[i+lb, i+ub]$. This guarantee is the result of R2U2's write operation [33] and the SCQ sizing discussed later in Sect. 3.3. To calculate the probability, the equation $\Pr\left(\bigvee_{j=i+lb}^{i+ub}\left((\bigwedge_{k=i+lb}^{j-1} \pi, k, d \models \psi) \wedge \pi, j, d \models \xi\right)\right)$ expands to the following:

$\Pr(\pi, i+lb, d \models \xi \vee (\pi, i+lb, d \models \psi \wedge \pi, i+lb+1, d \models \xi) \vee$
$\qquad (\pi, lb, d \models \psi \wedge \pi, i+lb+1, d \models \psi \wedge \pi, i+lb+2, d \models \xi) \vee ...$
$\vee (\pi, i+lb, d \models \psi \wedge \pi, i+lb+1, d \models \psi \wedge ... \wedge \pi, i+ub-1, d \models \psi \wedge \pi, i+ub, d \models \xi))$

which can be rewritten to the following form using the law of distribution:

$\Pr(\pi, i+lb, d \models \xi \vee (\pi, i+lb, d \models \psi \wedge (\pi, i+lb+1, d \models \xi \vee$
$\qquad (\pi, i+lb+1, d \models \psi \wedge (\pi, i+lb+2, d \models \xi \vee ...$
$\qquad (\pi, i+ub-2, d \models \psi \wedge (\pi, i+ub-1, d \models \xi \vee$
$\qquad (\pi, i+ub-1, d \models \psi \wedge \pi, i+ub, d \models \xi)))))))...)$

Utilizing this form, the probability of $\pi, i, d \models \psi \, \mathcal{U}_{[lb,ub]} \, \xi$ is calculated starting from the deepest nested parentheses (i.e., $\pi, i+ub, d \models \xi$) on line 3 and iterating outward on lines 4–6 by iterating backward through the children SCQs from $T_\psi.\tau - ub - 1$ to $T_\psi.\tau - ub + lb$ (e.g., next is $\pi, i+ub-1, d \models \xi \vee (\pi, i+ub-1, d \models \psi \wedge$ *previous*)). Lastly, the probability-timestamp tuple is returned (line 7) such that $T_\varphi = \left(\Pr\left(\bigvee_{j=i+lb}^{i+ub}\left((\bigwedge_{k=i+lb}^{j-1} \pi, k, d \models \psi) \wedge \pi, j, d \models \xi\right)\right), i\right)$. □

3.3 Memory Requirements for MMPRV

MMPRV determines verdicts based on maximum observed data. Additionally, R2U2 utilizes Common Subexpression Elimination (CSE) to reduce memory requirements for sets of PMLTL formulas, where common subexpressions share a singular SCQ node [29,33], but taking advantage of this reduction requires that predicted data doesn't overwrite observed data still relevant to other subexpressions. Therefore, to prevent overwriting any relevant observed data with predicted data, extra slots must be added to the SCQ size (as defined in Eq. 1). In [65], the SCQ size increased linearly with $max(H_p)$ as given by Eq. 2, but this was an overestimate that can be minimized. On the other hand, the addition of probabilistic operators requires the children of probabilistic temporal operators (e.g., Until) to store results for the entire interval from $[i+lb, i+ub]$ for consumption by the parent (as discussed in Algorithm 6 and Theorem 2). Therefore, the SCQ size is minimized and redefined in Eq. 3.

Theorem 3 (MMPRV SCQ Size). *Consider an AST representing PMLTL formula(s). Let $\mathbb{S}_g$ be the set of all sibling nodes of g, $\mathbb{TP}_g$ be the set of all probabilistic temporal parent nodes of g, and $max(H_p)$ be the maximum prediction horizon of g's parent* *formula(s). Then, the minimum size of g's SCQ required for MMPRV is given by the following:*

$$SCQ_{size}(g) = max(max\{s.wpd - s \in \mathbb{S}_g\} - g.bpd, 0) + max\{p.ub - p.lb - p \in \mathbb{TP}_g\}$$
$$+ min\Big(max(max\{s.wpd - s \in \mathbb{S}_g\} - g.bpd, 0) + max\{p.ub - p.lb - p \in \mathbb{TP}_g\}, \quad (3)$$
$$max(max(H_p) - 1, 0)\Big) + 1$$

Proof. Without prediction or probabilistic operators, $SCQ_{size}(g) = max(max\{s.wpd - s \in \mathbb{S}_g\} - g.bpd, 0) + 1$ (Eq. 1) has already been proven in [65]. In Eq. 1, $max(max\{s.wpd|s \in \mathbb{S}_g\} - g.bpd, 0)$ represents the maximum timestamp mismatch between g and its sibling nodes; node g may have to buffer this many tuples before they are consumed by the parent node. $+1$ extra SCQ slot is added to the size to account for the implementation requirement that a tuple must be buffered at least one cycle before it is consumed by a parent node(s). With the addition of probabilistic operators, children of probabilistic temporal operators must buffer $max\{p.ub - p.lb|p \in \mathbb{TP}_g\} + 1$ extra SCQ slots (instead of just $+1$) as required by Algorithm 6. Since observed data is always fully evaluated before predicted data enters the SCQ, this $+1$ extra slot can be reused for predicted data without overwriting relevant observed data (i.e., this slot will never be required after prediction starts). Therefore, to store predicted data without overwriting relevant observed data, at most $max(max(H_p) - 1, 0)$ extra slots need to be added to g's SCQ as at most $max(H_p)$ predicted verdict-timestamp tuples ever enter the SCQ. On the other hand, at most $max(max\{s.wpd|s \in \mathbb{S}_g\} - g.bpd, 0) + max\{p.ub - p.lb|p \in \mathbb{TP}_g\}$ extra slots are required to be added to g's SCQ; any predicted data that needs to be stored is limited by the timestamp mismatch between node g and its siblings (following from the proof in [65]) and the temporal interval $[i + lb, i + ub]$ of its parent node(s). Therefore, only $min\big(max(max\{s.wpd|s \in \mathbb{S}_g\} - g.bpd, 0) + max\{p.ub - p.lb|p \in \mathbb{TP}_g\}, max(max(H_p) - 1, 0)\big)$ extra slots are required for proper storage of predicted data. □

MMPRV Total Memory Size. PMLTL specifications that utilize the probability operator P_δ have larger memory requirements than similarly structured formulas that do not utilize P_δ (as shown in Table 1). The reason for the larger memory requirement is twofold: (i) children of probabilistic temporal operators may be required to store additional tuples for consumption by their parents as defined in Eq. 3 and (ii) probabilistic operators have to store probability-timestamp tuples. Let's assume verdicts are single-byte boolean values, probabilities are stored as 8-byte doubles, and the timestamp is stored as a 4-byte integer. Therefore, a verdict-timestamp tuple requires 5 bytes and a probability-timestamp tuple requires 12 bytes, and the memory size in bytes of a single node g's SCQ is given by the following:

$$SCQ_{memory}(g) = \begin{cases} 12 * SCQ_{size}(g), & \text{descendant of } P_\delta \\ 5 * SCQ_{size}(g), & \text{otherwise} \end{cases} \quad (4)$$

Furthermore, the total memory size in bytes of the entire AST is given by the following[3]:

$$AST_{memory} = \sum_{g \in AST} SCQ_{memory}(g) \quad (5)$$

Following Eq. 5, Table 1 provides the memory required in bytes for the AST of various PMLTL formulas. Based on the deadline d (which determines $max(H_p)$), there is a minimum and maximum size for each node such that $max(max\{s.wpd - s \in \mathbb{S}_g\} - g.bpd, 0) + max\{p.ub - p.lb - p \in \mathbb{TP}_g\} + 1 \leq SCQ_{size}(g) \leq 2*(max(max\{s.wpd - s \in \mathbb{S}_g\} - g.bpd, 0) + max\{p.ub - p.lb - p \in \mathbb{TP}_g\}) + 1$. While probabilistic operators increase the size of the AST, the sizing equation has a fixed upper bound (compared to linearly increasing with $max(H_p)$ as in [65]) such that we can look as far into the future as desired without increasing the SCQ size beyond this upper bound.

Table 1. AST_{memory} (in bytes) of example PMLTL formulas where $a_0, a_1, a_2, a_3 \in \mathcal{AP}$

Example PMLTL formulas	Deadline d						
	−15	−5	0	5	15	30	45
$\square_{[0,30]} a_0$	10	10	10	10	10	10	10
$P_{0.80}(\square_{[0,30]} a_0)$	749	749	737	677	557	389	389
$\square_{[0,10]} a_0 \wedge \Diamond_{[0,20]} a_1$	125	125	125	125	95	75	75
$P_{0.95}(\square_{[0,10]} a_0 \wedge \Diamond_{[0,20]} a_1)$	1025	1025	1013	953	689	545	545
$((\square_{[0,5]} a_0)\mathcal{U}_{[0,10]} a_1) \vee ((\square_{[0,5]} a_2)\mathcal{U}_{[0,10]} a_3)$	445	445	435	385	245	245	245
$P_{0.85}((\square_{[0,5]} a_0)\mathcal{U}_{[0,10]} a_1) \vee P_{0.98}((\square_{[0,5]} a_2)\mathcal{U}_{[0,10]} a_3)$	1551	1551	1527	1383	831	831	831

4 Autonomous Vehicle Case Study

Autonomous vehicles (AVs) are common targets of multimodal prediction research due to the safety-critical and multimodal nature of vehicles and other road agents (e.g., pedestrians). Conventionally, multimodal prediction has been produced by purely physics-based approaches (e.g., Monte Carlo [11,60]). Physics-based approaches are known for having low computational cost but are only valid for short prediction horizons (i.e., less than one second). For this reason, deep learning methods have gained recent popularity as they can accurately predict longer prediction horizons (i.e., several seconds); however, deep learning methods experience a higher computational cost in terms of memory requirements and latency [27,44]. In this section, we utilize a physics-based and deep learning-based multimodal model predictor.

---

[3] This only includes the memory requirement of the SCQs and doesn't consider the node's metadata.

4.1 F1Tenth Autonomous Racing

System Description. The F1Tenth platform is a ROS-based 1/10th scale autonomous racing vehicle equipped with a NVIDIA® Jetson Xavier NX, LiDAR, and vehicle electronic speed controller (VESC) as shown in Fig. 4. For our experiments, we utilize the OpenAI Gym simulator provided by the creators of the F1Tenth platform [45]. The simulator models up to two vehicles utilizing the single-track model from [2] along with parameters derived from the physical F1Tenth platform. The VESC and LiDAR for each vehicle are directly simulated within the simulator, and although the LiDAR can be utilized to provide vehicle localization (e.g., the particle filter in [61]), the simulator broadcasts the ground truth odometry for each vehicle.

Fig. 4. F1Tenth autonomous vehicle.

Implementation. We simulate a multi-agent race on the NVIDIA® Jetson Xavier NX, where an ego-vehicle (i.e., the vehicle operating MMPRV) races against an opponent vehicle. The ego-vehicle monitors the following safety specification utilizing MMPRV:

$$\varphi = a_0 \, \mathcal{U}_{[0,15]} \, P_{0.98}(a_1 \vee a_2) \tag{6}$$

where $a_0, a_1, a_2 \in \mathcal{AP}$ defined in Table 2 such that v_{ego} is the ego-vehicle's velocity, and $x_{ego}, y_{ego}, x_{opp}$, and y_{opp} are the x- and y-coordinates of the ego-vehicle and opponent vehicle, respectively. The specification φ aims to ensure that "the ego-vehicle decelerates for the next 15 time steps until the probability that either the ego-vehicle comes to a complete stop or the vehicles being greater than 0.58 m apart is greater than or equal to 98%", where 0.58 m is the F1Tenth platform's length. Note that φ is reevaluated for each time index, creating an implicit global operator $\Box_{[0,M]}\varphi$ (i.e., M is the end of mission-time).

Table 2. Atomic Propositions in Eq. 6

Atomic	Atomic Proposition	English Translation
a_0	$v_{ego}[i] - v_{ego}[i-1] < 0.0$	Ego-vehicle is decelerating
a_1	$v_{ego} == 0.0$	Ego-vehicle is stopped
a_2	$\sqrt{(x_{ego} - x_{opp})^2 + (y_{ego} - y_{opp})^2} > 0.58$	Ego-vehicle and opponent do not collide

The ego-vehicle utilizes a Model Predictive Control (MPC) controller to minimize its deviation from the reference trajectory (i.e., the track centerline). The overall goal of MPC is to minimize a cost function while also following a series of given constraints (e.g., physical dynamics and limitations of a system) [54]; therefore, the ego-vehicle's objective cost function is as follows[4]:

$$\min_{\mathbf{X},\mathbf{U}} \sum_{k=0}^{N-1} \left((\mathbf{X}_k - \mathbf{X}_{ref,k})^T \mathbf{Q} (\mathbf{X}_k - \mathbf{X}_{ref,k}) + \mathbf{U}_k^T \mathbf{R} \mathbf{U}_k \right) + (\mathbf{X}_N - \mathbf{X}_{ref,N})^T \mathbf{Q} (\mathbf{X}_N - \mathbf{X}_{ref,N}) \quad (7)$$

such that: $\mathbf{X}_0 = $ current state and $\mathbf{X}_{k+1} = \mathbf{A}\mathbf{X}_k + \mathbf{B}\mathbf{U}_k + \mathbf{C} \quad \forall k \in 0, 1, 2, \ldots, N$

$$0.5 \frac{m}{s} \le V_k \le 5.0 \frac{m}{s} \text{ and } -25° \le \delta_k \le 25° \quad \forall k \in 0, 1, 2, \ldots, N$$

where N is the prediction horizon, $\mathbf{X}_k^T = [x_k, y_k, \psi_k]^T$, $\mathbf{U}_k^T = [V_k, \delta_k]^T$, $\mathbf{X}_{ref,k}$ is the reference trajectory, x and y are the x- and y-coordinates of the center of gravity of the vehicle in the global frame, ψ is the angle of the vehicle relative to the x-axis, V is the velocity, δ is the steering angle, $\mathbf{Q}$ is a positive semi-definite weight matrix of size 3 × 3, and $\mathbf{R}$ is a positive definite weight matrix of size 2 × 2. To define $\mathbf{A}$, $\mathbf{B}$, and $\mathbf{C}$, the kinematic bicycle model derived from [48] is discretized and linearized around a reference point to the following form:

$$\begin{bmatrix} x_{k+1} \\ y_{k+1} \\ \psi_{k+1} \end{bmatrix} = \begin{bmatrix} 1 & 0 & -V_{ref} sin(\psi_{ref} + \beta_{ref}) dt \\ 0 & 1 & V_{ref} cos(\psi_{ref} + \beta_{ref}) dt \\ 0 & 0 & 1 \end{bmatrix} \begin{bmatrix} x_k \\ y_k \\ \psi_k \end{bmatrix} +$$
$$\begin{bmatrix} cos(\psi_{ref} + \beta_{ref}) dt & 0 \\ sin(\psi_{ref} + \beta_{ref}) dt & 0 \\ \frac{cos(\beta_{ref})}{\ell_f + \ell_r} tan(\delta_{ref}) dt & \frac{V_{ref} cos(\beta_{ref})}{(\ell_f + \ell_r) cos^2(\delta_{ref})} dt \end{bmatrix} \begin{bmatrix} V_k \\ \delta_k \end{bmatrix} + \begin{bmatrix} V_{ref} \psi_{ref} sin(\psi_{ref} + \beta_{ref}) dt \\ -V_{ref} \psi_{ref} cos(\psi_{ref} + \beta_{ref}) dt \\ \frac{-V_{ref} \delta_{ref} cos(\beta_{ref})}{(\ell_f + \ell_r) cos^2(\delta_{ref})} dt \end{bmatrix}$$
(8)

where β is the slip angle and ℓ_f and ℓ_r are the distances from the center of gravity to the front and rear axles. The ego-vehicle utilizes the operator splitting quadratic program (OSQP) [56] to solve the cost function (Eq. 7), and the output is a sequence of states ($\mathbf{X}_k$) and inputs ($\mathbf{U}_k$) for the next N time steps that minimize the cost function. Only the first inputs are applied to the ego-vehicle as MPC is recalculated for each timestamp (i.e., receding horizon control), but these predicted inputs and states are utilized as the predicted velocity and trajectory for the ego-vehicle (similar to [65]).

The opponent vehicle utilizes Rapidly exploring Random Trees (RRT*) to select the path that avoids obstacles and maximizes the progress along the centerline [32] and the pure pursuit algorithm to follow this path [18]. The opponent vehicle's current position is broadcast to the ego-vehicle, but the ego-vehicle is unaware of the opponent vehicle's control strategy. As a result, the ego-vehicle utilizes a naïve approach where k_{opp} possible future trajectories of the opponent's vehicle are generated based on random behavior modes [11] produced by Monte Carlo (MC) random sampling [25] over the model's input space in Eq. 8.

To determine the verdict of $a_2 \in \mathcal{AP}$ in Eq. 6, the single predicted trajectory of the ego-vehicle's MPC controller and the k_{opp} predicted opponent vehicle trajectories produce $1 * k_{opp}$ signal tuples (v_{ego}, x_{ego}, y_{ego}, x_{opp}, y_{opp}) for each predicted time step. R2U2's booleanizer [29] produces boolean atomics from these signal values to populate $K = 1 * k_{opp}$ finite traces with prediction until the verdict of φ is determinable.

---

[4] Additional details available at https://temporallogic.org/research/MMPRV/MPC.pdf.

Note that equal likelihood is assumed for this approach; therefore, the probability space $(\Omega_i, \mathcal{F}_i, \mathbb{P}_i)$ is defined according to Definition 12 such that $\forall j \in [0, K-1]\ \mathbb{P}_i(\{a \in \hat{\pi}_j(i)\}) = \frac{1}{K}$ and $\mathbb{P}_i(\{a \notin \hat{\pi}_j(i)\}) = 0$.

Real-Time Feasibility. To evaluate the real-time feasibility of our implementation, we record the 90% tail latency over 10,000 time steps (i.e., 90% of reported latencies are less than or equal to the given latency) of the MPC controller, MC multimodal predictor, and R2U2 (i.e., the latency of MMPRV not including the prediction time) for varying values of K and N; the latency increases linearly with increasing values of K and N as one would intuitively expect as shown in Fig. 5. The F1Tenth vehicle has an update rate of 20 Hz; therefore, we assume the ego-vehicle's control loop must also operate at 20 Hz (i.e.,

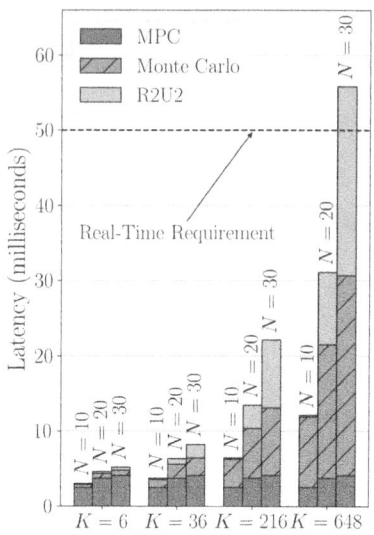

Fig. 5. 90% tail latency for varying values of K and N.

every 50 ms) as shown by the dashed line in Fig. 5. Even though we only consider MMPRV and the associated predictors in our latency analysis, it's important to note that the control loop includes other processes such as sensor processing and localization. Furthermore, although the latencies of the model predictors are specific to our implementation, MMPRV allows for *any* user-defined model predictor to be utilized with *any* values of K and N. While the chosen model predictor(s) must be feasible in real-time, R2U2 must also be able to run in real-time to produce verdicts without delay. Generally, with low values of K and N, R2U2 performs relatively quickly (e.g., if $K = 36$ and $N = max(H_p) = 30$, R2U2 has a 90% tail latency of 0.759 ms).

MMPRV Results. For simplicity, we will assume that when the ego-vehicle detects violations of φ (Eq. 6), the chosen mitigation action is to apply the brakes where a deadline $d = -15$ is required. Figure 6a displays the evaluation of $\pi, i, -15 \models \varphi$ for time index i reported by MMPRV at timestamp t_R. Note that for every timestamp t_R, the verdict of $\pi, i, -15 \models \varphi$ is reported fifteen time steps before i such that $i = t_R - d = t_R - (-15)$. For example, when $t_R = 148$, the verdict was reported for $i = 163$ such that $163 = 148 - (-15)$. Figures 6b, 6c, 6d, and 6e display trajectory predictions with a $N = max(H_p) = \varphi.wpd - d = 15 - (-15) = 30$ that were utilized to populate $K = 216$ finite traces with prediction for evaluation of $\pi, i, -15 \models \varphi$. Note, that $K = 216$ and $N = 30$ meets the real-time requirement according to Fig. 5.

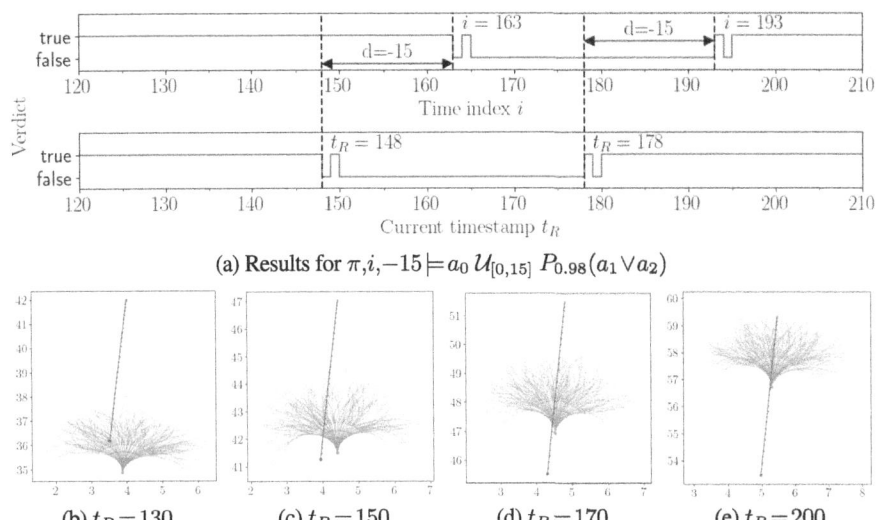

Fig. 6. MMPRV results. (a) displays the verdicts for time index i returned at timestamp t_R. (b), (c), (d), and (e) show the trajectory predictions for the ego-vehicle (blue) and opponent vehicle (orange) with $N = 30$. (Color figure online)

4.2 Argoverse Autonomous Driving

SOTA Multimodal Models. The Argoverse motion forecasting dataset [14] contains 323,557 traffic scenarios captured in Miami and Pittsburgh. Each scenario captures five seconds at 10 Hz such that each model is expected to predict the future three seconds (i.e., $N = 30$) given the past two seconds of observed trajectories. We examine six SOTA open-source deep neural network (DNN) multimodal predictors trained and evaluated on the Argoverse dataset: LaneGCN [37],

Table 3. Accuracy on Argoverse test set [14] ($k = 6$)

Model	minADE	minFDE	MR
LaneGCN [37]	0.870	1.362	16.2%
LAformer [40]	0.772	1.163	12.5%
mmTransformer [41]	0.844	1.338	15.4%
Lane Transformer [62]	0.866	1.316	15.2%
HiVT-64 [67]	0.807	1.243	14.0%
HiVT-128 [67]	0.774	1.169	12.7%

LAformer [40], mmTransformer [41], Lane Transformer [62], HiVT-64 [67], and HiVT-128 [67]. Each of these DNNs produces $k = 6$ multimodal predictions for each vehicle in the traffic scene, and Table 3 displays the accuracy of these predictions based on standard metrics. The minimum Average Displacement Error (minADE) and minimum Final Displacement Error (minFDE) are the average and endpoint L_2 distance errors, respectively, between the best-predicted and ground truth trajectories, and the Miss Rate (MR) is the percentage where none of the predicted trajectories have an endpoint L_2 distance error within two meters from the ground truth.

Real-Time Feasibility. Deep learning models are known to have large variations in latency based on several factors such as input/output data, model architecture, hardware platform, etc. [39]; therefore, we deploy all six models on four different hardware platforms: a laptop with a 2.8 GHz Quad-Core Intel® Core i7 CPU (Laptop CPU), the NVIDIA® Jetson Xavier NX with its GPU enabled (Jetson GPU), a desktop with a 3.00 GHz 8-core Intel® Xeon® Gold 6354 CPU (Desktop CPU), and that same desktop with the NVIDIA® A40 GPU enabled (Desktop GPU). To simulate predicting the multimodal trajectories of 16 vehicles in a given city traffic scene, each of these models (except HiVT-64 and HiVT-128) are run with a batch size of 16. HiVT-64 and HiVT-128 uniquely compute the multimodal predictions for *all* agents in a given traffic scene within a single forward pass; therefore, they are run with a batch size of one to provide an accurate comparison. The latencies of these models are captured utilizing the official open-source implementations, and the standard 90% tail latency [49] is reported in Fig. 7.

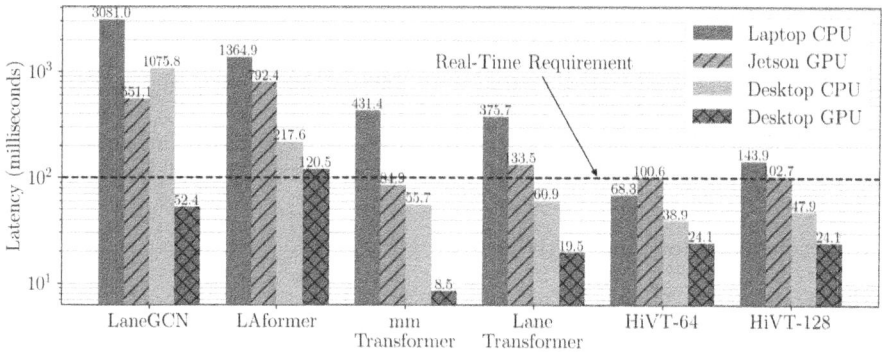

Fig. 7. 90% tail latency of SOTA models on the Argoverse validation set [14] ($k = 6$)

Since the Argoverse dataset was captured at 10 Hz, we assume the control loop must also operate at 10 Hz (i.e., every 100 ms) as indicated by the dashed line in Fig. 7. While we only analyze the latency of the multimodal predictor, the control loop also includes tasks such as localization, object detection, lane detection, planning, etc. [39]. Consequently, these SOTA multimodal predictors must operate with a latency much less than 100 ms to allow these other tasks enough time to execute; therefore, according to Fig. 7, there are only a few cases that meet this real-time requirement. When these SOTA DNNs target the NVIDIA® Jetson Xavier NX, they all fall short of this real-time requirement; instead, these models generally require the computing capabilities of the Desktop GPU to be feasible in real-time.

To compare our physics-based predictor in Sect. 4.1 and the SOTA DNNs, we reran the DNNs on the NVIDIA® Jetson Xavier NX to simulate predicting the multimodal trajectories of a single opponent vehicle (i.e., batch size of one), and mmTransformer had the lowest latency with 37.8 ms. Therefore, in order to achieve SOTA accuracy, we must experience a 55× slowdown from our Monte Carlo approach (i.e., Fig. 5: $K = 6$, $N = 30 \mapsto 0.69$ ms).

MMPRV Results. MMPRV determines the verdict of the following safety specification by deadline $d = 0$ (with $max(H_p) = 30$):

$$\varphi = P_{0.90}(\square_{[0,30]}a), \text{ where } a = \sqrt{(x_1 - x_2)^2 + (y_1 - y_2)^2} > 1.7$$

where a is an atomic proposition and x_1, y_1, x_2, and y_2 are the x- and y-coordinates of Vehicle 1 and Vehicle 2, respectively. The specification φ aims to ensure that "the probability of the distance between two vehicles being greater than 1.7 m for the next 30 time steps (i.e., next 3 s) is greater than or equal to 90%", where 1.7 m is the average width of a vehicle.

The mmTransformer is utilized to predict $k_{veh1} = 6$ and $k_{veh2} = 6$ multimodal trajectories for two nearby vehicles labeled Vehicle 1 and Vehicle 2, respectively. This produces $k_{veh1} * k_{veh2} = 36$ signal tuples (x_1, y_1, x_2, y_2) which are input as raw float values into R2U2's booleanizer [29] to populate $K = 36$ finite traces with prediction. Each multimodal trajectory produced by mmTransformer also has an associated probability; therefore, the probability space $(\Omega_i, \mathcal{F}_i, \mathbb{P}_i)$ is defined according to Definition 12 such that $\forall j \in [0, K - 1]$ $\mathbb{P}_i(\{a \in \hat{\pi}_j(i)\}) = \Pr(x_1, y_1) * \Pr(x_2, y_2)$ and $\mathbb{P}_i(\{a \notin \hat{\pi}_j(i)\}) = 0$ where $\Pr(x_1, y_1)$ and $\Pr(x_2, y_2)$ are the probabilities of (x_1, y_1) and (x_2, y_2) being the ground truth.

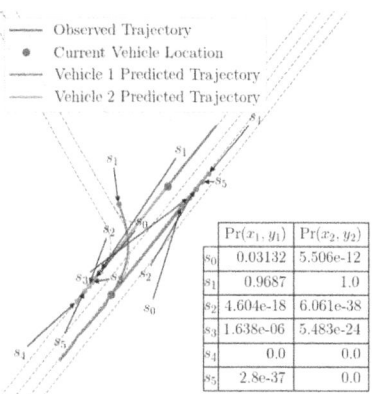

Fig. 8. Multimodal trajectory prediction for Vehicle 1 and 2. s_j is the trajectory produced by the jth multimodal prediction.

Figure 8 illustrates an interaction between Vehicle 1 and 2 at an intersection that results in $\pi, i, d \not\models \varphi$. According to the predictions of mmTransformer, Vehicle 1 might make a left turn (with $\Pr(x_1, y_1) = 0.9687$) that will result in a collision with Vehicle 2 whose predicted trajectories are straight. Note that the verdict is still a predicted result that is only as accurate as the prediction.

5 Conclusion and Future Work

MMPRV allows for *any* user-defined model predictor, including both unimodal and multimodal model predictors, while guaranteeing a verdict for a given PMLTL specification by a given deadline. The additional support of multimodal prediction allows for applicability to complex systems where multiple future behavior modes are plausible. As shown through our case studies, SOTA DNN multimodal predictors struggle to meet real-time requirements, especially when targeting embedded computing platforms. This motivates future work to continue investigating computationally lighter methods (e.g., Interacting Multiple Model Kalman Filters [31] or maneuver-based recurrent neural networks [21]) and investigate potential avenues for acceleration of these SOTA DNNs through techniques such as pruning or precision reduction [57]. Additionally, while we primarily focused on quantifying probabilistic multimodal predictions, future work includes quantifying distributed signal values within PMLTL specifications through techniques such as chance constraints [28, 34, 36] and conformal prediction [38].

References

1. Althoff, M., Dolan, J.M.: Online verification of automated road vehicles using reachability analysis. IEEE Trans. Robot. **30**(4), 903–918 (2014). https://doi.org/10.1109/TRO.2014.2312453
2. Althoff, M., Koschi, M., Manzinger, S.: Commonroad: composable benchmarks for motion planning on roads. In: 2017 IEEE Intelligent Vehicles Symposium (IV), pp. 719–726. IEEE (2017). https://doi.org/10.1109/IVS.2017.7995802
3. Althoff, M., Stursberg, O., Buss, M.: Model-based probabilistic collision detection in autonomous driving. IEEE Trans. Intell. Transp. Syst. **10**(2), 299–310 (2009). https://doi.org/10.1109/TITS.2009.2018966
4. Alur, R., Henzinger, T.A.: Real-time logics: complexity and expressiveness. In: LICS, pp. 390–401. IEEE (1990)
5. Aurandt, A., Jones, P.H., Rozier, K.Y.: Runtime verification triggers real-time, autonomous fault recovery on the CySat-I. In: Deshmukh, J.V., Havelund, K., Perez, I. (eds.) NASA Formal Methods. NFM 2022. LNCS, vol. 13260, pp. 816–825. Springer, Cham (2022). https://doi.org/10.1007/978-3-031-06773-0_45, https://temporallogic.org/research/CySat-NFM22/CySat-NFM22.pdf
6. Babaee, R., Ganesh, V., Sedwards, S.: Accelerated learning of predictive runtime monitors for rare failure. In: Finkbeiner, B., Mariani, L. (eds.) Runtime Verification. RV 2019. LNCS, vol. 11757, pp. 111–128. Springer, Cham (2019). https://doi.org/10.1007/978-3-030-32079-9_7
7. Babaee, R., Gurfinkel, A., Fischmeister, S.: 𝒫revent: a predictive run-time verification framework using statistical learning. In: Johnsen, E., Schaefer, I. (eds.) Software Engineering and Formal Methods. SEFM 2018. LNCS, vol. 10886, pp. 205–220. Springer, Cham (2018). https://doi.org/10.1007/978-3-319-92970-5_13
8. Babaee, R., Gurfinkel, A., Fischmeister, S.: Predictive run-time verification of discrete-time reachability properties in black-box systems using trace-level abstraction and statistical learning. In: Colombo, C., Leucker, M. (eds.) Runtime Verification. RV 2018. LNCS, vol. 11237, pp. 187–204. Springer, Cham (2018). https://doi.org/10.1007/978-3-030-03769-7_11
9. Bartocci, E., et al.: Specification-based monitoring of cyber-physical systems: a survey on theory, tools and applications. Lectures on Runtime Verification: Introductory and Advanced Topics, pp. 135–175 (2018). https://doi.org/10.1007/978-3-319-75632-5_5
10. Bortolussi, L., Cairoli, F., Paoletti, N., Smolka, S.A., Stoller, S.D.: Neural predictive monitoring. In: Finkbeiner, B., Mariani, L. (eds.) Runtime Verification. RV 2019. LNCS, vol. 11757, pp. 129–147. Springer, Cham (2019). https://doi.org/10.1007/978-3-030-32079-9_8
11. Broadhurst, A., Baker, S., Kanade, T.: Monte Carlo road safety reasoning. In: IEEE Proceedings. Intelligent Vehicles Symposium, 2005, pp. 319–324. IEEE (2005). https://doi.org/10.1109/IVS.2005.1505122
12. Cairoli, F., Bortolussi, L., Paoletti, N.: Neural predictive monitoring under partial observability. In: Feng, L., Fisman, D. (eds.) Runtime Verification. RV 2021. LNCS, vol. 12974, pp. 121–141. Springer, Cham (2021). https://doi.org/10.1007/978-3-030-88494-9_7
13. Cauwels, M., Hammer, A., Hertz, B., Jones, P., Rozier, K.Y.: Integrating runtime verification into an automated UAS traffic management system. In: DETECT. Springer, L'Aquila, Italy, September 2020. https://r2u2.temporallogic.org/wp-content/uploads/2020/12/CHHJR20.pdf

14. Chang, M.F., et al.: Argoverse: 3d tracking and forecasting with rich maps. In: Proceedings of the IEEE/CVF Conference on Computer Vision and Pattern Recognition, pp. 8748–8757 (2019). https://doi.org/10.1109/CVPR.2019.00895
15. Chou, Y., Yoon, H., Sankaranarayanan, S.: Predictive runtime monitoring of vehicle models using Bayesian estimation and reachability analysis. In: 2020 IEEE/RSJ International Conference on Intelligent Robots and Systems (IROS), pp. 2111–2118. IEEE (2020). https://doi.org/10.1109/IROS45743.2020.9340755
16. Cimatti, A., Tian, C., Tonetta, S.: Assumption-based runtime verification with partial observability and resets. In: Finkbeiner, B., Mariani, L. (eds.) Runtime Verification. RV 2019. LNCS, vol. 11757, pp. 165–184. Springer, Cham (2019). https://doi.org/10.1007/978-3-030-32079-9_10
17. Cleaveland, M., Sokolsky, O., Lee, I., Ruchkin, I.: Conservative safety monitors of stochastic dynamical systems. In: Rozier, K.Y., Chaudhuri, S. (eds.) NASA Formal Methods. NFM 2023. LNCS, vol. 13903, pp. 140–156. Springer, Cham (2023). https://doi.org/10.1007/978-3-031-33170-1_9
18. Coulter, R.C.: Implementation of the pure pursuit path tracking algorithm. Carnegie Mellon University, The Robotics Institute (1992)
19. Dabney, J.B., Badger, J.M., Rajagopal, P.: Adding a verification view for an autonomous real-time system architecture. In: Proceedings of SciTech Forum, pp. 2021-0566, AIAA, January 2021. https://doi.org/10.2514/6.2021-0566. Online
20. Dabney, J.B., Badger, J.M., Rajagopal, P.: Trustworthy autonomy for gateway vehicle system manager. In: 2023 IEEE Space Computing Conference (SCC), pp. 57–62. IEEE (2023). https://doi.org/10.1109/SCC57168.2023.00018
21. Deo, N., Trivedi, M.M.: Multi-modal trajectory prediction of surrounding vehicles with maneuver based LSTMs. In: 2018 IEEE Intelligent Vehicles Symposium (IV), pp. 1179–1184. IEEE (2018). https://doi.org/10.1109/IVS.2018.8500493
22. Ferrando, A., et al.: Bridging the gap between single-and multi-model predictive runtime verification. Form. Methods Syst. Des. 1–33 (2022). https://doi.org/10.1007/s10703-022-00395-7
23. Ferrando, A., Delzanno, G.: Incrementally predictive runtime verification. In: CILC, pp. 92–106 (2021)
24. Fisher, M., Mascardi, V., Rozier, K.Y., Schlingloff, B.H., Winikoff, M., Yorke-Smith, N.: Towards a framework for certification of reliable autonomous systems. Auton. Agent. Multi-Agent Syst. **35**, 1–65 (2021). https://doi.org/10.1007/s10458-020-09487-2
25. Hammersley, J.M.: Monte Carlo methods for solving multivariable problems. Ann. N. Y. Acad. Sci. **86**(3), 844–874 (1960)
26. Hertz, B., Luppen, Z., Rozier, K.Y.: Integrating runtime verification into a sounding rocket control system. In: Dutle, A., Moscato, M.M., Titolo, L., Muñoz, C.A., Perez, I. (eds.) NASA Formal Methods. NFM 2021. LNCS, vol. 12673, pp. 151–159. Springer, Cham (2021). https://doi.org/10.1007/978-3-030-76384-8_10
27. Huang, Y., Du, J., Yang, Z., Zhou, Z., Zhang, L., Chen, H.: A survey on trajectory-prediction methods for autonomous driving. IEEE Trans. Intell. Veh. **7**(3), 652–674 (2022). https://doi.org/10.1109/TIV.2022.3167103
28. Jha, S., Raman, V., Sadigh, D., Seshia, S.A.: Safe autonomy under perception uncertainty using chance-constrained temporal logic. J. Autom. Reason. **60**, 43–62 (2018). https://doi.org/10.1007/s10817-017-9413-9
29. Johannsen, C., Jones, P., Kempa, B., Rozier, K.Y., Zhang, P.: R2U2 version 3.0: re-imagining a toolchain for specification, resource estimation, and optimized observer generation for runtime verification in hardware and software. In: Enea, C., Lal, A. (eds.) Computer Aided Verification. CAV 2023. LNCS, vol. 13966, pp. 483–497. Springer, Cham (2023). https://doi.org/10.1007/978-3-031-37709-9_23, https://research.temporallogic.org/papers/JJKRZ23.pdf

30. Johannsen, C., Kempa, B., Jones, P.H., Rozier, K.Y., Wongpiromsarn, T.: Impossible made possible: encoding intractable specifications via implied domain constraints. In: Cimatti, A., Titolo, L. (eds.) Formal Methods for Industrial Critical Systems. FMICS 2023. LNCS, vol. 14290, pp. 151–169. Springer, Cham (2023). https://doi.org/10.1007/978-3-031-43681-9_9, https://research.temporallogic.org/papers/JKJRW23.pdf
31. Kaempchen, N., Weiss, K., Schaefer, M., Dietmayer, K.C.: Imm object tracking for high dynamic driving maneuvers. In: IEEE Intelligent Vehicles Symposium, 2004, pp. 825–830. IEEE (2004). https://doi.org/10.1109/IVS.2004.1336491
32. Karaman, S., Frazzoli, E.: Sampling-based algorithms for optimal motion planning. Int. J. Robot. Res. **30**(7), 846–894 (2011). https://doi.org/10.1177/0278364911406761
33. Kempa, B., Zhang, P., Jones, P.H., Zambreno, J., Rozier, K.Y.: Embedding online runtime verification for fault disambiguation on Robonaut2. In: Bertrand, N., Jansen, N. (eds.) Formal Modeling and Analysis of Timed Systems. FORMATS 2020. LNCS, vol. 12288, pp. 196–214. Springer, Cham (2020). https://doi.org/10.1007/978-3-030-57628-8_12, http://research.temporallogic.org/papers/KZJZR20.pdf
34. Kyriakis, P., Deshmukh, J.V., Bogdan, P.: Specification mining and robust design under uncertainty: a stochastic temporal logic approach. ACM Trans. Embed. Comput. Syst. (TECS) **18**(5s), 1–21 (2019). https://doi.org/10.1145/3358231
35. Li, J., Vardi, M.Y., Rozier, K.Y.: Satisfiability checking for mission-time LTL. In: Dillig, I., Tasiran, S. (eds.) Computer Aided Verification. CAV 2019. LNCS, vol. 11562, pp. 3–22. Springer, Cham (2019). https://doi.org/10.1007/978-3-030-25543-5_1
36. Li, J., Nuzzo, P., Sangiovanni-Vincentelli, A., Xi, Y., Li, D.: Stochastic contracts for cyber-physical system design under probabilistic requirements. In: Proceedings of the 15th ACM-IEEE International Conference on Formal Methods and Models for System Design, pp. 5–14 (2017). https://doi.org/10.1145/3127041.3127045
37. Liang, M., et al.: Learning lane graph representations for motion forecasting. In: Vedaldi, A., Bischof, H., Brox, T., Frahm, JM. (eds.) Computer Vision – ECCV 2020. ECCV 2020. LNCS, vol. 12347, pp. 541–556. Springer, Cham (2020). https://doi.org/10.1007/978-3-030-58536-5_32
38. Lindemann, L., Qin, X., Deshmukh, J.V., Pappas, G.J.: Conformal prediction for stl runtime verification. In: Proceedings of the ACM/IEEE 14th International Conference on Cyber-Physical Systems (with CPS-IoT Week 2023), pp. 142–153 (2023). https://doi.org/10.1145/3576841.3585927
39. Liu, L., Wang, Y., Shi, W.: Understanding time variations of DNN inference in autonomous driving. arXiv preprint arXiv:2209.05487 (2022). https://doi.org/10.48550/arXiv.2209.05487
40. Liu, M., et al.: Laformer: trajectory prediction for autonomous driving with lane-aware scene constraints. arXiv preprint arXiv:2302.13933 (2023)
41. Liu, Y., Zhang, J., Fang, L., Jiang, Q., Zhou, B.: Multimodal motion prediction with stacked transformers. In: Proceedings of the IEEE/CVF Conference on Computer Vision and Pattern Recognition, pp. 7577–7586 (2021). https://doi.org/10.1109/CVPR46437.2021.00749
42. Ma, M., Stankovic, J., Bartocci, E., Feng, L.: Predictive monitoring with logic-calibrated uncertainty for cyber-physical systems. ACM Trans. Embed. Comput. Syst. (TECS) **20**(5s), 1–25 (2021). https://doi.org/10.1145/3477032
43. Maler, O., Nickovic, D.: Monitoring temporal properties of continuous signals. In: Lakhnech, Y., Yovine, S. (eds.) Formal Techniques, Modelling and Analysis of Timed and Fault-Tolerant Systems. FTRTFT FORMATS 2004 2004. LNCS, vol. 3253, pp. 152–166. Springer, Berlin, Heidelberg (2004). https://doi.org/10.1007/978-3-540-30206-3_12
44. Mozaffari, S., Al-Jarrah, O.Y., Dianati, M., Jennings, P., Mouzakitis, A.: Deep learning-based vehicle behavior prediction for autonomous driving applications: a review. IEEE Trans. Intell. Transp. Syst. **23**(1), 33–47 (2020). https://doi.org/10.1109/TITS.2020.3012034

45. O'Kelly, M., Zheng, H., Karthik, D., Mangharam, R.: F1tenth: an open-source evaluation environment for continuous control and reinforcement learning. In: NeurIPS 2019 Competition and Demonstration Track, pp. 77–89. PMLR (2020)
46. Pinisetty, S., Jéron, T., Tripakis, S., Falcone, Y., Marchand, H., Preoteasa, V.: Predictive runtime verification of timed properties. J. Syst. Softw. **132**, 353–365 (2017). https://doi.org/10.1016/j.jss.2017.06.060
47. Qin, X., Deshmukh, J.V.: Clairvoyant monitoring for signal temporal logic. In: Bertrand, N., Jansen, N. (eds.) Formal Modeling and Analysis of Timed Systems. FORMATS 2020. LNCS, vol. 12288, pp. 178–195. Springer, Cham (2020). https://doi.org/10.1007/978-3-030-57628-8_11
48. Rajamani, R.: Vehicle Dynamics and Control. Springer, New York (2011). https://doi.org/10.1007/978-1-4614-1433-9
49. Reddi, V.J., et al.: MLPerf inference benchmark. In: 2020 ACM/IEEE 47th Annual International Symposium on Computer Architecture (ISCA), pp. 446–459. IEEE (2020). https://doi.org/10.1109/ISCA45697.2020.00045
50. Reinbacher, T., Rozier, K.Y., Schumann, J.: Temporal-logic based runtime observer pairs for system health management of real-time systems. In: Ábrahám, E., Havelund, K. (eds.) Tools and Algorithms for the Construction and Analysis of Systems. TACAS 2014. LNCS, vol. 8413, pp. 357–372. Springer, Berlin, Heidelberg (2014). https://doi.org/10.1007/978-3-642-54862-8_24
51. Rozier, K.Y., Schumann, J.: R2U2: tool overview. In: Proceedings of International Workshop on Competitions, Usability, Benchmarks, Evaluation, and Standardisation for Runtime Verification Tools (RV-CUBES), vol. 3, pp. 138–156. Kalpa Publications, Seattle, WA, USA, September 2017. https://research.temporallogic.org/papers/RS2017_RV.pdf
52. Sadigh, D., Kapoor, A.: Safe control under uncertainty with probabilistic signal temporal logic. In: Proceedings of Robotics: Science and Systems XII (2016). https://doi.org/10.15607/RSS.2016.XII.017
53. Schumann, J., Rozier, K.Y., Reinbacher, T., Mengshoel, O.J., Mbaya, T., Ippolito, C.: Towards real-time, on-board, hardware-supported sensor and software health management for unmanned aerial systems. In: PHM, pp. 381–401, October 2013. https://research.temporallogic.org/papers/SRRMMI15.pdf
54. Schwenzer, M., Ay, M., Bergs, T., Abel, D.: Review on model predictive control: an engineering perspective. Int. J. Adv. Manuf. Technol. **117**(5–6), 1327–1349 (2021). https://doi.org/10.1007/s00170-021-07682-3
55. Stahl, T., Diermeyer, F.: Online verification enabling approval of driving functions–implementation for a planner of an autonomous race vehicle. IEEE Open J. Intell. Transp. Syst. **2**, 97–110 (2021). https://doi.org/10.1109/OJITS.2021.3078121
56. Stellato, B., Banjac, G., Goulart, P., Bemporad, A., Boyd, S.: OSQP: an operator splitting solver for quadratic programs. Math. Program. Comput. **12**(4), 637–672 (2020). https://doi.org/10.1007/s12532-020-00179-2
57. Sze, V., Chen, Y.H., Yang, T.J., Emer, J.S.: Efficient processing of deep neural networks: a tutorial and survey. Proc. IEEE **105**(12), 2295–2329 (2017). https://doi.org/10.1109/JPROC.2017.2761740
58. Tiger, M., Heintz, F.: Stream reasoning using temporal logic and predictive probabilistic state models. In: 2016 23rd International Symposium on Temporal Representation and Reasoning (TIME), pp. 196–205. IEEE (2016). https://doi.org/10.1109/TIME.2016.28
59. Tiger, M., Heintz, F.: Incremental reasoning in probabilistic signal temporal logic. Int. J. Approx. Reason. **119**, 325–352 (2020). https://doi.org/10.1016/j.ijar.2020.01.009
60. Tran, Q., Firl, J.: Online maneuver recognition and multimodal trajectory prediction for intersection assistance using non-parametric regression. In: 2014 IEEE Intelligent Vehicles Symposium Proceedings, pp. 918–923. IEEE (2014). https://doi.org/10.1109/IVS.2014.6856480

61. Walsh, C.H., Karaman, S.: CDDT: fast approximate 2d ray casting for accelerated localization. In: 2018 IEEE International Conference on Robotics and Automation (ICRA), pp. 3677–3684. IEEE (2018). https://doi.org/10.1109/ICRA.2018.8460743
62. Wang, Z., Guo, J., Hu, Z., Zhang, H., Zhang, J., Pu, J.: Lane transformer: a high-efficiency trajectory prediction model. IEEE Open J. Intell. Transp. Syst. **4**, 2–13 (2023). https://doi.org/10.1109/OJITS.2023.3233952
63. Yoon, H., Chou, Y., Chen, X., Frew, E., Sankaranarayanan, S.: Predictive runtime monitoring for linear stochastic systems and applications to geofence enforcement for UAVs. In: Finkbeiner, B., Mariani, L. (eds.) Runtime Verification. RV 2019. LNCS, vol. 11757, pp. 349–367. Springer, Cham (2019). https://doi.org/10.1007/978-3-030-32079-9_20
64. Yu, X., Dong, W., Li, S., Yin, X.: Model predictive monitoring of dynamical systems for signal temporal logic specifications. Automatica **160**, 111445 (2024). https://doi.org/10.1016/j.automatica.2023.111445
65. Zhang, P., Aurandt, A., Dureja, R., Jones, P.H., Rozier, K.Y.: Model predictive runtime verification for cyber-physical systems with real-time deadlines. In: Petrucci, L., Sproston, J. (eds.) Formal Modeling and Analysis of Timed Systems. FORMATS 2023. LNCS, vol. 14138, pp. 158–180. Springer, Cham (2023). https://doi.org/10.1007/978-3-031-42626-1_10, https://research.temporallogic.org/papers/ZADJR23.pdf
66. Zhang, X., Leucker, M., Dong, W.: Runtime verification with predictive semantics. In: Goodloe, A.E., Person, S. (eds.) NASA Formal Methods. NFM 2012. LNCS, vol. 7226, pp. 418–432. Springer, Berlin, Heidelberg (2012). https://doi.org/10.1007/978-3-642-28891-3_37
67. Zhou, Z., Ye, L., Wang, J., Wu, K., Lu, K.: HIVT: hierarchical vector transformer for multi-agent motion prediction. In: Proceedings of the IEEE/CVF Conference on Computer Vision and Pattern Recognition, pp. 8823–8833 (2022). https://doi.org/10.1109/CVPR52688.2022.00862

Surrogate Neural Networks Local Stability for Aircraft Predictive Maintenance

Mélanie Ducoffe[1], Guillaume Povéda[1], Audrey Galametz[2(✉)],
Ryma Boumazouza[1], Marion-Cécile Martin[2], Julien Baris[1], Derk Daverschot[2],
and Eugene O'Higgins[2]

[1] Airbus Operations SAS, Toulouse, France
[2] Airbus Operations GmbH, Ottobrunn, Germany
audrey.galametz@airbus.com

Abstract. Surrogate Neural Networks are nowadays routinely used in industry as substitutes for computationally demanding engineering simulations (e.g., in structural analysis). They allow to generate faster predictions and thus analyses in industrial applications e.g., during a product design, testing or monitoring phases. Due to their performance and time-efficiency, these surrogate models are now being developed for use in safety-critical applications. Neural network verification and in particular the assessment of their robustness (e.g., to perturbations) is the next critical step to allow their inclusion in real-life applications and certification. We assess the applicability and scalability of empirical and formal methods in the context of aircraft predictive maintenance for surrogate neural networks designed to predict the stress sustained by an aircraft part from external loads. The case study covers a high-dimensional input and output space and the verification process thus accommodates multi-objective constraints. We explore the complementarity of verification methods in assessing the local stability property of such surrogate models to input noise. We showcase the effectiveness of sequentially combining methods in one verification 'pipeline' and demonstrating the subsequent gain in runtime required to assess the targeted property.

Keywords: Formal Verification · Neural Networks · Surrogate Models · Industrial Application · Aircraft Predictive Maintenance

1 Introduction

There have been significant advances in the development of verification methods to assess the robustness of neural networks (NN). Formal methods are, in particular, considered as key approaches to be explored and matured (see Sect. 2). They are expected to provide model guarantees that could allow industries, such as aviation, to meet the emerging certification requirements for the use of NN, in particular for safety-critical systems. Notable references, including guidelines from certification and aviation standardization entities, are advocating for the use of formal methods as a mean of compliance during the learning process management and inference model verification phases (see, e.g. the European Aviation Safety Agency (EASA) recent concept paper 'First usable guidance for Level 1 machine learning applications[1]). A concrete example of this use is introduced in the ForMuLA report (Formal Methods use for Learning Assurance), published from the partnership between EASA and Collins Aerospace [3]. It includes an application of formal methods to an industrial use case of prediction of the remaining life of aeronautical components and illustrates how these techniques can be used to assess the safety of machine-learning (ML) based systems.

The focus of published works on the applications of formal methods to ML models has predominantly been on classification tasks. There has been comparatively less emphasis on regression tasks, especially those tailored for industrial applications. It is however crucial to extend the implementation of these methods to regression challenges in regard to the increasing use of neural network surrogate models in industry, in particular in aviation where many are developed to act as substitute to computationally-demanding simulations (see Sect. 3).

In this paper, we are conducting the robustness assessment of NN surrogate models designed in the context of civil aviation and predictive aircraft maintenance. The case study presents unique specificities (e.g. regression task, multiple inputs and outputs etc.), rarely explored in the current literature. In this case study, we explore the adaptability and scalability of several families of verification techniques to the use case at hand. We further build upon their strengths and limitations to optimise their sequential and complementary use in order to perform the complete NN robustness assessment on a representative test set.

Section 2 summarizes the recent advances in NN verification. Section 3 introduces the case study of aircraft loads-to-stress prediction along with the tested models and stability property to be ensured. Section 4 describes the combination via the sequential use of techniques we employ in order to perform the NN stability assessment. Section 5 details the experiments and illustrates the verification process on a few NN models. Sections 6 and 7 present findings and conclusions.

2 Related Work

NN are brittle. The emergence of the field of adversarial machine-learning has shown that models can be easily fooled, even by small perturbations to input data [4]. A series of work has subsequently attempted to craft defense mechanisms against adversarial attacks e.g., [9]. Ultimately, however, these techniques do not provide guarantee that a neural network is robust to perturbations but only that counterexamples to a robustness requirement to be guaranteed can be generated.

The introduction of adversarial attacks has motivated the ramp-up of the applicability of formal methods to AI models, in particular to assess the robustness of neural networks against small 'local' perturbations, often represented by

---
[1] https://www.easa.europa.eu/en/easa-concept-paper-first-usable-guidance-level-1-machine-learning-applications-proposed-issue-01pdf.

l_p norm balls. Two families of verification methods have since been matured: *(i)* incomplete techniques e.g., [5–7] that can prove the presence/absence of counterexamples to a given property. They are usually computationally expensive and scale poorly with large networks. *(ii)* complete techniques, e.g., [11,12,16,17], that provide approximated bounds to model prediction. They commonly perform faster and thus scale better with larger models. They can however severely over approximate bound estimates of model output, leading to their lack of convergence for a given robustness status.

Verification tools are now commonly combining complete and incomplete techniques [15] in order to speed the verification process. However, to the best of our knowledge, there has been very limited published works illustrating and quantifying the impact (e.g. on computing time) this combination brings. As model size and input dimensionality keep increasing, scalability and verification optimisation will however be of essence for the adoption of formal methods in the verification, validation and certification processes of AI-based industrial systems.

3 Case Study: Aircraft Loads-to-Stress Prediction

3.1 Description

In aeronautics, numerical simulations are regularly used to model complex physical phenomena in systems or structures (using, e.g. a finite element discretization approach) and understand and anticipate their behaviour. The computational cost of such simulations has however prevented their use in real-time, including their embeddability in products or on-line processes. Their application therefore remains limited e.g. to a system design phase. The use of such simulation could however greatly improve productivity and operational cost, e.g. in the domain of aircraft predictive maintenance.

Structural maintenance programs (e.g. replacement of parts etc.) are currently based on conservative assumptions: they often assume aircrafts of a fleet have sustained a similar flight history and, thus, operational fatigue, and adopt worse case scenario, often overly preventive, maintenance actions for the whole fleet. One can therefore see the benefit in introducing a more optimised maintenance program, tailored to individual aircraft in order to reduce individual maintenance cost while ensuring that the safety of operations is maintained at the highest level. Such custom solutions, however, require the analysis of large amount of operational data from flight past history, the complete modelisation of the sustained aircraft fatigue and the prediction of the impact it had on its different parts in order to anticipate the required maintenance operations. These simulations involve computationally-demanding physics and mathematical modeling that may be unfeasible to use in real-life operational settings.

NN are a game changer. More and more studies are showing the value of NN-based surrogates to approximate numerical simulators [13]. Their more systematic use in industry however requires the maturation of new verification processes, specific to machine-learning components. The current lack of consensus on the tools to conduct such verification dramatically limits their applications, especially as components or enablers of safety critical applications. In this analysis, we investigate an example of NN surrogate models trained to predict the level of stress in different parts of an aircraft structure from sustained external loads. More details on the model function is provided in [10]. The accurate evaluation of the stresses is a key enabler for maintenance optimization.

3.2 Tested Models

We evaluate NNs composed of two hidden layers (h) with 165 neurons (r) and a dense output layer of size 81. Each hidden layer is followed by $ReLU$ activation functions. The NNs predict 81 normalised stress outputs (k) from 216 normalised loads input variables (n). In order to investigate the potential impact of training epochs on model robustness, we train a series of models with increasing number of epochs (5 models from 2 to 10000 epochs). These feed-forward NNs are functions $f : \mathbb{R}^n \mapsto \mathbb{R}^k$. Let x be an input vector of dimension n and W and b the weights and biases of the network respectively. f is the composition of linear functions denoted $l_i : x \mapsto W_i \cdot x + b_i$, followed by element-wise non linear activation functions denoted σ. We only consider $ReLU$ activations, such that $\sigma : x \in \mathbb{R}^n \mapsto [max(x_j, 0)]_{j=1}^r$.

The NN tested in the present study are research prototypes and earlier, less mature versions of the models currently pushed at Airbus. The models that will be used in predictive maintenance settings are currently being optimised, in part supported by robustness analysis such as the one presented here.

3.3 Property to be Ensured: Local Stability

A NN is locally stable if its predictions in the immediate vicinity of a test data point are consistent i.e., within a small value range allowed by the safety constrains. In engineering-driven domains such as aeronautics, the need for local stability of NN prediction is obvious and thus, a critical requirement. Model designers indeed want to ensure that a model reflects the continuous characteristics of physics-driven systems and phenomena. In the present case study, equivalent load values should cause equivalent stress intensities sustained by an aircraft part. The assessment of local stability is one of the robustness properties EASA lists as part of a model learning process verification phase (see Sect. 3).

Local stability (and thus safety) requirements for the case study at hand are enunciated in Property 1. In this particular case study, they are essentially split in two zones. We will refer to this property as the 'bow tie' owing to its distinctive shape. The belonging to a given zone ('Knot' or 'Wing') for a data point x and a given output index i is defined by the output value $f_i(x)$.

Property 1. Local stability property a.k.a., the 'bow tie'
Consider:

- a neural network f,
- an input sample $x \in \mathbb{R}^n$,

- i, the ith output of the network $f_i(x)$ where $i \in [1, k]$,
- p_{inp}, a local input perturbation and
- x', a perturbed input such that $x' \in [x - p_{inp}.|x|, x + p_{inp}.|x|]$

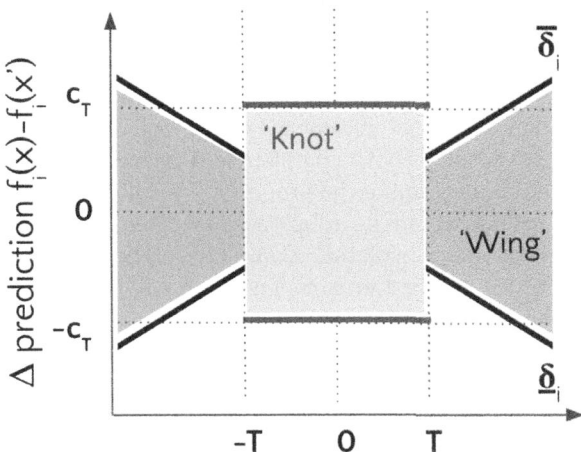

The NN local stability is ensured if, for any x':

$$\forall i \in [1, k], \underline{\delta_i} \leq f_i(x') - f_i(x) \leq \overline{\delta_i}$$

$$\text{with } [\underline{\delta_i}, \overline{\delta_i}] = \begin{cases} [-c_T, c_T] & \text{if } |f_i(x)| \leq T \\ & (\text{'Knot'}) \\ [-p_{out}.|f_i(x)|, p_{out}.|f_i(x)|] & \text{else} \\ & (\text{'Wings'}) \end{cases}$$

where

- $\underline{\delta_i}$ and $\overline{\delta_i}$ are respectively upper and lower constrains on deviation from original prediction,
- T is a threshold defining two zones of the output space with distinct requirements on stability i.e., $|f_i(x)| \leq T$ ('Knot') and $|f_i(x)| > T$ ('Wings'),
- c_T is the set constraint on δ_i in the knot and
- p_{out} are constrains on output perturbation in the wings.

We adopt $T = 10$ ($T < 10$ is considered as the small loads regime), $c_T = 1$ and $p_{inp} = p_{out} = 0.05$, taking into account safety requirements derived from the domain expertise of aircraft structure experts involved in the development of the maintenance solution. In the present work, we adopt constrains that are index-independent i.e., T, c_T, p_{inp} and p_{out} have the same value for all output indexes. We also adopt a direct match between input perturbations and output constrains ($p_{inp} = p_{out}$). The implemented solution is however highly parameterised and the verification procedure can easily be adapted as the stability property is refined and optimised by domain experts.

4 Method Combination for Local Stability Assessment

Before the advent of formal NN verification methods, the model local stability was assessed at Airbus via a random sampling of its immediate 'neighborhood' and corresponding predictions. This 'brute force' approach is both partial and computational expensive due to the necessity to homogeneously cover via sampling a high number of perturbed input variables. There was therefore a crucial need for formal, sound and time-efficient means to assess the NN stability.

Formal verification involves both complete and incomplete methods. Incomplete methods can either determine the property is verified for a given test point or are unable to conclude about its robustness i.e., it can not provide definite guarantees that a property is violated. Complete methods provide guarantees that a property is either verified or not. They are only inconclusive when the verification time required to reach a conclusion exceeds the time limit ('timeout') set for the verification. Both are 'sound' techniques meaning that they can never provide an incorrect answer. In a complementary manner, empirical techniques such as adversarial attacks exploit model vulnerabilities and find small input perturbations that will make a model produce incorrect and/or unsafe outputs.

Exploring a combination of techniques and using their strengths and limitations to optimise the verification assessment seemed like a promising direction to fulfill the requirements of soundness and time-efficiency. We converge towards the sequential use of the following techniques:

A- Empirical approaches:

To minimize the need for time-consuming formal approaches, the first verification step relies on generating adversarial attacks. If an attack is generated and successful on at least one of the 81 outputs, the stability of the test point is proven wrong. Attacks intent to 'push' the model predictions beyond the bow tie bounds while ensuring that the added perturbations stays within the allowed input noise defined in Sect. 3.3. They are performed for each output i separately i.e., we intend to increase $|f_i(x) - f_i(x')|$, independently of the effect on other output indexes. The attack implementation is designed to create a property violation, either a positive (beyond $\overline{\delta_i}$) or a negative one (beyond $\underline{\delta_i}$).

We conduct experiments generating several types of classical adversarial attacks, e.g. Projected Gradient Descent approach (PGD) [8] or Fast Gradient Sign Method (FGSM) [4] specifically designed to find local violation of model stability. We make use of the cleverhans library[2] and adapt the adversarial loss function to the given local stability property. The goal of this step A is to quickly find examples of model local instability. We notice that a simple attack generation technique such as PGD is sufficient to determine all test points whose local stability property is violated. We do not discard that more advanced attack generation techniques might be required as the models become more locally stable (e.g. via local stability training). The stability of test points for which no attack was generated is assessed using formal methods.

---

[2] https://github.com/cleverhans-lab/cleverhans.

B- Incomplete formal methods:

We leverage the less computationally-demanding nature of incomplete methods in order to assess test points whose stability might be less challenging to guarantee. We intend to provide lower and upper bound estimates of the model outputs to perturbed inputs. To do so, we make use of the linear relaxation-based perturbation analysis (LiRPA) verification bound method CROWN [17].

CROWN (or its equivalent DeepPoly [12]) is a commonly adopted bound propagation method. It has been shown to provide tighter bounds compared to previously developed techniques by means of linear and quadratic functions which enhance its effectiveness on many activation functions including ReLUs (used in our models). We make use of the version of CROWN implemented within the Airbus open-source decomon[3] library [2].

C- Complete formal methods:

To evaluate test points whose stability is neither refuted nor guaranteed by the previous methods, we use an in-house Mixed-Integer Linear Program (MILP)-based verifier. Encoding of the network into variables and constraints is done similarly to the Venus library [1].

The MILP encoding makes use of bounds computed by symbolic interval propagation [14]. For each layer i and neuron j in the layer i, two continuous variables are created: $y_{i,j,-}, y_{i,j,+}$ which corresponds to pre-activation and post-activation values of the neurons. Bounds of these variables are known thanks to the bound propagation function. Layer $i = 0$ corresponds to input values. The MILP is encoded as follow:

1. $\forall i \in [1, n_{layers}], j \in [0, n_i], y_{i,j,-} = W_i[j, :] \cdot y_{i-1,:,+} + b_{i,j}$, where W_i and b_i are respectively the model weights and bias of layer i
2. $\forall i \in [1, n_{layers}]$, if layer i is activated by a $ReLU$, $y_{i,j,+} = max(y_{i,j,-}, 0)$ else $y_{i,j,+} = y_{i,j,-}$

The max constraint is native into the Gurobi library and can also be chosen instead of the classically used Big-M constraint [1].

The negation of the stability property is encoded as follows. Given $x, f(x), \underline{\delta}, \overline{\delta}$ defined in Property 1:

1. Let $\forall j \in [1, 81], indic_{-,j}, indic_{+,j}$ be binary variables.
2. $\forall j, indic_{-,j} \rightarrow y_{n_{layers}, j, +} \leq f_j(x) + \underline{\delta}_j$
3. $\forall j, indic_{+,j} \rightarrow y_{n_{layers}, j, +} \geq f_j(x) + \overline{\delta}_j$
4. $\sum_j (indic_{+,j} + indic_{-,j}) \geq 1$

---

[3] https://github.com/airbus/decomon.

Each indicator variable will encode the fact that, for one output index, the perturbed NN prediction goes out of the bow-tie property. The last constraint thus encodes that the solver has to find a counterexample violating the property. If the MILP solver finds a solution, we conclude that the property is 'False'. If the solver shows the absence of counterexample, we conclude that the property is 'True'.

The sequence of these verification techniques is illustrated in Fig. 1. While we evaluate the efficiency of this verification process via this specific set of techniques (see Sect. 5), we expect that similar analysis can be conducted by removing bricks, sequentially combining techniques in another order (e.g. B+A+C instead of A+B+C) or replacing each brick by any technique falling into the same family (incomplete by incomplete etc.).

In order for the community to be able to perform similar verification technique combination and benchmarking, Airbus has made the verification pipeline open-source. Link and details on the source code are provided in Appendix A.

5 Experiments

The assessment of local stability (Sect. 3) is performed on 1000 test points[4] whose distribution matches the one of the training set and is representative of the operating domain.

The stability evaluation of the 5 models and 1000 points are conducted on a machine equipped with an Apple M2 Pro processor and 32 GB of memory. The MILP-based solver is running with Gurobi 10.0 version.

Figure 1 illustrates the sequence of techniques (empirical, incomplete and complete) used to assess the NN local stability. It also shows how the NN verification unfolds for the model which was trained for 2 epochs ('2-epoch') i.e., it shows the subsets of the 1000 test points progressing through the different stages (A+B+C), indicating whether their stability property is True (✓), False (X), or unknown (?). We see in this example that adversarial attack generation (A) is successful for 442/1000 test points. The stability of 554 of the remaining 558 test points is then proven via incomplete verification (B). The stability of the last 4 points is guaranteed via complete verification (C).

Attacks are generated using the PGD technique using 20 iterations of step size $\epsilon = 0.01$. The MILP verifier is run with a timeout $t = 300\,\text{s}$ per point. None of the test points' verification exceeded this timeout.

---

[4] We acknowledge that the present techniques allow the verification of the local stability property of a finite number of points in the input domain and do not permit in their current implementation to prove the global robustness of a continuous input domain. Work is currently being pushed by the formal method community towards exploring the extension of these techniques to global robustness verification.

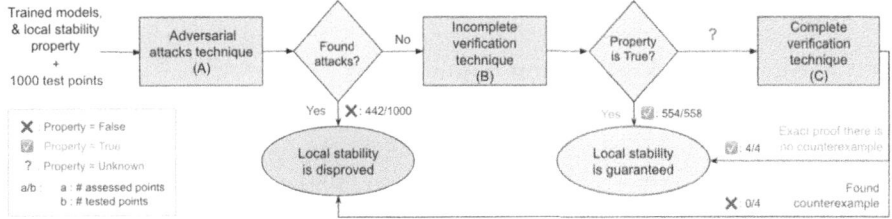

Fig. 1. Verification pipeline for NN stability assessment.

Table 1 summarises the stability assessment performed on two of the models (trained with 2 and 500 epochs) using the verification pipeline. As stated earlier, adversarial attack generation can only provide 'False' status, but cannot guarantee the property is 'True'. Incomplete/CROWN, on the opposite, can only prove that the property is 'True' for some test points i.e., they guarantee stability but not its lack of. Only complete techniques can unequivocally prove that a point stability is either guaranteed or disproved.

Table 1. Stability assessment of 2 and 500-epoch models. Columns 1–3 correspond to experiments with only A- adversarial, B- incomplete and C- complete techniques. Columns 4–6 show combinations of these. '#Tested' refers to the number of data entering a verification brick. '#True' refers to number of points whose property is guaranteed and '#False' to the fact that a counterexample is found i.e., the NN is not stable. '–' means the technique can not prove the property status. '0' shows it can but did not. Runtimes are provided in seconds.

		(1) A	(2) B	(3) C	(4) A+C	(5) B+C	(6) Pipeline A+B+C
model 2	#Tested	1000	1000	1000	1000/558	1000/446	1000/558/4
	#True	–	554	558	558	558	–/554/4 = 558
	#False	442	–	442	442	442	442/–/0 = 442
	Runtime	10.7	3.3	267	19.8	267	10.7/1.96/3.91 = 16.6
model 500	#Tested	1000	1000	1000	1000/552	1000/471	1000/552/23
	#True	–	529	552	552	552	–/529/23 = 552
	#False	448	–	448	448	448	448/–/0 = 448
	Runtime	11.5	3.4	1091	580	827	11.5/1.9/307 = 320

We see that we can generate attacks for 442 (448) out of 1000 test points for the 2-epoch (500-epoch) model. We can provide local stability guarantees for 554 (529) of the remaining 558 (552) test points. When combining bricks A+B+C, we only have to perform complete verification on the last 4 (23) test points.

6 Results

6.1 A Significant Verification Time Gain

The stability assessment on the 1000 test dataset was 3 to 16 times faster by combining verification methods instead of solely using complete approaches. The use of MILP-only verification takes 267 s (resp. 1091 s) for the 2- (resp. 500-) epoch model. In contrast, the cumulative time for the full pipeline is only 16.6 s (320 s).

Similarly, the three-stage pipeline has a significantly faster runtime than a portion of it (e.g. Bricks A+C) which further shows the effectiveness of combining techniques, thereby reducing the call to time-demanding exact computations. The use of incomplete methods as Brick B allows, e.g. to converge towards a guarantee of local stability for the large majority of the test data that were still to be evaluated after the adversarial attack stage (e.g. 554/558 and 529/552 for 2-epoch and 500-epoch models respectively).

A subtlety of the complete MILP-based method implemented in the present analysis is that it uses bound propagation [14] in order to provide lower and upper values to neurons in the network. When the bound propagation already allow to reach a definite conclusion on the stability property status, there is no call to the MILP solver (see Fig. 2). We acknowledge that the derivation of these bounds are conceptually similar to bounds derived using incomplete methods. While this part of brick C is here performed using symbolic interval analysis that provides tight but potentially looser bounds than CROWD, we are exploring the feasibility of using bounds derived by method B as inputs to C.

An example can be seen in the time of method A+C for the 2-epoch model competitive with respect to the full pipeline (Table 1, column 4 vs. column 6). On this lightly trained model, the first step of bound propagation estimation already concludes on the stability of all but four test points, without the need for additional MILP computations. On the contrary, when using method B+C (column 5), most of the points entering the complete method are not locally stable. They would have been identified during the adversarial attack phase (not used in B+C) and the MILP-based solver has to be called to find or not counter-examples to the property.

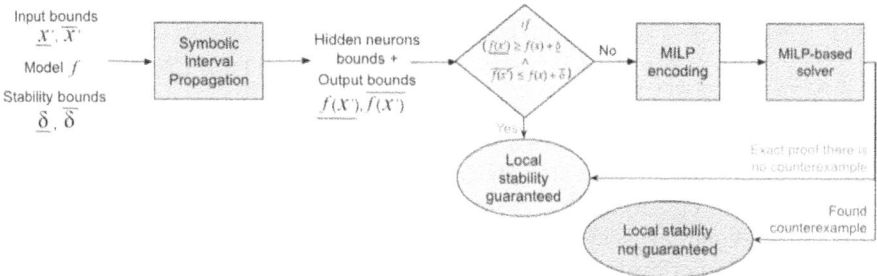

Fig. 2. Sub-pipeline included in the MILP-based approach

We are currently working on making the models more locally stable e.g. by using stability constrains as part of the training objectives. As the model becomes more and more robust, it will become more challenging to find counterexamples and runtime will increase with the use of formal techniques.

6.2 Insights into the Models

Up to 45% of the test data could be attacked (with some model-to-model variation). Figure 3 shows the percentage of successful PGD attacks for a given output index. Results are shown for the 50-epoch model. Attacks are generated for the 1000 test points and each output index was attacked twice per test point (towards a positive or negative violation) resulting in a total of 2000 attack attempts.

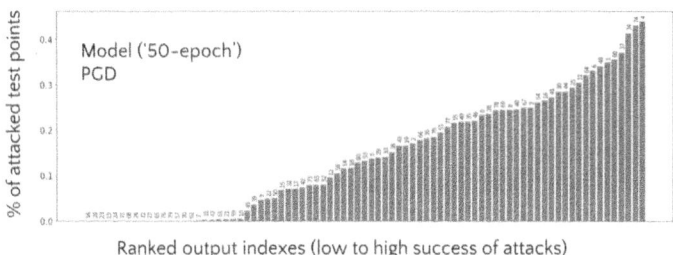

Fig. 3. Percentage of successful PGD attacks for a given targeted output index (from 0 to 80; ranked with increasing success).

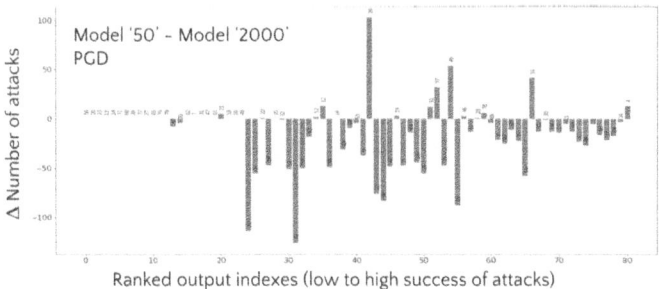

Fig. 4. Difference of number of attacks (out of 2000 attempts; see Fig. 3) between the 50-epoch and 2000-epoch models.

We first observe that some output indexes are more vulnerable than others, a result that is being used for the on-going model strengthening. Indeed, if the local stability is disproved for at least one output index, the test point is considered as not meeting the safety requirement. If some indexes are systematically shown to be vulnerable, the pertinence of these indexes might be re-evaluated.

In this analysis, the adversarial attacks are performed in order of output indexes. We can also greatly benefit from the fact that we can anticipate which indexes are more easily attackable than others to optimise the attack generation on subsequent generation of models and gain time on future robustness assessment.

We observe that the increase of training epochs does not make the models more stable. Table 1 shows that the predictions of the 500-epoch model can be attacked 44.8% of the time versus 44.2% for the 2-epoch model. A similar conclusion is reached from Fig. 4 which shows the difference of attacks generated for the 50 and 2000-epoch models. We observe however that the stability property is very dependent on the targeted output index. This shows that, in order to build models that are inherently stable (or in general robust to local perturbations), robustness should be part of the training objective and while training with more epochs surely increases performance (up to the point when the model starts overfitting), it does unfortunately not prevent local vulnerabilities.

It is also worth noting that the number of epochs negatively affects the performance of incomplete methods, leading to a longer verification time.

The experiments also show that counterexamples are preferentially found for $|f_i(x)| > 10$. The requirement in the 'knot' stress regime is conservative enough that the property is almost never infringed in the small loads regime.

7 Conclusions and Future Work

This case study analysis presents the implementation of a sound multi-technique pipeline for the a posteriori assessment of the local stability property of surrogate NN. By combining the strengths and mitigating the limitations of a number of techniques including adversarial attacks and complete and incomplete formal verification methods, we have not only managed to successfully perform a complete NN stability assessment of the models over the test dataset but also reduced the runtime of the required experiments to do so. Furthermore, the experiments have also shone light on model vulnerabilities and the necessity to investigate the feasibility of looser constraints for the local stability property itself.

This case study and technique configuration only begins to explore what such a verification pipeline can offer; further tuning of the techniques could indeed lead to an even more time-efficient verification. We performed a number of optimisation experiments e.g., hyperparameters tuning for adversarial attacks, MILP-computation etc. But further optimisation work could be done in that respect. As far as the implementation of the MILP solver is concerned (see Sect. 4), the present analysis uses symbolic interval propagation in order to provide starting bounds and restrict the input domain to be verified. For more complex NN however, interval arithmetic could provide excessively conservative bounds that may slow the verification. We will be exploring the use of bounds derived from an incomplete verification tool (e.g. CROWN) in order to feed them as initial bounds to the complete verifier.

The next step is to enhance NN surrogate models through the integration of empirical and formal components as part of the model design phase (e.g. during training), moving beyond the sole a posteriori evaluation of its local stability.

Appendix

A Open-Source Verification Pipeline

The open-source code of the verification pipeline (AIROBAS) is made available on github.
It provides functionalities to:

- load input data and models,
- define a robustness property to be verified. The code has been implemented to be as generic as possible and highly parametrizable regarding property definition,
- design customized verification pipeline,
- run verification with a default set of empirical and formal methods e.g., attacks using the cleverhans library, incomplete verification using LiRPA-based functionalities implemented in decomon etc.,
- append new verification functions or link the code to open-source libraries of one's choice.

It also provides a set of step-by-step notebooks to train a number of NN surrogate models (e.g., surrogate to the Rosenbrock analytic function, a runway braking distance estimate etc.), define robustness properties to be assessed and proceed to prove or disprove such properties for a set of test data.

References

1. Botoeva, E., Kouvaros, P., Kronqvist, J., Lomuscio, A., Misener, R.: Efficient verification of relu-based neural networks via dependency analysis. In: Proceedings of the AAAI Conference on Artificial Intelligence, vol. 34, pp. 3291–3299 (2020)
2. Ducoffe, M.: Decomon: automatic certified perturbation analysis of neural networks (2021). https://github.com/airbus/decomon
3. ForMuLA: Formal methods use for learning assurance. Technical report (2023)
4. Goodfellow, I.J., Shlens, J., Szegedy, C.: Explaining and harnessing adversarial examples. arXiv preprint arXiv:1412.6572 (2014)
5. Katz, G., Barrett, C., Dill, D.L., Julian, K., Kochenderfer, M.J.: Reluplex: an efficient SMT solver for verifying deep neural networks. In: Majumdar, R., Kunčak, V. (eds.) Computer Aided Verification. CAV 2017. LNC, vol. 10426, pp. 97–117. Springer, Cham (2017). https://doi.org/10.1007/978-3-319-63387-9_5
6. Katz, G., et al.: The Marabou framework for verification and analysis of deep neural networks. In: Dillig, I., Tasiran, S. (eds.) Computer Aided Verification. CAV 2019. LNCS, vol. 11561, pp. 443–452. Springer, Cham (2019). https://doi.org/10.1007/978-3-030-25540-4_26

7. Kouvaros, P., Lomuscio, A.: Towards scalable complete verification of relu nn via dependency-based branching. In: IJCAI, pp. 2643–2650 (2021)
8. Madry, A., Makelov, A., Schmidt, L., Tsipras, D., Vladu, A.: Towards dl models resistant to adversarial attacks. arXiv:1706.06083 (2017)
9. Madry, A., Makelov, A., Schmidt, L., Tsipras, D., Vladu, A.: Towards deep learning models resistant to adversarial attacks (2019)
10. O'iggins, E., Graham, K., Daverschot, D., Baris, J.: Machine Learning Application on Aircraft Fatigue Stress Predictions, pp. 1031–1042, January 2020. https://doi.org/10.1007/978-3-030-21503-3_81
11. Singh, G., Gehr, T., Mirman, M., Püschel, M., Vechev, M.: Fast and effective robustness certification. In: Bengio, S., Wallach, H., Larochelle, H., Grauman, K., Cesa-Bianchi, N., Garnett, R. (eds.) Advances in Neural Information Processing Systems, vol. 31. Curran Associates, Inc. (2018). https://proceedings.neurips.cc/paper_files/paper/2018/file/f2f446980d8e971ef3da97af089481c3-Paper.pdf
12. Singh, G., Gehr, T., Püschel, M., Vechev, M.T.: An abstract domain for certifying neural networks. Proc. ACM Program. Lang. **3**(POPL), 41:1–41:30 (2019). https://doi.org/10.1145/3290354
13. Sudakov, O., Koroteev, D., Belozerov, B., Burnaev, E.: Artificial neural network surrogate modeling of oil reservoir: a case study. In: Lu, H., Tang, H., Wang, Z. (eds.) Advances in Neural Networks – ISNN 2019. ISNN 2019. LNCS, vol. 11555, pp. 232–241. Springer, Cham (2019). https://doi.org/10.1007/978-3-030-22808-8_24
14. Wang, S., Pei, K., Whitehouse, J., Yang, J., Jana, S.: Formal security analysis of neural networks using symbolic intervals. CoRR (2018)
15. Wu, H., et al.: Marabou 2.0: a versatile formal analyzer of neural networks (2024)
16. Xu, K., et al.: Fast and complete: enabling complete neural network verification with rapid and massively parallel incomplete verifiers (2021)
17. Zhang, H., Weng, T.W., Chen, P.Y., Hsieh, C.J., Daniel, L.: Efficient neural network robustness certification with general activation functions. Adv. Neural Inf. Process. Syst. **31** (2018)

Author Index

A
Afzal, Mohammad 201
Almeida, Dalay 182
Aurandt, Alexis 220

B
Baranov, Eduard 119
Baris, Julien 245
Becker, Jan Steffen 3
Belt, Jason 97
Bøgedal, Tobias Worm 136
Bonafini, Federico 170
Boumazouza, Ryma 245
Bunte, Olav 63

C
Campidelli, Matteo 170
Castiglioni, Valentina 21
Cavada, Roberto 170
Cimatti, Alessandro 170

D
Daverschot, Derk 245
Ducoffe, Mélanie 245
Dust, Lukas 40

E
Ekström, Mikael 40

G
Galametz, Audrey 245
Gehlert, Lise Bech 136
Griggio, Alberto 170
Gu, Rong 40

H
Hansen, René Rydhof 136
Hatcliff, John 97
Huisman, Marieke 152

J
Jamain, Florian 182
Jimenez-Roa, Lisandro A. 80
Jones, Phillip H. 220
Jørgensen, Malthe Peter Højen 136

K
Karmarkar, Hrishikesh 201
Koch, Christoffer Brejnholm 136

L
Lanotte, Ruggero 21
Lecomte, Thierry 182
Legay, Axel 119
Loreti, Michele 21
Lux, Daniel 136

M
Madhukar, Kumar 201
Martin, Marion-Cécile 245
Møller, Tobias 136
Mubeen, Saad 40
Mukhopadhyay, Diganta 201

O
O'Higgins, Eugene 245

P
Poulsen, Danny Bøgsted 136
Povéda, Guillaume 245

R
Robby, 97
Rozier, Kristin Yvonne 220
Rusbjerg, Signe Kirstine 136
Rusnac, Nicolae 80

S
Seceleanu, Cristina 40
Siddiqui, Sanaa 201
Stoelinga, Mariëlle 80

T
Tini, Simone   21
Tonetta, Stefano   170

V
van den Brand, Mark   152
van den Haak, Lars B.   152
van Gool, Louis C. M.   63
van Laarhoven, Jordi E. P. M.   63

Vivian, Martin   119
Volk, Matthias   80

W
Wijs, Anton   152
Willemse, Tim A. C.   63
Wongpiromsarn, Tichakorn   220

Z
Zasa, Andrea   170

SPRINGER NATURE

GPSR Compliance

The European Union's (EU) General Product Safety Regulation (GPSR) is a set of rules that requires consumer products to be safe and our obligations to ensure this.

If you have any concerns about our products, you can contact us on ProductSafety@springernature.com

In case Publisher is established outside the EU, the EU authorized representative is:

Springer Nature Customer Service Center GmbH
Europaplatz 3
69115 Heidelberg, Germany

The manufacturer's authorised representative in the EU is Springer
Nature Customer Service Centre GmbH, Europaplatz 3, 69115 Heidelberg,
Germany. If you have any concerns regarding our products, please
contact ProductSafety@springernature.com

Printed and bound by CPI Group (UK) Ltd, Croydon, CR0 4YY
25/03/2026
02078185-0011